No There There

The publisher gratefully acknowledges the generous contribution to this book provided by the General Endowment Fund of the University of California Press Associates.

No There There

Race, Class, and Political Community in Oakland

CHRIS RHOMBERG

University of California Press

BERKELEY   LOS ANGELES   LONDON

This book was published with the assistance of the Frederick W. Hilles Publication Fund at the Whitney Humanities Center, Yale University.

University of California Press
Berkeley and Los Angeles, California

University of California Press, Ltd.
London, England

Library of Congress Cataloging-in-Publication Data

Rhomberg, Chris, 1959–
    No there there : race, class, and political community in Oakland / Chris Rhomberg.
      p.   cm.
    Includes bibliographical references and index.
    ISBN 0-520-23618-1 (alk. paper)
    1. Oakland (Calif.)—Race relations.   2. Oakland (Calif.)—Politics and government—20th century.   3. Oakland (Calif.)—Social conditions—20th century.   4. African Americans—Civil rights—California—Oakland—History—20th century.   5. Black power—California—Oakland—History—20th century.   6. Social classes—California—Oakland—History—20th century.   7. General strikes—California—Oakland—History—20th century.   8. Ku Klux Klan (1915–)—California—Oakland—History—20th century.   9. Social conflict—California—Oakland—History—20th century.   I. Title.
    F869.O2R48   2004
    979.4'6605—dc21   2003000598

Manufactured in the United States of America
13   12   11   10   09   08   07   06   05   04
10 9 8 7 6 5 4 3 2 1

Contents

Maps

Preface and Acknowledgments

> What was the use of my having come from Oakland it was not natural to have come from there yes write about it if I like or anything if I like but not there, there is no there there.

Gertrude Stein wrote those lines in her memoir, *Everybody's Autobiography*, published in the United States in 1937. Ever since then, it seems, the city of Oakland has suffered from a certain image problem. The usual stereotype casts the East Bay hub as a gray, industrial Second City to San Francisco, hardworking but dull in comparison to its more glamorous, sophisticated (and European) neighbor on the western side of the bay. Other versions paint an even gloomier picture of the quintessential American urban wasteland, a desultory sprawl of congestion and decay, faceless and culturally vacant. A city with no there there, a nonplace where nothing ever really happens.

This stereotype is not only false about Oakland, it is not even true to Stein's text. The celebrated author and critic lived in the city as a young girl, growing up on a ten-acre garden estate that her family rented in an area east of Lake Merritt. Late in her life, after many years' absence, she returned to find her childhood environment vanished, the house and the fields long since overcome by real-estate speculation, the grassy hillside replaced by a dense residential tract. Stein's lament echoes a lost world of memory, the disappearance of the physical landmarks of identity, an alienation from the spaces of one's being. For many readers, the sense of strangeness and misrecognition on revisiting the places of one's past may be disturbingly familiar.

It is a play on this meaning that I take as the inspiration for the title of this book. In Oakland—and, I would argue, in American cities generally—what have all too frequently been lost are the worlds of collective memory, the spaces of social being. As I hope to be able to show, an enormous variety of often extraordinary things have in fact happened in Oakland as its citizens have struggled to create an urban community. Nevertheless, the difficulties that Oaklanders have faced, and the equally extraordinary discontinuities that they have experienced in their pursuit of community, form the central problem for this study.

Questions about urban community have intrigued me through most of my adult life. I grew up in the American Midwest, near a cluster of manufacturing towns on the Mississippi River that endured a wave of plant closings in the 1980s. While still in high school, I moved with my family to Louisiana, where I started college, earning work-study dollars as a counselor in an after-school program for kids in a large settlement house in New Orleans. I finished college in Massachusetts, and stayed on for a couple of years doing door-to-door outreach for a community organization in Boston. I then spent three years studying sociology and urban planning at Rutgers University, amid the expansive suburban environment of central New Jersey.

When I finally arrived in the Bay Area, I was like many Californians, that is, originally from out of state. I lived in Oakland for six years, first in North Oakland and then in East Oakland in an area near Clinton Park. The neighborhood around my apartment was then undergoing rapid transition; once nearly all white, in the '60s and '70s it had become mainly black and Latino, and in the '90s it was quickly absorbing a large population of new Asian immigrants. No fewer than eleven native languages besides English were spoken among the students at the local elementary school.

I was interested in problems of race, class, and urban politics in the United States, and Oakland seemed like a promising case study. I already knew that the city had been the birthplace of the Black Panther Party in the '60s. As I began to look into the background for that period, however, I soon discovered that there had been a general strike in the city in 1946. And as I started to dig even further, I found that the Ku Klux Klan had been a powerful force locally in the '20s. What a remarkable sequence of events to have transpired in a single place! I wondered what could possibly account for it. How had such a past affected the city's destiny, and what traces of it still remained? How could one even begin to tell a historical narrative that would encompass all of it in one story?

These were some of the thoughts that led me to undertake this project. Between those beginnings and the book you now hold lay a collaborative process that included the contributions of a great many people along the way. It began as a doctoral dissertation in the Sociology Department at the University of California at Berkeley. I am deeply grateful to the members of my thesis committee, particularly my chair, Michael Burawoy—a committed teacher, determined interlocutor, and staunch supporter throughout.

Victoria Bonnell was an astute critic and tutor in the historian's craft, and Michael Omi offered perceptive comments and welcome collegiality. Other Berkeley faculty also read various drafts of articles or chapters based on the research, including Dick Walker, Manuel Castells, Claude Fischer, Victor Rubin, Martin Sanchez-Jankowski, Bob Blauner, Krista Luker, Jerry Karabel, Percy Hintzen, and Robert Allen. I was fortunate to take part in a wonderfully cooperative graduate-student culture at Berkeley, and my thanks go to friends and colleagues Joe Blum, Deborah Gerson, Eric Brown, Steve Lopez, Hyun Ok Park, Pamela Perry, John Talbot, Ricky Bluthenthal, Rich Wood, and the members of the "Smith" dissertation group, who shall know themselves by their eponymous leader.

Since coming to New Haven, I have had the opportunity to work and learn with many outstanding scholars at Yale University. In particular, I would like to thank Chick Perrow, Kai Erickson, Peter Marris, and Robert Johnston for their comments and criticisms on selected chapter drafts. In the Political Science Department, the colloquium on Race, Inequality, and Politics, led by Rogers Smith and Cathy Cohen, was a lively source of ideas and intellectual exchange. Thanks also to the participants in the Ethnicity, Race, and Migration brown-bag group, including Michael Denning, Alicia Schmidt Camacho, Alethia Jones, and especially Jen Tilton, as well as to the students in my graduate political sociology seminar, Lisa McCormick, Gabriela Garciaperez, Martin De Santos, Abby Levine, Yasemin Bilgel, Joanna Mosser, John Phillips, Ling-Yun Tang, Mette Bastholm, Bill Mangino, Anthony Spires, and Forest Zhang, all of whom patiently taught their professor as much as he taught them.

In addition, Stan Oden, Peter Solomon, Joseph Rodriguez, and Michael Maly shared their knowledge and insights on the East Bay with me, and I received valuable research assistance from Julie Sadigursky. My editor at the University of California Press, Naomi Schneider, showed an immediate enthusiasm for the manuscript and, along with Laura Harger, helped me make it into a better book. Special thanks are due to Charles Tilly for his judicious review of the draft version, and to Ira Katznelson and Doug McAdam for their interest in and encouragement of the project at key points in its development.

The real labor of historical research relies heavily on the work of dedicated archivists, curators, librarians, and clerical workers. I would like to thank Jack Van Euw, Bill Roberts, and all of the staff of the Bancroft Library for their help during my time there as a fellow and in many visits since. I spent many fruitful hours in the History Room of the Oakland Public Library, aided by the estimable Bill Sturm (now retired), Kathleen DiGiovanni, and Steven LaVoie. I am further indebted to the staffs of the African American Museum and Library at Oakland, including Veronica Lee and former director Robert Haynes, and the Oakland Museum of California, where Diane Curry and Marcia Eymann were more than kind. At the Oakland City Hall, Michelle Abney and the employees in the Office of the City Clerk were reliably courteous and helpful, despite their temporary dislocation by the 1989 Loma Prieta earthquake. Across the bay, the Labor Archives and Research Center at San Francisco State University is a local treasure, in no small part owing to Lynn Bonfield and all the librarians who care for it. I am grateful also to Susan Goldstein and Patricia Akre at the San Francisco Public Library, and to Eugene Vrana of the Research and Education Department at the International Longshore and Warehouse Union, for permissions to use photographs from their collections.

The Bay Area has an active community of labor, ethnic, and social historians. Among them, I met Richard Boyden, Gretchen Lemke-Santangelo, Jim Rose, and Nancy Quam-Wickham through the Bay Area Labor History Workshop, which celebrated its twenty-second anniversary in 2002. As coordinator of labor studies at Laney College, Albert Vetere Lannon led me and several other students on a walking tour of the sites of the Oakland General Strike. I also had the pleasure of working with Fred Glass, communications director for the California Federation of Teachers, on its Golden Lands, Working Hands project. Golden Lands is an award-winning, multicultural educational curriculum on California labor history and features a ten-part, three-hour video series along with readings and lesson plans suitable for high-school classrooms or union education programs.

I have learned much from my own participation in the union labor movement and gladly acknowledge solidarity with my brothers and sisters from the Association of Graduate Student Employees at the University of California, now part of United Auto Workers Local 2865. From 1993 to 1996, I served on the UAW Region Five Northern Area Community Action Program Council, and I give credit to Mary Ann Massenburg, Al Ybarra, Debbie Williams, Carl Jaramillo, and Gus Billy for their experience and leadership. I also recall working with the many leaders and members of other unions at the University of California and in my time as a delegate to the Alameda County Central Labor Council. I continue to participate in the labor movement now as a member of the National Writers Union/UAW Local 1981.

My work would not have been possible without generous financial support from many sources. At the University of California, I was aided by a University Regents-Intern fellowship, an Allan Sharlin Memorial fellowship, a Bancroft Library Study award, and a Humanities Graduate Research grant. At Yale University, I am grateful for support from the Social Science Faculty Research Fund and from the Frederick W. Hilles Fund. In the Berkeley Sociology Department, Judy Haier and Elsa Tranter helped me navigate innumerable organizational tasks, while at Yale, Pam Colesworthy provided similar assistance and Ann Fitzpatrick ably transcribed interview tapes and helped prepare the manuscript. Finally, I especially want to thank Maida Rosenstein for sharing with me her intellectual and practical commitment, and her constant love and companionship. This one is for her.

1 No There There

Social Movements and Urban Political Community

On the night of May 5, 1922, a crowd of some fifteen hundred men wearing white robes and masks gathered silently in a valley in the hills above Oakland, California. Rows of parked cars lined the nearby road, and two searchlights beamed across the sky as a fiery cross burned behind an altar draped with the American flag. At a given signal, five hundred more unmasked men marched four abreast toward the altar to take their oaths and be initiated into the order of the Knights of the Ku Klux Klan. Newspaper reporters were brought in to record the scene, and hooded Klansmen from as far away as San Francisco, Sacramento, Fresno, San Jose, and Los Angeles came to join their Oakland brethren for the ceremony.[1]

In the early 1920s, a powerful Ku Klux Klan movement burst forth in many American cities, targeting immigrant Jews and Catholics as well as people of color and attracting an estimated four to six million members, in what some consider to be the largest right-wing movement in our nation's history.[2] By 1924, the Oakland Klan alone enrolled at least two thousand members, including such prominent and ordinary citizens as Protestant clergy, small businessmen, professionals and managers, salesmen, skilled workers, public employees, and even the son of a U.S. Congressman. A year later, the *Oakland Tribune* reported that eighty-five hundred Klansmen and women and their supporters from across the country filled the Oakland Auditorium to witness the swearing-in of five hundred members joining the national order.[3]

Blending prejudice with advocacy on issues like Prohibition and opposition to urban machine politics, the Klan enjoyed significant support in Oakland, a city whose population in 1920 was more than 90 percent white. Local Klan leaders won election as county sheriff in 1926 and city commissioner of streets in 1927, and quickly established their own patronage networks in city hall. Their power was finally broken in a celebrated graft trial prosecuted by Alameda County District Attorney (and later U.S. Supreme Court Chief Justice) Earl Warren. The scandal achieved such notoriety that it led directly to a major reform of the Oakland city charter in 1930 that abolished the city commissions and created a city-manager form of government.

Fast-forward to 1946. By this time, Oakland had already experienced the economic and political upheavals of the Great Depression and New Deal eras, including the 1934 General Strike across the bay in nearby San Francisco. World War II accelerated the process of change, stimulating production in local shipyards and factories and attracting a massive influx of new workers to labor in the defense industries. By 1945, Oakland's population had increased by as much as a third and its black population had more than tripled, reaching almost 10 percent of the total number of city residents.[4]

Nationally, the end of the war was followed in 1946 by a wave of strikes, the largest in American history, involving more than four million workers.[5] In Oakland, however, class polarization emerged not from the factories or the waterfront but from a strike of downtown retail clerks, most of whom were women. In late 1946, a majority of workers at Kahn's, a department store, and Hastings, a men's store, struck to demand recognition of their union. Local drivers from the International Brotherhood of Teamsters honored their picket line and refused to deliver goods to the stores during a busy holiday season. The retail business elites then pressured the city government to break the picket, and a massive display of police force sparked a citywide General Strike by the city's American Federation of Labor (AFL) unions in protest. For two and a half days, an estimated one hundred thousand striking workers from 142 unions shut down factories, shipyards, construction sites, most retail shops, and virtually all transportation in the city. Crowds estimated at between five thousand and twenty thousand people rallied in downtown Oakland in largely peaceful demonstrations outside the struck stores.

Labor insurgency carried over through the following spring, when four union-endorsed candidates won upset elections to the city council, despite a vigorous Red-baiting campaign led by the *Oakland Tribune*. The popular challenge in city government lasted until 1950, when politics in Oakland again split into two camps. Backed by the AFL Central Labor Council, the local Congress of Industrial Organizations (CIO), and the National Association for the Advancement of Colored People (NAACP), the city council voted to authorize the construction of three thousand units of federally subsidized public housing, as part of a comprehensive plan to remove urban "blight" in the central city. Opponents attacked the plan as "socialistic" and, led by the Apartment House Owners Association and the Oakland Real Estate Board, launched a recall campaign against the progressive councillors. The result was the defeat of one of the councillors, the withdrawal of the housing proposal, and the end of the liberal coalition on the city council.[6]

Turn again to twenty years later. The city's African American population had grown steadily during the postwar decades, but racial segregation in housing kept it concentrated initially in the West Oakland ghetto, where unemployment and poverty were at least two to three times the city average.[7] By the 1960s, however, continued population growth, along with displacements resulting from highway construction and urban renewal projects, pushed black residents toward other areas of the city. Tensions in racially transitional neighborhoods led to increased intervention by the city's social service and law enforcement agencies to control juvenile delinquency and manage problems of "social disorganization." These early efforts in Oakland later expanded under (and served as a model for) national urban social programs sponsored by the Ford Foundation and the federal government's War on Poverty.[8]

As the civil rights movement of the '6os spread from the southern states to cities in the North and West, such programs frequently became the catalysts for black community organization and political mobilization.[9] In Oakland, struggles emerged for control of the city's Community Action Agency and Model Cities programs, centering on demands for jobs, housing, and social services, as well as long-standing grievances over police conduct in the black community. The latter, especially, helped give rise to the Black Panther Party for Self-Defense, founded in Oakland in 1966.[10]

Racial polarization persisted for years in Oakland, as a conservative white political elite held on to power in city government and black community organizations engaged in a "long march" through the corridors of an array of urban public bureaucracies. Unlike many other American cities, no major riot occurred in Oakland during the period, but the city did not escape violence, including several fatal shootouts between Black Panther members and police. Yet despite the imprisonment or exile of many leading members between 1967 and 1973, Black Panther Party chair Bobby Seale's 1973 campaign for mayor won a stunning 37 percent of the vote, in the largest turnout for a regular municipal election in Oakland's history.[11]

WHAT'S GOIN' ON?
PROTEST AND DISCONTINUITY IN AMERICAN SOCIETY

One city, three periods of popular insurgency. Each movement touched on above is radically different from the others; each one arises from a different social location or base, adopts a different form, and articulates a differ-ent collective identity, centered on ethnicity, class, and race, respectively. Yet all three occurred in the same place and within a relatively short span of about fifty years—in effect, one person's adult lifetime. How could that be? We are accustomed to thinking of cities as almost organic entities, each with its own unique biography and personality, the history of their physical de-velopment embodied in their streets, skylines, and neighborhoods, their col-lective memory held together by the accumulated ties of community. But what kind of community could repeatedly undergo such diverse moments of mass polarization? It is almost as if we were talking about three differ-ent cities. The sheer juxtaposition of these movements in one place chal-lenges our understanding and raises at least two questions. First, what ex-plains their rapid disjuncture? Even if we allow for substantial social change in Oakland between periods, that only begs the second question: What were the lasting effects, if any, of each movement on subsequent periods and on the local community?

These questions are not just a puzzle for sociological theory, nor is Oak-land an isolated case. Each one of these episodes occurred as part of nation-wide social and political mobilizations that swept across twentieth-century urban America. In the 1920s, a resurgent white nativist (or "Second") Klan prospered not only in the Old South but also in Indianapolis, Denver, Los Angeles, and other cities and towns across the northern and western United States. Contrary to popular perceptions, urban Klan members came from a wide range of socioeconomic strata; many had solid social standing, and the movement was strongest where native white Protestants were a majority or rising group, not a backward or declining one. Alongside racial and eth-nic intolerance, Klan leaders frequently espoused mainstream middle-class values, calling for good government, better law enforcement, and improve-ments in public schools and city services, and they gained considerable sup-port through participation in electoral politics.[12]

A few years later, urban workers were at the forefront of protests against the economic crisis of the 1930s. In 1934, strikes of factory hands in Toledo, truck drivers in Minneapolis, and stevedores in San Francisco sparked mass uprisings and bore witness to the revival of labor militancy throughout the country. In the mill towns of New England and in the auto and steel hubs of the industrial Midwest, CIO union drives galvanized virtually entire com-munities, while in the metropolitan port cities of the West and East, long-shore, maritime, and transportation workers challenged local elites for power. With the end of World War II, the nation's streets filled with dis-charged soldiers, migrant war workers, and striking union members, and in

1946, citywide general strikes broke out not just in Oakland but also in Stamford, Connecticut; Lancaster and Pittsburgh, Pennsylvania; Houston, Texas; and Rochester, New York.[13]

Finally, African American experiences of migration and urbanization in the postwar period formed the social bases for the rise of the modern civil rights movement. Urban black communities provided the crucible, as sociologist Aldon Morris observes, for the "institutional building and the proliferation of dense social networks across localities and across neighborhoods in cities through which the movement was mobilized and sustained."[14] Conditions in cities also transformed the movement as it spread from the South to the racial ghettoes of the North, charting a trajectory of protest from civil rights to black power. Across the era as a whole, these changes are remembered by their urban landmarks: Montgomery and Greensboro; Birmingham and Selma; Watts, Newark, and Detroit.

"As an urban nation," political scientist John Mollenkopf writes, "urban development issues have been a primary, if not exclusive, factor in our national political development."[15] Similarly, in this book I argue that each one of these movements both reflected and called into question the experience of urban political community at distinct moments in the past century. Each represented a crucial struggle over the boundaries of the polity and the meaning of popular civic participation, and all were pivotal historical junctures in the patterning of race, class, and urban politics in the United States. Each is significant in its own right, but my aim here is to bring all three together in one place, in order to examine their relationships with one another and the dynamics of mobilization and community in urban space. And by focusing on the puzzle of their *discontinuity*, I believe an analysis of these movements can help shed light on the conditions of political community in our country today.

SOCIAL MOVEMENTS AND POLITICAL COMMUNITY: AN ANALYTIC FRAMEWORK

If the theme of this study is discontinuity, then what do these diverse movements have in common? What theoretical guidelines or tools can we use to trace their causes and consequences, and to fit them into a comparative frame? How may we identify the key actors, the conditions affecting them, and the outcomes of their interaction? In this book, I employ an explanatory framework built on three basic analytic dimensions: socioeconomic structure, institutional politics, and urban civil society.[16] To specify these I introduce here concepts drawn from three corresponding, well-known paradigms in sociology and political science: (1) traditional political sociology, grounded in the social bases of groups; (2) the "new institutionalism," with its central focus on the state; and (3) social movement theory, highlighting processes of group formation and mobilization in civil society. Each of these theoretical approaches helps explain part of the story, but each is by itself incomplete. Only by looking at it from all three perspectives together can we fully grasp the historical relationship between social movements and political community.

Socioeconomic Structure: Traditional Political Sociology

Let us begin with the old school. Traditionally, the field of political sociology took as its starting point the social origins of politics, and specifically the emergence of groups and interests from positions in an underlying social structure. This was true of classical Marxism, with its antagonistic classes arising from the societal division of labor; but it was no less true for the American pluralist social science of the 1950s and '60s, in which groups of individuals from various social strata developed different political values and interests, expressed in voting preferences and other behavior.[17] For both, macrostructural conditions in the economy and society produced the bases for the formation of groups, whose interests were translated more or less directly into the polity and into political outcomes.[18]

This approach has been subject to much criticism, of course, most often for its "reduction" of politics and culture to mere reflections of socioeconomic structure. Notwithstanding these criticisms, for our purposes the traditional paradigm continues to offer an essential point of departure. The analysis of social structure calls attention to categorical inequalities among groups, in terms of their access to and control over resources.[19] Structures embody enduring, unequal, and contradictory relationships, and therefore generate recurring problems of integration and social order, the solutions to which raise questions of political power.[20] Thus, a structure of wage labor creates problems for employers of recruiting, paying, and controlling a labor force, and problems for workers of securing jobs, income, and the regulation of work. Structures of urban settlement create shared circumstances of collective consumption for residents of an area, as well as competition with other users of the spatial environment. In each case, the structural position of actors may systematically afford or deprive them of resources or advantages in pursuing different goals.

Processes of structural change likewise affect the configuration of social relations found in the city. Geographers have examined the ways in which mobile capital investment and successive rounds of development produce uneven "layers" of urban economic and spatial structure.[21] Others have studied the entry of generations of urban migrants and their descendants into various occupational or labor market niches.[22] The distribution of residential housing also defines groups through the segregation of urban neighborhoods by class and race or ethnicity.[23] These processes are all visibly illustrated in Oakland, where the peculiarities of the city's industrial and occupational structure, the means of access to its labor and housing markets, and its patterns of migration and urban growth produced the bases for spatial differentiation and social inequality among groups.

A structural approach, therefore, identifies important societal cleavages and the unequal conditions affecting different groups. By itself, however, structural analysis does not explain each group's concrete political *interests*, their alignment with or against other groups, the strategic opportunities for action, or the particular shape of state institutions or policy. Nor does it explain processes of group formation and mobilization, or the outcomes of actual events of collective action. In short, socioeconomic structures are necessary but insufficient determinants of group formation and political conflict. Throughout the twentieth century, the city of Oakland underwent substantial structural change, much of it driven by external forces, as during the rapid transformation of the region during World War II. Nevertheless, local actors still had to negotiate the form and impact of these changes within the community. How they did so must be explained with reference to the other two analytic dimensions.

The State:
The "New Institutionalism"

More recent generations of political theorists have developed an alternative perspective, sometimes referred to as the *new institutionalism*.[24] This paradigm shifts the burden of explanation from the structural bases of groups to the organizational field of politics, centered on the institutions of the state. In this view, state actors and political institutions do not simply reflect social forces but possess powers and interests of their own, and actively shape the political terrain for all groups. Unlike traditional political sociology, this theory holds that groups do not enter the political arena with predetermined capacities or goals. Rather, the political terrain itself determines the prevailing "rules of the game," deciding who counts as an actor, what is or can become an "issue," and how power is to be exercised.[25]

At the level of the city, this approach may be specified using the concept of urban political "regimes," as developed by political scientist Clarence Stone and others.[26] In this model, local political actors build alliances with private economic and social groups in order to promote urban development and govern more effectively. Power is viewed as coordinating capacity within governing coalitions, rather than as direct command or control; constituent group interests are negotiated within the dominant coalition, which determines those policy alternatives that are deemed practically achievable and how groups may benefit from them. The alliances in the regime are held together by formal and informal ties extending into civil society, which facilitate the cooperation of actors around a unifying policy agenda and overall political project.[27]

The regime model links the formal institutions of the state with the composition of its constituent groups, their mode of cooperation, and the resources they can coordinate.[28] Established regimes are self-reinforcing, with considerable power to suppress opposing interests, not so much through direct force as through the preemptive weight of the regime's accumulated relations of coordination. Subordinate or excluded groups face the daunting task of contesting not only more powerful actors but also the principles of organization in the regime. As Stone writes, "Challenging a regime is not simply a question of mobilizing opposition. It means restructuring the ways in which people and groups are related to one another and providing new avenues of cooperation between them."[29]

The periods of protest in Oakland, I will argue, each occurred under distinct urban political regimes. The Klan mobilized against a regime characterized by *machine patronage*, organized by ethnic politicians like Alameda County boss Michael Kelly. In the '30s and 40s, labor insurgency rose up against the power of what I call *business managerialism*, personified in the figure of J. R. Knowland, the conservative Republican publisher of the *Oakland Tribune*. In the '60s, the civil rights and black power movements encountered a racial order regulated by *bureaucratic insulation*, administered through the city government, quasi-independent local authorities, and federal programs. In each case, the organization of the regime embodied a specific set of political alliances and defined the dominant terrain of politics for the period.

Institutionalist state and urban regime theories tell us much about the boundaries of inclusion and exclusion in the polity, the interests and alignments among political actors, and how groups become established or hegemonic in different political or governmental arenas. But they still do not explain the *origins* of insurgent movements, how oppositional identity develops within excluded groups, or how the latter sometimes do in fact challenge regimes. Neither structural change nor political institutions alone can explain mobilization, as it develops through a historical process of self-organization among groups, and as it is revealed in the episodic pattern of collective action observed in Oakland. To understand this process we must look to the third analytical dimension, the arena of civil society, using social movement theory as a guide.

Civil Society:
Social Movement Theory

Current sociological theories of social movements generally incorporate elements of the structural and political-institutional perspectives described above, as causal factors shaping the context for mobilization. Thus macrosocial changes like urbanization, industrialization, and migration affect groups' mobilization potential through changes in population size and demographic patterns, relative societal location, spatial concentration, and means of communication.[30] Similarly, the political terrain affects the strategic opportunities for action and the articulation of concrete issues and interests. Where social movement theory makes a distinctive contribution, however, is in its focus on processes of mobilization in civil society.

By *civil society* I mean the "middle ground" of social relations between the socioeconomic structure and the state. This refers to the broad field of private, formal voluntary association—including the variety of social, cultural, and community organizations, churches, labor unions, neighborhood associations, advocacy groups, and others—as well as the more informal world of family and friends, personal networks of mutual dependency and support, and the spontaneous conviviality of the "daily round."[31] Relations in civil society support the emergence of various public spaces in which people learn about, discuss, and form opinions on social and political concerns independently of the state and of the formal institutions of the public sphere (e.g., mass media, legislatures, courts).[32]

These social spaces correspond to what social movement theorists call "micromobilization contexts," and they function as arenas or sites for the collective formation of social identity and political opinion.[33] Participants in these spaces engage in an open-ended "cultural and ideological contest or negotiation" that includes the content of public affairs, their identities as speakers, and the location of boundaries between the public and private worlds. As a whole, civil society is a "multi-organizational field" that encompasses diverse streams of public discourse, whose interactions create the possibility for innovative or oppositional cultures.[34]

In the urban environment, two crucial arenas where association and group formation occur are the workplace and the neighborhood.[35] In the railroads and shipyards, machine shops and warehouses, canneries and department stores, and street corners and agency offices, groups of Oakland workers interacted with one another and developed traditions and habits of organization and collective identity. At the same time, uneven patterns of housing and urban development both united and divided groups, from the old ethnic working-class neighborhood in West Oakland, to the white middle-class housing tracts in the foothills of East Oakland, to the growing division by race throughout the city after World War II. These spatial settings formed the scene for the routines of everyday life and the experience of urban community.

Social movements are constituted in and through this medium of civil society, through the collective working out of constructions of identity, solidarity, and public awareness. But civil society does not automatically produce political insurgency. Subordinate groups may be internally stratified, fractured by structural contradictions, or divided by legacies of prior organization and political conflict.[36] Public spheres are often fragmented or dominated by elite interests, while civil society itself harbors exclusionary and hierarchical relations of private power.[37] The ambivalence of civil society underlines the importance of specialized social movement organizations as strategic agents, who intervene in civil society to make groups into collective *actors*.

Movement organizations do this by employing select repertoires of associational forms, resources, and tactics, including the cultural symbols deployed to inspire and maintain group solidarity.[38] Resources are concentrated through an often difficult process of organization building, alliance formation, and outreach among the indigenous networks and relationships of persons within subordinate populations.[39] At the same time, movement organizers try to unify the group through discursive strategies of "framing"—articulating a sense of collective identity and shared grievance—that draws on the group's own culture and the discursive possibilities in the public sphere.[40] Movement organizations act as intermediaries between the mobilization of identity in society and the negotiation of interests in the polity. To paraphrase sociologist C. Wright Mills, they turn private troubles into public issues, transforming common experiences of group inequality into cohesive oppositional identities and specific goals, alliances, and political demands.

My analysis of Oakland focuses especially on the role played by social movement organizations against the backdrop of group formation in civil society. So, for example, the Klan used the familiar model of the secret fraternal society to promote a nativist ideology that combined Protestant moralism, urban reformism, and racial and ethnic chauvinism into a persuasive collective identity and mobilizing force. Labor unions gave an organizational form and voice to workers who had endured the Depression, migration, and war, transforming their hopes and fears into mass militancy and political action. The civil rights and black power movements drew on forms of ghetto neighborhood organization and racial solidarity to unite African American residents and challenge the city to overcome racial segregation and inequality.

This brings us to the question of urban political community. As we have seen, structural forces concentrate diverse populations in urban space, creating interdependencies of work, consumption, and residence in a local economic area, as well as shared interactions with local government and political institutions. Beyond these linkages, such populations form a political community through their formal and informal recognition of mutual rights and responsibilities to participate in collective self-governance.[41] The *content* of their community, however—its meaning and boundaries—remains historically variable and often politically contested. Who belongs to the community and how they recognize their rights and responsibilities to one another are critical questions not only for analysis but for the participants themselves. For us, the answers to these questions will be most clearly revealed in events of collective action.

COLLECTIVE ACTION AND THE STRUGGLE FOR POLITICAL COMMUNITY

The analytic dimensions of socioeconomic structure, institutional politics, and civil society provide the theoretical scaffolding for my narrative account of events in Oakland. Within this framework, a comparison of the three movements reveals not an invariant outcome but a recurring problem. Urban political elites govern through the construction of regimes, organizing selective ties among actors in the state and society through the mechanisms of machine patronage, business management, or bureaucratic insulation. These regimes define the boundaries of community and the dominant terrain of political power, in the cases described here along the lines of ethnicity, class, and race. Structural changes can and do destabilize regimes, however, creating opportunities for excluded groups. Challenging actors mobilize on the field of civil society, building up group solidarity, articulating their collective identity, and reaching out to a larger public. In the course of insurgency, challengers bring to bear strong new claims of political community on actors in the urban setting, in order to win recognition and achieve their demands.

In so doing, movement actors must create or expand the public spaces needed to make their challenges heard. Yet these public spaces are highly fragile, political institutions are normally exclusive, and privileged groups turn away from public dialogue toward the protection of private interests and domains. Under normal conditions, regime hegemony rests not on any strong consensus but on the demobilization or dispersal of opposition— hence the explosiveness of polarization when it occurs. And urban civil society in the United States is itself a deeply fragmented terrain, divided historically by race, class, and other social fissures. The fragmentation of urban civil society undermines the capacity of the local civic arena to bind actors together in a mutually responsive political community.

Social movement organizers maneuvering on this terrain face difficult tasks: maintaining group unity, keeping coalitions together, and contending with more powerful actors. Moments of collective action are inevitably uncertain and involve real risks of repression, disintegration, or defeat. In the absence of a strong civic community, movement organizers turn instead to institutional strategies, attempting to secure their gains by incorporating group demands into the political fabric of the regime. The turn to institutionalization leads on the one hand to the decline of mobilization, and on the other to the redrawing of the boundaries of institutional power. Subsequent challenges, then, emerge from groups with different identities affected by different dimensions of exclusion, who face the legacy, and the limits, of previous rounds of reform. Thus discontinuity.

Again and again—through protests and strikes, and in key local elections—challenging actors in Oakland sought to enlarge the sphere of public discourse, and to gain access and entry to the polity. Yet, as often, the strength of the political community was insufficient to sustain the actors' engagement with one another. There was not enough *there* there; civil society remained divided, coalitions broke apart, and participation declined as movement actors settled into institutional reform. The outcomes produced the demobilization of collective actors and the reconstitution of urban regimes, not a continuing dialogue among groups in a dynamic political community.

Discontinuity, however, also means that boundaries and identities are not fixed. The institutional settlements affected the formation of actors but failed to eliminate the structures of inequality. As new structural changes occurred, or as relations among groups broke down, so the conditions of political community were again transformed. Social movements remained crucial vehicles in this process, reconfiguring identities and mobilizing collective actors in new forms.

THE PROBLEM OF DISCONTINUITY: HISTORICAL PERSPECTIVES

In a nutshell, this model describes the relationship I observe in Oakland between social movements and urban political community. How does my analysis compare to other accounts of these dynamics? To be sure, more traditional interpretations take a different view. Among the latter are what might be called the assimilationist, cyclical disorder, and social capital models of political community. Each of these draws from and lends itself to broad historical readings of American politics and society, and each offers a different explanation for social movement discontinuity. Yet none adequately distinguishes the three dimensions of socioeconomic structure, institutional politics, and civil society.

The Traditional Paradigm: Assimilationism

Perhaps the most familiar version is the traditional assimilationist paradigm, in which periods of mobilization merely reflect the temporary pressures associated with the accommodation or entry of new groups into the American polity. In this model, cities are the great melting pots of American democracy, where members of incoming groups find opportunities for education and social mobility; develop multiple, cross-cutting social ties; and learn to participate in a unifying, public-regarding "civic culture."[42] Movements are but symptoms of the individual and social adjustments that occur in this process, which results in the progressive incorporation of groups into an open, liberal, and pluralist institutional arena.

In this view, the Klan serves as a negative case: Traditional accounts portray it as a reactionary extremist movement, the "last desperate protest of a nineteenth-century Protestantism in the course of eclipse."[43] Attracting mainly isolated, downwardly mobile or lower-middle-class persons on the margins of urban society, the Klan's bigotry and intolerance offered symbolic relief for its supporters' status anxieties, but the organization ultimately collapsed, along with its disappearing social base. By contrast, the labor struggles of the '30s and 40s captured the democratic aspirations of the rising urban immigrant working classes and delivered them into the high tide of political incorporation under the New Deal. Under the auspices of the 1935

National Labor Relations Act, unions became partners in the formation of an industrial welfare state, gaining a permanent status as an interest group aligned with the Democratic Party.[44]

What the labor movement did for ethnic working classes, by analogy, the civil rights movement did for blacks. As African Americans migrated from the rural South to the urban centers, they followed in the footsteps of the European immigrants, first organizing in their own communities and eventually pressing for the recognition of their rights. The civil rights movement won by appealing to established democratic values, earning northern liberal support against the archaic racial caste system of the Old South. With the passage of federal civil and voting rights laws in the 1960s, African Americans finally secured entry as equal members of the polity, fulfilling the promise of American democracy.[45]

The assimilationist tradition rightly puts social movements in the context of macrostructural processes and periods of institutional change. But the ideology of progressive liberal incorporation often fails to understand how structural forces affect the social bases of groups, both before and after the process of "entry." A growing body of historical research now shows that urban Klansmen were *not* disproportionally lower-class or marginal individuals, but instead roughly paralleled the general population in their communities.[46] The organization of labor unions often both reflected and reinforced exclusionary labor markets and racial-ethnic divisions within the urban working class. And behind the achievements of the civil rights movement were persistent patterns of socioeconomic stratification, between blacks and whites and within the black population, some of which have since become even more pronounced.[47]

Just as important, the concept of an integrative civic culture presupposes that interests are represented more or less equally or transparently within a liberal political sphere. But civic and political institutions can be highly selective about which interests gain access and how they are represented. In the '20s, the Klan's racial and ethnic prejudice often proved no barrier to its political legitimacy, but rather mirrored prevailing public opinion among white Protestant middle classes, merging rhetorically with other elements of so-called progressive municipal reform. Conversely, labor historians have observed the institutional constraints imposed by the legal regulation of collective bargaining, notwithstanding the real gains that workers achieved. Capital mobility and limitations on workers' rights to organize meant that firms could abandon older unionized industrial cities and states for nonunion areas in the suburbs and in the South and West, where rapid postwar growth sustained the regional bases for the alliance of conservative Republicans and southern Democrats in the U.S. Congress. Throughout the postwar era, the unions were unable to alter these substantive constraints, despite their allegiance to the majority Democratic Party.[48]

Other scholars have emphasized the racial boundaries that characterized New Deal politics and policies from their beginnings.[49] Later, as black migration increased to the urban North and West, federal and local housing and urban renewal programs systematically segregated or discriminated against African Americans.[50] These and other government actions served to perpetuate informal but entrenched societal relations of racial exclusion in housing, employment, and education. Nondiscrimination laws alone proved insufficient to undo these relations, leading to the introduction of affirmative action and other types of state intervention to achieve integration and racial equality. These policies have had mixed success, however, and are themselves now increasingly under attack.[51]

In short, the simple ebb and flow of mobilization cannot be taken as a sign of stable liberal assimilation. The fate of the New Deal and civil rights coalitions underlines the impermanence of their political settlements; contrary to the image of steady, progressive inclusion, relations among groups have seen periods of democratic expansion and conservative retrenchment. In the city, actors are made, unmade, and remade, altering not only the balance of power among interests but also the culture of the civic community.

The Limits of Assimilation: Cyclical Disorder Theory

A second, more skeptical, view of discontinuity might be labeled *cyclical disorder* theory. In this model, democratic institutions are if anything *too* open and subject to popular pressures. For political scientist Samuel Huntington, American political culture is defined by a historically constant system of beliefs or "creed," identified with values of liberty, equality, individualism, and democracy. Periodically, Americans are seized by an intense moral fervor for these ideals, yet such moments of "creedal passion" raise excessive and contradictory demands that no government can practically satisfy. The result is an inevitable cycle of disappointment, cynicism, and political retreat, which then prepares the ground for renewed outbursts of creedal intensity.[52] Political scientist James Morone argues that reformers in American politics win support by invoking a myth of "the people" as a united community, participating directly in the control of their own affairs. Once the desired reforms are actually implemented, however, the image of community dissolves into a maze of fragmented government bureaucracies and competing, self-interested groups.[53] In these theories, democratic participation leads not to assimilation but to conflict and political gridlock, while collective action ends mainly in unintended consequences. Radical protest undermines established authority without realizing the reformers' ideals, and other critics have blamed social movements, particularly those of the '60s, for contributing to the breakdown of civic solidarity and urban moral order.[54]

Cyclical disorder theorists correctly point to the limits of assimilation, and of the political system's capacity to mediate contradictory demands. But they do not adequately explain how or why political institutions have the distinct capacities that they do. In Oakland, as we shall see, the machine politics of the '20s, the business managerialism of the '30s and 40s, and the large-scale bureaucratic administration of the '60s were all different ways of organizing the polity, and each generated different kinds of responses. By contrast, the idea of a constant, invariant cycle does not capture the historical stakes involved in each period, and obscures significant differences in the development of political institutions and their relation to groups in society.[55]

Similarly, broad, abstract notions of "creed" or "people" do not account well for the complex ways in which ethnic, class, and racial identities operated at each juncture. After all, the Klan was hardly egalitarian, unions did not preach individualism, and the civil rights movement showed no liberal fear of government. Likewise, pessimism about protest does not allow for how mobilization might actually express collective agency or effectively bring about change, notwithstanding its varied consequences. In each period, movement actors articulated specific identities, grievances, and alternative visions of the urban future. We will do better to trace more closely who the actors were in each case, their paths of formation, and their roles in the struggle to define their political community.

The Collapse of Community?
Social Capital and Civic Engagement

Over the past decade, scholarly and public debates in the United States have again turned to problems of community and politics, although this time for very different reasons. Unlike the earlier periods of mobilization, in the 1990s researchers were more likely to note a disturbing *decline* in popular civic and political participation.[56] In contrast to both the assimilationist faith in liberal integration and the cyclical theorists' distrust of democracy, Americans seemed to be losing their sense of political community altogether.

One of the more prominent figures in this "civic disengagement" debate has been political scientist Robert Putnam. In a series of publications, Putnam has argued that Americans have experienced a historic loss of individuals' "social capital," by which he means those "features of social life—networks, norms, and trust—that enable participants to act together more effectively to pursue shared objectives." For Putnam, social capital is the key to a healthy civil society, the essential precondition for bringing citizen action together with public policy and "making democracy work." The collapse of a broad social connectedness has deprived citizens of vital links with their communities, thereby diminishing their attachment to public concerns.[57]

What has caused this decline of community? The demands of modern organizations of work, the sprawling pattern of urban growth, and the effects of television and mass media on leisure time have all played a part in eroding the ties among individuals. But for Putnam the most important factor is a generational gap in the socialization of persons into the norms and networks of social trust. In order to revive democratic participation, Putnam advocates revitalizing local grassroots forms of voluntary association, as a way to increase social capital and as a forum for popular civic education.[58]

The debate over civic engagement has raised serious questions about the current state of American political community, yet the analysis of social capital shares some of the weaknesses of the earlier theoretical approaches. The benign vision of local civil society discounts the historical weight of both structural group conflict and institutional power.[59] Putnam's model implicitly recalls the older sociological theory of social disorganization, in which individuals' atomization leads to anomic dysfunctions and the failure to integrate into a consensual civic culture. Correspondingly, his programmatic stress falls on the education and socialization of individuals, not on the structural forces that unequally distribute resources and actively produce disorganization, or on the institutional barriers that discourage participation and disempower certain groups. Indeed, under some circumstances, comparatively higher levels of civic engagement might well take the form of polarization and mass protest, as we will see in Oakland.

The metaphor of social capital makes community a marketlike commodity, but the logic of markets does not spontaneously create democratic institutions.[60] Putnam is right to bring our attention to the lived experience of everyday life in neighborhoods, workplaces, and other "face-to-face" associational settings typical of urban civil society.[61] But the social capital approach blurs the transition from private voluntarism to political action, from civil society to public politics. The focus on individuals' norms and behavior neglects the role of *collective* actors in sustaining participation and in forging the bonds of political community. People engage in the life of their communities not only through private affiliations but also as members of mobilized groups, through strikes, demonstrations, elections, and other forms of collective action in the public sphere. These are often concentrated in highly contentious and pivotal events, whose outcomes shape our understanding of the *content* of political community.

The assimilationist, cyclical disorder, and social capital theories all fail to account adequately for the problem of social movement discontinuity. All underestimate the effect of structural forces on the social bases of groups, and on the resources available to them. All presume an open, neutral, and liberal civic and political arena, without adequately theorizing the institutional capacities, organization, or biases of the state. Finally, none provides an appropriate framework for understanding social movements, or political community, as a relationship among collective actors.

OAKLAND: A CASE STUDY

This book offers a case study of these three social movements in Oakland, from the point of view of urban political development in twentieth-century America. As a case study, it draws on that tradition of social research, associated with Max Weber, which is grounded in the causal explanation of social action in specific historical contexts.[62] In this tradition, as Charles Ragin writes, sociological analysis aims at generating "limited historical generalizations that are objectively possible and cognizant of enabling conditions and limiting means—of context." The approach is case-oriented because it looks to the configuration of causes and conditions in a given historical setting, interpreted as a whole. The in-depth study of particular cases can allow us to uncover those social mechanisms—or what Charles Tilly calls "recurrent causal sequences of general scope"—that are analogous across cases or relevant in other settings.[63]

My focus is on the struggles of groups and actors to forge a political solidarity and community in an urban context. As a window onto these processes, the city of Oakland has certain advantages. Founded in the middle of the nineteenth century, it grew rapidly to its mature size during the period of this research, in the early and mid twentieth century. A medium-size city, with a population of 384,575 in 1950, it is large enough to feature problems of concentration, industrialization, and population change typical of American urban centers, yet small enough to permit observation of its social and political relations more or less as a whole. Moreover, the prominence of all three movements in the city's history makes it an especially useful case, displaying the more pronounced aspects of polarization and discontinuity that are my specific concerns.

At the same time, no claim is made here that Oakland is representative, statistically or otherwise, of all American cities. By identifying its unique circumstances, however, we can establish comparative standards for analyzing similar and different conditions in other cities and regions in the United States. Nor do I assume that all relevant contextual factors are enclosed within the city itself: Larger economic forces, state and national politics, broader cultural traditions, and even global events like World War II— all exerted enormous influence. But whatever these external forces were, local actors still had to negotiate their impact on group relations and politics within Oakland, and they often did so in highly conscious and deliberate ways. That is the process that I will examine here.

Because of my interest in mobilization, I divide the overall time frame in Oakland into three periods, each associated with a specific movement and its dominant political terrain: roughly 1900 to 1930, 1930 to 1950, and 1950 to 1977. Although these periods do not perfectly separate each movement in time, arranging Oakland history in this manner serves my analytical purposes in two ways: First, it allows for an individualizing comparison between periods, calling attention to their distinctive characteristics and differences; and second, it provides a longitudinal comparative design for inquiry into the sequential relationship between periods of movement activity.[64]

My central problem is to explain change—discontinuity—across periods in the same place, and correlatively to ask what effects earlier periods had on later ones. Hence, I depart from the traditional variable-based causal models that are standard in much of contemporary social science. Such models require strong assumptions of equivalence and independence between cases in order to test the validity of uniform hypotheses generalized for all cases. This would require assuming, at the outset, that each period had no effect on the others—in other words, that at three successive times, Oakland really was simply three different cities, all subject to the same causal forces. Regardless of whether such a claim were plausible, it would immediately assume away an investigation into what I am really interested in— namely, the discontinuity and sequence, or change, between periods.[65]

Moreover, in variable-based methods, cases do not operate as *contexts,* or configurations of parts in interrelated wholes, that are subject to reflexive action or internal transformation. Instead, cases are assumed to be drawn from a population of fixed entities with analytically separate attributes. The researcher hypothesizes that some of these attributes affect other attributes, and the hypothesized causal factors act largely independently from one another to produce constant effects across all cases.[66] Again, this abstracts from the very features with which I am most concerned: the relations between groups and actors in the temporal unfolding of events.

Therefore, I adopt a narrative analytic method, in order to capture what sociologist Larry Griffin describes as "the mutually constitutive interplay of agency and social structure, a dynamic continuously occurring in time and through time."[67] From this perspective, causal social forces are embedded in the sequences of interactions between actors and their historical context, understood as a set of enabling conditions, influences, and constraints. This approach allows for the possibility that actors and events may alter their environments, that outcomes in earlier periods may affect conditions for later ones, and that the institutional settings for and meanings of action can change, for example, as the central axis of political conflict shifts from one set of identities to another (see the methodological appendix).

THE PLAN OF THIS BOOK

In the story that follows, I begin my study of each period by surveying the socioeconomic structural conditions generating the social bases of unequal groups. I then describe the organization of the dominant political regime, its member groups and their mode of coordination, and the ways these factors define the boundaries of inclusion and exclusion in the urban polity. I observe the paths of group formation on the field of urban civil society, focusing especially on the rise of new or newly mobilized collective identities and forms of organization.

At crucial junctures, the paths of these groups intersect in urban public space. I follow the interactions of movement actors and established elites in sequences of mobilization and conflict, tracing the steps that lead to polarization and political crisis. In such moments, the opposition between the goals of the movement and the mechanisms of reproduction in the regime highlight the choices at stake and their implications for the future pattern of urban development. The outcomes of these events, in turn, shape the political terrain for subsequent periods of regime-making and social movement challenge.

For clarity of exposition, each period is divided into two chapters. The first describes the context of mobilization under the existing regime, and the second concentrates on events leading to increasing polarization and its outcomes. Chapter 2 begins by drawing a baseline of economic, political, and social development in Oakland from the beginning of the twentieth century to 1920, showing how these forces generated the principal contending groups and the dominant political terrain. On the one hand, an old corporate elite and an ethnic (Catholic) working class were united through a system of urban machine patronage, while on the other, a rising downtown merchant class and white Protestant middle class experienced exclusion from this regime and increasingly mobilized for reform. Structural changes up through World War I destabilized these actors and their alliances, leading to a brief upsurge of working-class militancy, which was largely defeated after the war.

This review sets the stage for the events of the '20s, described in chapter 3. Rapid commercial and residential growth greatly increased the size and strength of both downtown business and the white middle class, the latter providing the social base for the emergence of the Ku Klux Klan. Taking the form of a secret fraternal society (a common form of grassroots social and political organization at the time), the Klan mobilized opposition to the machine using a discourse of ethnic nativism. Once in power, however, the Klan leaders themselves succumbed to the institutions of machine politics, becoming simply one more corrupt faction. Middle-class whites then transferred their allegiance from the Klan to the downtown business leaders, who pushed through a series of reforms that effectively eliminated machine politics from city government.

These reforms produced a major break and reorientation in the relations between the local government and societal actors. Oakland shifted from a political terrain dominated by ethnicity to one more strongly defined by class power. Chapter 4 begins with the consolidation of a new regime, which I describe here as business managerialism. Led by *Oakland Tribune* publisher Joseph Knowland, the downtown elite intervened more or less directly in the control of Oakland's economic development, while the reformed city council maintained a middle-class "caretaker" government oriented toward low taxes and homeowner services. At the same time, the crisis of the Great Depression stimulated a return of working-class militancy, marked by the rise of unions affiliated with the CIO. During the '30s, however, organizational rivalry between the CIO and the older, larger AFL unions kept the working-class challenge in check, helping to preserve the power of the urban regime.

In the 40s, wartime industrialization brought a massive new influx of working-class population, socially isolating the business regime and creating the conditions for class polarization. In chapter 5, I analyze the events leading up to and during the General Strike, and the political mobilization that followed. In the General Strike, Oakland workers demonstrated an extraordinary class solidarity, allowing the unions to defend themselves successfully in a showdown with the downtown elite. The pursuit of democratic reform in city government, however, called for more complex alliances on a difficult terrain, and the unions' inability to bridge divisions of class and race, even within their own ranks, limited their ability to achieve broader institutional change.

Chapter 6 picks up the third case. By the early '50s, the downtown elites had weathered the postwar working-class challenge, and they began to pursue their own agenda of urban and regional redevelopment. This included major changes in housing, economic, and transportation infrastructures, administered by an array of new bureaucratic public authorities. Redevelopment led to the displacement of the growing yet politically excluded black population and to the dissatisfaction of white homeowners who opposed the movement of black residents into their neighborhoods. Political elites responded by adding separate layers of administrative social programs, largely funded by the federal government and premised on the principle of bureaucratic insulation. While offering opportunities, these programs also channeled black mobilization toward a parallel form of bureaucratic enfranchisement and reinforced the compartmentalization of black demands.[68]

The failures of this form of incorporation helped drive the racial polarization of the late '60s, discussed in chapter 7. In particular, controversies surrounding the issues of unemployment and relations between police and the community formed the local context for the emergence of the black power movement. This took shape in several forms: in the rise of the Black Panther Party among black youth, in the radicalization of protest in the city's federal Community Action and Model Cities programs, and in the turn to demands for community control. Official resistance on the part of the city government to these pressures maintained the atmosphere of racial polarization in Oakland, setting the stage for the electoral campaigns of Bobby Seale for mayor and Elaine Brown for city councillor in 1973.

The final chapter recaps the dynamics that lead to social movement discontinuity, focusing on the problem of urban political community, and explores some of the theoretical implications of the results. I compare the historical experiences in Oakland with those in other American cities and examine some of the changes that have occurred in Oakland in the 1980s and '90s. Finally, I reflect on the significance of the analysis for current debates on civic and political engagement and the future of democratic participation in the United States. Throughout the book, my deepest concern will be to understand not only the way things are, but how they can change.

2　Corporate Power and Ethnic Patronage

Machine Politics in Oakland

Overlooking the eastern side of San Francisco Bay, the Contra Costa hills of the California Coastal Range rise gently more than fifteen hundred feet above sea level and the city of Oakland. On their western slope, the landscape descends from the top of the ridge into gravelly, brush-covered hillsides, interspersed with wooded canyons and arroyos, before giving way to a narrow coastal plain of grassy foothills, flats, and wetland marshes near the shore. Several mountain creeks carve their way down through the hills; one of them, San Antonio Creek, turns into a broad estuary that flows into the bay, marking the city's southern boundary. Midway along its northern side, an arm of the estuary reaches inland to form a wide, shallow tidal slough, attracting ducks, geese, pelicans, and other waterfowl. To the south lies a thumblike protrusion of land, upon which sits the town of Alameda. Beyond the mouth of the estuary, the shoreline curves northward along a western waterfront facing the bay.

Today, much of this environment bears the mark of human intervention. At the crest of the hills once stood a magnificent grove of redwood trees, visible to ships' captains for miles, and almost entirely felled for timber by the middle of the nineteenth century. Rows of houses now perch across the higher elevations, while the lower hills and flats are carpeted with residential tracts, paved streets, and industrial and commercial land uses. In 1869, the inlet to the slough was dammed to create a 155-acre saltwater lake, now known as Lake Merritt, in the center of the city. Thirty-five years later, U.S. Army engineers opened a canal between the estuary and San Leandro Bay, clearing the channel and turning Alameda into an island. More than a century of improvements have transformed the estuary into the Oakland Inner Harbor, while the western marshes are now mostly filled, given over to the giant cranes and container terminals of the port of Oakland and the highway approaches to the San Francisco–Oakland Bay Bridge.[1]

So the history of urban development is continually imprinted on the physical landscape. In order to observe better the process and shape of change, this chapter sets a historical baseline, from the city's origins to the first decades of the twentieth century. Using the terms of my narrative analytical framework, I describe the structural and conjunctural conditions that affected the formation of actors, including the dominant forms of capitalist economic development and the political and social institutions linked in the organization of the urban regime. The key actors in this regime are large corporate enterprises, machine politicians, and immigrant ethnic groups, united through the medium of ethnic patronage. While ethnicity forms the dominant terrain of urban politics in this period, I also trace simultaneous patterns of group formation defined by class and race. Alongside, intertwined, and ultimately in conflict with the regime, these patterns generate other nascent actors, among them a union labor movement, a downtown merchant elite, and a Protestant white middle class.

Only after having first introduced the relations among these actors and their historical trajectories, I argue, can we make sense of the Oakland Klan movement of the 1920s. Beginning roughly with the 1906 San Francisco earthquake and continuing through the First World War, a series of structural and developmental changes pushed the existing urban regime toward a crisis. The machine survived early efforts at reform by business and middle-class leaders, as well as a wave of working-class insurgency during and after the war. These events set the political context for the start of the '20s, described in the next chapter. By that time, economic prosperity had contributed to the growth of downtown business and of the middle-class population, particularly in the newer areas of the city like East Oakland. These new middle classes, especially, would form the social bases for the emergence of a white nativist movement, led by the Ku Klux Klan.

SOCIOECONOMIC STRUCTURE:
URBAN AND INDUSTRIAL DEVELOPMENT

Like many American cities, Oakland was born of speculation. In 1850, during the heady days of the California gold rush, three Yankee entrepreneurs sailed from San Francisco across the bay to the mainland on its eastern side, landing in a shoreline area owned by ranchero Don Vicente Peralta, heir to an original land grant from the Spanish crown. Businessmen Edson Adams and Andrew Moon, and a young attorney named Horace Carpentier, each laid claim to 160 acres of Peralta's land, amid the handful of settlers and sawmills already squatting in the vicinity. With the Mexican-American War and the entry of California into U.S. statehood, the three Americans had little trouble maneuvering their way into control of the property, and in a short time they had hired a surveyor and begun selling lots. Within four years, Carpentier had overseen the incorporation of Oakland as a town and then a city, and gotten himself elected as Oakland's first mayor. Finally, in exchange for his promise to build a schoolhouse and three small wharves and to share a small percentage of his revenues, he convinced the town's board of trustees to grant him legal title to the entire city waterfront, comprising ten thousand acres of overflowed land, with exclusive rights to construct wharves, piers, and docks and to collect fees from the same.[2]

Notwithstanding its founders' ambitions, for most of its first two decades Oakland remained a small village while San Francisco, at the tip of the peninsula and blessed with a deep-water port, quickly became the economic capital and metropolitan center of the region. Oakland's fortunes, however, began to change by the end of the 1860s. On March 31, 1868, Carpentier transferred his control of the Oakland harbor to the recently formed Oakland Waterfront Company, whose officers included Carpentier and his brother Edward, Oakland mayor Samuel Merritt, investors Lloyd Tevis and John Felton, and Leland Stanford, president of the Central Pacific Railroad. The next day, for a price of five dollars, the Oakland Waterfront Company sold five hundred acres of bay frontage and two strips of land for rights-of-way to the Western Pacific Railroad, an affiliate of the Central Pacific. Taking advantage of Oakland's location on the mainland side of the bay, the railroad then chose it as the West Coast terminus for its new transcontinental line. In May 1869, the Central Pacific joined the westbound Union Pacific at Promontory, Utah, linking California by rail with the rest of the nation, and by November the first overland passenger trains had arrived in Oakland.[3]

Initially situated on the estuary between the tidal slough and the bay, with the arrival of the Central Pacific the city grew westward, out to the end of Seventh Street, where the railroad built a long wharf and a passenger-ferry mole, extending out past the mud flats into deep water in the bay.[4] By 1900, Oakland was divided into seven wards (see map 1). The industrial and working-class neighborhoods near the waterfront and the railroads formed the old Fourth and Sixth Wards below Twelfth Street in West Oakland, backed by the Third Ward, which extended up to Twenty-second Street. As the city expanded, it moved north and east: The area that became the Sec-

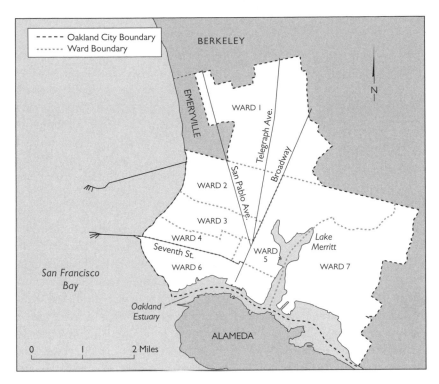

Map 1. Oakland wards, circa 1905.

ond Ward was incorporated in 1872, reaching north from Twenty-second Street to Thirty-sixth Street and the border of the town of Emeryville. That same year, residents of the town of Brooklyn on the east side of Lake Merritt voted to merge with Oakland, creating the East Oakland Seventh Ward. The hills above Lake Merritt, known as Vernon Heights, were added in 1891 to the downtown Fifth Ward, and the remaining areas between College Avenue and Emeryville up to the Berkeley city line were annexed in 1897 to become the North Oakland First Ward.[5] To the east, beyond the boundary of Twenty-third Avenue, lay the independent, largely rural villages of Fruit Vale and San Leandro.

At the turn of the twentieth century, Oakland's economic structure reflected the Bay Area's regional concentration in the manufacture of machinery, construction, coastal trade, and the processing of products from the area's rural hinterland. By 1911, Oakland was the West Coast terminus for three transcontinental rail lines, and as many as sixteen hundred trains a day moved through the city. The largest railroad was the Southern Pacific, successor to the old Central Pacific, and a substantial property owner and employer in its West Oakland yards. Shipbuilding began in earnest about 1910 and took off during World War I, and work in the shipyards, on the railroads, and in the mining equipment industry supported many smaller metal foundries and machine shops. Clustered near the rail lines were various processing industries, including textile mills for cotton and jute and numerous fruit and vegetable canneries, each giving seasonal employment to hundreds of men, women, and children. Finally, the city was fast becoming a branch plant center for several nationwide manufacturing firms, particularly in the emerging automobile industry, with factories for Chevrolet, Fisher Body, Fageol trucks, and Willys-Overland.[6]

Alongside industrial development came population growth. The city experienced a huge increase in the wake of the 1906 San Francisco earthquake, as an estimated 65,000 refugees settled permanently in the comparatively undamaged East Bay. The massive relocation following the quake transformed the local economy and stimulated the construction of many new residential districts in Oakland and its surrounding areas. In 1909, Oakland annexed the vast, rapidly developing territory east of Twenty-third Avenue, expanding the East Oakland Seventh Ward and more than doubling the city population, from 66,960 in 1900 to 150,174 in 1910. Spurred again by the economic boom of World War I, growth continued within these new boundaries, reaching 216,261 people by 1920 (see map 2).[7]

The majority of the population was of northern European origin, including immigrants and native-born descendants of the United Kingdom, Germany, and Scandinavia. The city was also home to significant numbers of Irish, Italian, Portuguese, and other European Catholic immigrant groups. In a common pattern, these groups often established networks or niches in various occupations, resulting in a pattern of ethnically segmented labor markets.[8] Native-born Protestant men of Anglo-Saxon and Nordic descent dominated in small business and the skilled crafts, on the railroads and in the building trades, and as merchant seamen. Catholic Irish, along with southern and eastern European immigrants, often started out as common laborers on the railroads or in other industries, at a going rate of ten cents an hour, for a twelve-hour day and a six-day week. Ethnic Irish men also found work as carpenters or teamsters, while Italian men moved into wholesale produce and scavenging businesses, and Portuguese men worked in fishing and sailing. Women and children frequently performed unskilled factory work in the laundries, canneries, and textile mills for as little as forty cents a day; other women earned money by taking in boarders or working as seamstresses in the home.[9]

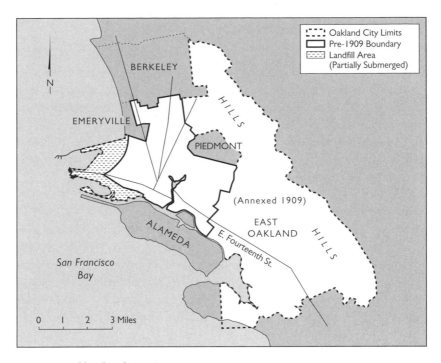

Map 2. Oakland and East Bay cities, 1920s.

These immigrant working-class groups were concentrated especially in the older, multiethnic West Oakland neighborhood near the rail yards and the waterfront. In addition, Italian ethnics settled in the Temescal neighborhood in North Oakland near Emeryville, while in East Oakland a Portuguese colony formed in the industrial flats at the foot of Twenty-third Avenue.[10] A small but well-established African American community also flourished in Oakland, composing less than 3 percent of the total city population but second in size within California only to black Los Angeles. Black men employed as Pullman porters, railroad laborers, and service workers anchored this community in West Oakland: Railroad operating employees were required to live near the yards in order to be on call for unscheduled duty. Between 1870 and 1930, perhaps a quarter to a third of all black workers in Oakland were employed in some fashion on the railroads. Other black men and women were limited mainly to jobs in domestic service or unskilled labor, while a small black business and professional class arose to serve the black community.[11]

The largest non-European population in Oakland was people of Asian descent, including Chinese and Japanese, together accounting for just over

3 percent of the population in 1920. Throughout the late nineteenth century, discrimination against the Chinese had led to their gradual expulsion from most occupations and their geographic restriction to a Chinatown district, centered below downtown around Eighth and Webster Streets. By the 1900s few Chinese could find work in the larger economy, apart from jobs in domestic service or in hazardous industries like the manufacture of explosives. Excluded from economic and political opportunities, the Chinese community turned inward, relying on ethnic enterprises such as commercial laundries, retail produce stores, and butcher shops, as well as criminalized activities like the opium trade, prostitution, and gambling.[12]

In many ways, then, Oakland at the beginning of the twentieth century resembled the archetypal railroad boom town of the American West.[13] In just a few decades, the city had grown dramatically, attracting a diverse population in search of fortune and opportunity. Yet just as quickly, Oakland residents found themselves contending with problems of rapid urban development, economic and social inequality, and concentrated political power. These problems were embodied in the two most important political institutions of the time, the franchise corporations and the political machine.

THE REGIME:
THE CORPORATIONS AND THE MACHINE

Politics in Oakland was traditionally dominated by its large "public-service" corporations. Early local government had made up for its lack of fiscal and administrative resources by granting monopoly franchises to private corporations to meet the city's infrastructural and service needs. Under this arrangement, entrepreneurs supplied the initial capital investment and organization and were in turn granted the rights to provide public services for a profit. In Oakland, private companies supplied water, power, traction (crosstown streetcar), and interurban railway service. Unfortunately, the practice quickly became so unregulated that Oakland was described as a "fountain of franchises." Long-term grants were assigned with minimal return to the city and no control over rates or quality of service. Speculators even formed a market in Oakland street rail franchises, anticipating profits for surrendering duplicate or overlapping rights for which they had paid nothing to the city. Thirty such franchises were granted from 1870 to 1883, none of which was ever built.[14]

As the city grew, the largest and most powerful franchise corporations soon monopolized control of Oakland's economic development. The Contra Costa Water Company owned much of the city's water supply, consolidating seven competitors before 1900. In 1902, Oakland residents paid more to the company for water than they did in property taxes to the city.[15] Among the more flamboyant of the franchise entrepreneurs was Francis M. "Borax" Smith, who arrived in Oakland in 1891 after accumulating a fortune from mining borax in the Southern California desert. With his partner, Frank Havens, Smith fashioned an empire of interlocking investments in transportation, real estate, and water. In 1893, Smith acquired a controlling interest in the Oakland Consolidated Street Railway Company, and over the next few years he absorbed several rival lines into a combined streetcar and transbay ferry service that became known as the Key System, so named because the company's three-mile-long pier out on the bay looked like an old-fashioned house key, with ferry slips for the teeth.

In 1895, Smith and Havens founded the Realty Syndicate and began reaping profits from real-estate development through their control of trolley line extensions. As one senior executive later testified, the relationship of the Key System and the Realty Syndicate was "very similar to the relation between two pockets in the same man's trousers." By 1900, the Realty Syndicate owned thirteen thousand acres of East Bay residential property and thousands of acres more of commercial and industrial land. The two men subsequently merged the Contra Costa Water Company and several others with their own People's Water Company, capitalized in 1906 at $20 million. By 1911, the Realty Syndicate owned $10 million worth of real estate and $8 million more of traction company stock.[16]

The premier economic and political force in Oakland, however, was undoubtedly the Southern Pacific Railroad. The Southern Pacific was the most powerful corporate actor in the state, the "Octopus" made famous in Frank Norris's 1901 muckraking novel of that name. In Oakland, the railroad's rights-of-way ran right down the center of the city's main streets, with grade crossings at nearly every intersection. Transcontinental and local trains roared through downtown, dominating traffic and street life, on their way out to the ferry mole at the end of Seventh Street. In 1895, the corporation's state baggage master was appointed president of the Oakland Board of Public Works, exercising authority over streets, public buildings, and the police and fire departments. As one resident later recalled, "The railroad's expanding gradually and employing thousands, had much to do in governing civic and political affairs and many a man in political life owed his start to his railroad connections."[17]

Along the waterfront, the Southern Pacific had amassed a giant complex of switching and maintenance yards, car building and repair shops, a creosoting plant, a prefabricated bridge and building department, a blacksmith's shop, and even a shipyard for its own ferry service. In the early years of the century, as many as half of the adult male residents of the adjacent neighborhoods in West Oakland worked in some capacity for the railroad, making the area a virtual company town. Finally, under a disputed legal title (originally held by Carpentier), the Southern Pacific controlled nearly all of the Oakland harbor area, preventing independent competition or public improvements on its property.

The franchise corporations formed the core of the urban regime in Oakland. Through them, local politicians satisfied public demands for both low taxes and basic city services. Corporate elites, in turn, protected their profits and privileges by forming alliances with the ward bosses who controlled the votes of the dependent working classes.[18] Throughout much of this period, the most prominent party machine leader in Alameda County was Michael J. "Mike" Kelly. Born in West Virginia in 1864, Kelly arrived in Oakland at age twenty-two, and began work as a nailmaker's apprentice in a West Oakland factory. In 1894, he was hired at the United States Mint in San Francisco and, rising through the political ranks, secured appointment as Alameda County treasurer in 1906 and as county tax collector in 1919. A Catholic, Kelly gained power by supporting Governor Hiram Johnson and the Republican progressives, who were often in bitter competition with the conservative party regulars. Access to the statehouse gave Kelly control over the Alameda County Board of Supervisors: Interim vacancies on the board were filled by gubernatorial appointment, with Kelly's approval. In 1921, Kelly himself was named superintendent of the San Francisco Mint, with the aid of Johnson, now a U.S. senator.[19]

Locally, the machine's control of public contracts allowed it to "have a say in whom the contractors hired, and which lawyers, insurance brokers, and small businessmen received a 'break' in penetrating the market for interstitial economic activities."[20] Notwithstanding the rules of civil service, the machine could still influence the hiring of police and firemen, so that these, too, owed political favor. In return, Kelly and his allies acquired the resources to mobilize campaign support at election time. Nevertheless, the limits of institutional politics in Oakland led to a weaker form of machine-building here than in other big cities of the time. Like most of California, Oakland and Alameda County were overwhelmingly Republican, and they shared features common to Republican Party urban machines: lower tax ceilings, smaller local public sectors, and greater dependence on state and federal party linkages for patronage than their Democratic Party counter-parts.[21] The low tax ceiling and underdeveloped city administrative capacity meant that local patronage relied not so much on an army of government workers as on the payrolls of the franchise corporations and other public contractors. At the same time, the threat of a middle-class tax revolt enforced fiscal discipline, limiting the resources available for expanding distributive benefits. Altogether, the dependence on external or private patronage, and the factional divisions within the party, prevented a strong centralization of the machine. Kelly remained the most powerful party leader, but even he had difficulty controlling rivals and sometimes even his own protégés.[22]

CIVIL SOCIETY:
PATRONAGE AND ETHNIC GROUP FORMATION

As in other American cities, machine politics was closely tied to the pattern of working-class and ethnic group formation.[23] In a competitive wage-labor market, one of the most basic structural problems facing workers was gaining access to work, especially during hard times.[24] The machine offered a solution through its system of patronage. William Denahy was an Irish American resident of West Oakland, from a family of neighborhood tavern-owners. He explained,

> In those days if somebody needed a job, if some kid got out of school, or got kicked out of school, the old mother would come down to my dad and say "Timmy needs a job." Well, they'd either go see some guy on the railroad or they'd get him some kind of city job—a policeman's job, or a fireman's job . . . they used to come to my dad because they knew my dad had [Kelly's] ear. He'd say, "So and so needs a job or something." "Did he ever do anything for us?" "Well, he's a pretty good guy, I know the family." "I'll see what I can do." If he said that he knew that he'd be taken care of.[25]

The elder Denahy's status as a tavern-owner underscores the link between the political machine and what was then a typical institution of urban civil society: the saloon. It is estimated that in the years before Prohibition, there were about 450 saloons in Oakland, for a population of less than 200,000 persons (by comparison, in the 1980s, just over 200 bars and restaurants in the city had full liquor licenses, for approximately 350,000 people).[26] Overwhelmingly male, saloon culture emphasized an ethic of masculine status honor, sociability, and reciprocity in rituals of communal drinking. As public places, saloons were familiar sites for economic and political mobilization and for the enactment of social identity, functioning as informal labor bureaus, immigrant assistance centers, and scenes for neighborhood conviviality.[27] The role of the saloon in the city's political culture is vividly conveyed by novelist and Socialist Party activist Jack London in *John Barleycorn*, a memoir of his youth in Oakland:

> In saloons I saw reporters, editors, lawyers, judges, whose names and faces I knew. They put the seal of approval on the saloon. . . . You see, in election time local politicians, aspirants for office, have a way of making the rounds of the saloons to get votes. . . . They have smiles and greetings for everybody—for you, without the price of a glass of beer in your pocket, for the timid hobo who lurks in the corner and who certainly hasn't a vote but who may establish a lodging-house registration. . . . And the next thing you know, you are lined up at the bar, pouring drinks down your throat and learning the gentlemen's names and the offices which they hope to fill.[28]

The system of patronage, however, extended beyond such venues and permeated the civil organization of the ethnic community, through institutions like the family and the Catholic Church. William Denahy recalled,

> Those old Irish priests were really political powers . . . [Father Mc-Nally] was an intimate of Leland Stanford, president of the Southern Pacific Railroad. . . . When he was the pastor at Old St. Mary's, there'd all be Irish gandy dancers, worked in the shops . . . some old Irish guy would get drunk or something, he wouldn't show up, and he'd lose his job. There was a fellow by the name of MacKenzie, and MacKenzie was the, I think, Superintendent of the S.P. of this division, and ran the shops down there. He was a Protestant. . . . Of course he knew that Leland Stanford was a buddy of McNally's. So Mary would come up and say, "Oh, Pat got fired," or something. MacKenzie would come off the streetcar and walk down to shops, and Father McNally would meet him on the corner. He'd walk down to the office with him, and the next day probably, Old Pat would be back to work. He had the juice. They were a power like that.[29]

Denahy's story may have the flavor of barroom lore, but Father McNally and Superintendent McKenzie were in fact well-known figures in the neighborhood, and it suggests the ways in which patronage was popularly understood.[30] Donald Mockel, a retired Oakland police officer, concurred:

> There was this priest at St. Patrick's at Tenth and Peralta Streets . . . he had an "in" with the Bell Telephone Company. There was an Irishman, or someone, was the president, I think his name was Flynn. And he

would get these girls—deserving girls—a job in the telephone company as operators. And then my mother, and my aunt, both went to work and got jobs from the priest at St. Patrick's.[31]

Relations of nepotism and personal favoritism provided access to jobs, creating distinct ethnic labor market niches within the corporations and city government, and reinforcing kin networks as a basis of ethnic group formation. Mockel remembered,

> Even the Water Company, years ago, here, if your father had worked for 'em, or was working, you had first preference, you know, to get a job, they tried to keep it in—and the scavenger company, the same thing. The Italians would buy shares, but then you would turn your shares to your son, and the business, and it would go right on down. And even in our Fire Department, my father was a fireman, and my stepfather was a fireman, my two brothers-in-law were firemen, my cousin's nephew—my cousin's son, is a fire chief out in Berkeley. We were police and firemen, my mother's brother was a policeman, her brother-in-law was a policeman who married my mother's sister, his son retired from the police department, and his two sons are now Oakland policemen.[32]

In this way, the organization of urban machine politics helped foster the process of ethnic group formation in civil society. Large monopoly franchise corporations furnished the resources for private and political patronage brokers to channel economic opportunities to members of favored ethnic groups. These resources were distributed through the private institutions within the ethnic community, including the family and the Catholic Church, as well as through public spaces like the saloon. Working-class dependence on patronage for access to jobs reinforced corporate loyalty, particularly for those with few alternatives, while reliance on kin networks and personal favoritism strengthened patrimonial "family values" and the tendency toward ethnic group closure.

The "values" of patronage, however, came not from any essential immigrant-group culture but from the institutional compromise embedded in the machine. Patronage offered a solution to the problems of economic uncertainty and group inequality. The machine politicians' desire for votes assured that local government would be responsive, at least in this sense, to the needs of its working-class constituents, who by their loyalty earned a means of making claims on more powerful elites. Thus, the regime embodied a specific relationship between the organization of local government and the pattern of group formation in civil society.

URBAN COMMUNITY AND THE LIMITS OF PATRONAGE

Social scientists and historians have sometimes credited urban political machines with achieving the swift assimilation of immigrant populations in the United States into a modern industrializing economic and political order.[33] In this view, the machine cushioned the shock of displacement and socialized successive waves of newcomers to American norms and institutions. At first glance, West Oakland in the early twentieth century appears to have been a successful case of such accommodation. Various personal accounts paint a picture of something like a genuine cultural pluralism, notwithstanding the more obvious biases of hometown boosterism or nostalgia. In 1927, a columnist for a black West Oakland newspaper wrote, "Here Briton, Teuton, Slav, yellow men, Latin and Black live and toil in an atmosphere of peace and harmony . . . good fellowship has grown among them that cannot be found in any other spot along the Pacific Coast." And in 1950, a former West Oakland native reminisced, "laborer, mechanic, business or professional man, all were neighbors. No class lines were drawn. No poverty, no bread lines, and few wealthy people. Wages were not large, hours of work rather long, but everyone was satisfied and happy."[34]

As a political institution, the machine may have succeeded in bringing order and managing the conflicts caused by the rapid socioeconomic development of the city. In the long run, however, the system of ethnic patronage was incapable of sustaining an urban community. Beyond access to jobs, patronage at best offered meager protections for most workers and their families. Wages remained low, and even the largest franchise corporations offered few benefits; most firms had none. On the railroads, disabling injury and death were constant hazards; one crossing near the Oakland mole had so many accidents that it was nicknamed the "Death Curve."[35] Vernon Sappers, a longtime West Oakland resident and railroad employee, described the working conditions on the Southern Pacific:

> There were a great many injuries among the railroad workers. The
> Southern Pacific had a hospital down there and it came in handy for
> men who were critically injured. Men were especially prone to losing
> limbs. . . . What the railroad would do is assign a man who lost an arm
> or a leg to work as a flagman at a crossing—back in the early Twenties
> I remember many flagmen who limped or had a wooden leg or were
> missing an arm. But work as a flagman didn't pay nearly as much as
> an engineer or mechanic—it didn't pay much at all. It was cheaper
> for the railroad than putting in automatic crossing gates.[36]

Similarly, Donald Mockel recalled,

They called [my uncle] "Rags" Murphy, because the railroad gave the oldest boy a job, to keep the family together when someone got killed—his father was killed on the railroad—and so my uncle Daniel J. Murphy went to work for the Southern Pacific, at 14 years old, and he'd go—at 50 cents a day, and there was about a ten hour day, so he'd have his overalls sewed so many times that it was rags, and my grandmother would sew 'em again, and he'd be polishing engines, and he'd have to get underneath the engine and wipe up all the grease and that sort of thing, so every time he'd come from under there he was in rags, so they called him "Rags" Murphy.[37]

Conditions in the factories were not much better. A 1902 newspaper story promoting the California Cotton Mills, "where 500 men, women and children spend their time during six days of the week," acknowledged that "as you enter the main working rooms the hum and buzz of a thousand wheels and spindles almost deafens you . . . many operators seem to be so accustomed to the din that they fail to notice it, but the noise is so great that it is difficult to carry on a conversation."[38] Child labor was not uncommon: In 1909, almost two-thirds of the workers employed in paper box manufacturing in Oakland were under the age of eighteen. In the canneries, a 1913 state Labor Bureau report found that adequate lighting, ventilation, drainage, and toilet facilities were often lacking; an independent 1928 study observed that bandaged hands were common among the women who peeled fruit, and infections and blood poisoning were frequent. A female cannery worker from Oakland later attested, "the hands of the workers are stained and from holding the knife, the fingers blister and the workers' palms get raw. The fruit acid eats right into the sores. . . . Many of the time slips of the knife cut the hands very severely."[39]

What benefits the machine did provide were distributed unequally, according to a hierarchy of ethnic group status and power.[40] Patronage presupposed the competition among groups for privileged access and promoted the hoarding of advantage, as in the ethnic labor market niche. William Denahy's remarks illustrate the order of group hierarchy: Asked if patronage crossed ethnic lines, he replied, "Sure. The Portuguese and a lot of the Italians came in just a little bit behind the Irish in West Oakland." Other groups received considerably less. While African Americans undoubtedly enjoyed greater social acceptance in West Oakland than in the Jim Crow South, their numbers were too small to receive more than token recognition from the machine, and for most black workers occupational segregation was a fact of life, reinforced by other groups' prior monopolization of ethnic labor markets.[41] At the bottom were the Chinese: Denied natural-ization and the right to vote, they remained outside the bounds of ethnic pluralism.

If patronage only marginally improved the lives of most workers, however, it had a decided effect on local government. City hall was plagued by charges of favoritism and corruption, especially in law enforcement and in street and sewer maintenance. Although Boss Kelly always maintained a reputation for personal honesty, others—including his own lieutenants—were less scrupulous, and bribery and graft were familiar practices.[42] Partly as a result, public administration was widely regarded as incompetent and untrustworthy, while the local franchise corporations were seen as equally inefficient, characterized by mismanagement, price gouging, and poor service. In any case, working-class West Oaklanders rarely saw public improvements of any kind; taxes were collected but usually spent on parks, streetlights, and paving in the newer, developing areas, while much of the western waterfront marsh still reeked from its use as a landfill or garbage dump.[43]

In short, the system of ethnic patronage failed to produce a lasting urban community in West Oakland. With the increasing availability of new housing in East Oakland and in the hills, the middle classes began to abandon the neighborhood as early as 1910. The machine did nothing to stop its subsequent decline, and as other parts of the city grew, residential areas in West Oakland were left with inadequate sewers and decaying, poorly paved streets that lacked curbs or sidewalks. Under these conditions, ethnic group solidarities could not hold on to the remaining population, and the old community fragmented and dispersed. When they could afford to, West Oakland ethnics, and their adult children, simply moved out.[44]

Throughout this period, the ethnic diversity and tolerance in West Oakland were at all times bounded by the simultaneous racial segregation of Chinatown. The Chinese were excluded from standard patronage, but the machine was hardly a stranger to the racial enclave. Through selective police enforcement, officially repressed "vice" activities (in particular, gambling) were dumped on the Chinese, while graft from Chinese lotteries provided lucrative returns for the machine.[45] Without access to other opportunities, gambling became a major source of jobs and income for the Chinese population, drawing in revenue from outside the community. According to one account,

> Large sums of money passed through the lottery houses each day,
> but the owners could hardly expect police protection from robbers. . . .
> In most cases, the lottery house owner would belong to a mutual aid
> society which would help regulate the gambling business and also
> provide the houses with protection. . . . The owners had high overhead—

the guards had to be paid, the mutual aid societies supported, and city officials had to be persuaded through bribery to ignore the existence of gambling . . . [but] it was one of the larger revenue-producing businesses in Chinatown, in many cases, providing food for the unemployed in the area.[46]

In an era in which the African American population in Oakland was still small and relatively diffused, Chinatown marked the visible cultural and spatial boundaries between respectable white, Christian society and the deviant, exoticized, "heathen" racial other. Between them, West Oakland and Chinatown symbolized the alternative social dimensions of ethnicity and race for both the native-born white and the European immigrant populations. As aspiring middle classes left ethnic West Oakland for the newer, outlying residential districts (and as new migrants arrived from the American midwestern states), they would have to choose what they would become. The rearticulation of a white racial identity was to play a crucial part in the new middle classes' path of group formation and in their redefinition of the urban community. Such a rearticulation, however, would take place against a backdrop of widening class conflict.

CROSS-CURRENTS IN CIVIL SOCIETY: THE EMERGENCE OF NEW ACTORS

Machine patronage and ethnic particularism were the dominant institutions shaping urban politics and community organization in Oakland during the first decades of the twentieth century. Yet these were not the only forces at work within urban civil society. Other paths of group formation, sometimes parallel and sometimes cross-cutting, were also emerging from socioeconomic conditions and giving rise to new actors. Two important instances were the mobilization of a union labor movement within the working class and a concurrent process of middle-class formation among local businesses and residential property owners. The interaction of the paths of these actors would lead to a conjunctural crisis in the years prior to and immediately after World War I and result in a transformation of class, racial, and ethnic identities in Oakland society and politics.

Working-Class Formation: The Labor Movement

With rapid industrialization came a growing working-class population and the rise of a union labor movement. In Oakland as in the rest of California, class formation coincided with racial formation. Organized labor bore the mark of its origins in the Workingmen's Party agitation of the 1870s, and anti-Chinese exclusionism remained a consistent theme in the movement's repertoire.[47] In this regard the labor movement shared an ideology common to all classes in the white majority, while introducing its own forms of working-class organization and identity into the community and into the public sphere.

The movement took shape first in the city's dominant industry, the railroads. Workers in West Oakland took an active role in the American Railway Union strike of 1894, led nationally by Eugene Debs. Though officially directed at the Pullman Car Company, the strike ignited long-standing local grievances against the Southern Pacific. An estimated one thousand workers left their jobs on the first day of the strike, as crowds of strikers and supporters spontaneously stopped trains and took possession of the Southern Pacific yards, shops, and roundhouses in what amounted to a communitywide uprising against the railroad. The strikers initially enjoyed the tacit acceptance of the local police, but Oakland mayor (and later California governor) George Pardee vigorously denounced their actions, and after two weeks the strikers were finally removed by federal troops.[48]

The West Oakland rail yards were the center of conflict again in 1911, when workers in the metal trades attempted to organize a national System Federation of unions in the repair shops of the Harriman lines. Led by socialist activists in the machinists' union, more than eight hundred machinists, boilermakers, blacksmiths, and helpers struck the Southern Pacific in Oakland. Although this time the strikers were more formally organized than in 1894, the company was likewise prepared. The railroad hired strikebreakers and armed guards to keep the shops open, and the striking metal workers were unable to rally the support of the engineers or operating unions. The conflict in Oakland dragged on for months, during which time one striker was killed and two hundred were arrested, and the company ultimately prevailed after a long and difficult fight.[49]

Outside of the railroads, the Bay Area's economic structure of skilled craft production, small firm size, and relatively insulated West Coast markets facilitated the growth of unions affiliated with the American Federation of Labor (AFL). In Oakland, countywide AFL building trades and central labor councils were organized by the turn of the century, along with councils of unions in the metal and printing trades; and an AFL-sponsored labor newspaper, the *Tri-City Labor Review*, began publishing in 1910. Union membership was strongest in the construction crafts, and from 1908 to 1915 membership in the Alameda County Building Trades Council and other nonrailroad unions rose and fell with the business cycle, ranging between nine thousand and fourteen thousand members.[50]

Craft unionism met the problem of labor market competition by controlling access to skill, and so it frequently paralleled or merged with segmented labor markets defined by ethnicity, race, and gender.[51] In 1920, 92 percent of all workers in transportation and "manufacturing and mechanical" jobs (including construction) in Oakland were men, and crafts like the machinists, electricians, plumbers, steamfitters, teamsters, and building painters were disproportionally native-born and white. By contrast, immigrant whites and people of color filled the majority of unskilled laborer jobs in the shipyards, railroads, canneries, and construction trades. And while the Industrial Workers of the World (IWW) carried on sporadic free speech campaigns in Oakland, that group never became a force among the city's factory workers, who remained largely unorganized.[52]

Based primarily among native-born white males in the skilled crafts, the AFL unions were poorly suited to challenge either the structure of labor market segmentation or the institutions of machine politics. In 1902, the Oakland unions organized a Union Labor Party, nominating their own candidate for mayor in 1903. The Oakland party lacked the resources of its more successful counterpart in San Francisco, however, and its role was reduced to endorsing other major party candidates.[53] The local Socialist Party ran candidates regularly in city, state, and national races, but except for a brief period (1910–1911), it won only a marginal vote, even with Jack London as its standard-bearer for mayor in 1903 and 1905.[54] Although Oakland served as the state headquarters for the party and published its newspaper *The World,* Oakland Socialists bitterly opposed the party fusionists and building-trades unionists in the Union Labor Party. Apart from a joint (and unsuccessful) recall campaign with the Central Labor Council against Mayor Frank Mott in 1912, the Oakland Socialists never built a lasting electoral alliance with the labor movement.

Instead, Oakland unions generally followed a conventional doctrine of AFL voluntarism, alternately bargaining, allying, or competing with machine politicians and reformers.[55] As a result, there was often no unified labor position in local politics. East Bay labor historian Robert Knight writes, "Several union leaders, principally Republicans from the Building Trades Council, held minor positions in the administrations of [Oakland Mayor] Frank Mott. . . . They were not in favor, however, with the many Alameda County Central Labor Council officers who joined the Socialists in denouncing Mott as a 'reactionary' representative of business interests."[56] Forced to contend with more conservative politicians in power, union lead-

ers often found themselves aligned with Kelly and others in support of Johnson and the progressives.[57] The weakness of this alliance, however, limited
the articulation of working-class interests within the regime.

Middle-Class Formation: Downtown and the Suburbs

"Oakland is a city controlled by several great corporations," wrote the Socialist Party *World* in 1909. "The Southern Pacific, the Western Pacific, the
Traction Company, the Water Company, the Realty Syndicate—these are
our lords and masters."[58] In fact, by that time traditional corporate dominance in Oakland was already beginning to break down. Decades of litigation had finally begun to loosen the grip of the Southern Pacific over the
Oakland harbor: In 1897, the California Supreme Court gave back to the
city the title to its waterfront land, and in 1907 the U.S. Court of Appeals
affirmed the city's power to grant wharfing rights to the competing Western Pacific railroad.[59] Meanwhile, the empire of "Borax" Smith fell apart
swiftly in a more spectacular manner. In 1910, Smith severed his connections with Havens and joined with W. S. Tevis and R. G. Hanford in the
United Properties Company, a colossal venture capitalized at $200 million
that was designed to monopolize water, electric power, real estate, and streetcar transit in the East Bay. Within two years, the financing for the project
collapsed, Smith was forced into bankruptcy, and his holdings were left in
disarray. The Key System continued to operate as a public franchise, but it
went through chronic fiscal difficulties and a series of financial reorganiza-
tions over the next two decades.[60]

The traditional franchise corporations had acted like colonial powers, mo-
nopolizing or exploiting the city's resources but otherwise not much interested in its independent economic development. As their power receded, they
gave way to an emerging class of city-based financial, mercantile, and industrial interests, including downtown bankers and retailers, real-estate developers, local manufacturers, and construction firms, all oriented toward
the Oakland market. In 1905 members of this business community founded
the Oakland Chamber of Commerce, the better to promote local economic
growth.[61] The following year saw the creation of an Oakland Real Estate
Board,[62] and in 1908 a chapter of the Rotary Club was formed, with Frank
Bilger—a leading local building and paving contractor—as its first president.[63] This new "growth coalition" was eager to break out of Oakland's
Second City status in the shadow of San Francisco, and develop the city as
an independent East Bay urban center.

In 1905, these elites united behind the election of Frank Mott as mayor.

Mott was a successful small merchant, real-estate developer, and director for the Security Bank and Trust Company; and later that year he joined his colleagues as a founding member of the Chamber of Commerce. Mott had first come to prominence in 1894, when he provided aid, in the form of ax handles from his hardware store, to Mayor George Pardee to help drive a Bay Area contingent of "Coxey's Army" of protesting unemployed workers out of the city. A veteran ward politician, Mott had served on the city council from 1894 to 1905, and his political base lay in the traditional machine Fourth and Sixth Wards and in the downtown "silk stocking" Fifth Ward near Lake Merritt. In Mott, the Oakland business community found among their own a machine leader who could effectively bargain their interests with the railroads and other franchise corporations. Coinciding with the burst of development after the 1906 earthquake, Mott established a "progressive" pro-business machine, aggressively pursuing civic improvements and economic growth.[64]

Mott and the new progrowth elite shared an expansionist economic vision for Oakland and were more willing to spend public funds on urban infrastructure—a departure from the traditional reliance on the low-tax franchise system. As recently as 1904–1905, Oakland voters had rejected bond issues of $2.5 million for a new city hall, parks, streets, and fire protection, and $6 million for the purchase of a municipal water supply. Under Mott's leadership, however, in 1906 the city passed its first nonschool bonds, worth $1.6 million, for parks and sewer construction.[65] Two years later, Mott negotiated a settlement with the Southern Pacific whereby the city would grant the railroad a long-term lease for a large part of the waterfront in exchange for recognition of the city's title and an end to litigation. In March 1909, Mott won reelection along with a platform of charter amendments ratifying the waterfront compromise and establishing a new Park Board and Library Board. Later that year, Mott and his allies placed on the November ballot a $3.73 million bond issue for harbor improvements, public safety, and a new city hall, together with a referendum to annex the huge unincorporated territory east of Lake Merritt, between Twenty-third Avenue and the town of San Leandro.

This area included the suburban localities of Fruitvale (now spelled as one word), Melrose, Fitchburg, and Elmhurst, all of which had grown rapidly after the earthquake and the extension of the Key System lines. Even though they were shortly to be included within Oakland, these communities had been and in effect remained "the suburbs," with their own distinct structure and identity. Physically separated from downtown and West Oakland by Lake Merritt, Trestle Glen canyon, and the Piedmont hills, the residents of these areas had only recently (in 1907) rejected an annexation effort. Led by maverick small businessman T. F. Marshall and his Alameda County Progress Club, antimachine reformers now successfully mobilized territory residents to demand a new city charter as a condition of annexation. The business elites, not wanting to lose another vote, agreed. In November 1909, the bond issue and annexation passed almost unanimously. Annexation more than tripled the total area of the city, from 16.6 to 60.1 square miles. The newly expanded East Oakland Seventh Ward alone accounted for 48,677 people in 1910, or nearly one-third of the city's total population.[66]

As promised during the campaign, the city agreed to hold an election on June 10, 1910, for a board of freeholders, which would have the authority to draft a new city charter. Marshall and his allies wanted to replace the ward-based mayor-council system with a commission form of government, which they believed would eliminate the power of machine politicians and the franchise corporations. With the support of progressive small businessmen and middle-class residents in East Oakland, Marshall organized the Greater Oakland Charter Convention, electing several candidates to the board of freeholders and influencing the provisions of the new charter. The final version abolished the ward system and established a nonpartisan city council composed of a weak mayor and four city commissioners, elected at-large to staggered four-year terms. Legislative and executive authority were combined in the new council, with commissioners heading city departments of revenue and finance, streets, health and public safety, and public works. The commission charter was ratified overwhelmingly by the voters in December 1910 and took effect the following year.[67]

With great cynicism, the Socialist Party *World* dismissed the charter reform movement as a dispute between the more pro-corporate downtown elites and the independent suburban petite bourgeoisie:

> On the one hand is arrayed the forces of Big Business such as the railroad companies, the Oakland Transit, the Water company, the gas and power companies, etc.—These are quietly working through the present [Mott] city administration. One the other hand are arrayed the merchants, landlords, and small business men who are working through what is known as the Marshall convention to secure a new charter that will protect their business interests by restricting the more successful and powerful corporations to the end that the middle class may secure a larger share of the surplus wealth created by the unpaid labor of the working class.[68]

The World may have oversimplified, but the victory of the new charter unmistakably heralded the emergence of "downtown" and "the suburbs" as important actors and demonstrated the power of their political alliance. In 1911, Mott was reelected mayor, and over the next four years he continued his program of ambitious public expenditure, overseeing passage of more than $6 million in bonds for a new municipal auditorium, schools, sewers, and other improvements. In June 1913, Mayor Mott proudly presided over the opening of the new fifteen-story, gleaming white granite City Hall, nicknamed "Mott's wedding cake" in honor of his recent marriage, in ceremonies that seemed to announce a bold, progressive, and prosperous future for Oakland.

THE CRISIS OF THE OLD ORDER:
WORLD WAR I AND AFTERWARD

The charter reform appeared to signify a victory for the new middle classes, but in practice, it proved to be an almost complete failure. Far from eliminating machine politics, the new commission government merely fragmented and multiplied it. Incumbent commissioners quickly learned to turn their administrative departments into political fiefdoms, in order to secure the resources necessary to run for reelection. Council business fell to logrolling among commissioners to meet their particular needs, and any combination of three (the mayor also had a vote) could form a majority clique to control votes in their favor. Such cliques formed and collapsed continually, and factional divisions were reproduced in rival patronage networks within departments.[69]

In 1915, John L. Davie defeated downtown businessman Bilger to become mayor of Oakland, and four years later he won reelection against Chamber of Commerce president Joseph King.[70] Davie was a former Populist and a colorful figure in Oakland politics, having first gained attention in the 1890s for his pitched battles with the Southern Pacific to establish an independent coal yard and competing ferry service on its waterfront property. His election marked a defeat for the new downtown coalition and a return to a more traditional style of machine governance. Unlike Mott, under Davie the city reverted to the decentralized system of subsidized private development, liberalizing the rules governing franchises and granting new leases for the waterfront.[71] These changes helped cement Davie's relations with the Kelly machine, and he held the mayor's office continuously for sixteen years, from 1915 until 1931. Known for his stylish dress and flowing moustache, Davie was a master both of public political spectacle and of the council's backroom dealings, and he maintained his stance as a populist outsider in part through his constant feuding with the other councillors.[72] His politics of personality allowed him to stay atop the city's factional instability, even as the latter undermined the regime's governing effectiveness and increasingly alienated public opinion.

By 1920, the machine as a whole was rapidly losing its capacity to hold together the actors in the urban polity. World War I accelerated changes in the economy that had been developing over the previous decades, including a growing level of industrialization and a widening class conflict. Between 1900 and 1920, the relative size of the manufacturing working class increased from 31 percent of the Oakland labor force to nearly 40 percent, as industrial development spread out along a perimeter from the bayside waterfront in West Oakland to the flats beside the estuary in East Oakland. In 1916, the *San Francisco Examiner* reported that twenty-five factories had opened or expanded in Oakland the previous year, including a new Chevrolet automobile assembly plant on Foothill Boulevard. Wartime production also boosted the city's food processing industries: Between 1917 and 1921 six major canning or packing firms were founded or significantly enlarged. Finally, shipbuilding took off in 1917, and in the peak year of 1920 the shipyards alone employed more than forty thousand men—more than all other local industries combined.[73]

The wartime boom brought with it a rising cost of living and a renewed militancy among Oakland workers, much of it centered on the waterfront. In March 1917, several hundred members of the new Shipyard Laborers' Union struck the two largest East Bay shipyards for more than two weeks, winning tacit union recognition and higher wages. In September, thirty thousand metal-trades workers shut down shipyards, foundries, and metal shops throughout the Bay Area, leading to an increased wage scale set by the federal Shipbuilding Labor Adjustment Board. The following year, the East Bay Boilermakers' Union struck again to enforce the pay scale in the Oakland and Alameda yards. By mid 1918, the Boilermakers, Shipyard Laborers, and Machinists were the three largest unions in East Bay, each with between fifteen hundred and five thousand members. That same year, the *Tri-City Labor Review* estimated that there were between thirty-five thousand and forty thousand union members in Alameda County as a whole.[74]

Labor militancy extended beyond the shipyards to include many previously unorganized or unskilled workers, and spontaneous strikes or new union activity appeared among railroad laborers, cannery workers, slaughterhouse butchers, building janitors, and female telephone operators. In July 1917, more than a thousand mainly Italian male and female workers belonging to the AFL-affiliated "Toilers of the World" struck against canneries in San Jose and San Francisco. A group of 150 strikers from San Francisco traveled across the bay twice to convince Oakland cannery workers to join the action, but were stopped and sent back each time by Oakland police. The next year, however, female fruit cutters at the Griffin and Skelley cannery in Oakland walked out on their own in protest against a speedup in piece rates.[75]

In 1918, the Central Labor Council chartered the Factory, Mill and Warehouse Employees' Union, an AFL federal union. As Knight observes, "Taking in men and women from groups not always welcome to established AFL unions—Portuguese immigrants, Mexicans, Negroes—the Factory, Mill and Warehouse Employees' Union by late 1918 had gained a foothold in a number of manufacturing industries. Its membership embraced workers in plants producing paper, paint, sulphur, fertilizer, textiles, and canned fruit and vegetables." Similarly, the militant Shipyard Laborers' Union "rejected the race barriers characteristic of AFL organizations. The union enrolled large numbers of Negroes, elected a Negro among its officers, and marched in the Oakland Labor Day Parade with a banner proclaiming its freedom from racial discrimination."[76]

The AFL unions' commitment to such initiatives was at best tentative, but the new militancy signified a widening of the labor movement's social base and its potential development as a working-class actor, beyond the limits of craft and ethnic segmentation. And though hardly revolutionary, the growing level of unionization stirred an immediate countermobilization from local businesses, which generated a reactive sequence of increasing labor repression and class polarization. The Oakland Chamber of Commerce followed its San Francisco counterpart in declaring itself in favor of the open shop, and in 1917 it successfully placed an antipicketing ordinance on the city ballot that passed by a slim margin. Local police and federal agents appeared at meetings of the Factory, Mill and Warehouse Employees' Union, allegedly at the behest of the employers, and on one occasion abruptly closed down a large mass meeting held for the cotton mill workers.[77]

These struggles intensified after the war. In October 1919, eleven hundred streetcar and ferry operators struck the Key System for ten days. The company hired 250 armed strikebreakers from the notorious "Black Jack" Jerome Detective Agency, and defied strikers by parading an armored streetcar down its main lines, accompanied by local police automobiles. In the violence that followed, forty people were seriously injured, several by gunshot wounds. Five men and two women were killed in a trolley accident, and police made forty-eight strike-related arrests. Union representatives appeared before a city council meeting and denounced Police Chief John Lynch for "beating men and women with a club while giving aid and protection to the thugs and gunmen of the street car company." The council responded by authorizing one hundred special police to control the strike.[78]

In the war industries, the withdrawal of federal mediation raised the stakes even higher. In September 1919, Bay Area longshore workers struck, advancing radical demands for employee stock ownership and a number of seats on the steamship company boards. After several months, the shipowners signed a closed-shop contract with a "blue book" (company-sponsored) union, locking out and effectively breaking the striking workers' union. In the winter of 1919–1920, some sixty thousand Bay Area shipyard workers struck for ten months—the fourth largest labor dispute of the national postwar strike wave.[79]

By 1921, however, the country had entered into a postwar economic recession, and rising unemployment shifted the advantage to the employers. In November 1921, Bay Area employers formed the Industrial Association and pledged one million dollars to a concerted drive to break the craft unions. The association organized banks and suppliers to discriminate against unionized building contractors, employed private labor spies and security forces, and maintained a hiring hall to recruit strikebreakers. Strikes by the building trades and the sailors' unions in 1921, and of the iron molders and the building trades again in 1922, all ended in defeat for the unions and the imposition of the open shop. By 1923, local Chamber of Commerce advertising was already boasting of general open-shop conditions in Oakland.[80]

CONCLUSION:
TRAJECTORIES AND TRANSFORMATIONS

The postwar strikes were extraordinarily hard-fought and bitter, with lasting effects in the local community. In the metal trades, the "molders' war" actually went on for years, during which time three men were killed, fifteen were seriously injured, and at least sixty-three acts of violence were reported.[81] The outcome, however, was a decisive victory for the employers, and a critical juncture in the relations among groups in Oakland politics and civil society. On the one hand, the fledgling industrial unions were destroyed, and the labor movement as a whole virtually collapsed as an actor in the urban polity. On the other, the open-shop drive gave an important stimulus to class organization for local businesses and employers, as we shall see. Between them, the machine's failure to mediate the escalating class conflict exposed a serious political weakness, and with the decline of the craft unions it lost an important organizational ally among the traditional working class.

In the aftermath of World War I, a period in Oakland's social and political history began to close. The first decades of the century had seen the forging of a durable alliance of structurally based groups, bound together through institutionalized relations in local politics and civil society. Corporate enterprises, machine politicians, and immigrant working classes were united through the medium of ethnic patronage. By the 1920s, however, changes in the structural bases and social composition of groups, in the institutions and opportunities for political action, and in the patterns of group formation in civil society all combined to undermine the old order.

These processes left the patronage regime increasingly vulnerable to opposition. With the defeat of the working-class challenge, other actors moved to center stage in Oakland politics. As the decade of the '20s began, Oakland swung into a new phase of urban development, one that was to create the conditions for another challenge to the ethnic machine. This time, however, popular insurgency took the form of a white nativist movement, embodied in the mobilization led by the Ku Klux Klan.

3   The Making of a White Middle Class
The Ku Klux Klan and Urban Reform

In the early twentieth century, corporate power, machine politics, and ethnic patronage were the dominant institutional forces affecting community life in Oakland. By the 1920s, however, all three had begun to break down. In the wake of structural and conjunctural changes stimulated by the 1906 earthquake and the First World War, new actors began to appear on the urban scene, including a militant union labor movement, a nascent downtown business elite, and a suburban middle class. The latter two came together in the 1910 commission charter reform, but their efforts failed to dislodge the power of machine politics. In the 1920s, however, these two groups were to play a decisive role in the transformation of the urban regime.

In this chapter, I focus on the political development of middle-class residents and downtown business elites as collective actors. I begin by examining the rise of the white Protestant middle-class population and its formation as a group. Concentrated especially in the newer residential areas in East Oakland, this group drew on racial, class, and moral discourses to define its own collective identity and distinguish itself from the ethnic working class. As it grew, its path of formation collided with the interests allied in the old regime over control of the urban environment. This trajectory of conflict created the opportunities for the emergence of the Ku Klux Klan as a social movement.

What was the content, or meaning, of this movement? As noted in chapter 1, traditional interpretations of the urban Second Klan of the '20s have portrayed it as a reactionary, antimodernist "status backlash" movement of a declining old Protestant middle class, left behind by the triumph of urban pluralism and liberal assimilation. More recently, a new body of empirical research has found a broader social base and ideological appeal in the movement, leading some historians to propose a more benign view of it as a kind of moderate and even progressive "civic populism."[1] Neither of these interpretations adequately accounts for the events in this case. White middle-class Protestants were a rising group in Oakland, and the issues that concerned them were as modern and contemporary as efficient public administration and city streets built to handle the traffic of automobiles. These civic issues, however, were inseparable from institutionalized patterns of urban racial and class formation.

In this way, I argue that notwithstanding its antiblack racism, the Oakland Klan movement had its greatest impact on the city's majority white population. Racial prejudice against nonwhites was already common across the mainstream political spectrum, and the small black and Asian populations in Oakland posed little competitive threat to most whites. Rather, the Klan crystallized emerging conflicts over the boundaries of local political community and over the definition of the rights and privileges associated with white racial identity. As such, the movement was an integral part of an important phase in the making of an urban white middle class.

By the mid '20s, the regime in Oakland faced several challenges, not only from the Klan but also from the new downtown business elite. The rise and fall of the Oakland Klan did not simply occur as an outcome of the interactions between movement and regime, but involved a conjunctural conflict among at least three actors: machine, Klan, and "downtown." Ultimately, the business elite succeeded in overthrowing machine politics, forging its own alliance with the Klan's constituency, and institutionalizing a new regime. The result shifted the terrain of local politics from a central axis of ethnicity to one defined by primarily by social relations of class.

SOCIAL STRUCTURE AND CIVIL SOCIETY: SPACE, CLASS, AND RACIAL FORMATION

The old political machine was built on the social base of the immigrant ethnic working classes in West Oakland. By the 1920s, however, those groups were no longer driving the new population growth in the city. In 1910, whites of "foreign stock" (foreign-born or native-born of foreign or mixed parents) had accounted for 61 percent of the white population in Oakland. With the decline of immigration during World War I and afterward, native-born whites of native parentage grew from 39 percent of all whites in 1910 to 44 percent in 1920, and continued rising to 49 percent by 1930.[2] At the same time, surveys by the U.S. Census Bureau show, the proportion of Roman Catholics among the city's total church membership fell, from 68 percent in 1916 to 54 percent in 1926.[3]

Moreover, despite its industrial expansion, the city as a whole was actually becoming more middle class. By 1922 the shipyard boom had ended, and commercial and residential growth rapidly took off. Professional, clerical, and trade employment climbed from 35 percent of the city's working population in 1920 to 42 percent in 1930, while industrial employment (including transportation and "mechanical and manufacturing" occupations) correspondingly fell, from 49 percent to 42 percent. The level of home ownership also increased: Owner occupancy rates rose from 41 percent of Oakland homes in 1920 to 49 percent in 1930.[4] Altogether, native white Protestant middle classes were hardly a declining group in Oakland. Rather, the data suggest more strongly the image of a rising group that was gradually acquiring the resources and capacity to make its presence felt in the political arena.

The path of formation for this group, however, departed from the traditional pattern in the city, and its social and spatial practice would radically transform the terrain of urban civil society. If areas like West Oakland were known for a degree of racial and ethnic tolerance, the residents of the new middle-class neighborhoods increasingly demanded a strict racial homogeneity as an essential part of their urban environment. Advertisements for the newer subdivisions boasted of housing covenants barring racial minorities. Promoters of the Maxwell Park district at Fifty-fifth Avenue assured buyers that "the property is restricted as to Orientals, Asiatics and Africans," while agents for the adjacent Central Terrace development stated bluntly, "No member of the African or Asiatic Races will be permitted to hold title or rental."[5] In 1918, an ordinance was introduced in the city council to prohibit blacks from buying property in the recently opened Santa Fe tract in North Oakland, but normally such official action was unnecessary, as homeowners' groups usually enforced covenants themselves.[6] White residents did not hesitate to act collectively to defend racial boundaries: In East Oakland, parents of public-school children organized a boycott to protest the presence of Chinese American students at the John Swett School on Thirteenth Avenue, while threats of violence were made against black homebuyers on Halliday Avenue in Eastmont and in the affluent Rockridge neighborhood in North Oakland. E. A. Daly, a black newspaper publisher and real-estate agent in Oakland, recalled,

> In 1923 Mr. Burt Powell . . . bought a house on Manila Avenue. We had to protect him for three or four weeks because the white people wanted to kill him because he moved in a white district. So we worked for him

to watch over him for a period of twenty-four hours for about three months. After then things kind of quieted down. . . . There was another one on Genoa Street in the 5700 block. They put up a new house there and a Negro moved in. The white people tried to run this colored man out and we had to watch over him for about a month, day and night, to keep the white people from molesting him.[7]

In Piedmont, a wealthy suburban enclave in the Oakland hills, police refused to provide protection for Sidney Dearing, the only black homeowner in town. When Dearing chose not to move, the city began condemnation proceedings against his property in order to force him out.[8] These actions were not without impact: By 1930, the population of East Oakland was less than 0.7 percent black, compared to 2.6 percent for the city as a whole.[9]

Along with racial homogeneity came demands for ethnic and cultural uniformity, as pressures for immigration restriction and "Americanization" became more prominent after World War I. The November 1921 issue of *The Crusader*, an Oakland monthly paper "published in the interests of American Principles and Ideals, Law Enforcement and Social and Moral Reform," editorialized, "The problem of immigration to the United States is as serious a problem for this country as Irish ascendancy. The dangers are the same. . . . The more we get of Southern Ireland and Southern Europe the quicker the control of the United States will pass into their hands." *The Crusader* offered a standard nativist solution for the nation's ills: "[If] this country corrects prevailing illiteracy, passes legislation in every state compelling all children between the ages of 7 and 16 years to attend the American Public School, and restricts immigration to those who are desirable and capable of assimilation, our crime sheets will be reduced by half, there will be little foreign agitation in our midst, and the political power of the Roman Catholic Church will wane to zero."[10]

Other public figures echoed these alarms. The Oakland superintendent of schools wrote in the *Oakland Tribune Yearbook* in 1920, "There are thousands of men in Oakland who, without the English language, or knowledge of citizenship, are sources of greatest danger to our government."[11] Shortly before his successful campaign for Congress in 1922, insurance salesman J. H. MacLafferty was touted in the same periodical as "[a believer] in the defense and perpetuation of American ideals as they were handed down by our forefathers . . . he stresses the need of protecting the Government from its enemies within—the 'reds'—and the enemies without—the Japanese. Americanism is his creed."[12]

Protestant nativism often found close company with Prohibitionism. The latter incorporated prejudice against lower-class ethnic and especially

Catholic morals and provided a key test of the probity of public officials.[13] More than a third of Oakland voters in 1910 had favored a dry amendment to the city charter reform, well before Prohibition took effect nationwide in 1920. The amendment, which would have banned saloons in residential neighborhoods, won 44 percent of the vote in the old East Oakland Seventh Ward and 46 percent in the North Oakland First Ward, compared to only 22 and 9 percent in the machine's West Oakland Fourth and Sixth Wards, respectively.[14] Opposition to booze went hand in hand with calls for greater control over other forms of deviance as well. In March 1921, residents in the vicinity of Twenty-ninth Avenue complained of gambling and loitering among young men attending night classes in Americanization at the Lazear public school in East Oakland. Despite school principal Thomas Hennessey's attempts to intercede, police arrested fourteen youths (with names like Gomez, Carelli, Cravalho, Souza, Pastaro, Duarte, Freitas, Ammeli, and Prussinovski) on charges of "vagrancy," with bail set at a hundred dollars each.[15]

Elements of nativism, Americanism, and Protestant moralism merged together to form a background for antimachine reformism. This can be seen in the rhetoric of good government groups like the Alameda County Federation, led by R. H. Marchant, president of the Marchant Calculating Machine Company, and J. L. Howard, vice president of the Chamber of Commerce. The federation's 1918 campaign literature railed against the "ring of professional politicians and their satellites 'bossed' by a politician who, by reason of his control of the voting element in certain sections of the city, can make or ruin an officeholder. . . . The platform of such 'rings' is graft, special privilege, and 'long live the saloon.'" According to the federation, "For many years the 'MIKE KELLY MACHINE' has been in control. . . . The bulk of its financial support has always come from the saloons, the liquor interests, the gambling joints, and the 'Red Light District.' It has consistently fought every DRY measure in the Legislature, and is now supporting WET candidates for County and State offices in an endeavor to save everything for the saloon." For the federation, moral and political reform were linked to lower taxes, a perennial middle-class goal: "The Alameda County Federation is a non-partisan, non-sectarian organization, formed by local business men for the purpose of securing better and CHEAPER government for Alameda County. . . . Stop the machine that has been joy-riding on the taxpayers' money! . . . Vote to put the same spirit of patriotic economy in the County that you show in your homes."[16]

These public discourses contributed to an emergent collective self-consciousness among the Protestant white middle classes in Oakland. Demands for racial, class, and moral homogeneity marked the boundaries of group cultural identity and articulated a sense of the rights and entitlements of first-class, white racial citizenship. Similarly, attacks on the Catholic Church, the saloon, and the machine targeted the institutional embodiments of rival, ethnic working-class formation and political power. For middle-class residents, racial and nativist constructions of identity affirmed their aspirations for upward social mobility and gave meaning to their experiences of living in the new neighborhoods. Their formation as a "community" was, in effect, the making of a white middle class. As this group began to mobilize politically, they began to define themselves in concrete struggles over the control of urban development, and particularly in the opposition of the suburbs toward the machine.

THE POLITICS OF URBAN DEVELOPMENT:
THE SUBURBS VERSUS THE MACHINE

In the '20s, the effects of rapid urban development were most pronounced in East Oakland, the fastest-growing area in the city. After years of shortage during the war, construction of residential housing in Oakland surged in the early '20s: 12,823 new single-family houses were built from 1921 to 1924, more than a 50 percent increase over the total for the previous ten years combined. According to estimates, almost 85 percent of these new homes were located in East Oakland. Rows of detached, one-story stucco houses known as California bungalows multiplied over the foothills and flatlands of Fruitvale, Melrose, and Elmhurst, while more expensive Mediterranean- and Tudor-style houses began to reach up into the steeper hill areas. Between 1920 and 1930 the population of East Oakland (Brooklyn Township) nearly doubled, from 76,174 to 146,938, surpassing the total (137,126) for the entire rest of the city.[17]

This explosive population growth upset the balance of power in city politics, as East Oakland became a substantial part of the potential electorate and a competitive ground for political entrepreneurs. Yet the area, which had only recently joined the city in 1909, was not easily incorporated within the institutional framework of the old machine. East Oaklanders were distant from the political networks based in the older and more ethnically diverse West Oakland.[18] Excluded from or simply less dependent on the machine's patronage for jobs, the middle-class residents in the newer sections of Oakland focused their concerns on lower taxes, city services, and the quality of life in their neighborhoods.

Booming growth conditions quickly led to accumulating grievances against the local authorities over basic services like sewers and street paving. Not coincidentally, the latter were prime sources of patronage for the machine, traditionally organized in cooperation with the private contractors' association or "paving combine." When letting contracts for new or resurfaced streets, the city specified the use of materials or paving processes owned or patented by members of the combine. The royalties for these would be set so high, however, that no builder could afford them except the other members of the combine, who secretly were allowed to pay a much lower fee. The leaders of the combine then decided which member would be the low bidder for each job, thus eliminating competition. Under the state's Vrooman Act, street contractors also hired temporary building inspectors who were not civil servants, thereby assuring their cooperation and providing additional patronage jobs.[19] Allegations of a paving combine arose during the administration of Commissioner of Streets William Baccus, himself a building contractor and a twenty-year veteran of the city council, who had first been elected in 1903 from the old machine Sixth Ward in West Oakland.[20]

The result of such collusion was often substandard work on the physical infrastructure of the new neighborhoods. Complaints of poor construction and rapid disintegration of pavements were made in 1925 by homeowners on 101st, 103rd, and 104th Avenues in East Oakland, while inadequate oil macadam streets on Eighty-first and Eighty-second Avenues collapsed under heavy auto and truck traffic.[21] Members of the Thirteenth Avenue Improvement Club claimed contractor overcharges of sixteen thousand dollars on their street, which reportedly began cracking only three months after completion. Club members demanded and got an investigation by the city council that lasted for seven weeks. When the council ultimately ruled against the residents, club president L. B. Self initiated an unsuccessful recall petition against Commissioner Baccus, accusing him of corruption, negligence, and having "used intoxicating liquors to excess."[22]

Such antagonisms contributed to a growing crisis of the regime's legitimacy in the new residential areas. In parts of East Oakland the city government barely maintained its authority over civil order: In 1921, residents of the Dimond district formed their own vigilante police force, and the following year Phillip Reilly, the iconoclastic editor of the weekly political broadside *Free Press*, was reportedly beaten, and then tarred and feathered by a mob, near his home on Ninety-third Avenue.[23] Three years later, homeowners in a marshy area in the flats of Elmhurst protested that a storm sewer built for the more affluent hill neighborhoods drained into an open ravine that ran through their property and flooded during the winter rains. When Commissioner Baccus refused their demands for action, the residents, led by the Reverend Henry Weimken of the Ninety-second Avenue Evangelical Lutheran Church, sealed off the sewer themselves and threatened to use shotguns against any city personnel invading their land. The city attorney could not confirm the legal status of the sewer, and the police department declined to intervene. After a prolonged standoff between armed homeowners and the Streets Department, the city finally agreed to build a culvert to protect the residents' property.[24]

These incidents gained significance from their structural and institutional context. The decade of the '20s in Oakland witnessed the rise of a native-born Protestant middle-class population, particularly in the rapidly developing suburban residential areas of the city. Alienated from or as yet weakly incorporated into municipal political institutions, these new middle classes increasingly defined their interests in opposition to the urban regime. Because the regime itself was organized in the framework of ethnic patronage, Protestant nativism offered a powerful ideological frame for uniting a range of middle-class grievances against the machine. In this context, the political mobilization of group identity took shape in an urban social movement, led by the Ku Klux Klan.

THE KU KLUX KLAN IN OAKLAND, 1921–1925

By August 1921, organizers W. G. McRae and R. M. Carruthers of the Knights of the Ku Klux Klan, Inc., had opened an office in downtown Oakland. Klan agents promoted the organization as a patriotic fraternal society, dedicated to "keep[ing] closer check upon public officials," to preventing "laxity in the discharging of the duties of public offices," and to "fix[ing] its attention on the prosecution of cases involving the honor of women."[25] Oakland Klan No. 9 was formally chartered in January 1922, and in March, reporters were brought secretly to bear witness as one thousand masked members initiated several hundred more in the rural Contra Costa hills north of the city. A week later, journalists were again invited to watch as six hooded Klansmen performed funeral services for a deceased member at a local crematorium.[26]

By 1924, Klan No. 9 had at least two thousand members and claimed a following of many thousands more. Newspaper reports along with civil and criminal case records reveal the names of sixty-nine local Klansmen in Oakland, of whom fifty-eight are identifiable through city directories and other sources. Though not a representative sample, these included some of the most prominent and active Klan members, and their characteristics are suggestive.[27] Klan members included Protestant churchmen, small businessmen, professionals, managers and salesmen, skilled workers, members of the Oakland Fire Department, and even the son of a congressman. Forty-nine of the known Klansmen lived in Oakland, with the remainder residing in Berkeley, Piedmont, or more distant suburbs. Among Oakland residents, twenty-nine (58 percent) lived in East Oakland, eight (16 percent) lived in North Oakland, and thirteen (26 percent) lived downtown or in West Oakland.[28] Together, only 23 percent of the known Klansmen lived in the old neighborhood of West Oakland, while three-quarters lived in the outer areas of the city or the suburbs.

These findings are consistent with other recent case studies that show a broad socioeconomic base of support for the movement. Moreover, Klan membership in Oakland does not appear to have been concentrated in declining older or ethnically changing neighborhoods, but rather in the newer, more homogeneous middle-class areas.[29] Nor was this an especially transient group: Household status was available for forty-nine members, and of these eight (16 percent) were roomers and boarders, while five times as many (forty-one, or 84 percent) lived in their own households. Altogether, the data suggest that Klan members were recruited mainly from independent or rising social strata, reflecting the broader trend in the Oakland population.

Growth in the California Klan was interrupted in the summer of 1922 when Los Angeles District Attorney Thomas Lee Woolwine raided Southern California Klan offices and uncovered membership lists for the entire Pacific Coast region. These lists were circulated to district attorneys throughout the state, and adverse publicity brought a reaction against the order and mass defections of exposed members. In Oakland, the city council unanimously passed an ordinance, introduced by Commissioner of Health and Safety Frank Colbourn, to ban masking in public. Yet although the names of some fifty Oakland residents (including current and former city police) were reportedly on the list, Alameda County District Attorney Ezra DeCoto never released the names, and the Oakland Klan was seemingly unaffected by the scandal.[30]

On the contrary, local Klan activity escalated with the November elections that fall. The state governor's race pitted the conservative dry Republican candidate Friend Richardson against District Attorney Woolwine, the Klan's hated adversary and a wet Catholic Democrat. The state Klan endorsed Richardson, who refused to comment during the campaign on his alleged ties to the order.[31] When Woolwine spoke in Oakland in October, a band of Klansmen rushed the stage and tried to place a Klan image on the platform. The following week, the Klan held their own rally at the Oakland Auditorium, where one speaker declared, "The election of Richardson is imperative if we are to remove the Jews, Catholics and Negroes from public life in California." Anti-Catholicism also played a role in local races, especially the campaign against Police Judge Edward Tyrrell. Opponents flooded the city with phony literature that endorsed candidates purportedly seeking to "Catholicize America," signed with false names suggesting a Catholic organization.[32] Tyrrell survived the challenge to his reelection, but Richardson won an overwhelming statewide majority to become the new governor.

A Klan flyer printed in Oakland tells us something of the ideological content of the movement's appeal and its vision of political community. Addressed to the "native-born, Protestant, gentile American," the flyer declared that

THE KU KLUX KLAN HAS PLEDGED
   ITSELF TO:
Uphold white supremacy;
Oppose entangling European alliances;
Encouragement of and belief in the free public
   schools;
The separation of church and state;
Restriction of immigration and the prompt deportation of alien criminals;
Insistance [sic] on and the support of law enforcement;
The open Bible;
The continuance of American ideals laid
   down by our forefathers;
Free speech; free press; one language; and one flag;
AMERICANIZATION OF ALL![33]

The values of white supremacy, isolationism, immigrant restriction, law enforcement, and the Christian Bible are familiar themes from Protestant nativism. The insistence on separation of church and state, though perhaps less transparent, may reflect fears of Catholic social and political power in the machine. But the demands for Americanization, free public schools, and "free speech; free press; one language; and one flag" perhaps best capture the Klan's ideal of a homogeneous cultural community of citizens of a white republic.[34] "If you believe in a Government of the people, for the people, and by the people," the flyer listed as one of its conditions—with little doubt about who constituted the "people"—"Then you are eligible to join the Knights of the Ku Klux Klan."

Locally, the Klan functioned as a semiofficial vigilante group, accompanying federal agents on prohibition raids, and as a secret fraternal society, in an era when fraternal societies were a common vehicle of grassroots political organization.[35] In 1923, Klan No. 9 Kligrapp (secretary) Ed L. Arnest and Exalted Cyclops (president) Leon C. Francis ran for city commissioner and school board member, respectively. Both candidates received the endorsement of *The Crusader*, and Francis was endorsed by the Christian Citizens' League, of which he was a member.[36] Despite crowded fields in both races, Arnest won 9 percent and Francis 18 percent of the vote in the primaries.[37]

The next summer, organizers planned a statewide convention in Oakland and secured a parade permit from the city for the Fourth of July. Citing the threat of violence, however, Commissioner Frank Colbourn later revoked the permit. Hundreds of Klan members and supporters protested at a city council hearing, but Colbourn remained firm. The convention and parade were relocated to the nearby city of Richmond, where a reported three thousand Klansmen marched on July 4, followed by an evening initiation ceremony in the El Cerrito hills.[38]

As late as October 1924, the Oakland Klan continued to grow, holding group initiations of fifty or more recruits. By the end of the year, however, tensions erupted between local activists and the Atlanta-based national organization over the latter's efforts to impose greater control over the California realm. At a meeting on November 28, 1924, some five hundred members of Klan No. 9 unanimously passed a resolution refusing to recognize the authority of Imperial representative G. W. Price and asking for his removal. The next day Price, acting for Imperial Wizard Hiram Evans, suspended the charter of Klan No. 9, and the following January the parent corporation filed suit to recover assets and the rights to its name. Klan No. 9 remained active through April 1925, when its property was seized as part of the protracted litigation. Although Klan No. 9 eventually won all of its legal battles (its suspension was ruled illegal on procedural grounds), its resources were exhausted and the organization thereafter disintegrated.[39]

This apparently was not the end of the Klan movement, however. Before their suspension, the Oakland leaders had transferred their group's funds to a parallel organization called the East Bay Club, Inc. Some months earlier, Southern California Klansmen J. F. DeBorde and Charles Hayes had organized a rival corporation under the laws of the state of Nevada called the Invisible Empire Knights of the Ku Klux Klan, Inc. Through late 1924 and into 1925, Klan No. 9 leaders collaborated with DeBorde and Hayes in recruiting their members to join the Nevada Klan. In February 1925, DeBorde, Hayes, and others organized a California corporation called the White Cross Clan. The organizers declared their purposes to be as follows:

1) To promote the welfare of the Caucasian race and to teach the doctrine of white supremacy, 2) To promote the doctrines and tenets of Protestant Christianity, 3) To promote and maintain the purity of white blood, and 4) To promote, develop, and safeguard the ideals of American citizens and the high standards in social and political relations, including the rightful use of ballots and the enforcement of law by regular constituted authorities.[40]

In May 1925 a charter was granted to Oakland Clan No. 9 of the White Cross Clan. By this time there were at least three organizations known as Klan (or Clan) No. 9 in Oakland, in addition to the East Bay Club.[41] Finally, in a show of strength by the national order, in August 1925 Great Titan T. S. Moodie held an initiation of five hundred "aliens" into the apparently loyal Oakland Klan Nos. 1 and 3. The ceremony was conducted in the Oakland Auditorium, attended by eighty-five hundred Klansmen and -women and their supporters, and featuring a seventy-five-piece band from the Oakland organization and drill teams from the national Klavaliers and Women of the Ku Klux Klan.[42]

Whether this signified the decline or proliferation of local Klan organization is unclear, as the fate of the other Klaverns is not known. In any case, the Oakland Klan's internal disputes evidently caused the movement no public discredit; on the contrary, hundreds of spectators packed the civil case hearings to show their support.[43] Moreover, Oakland Klan leaders remained active political entrepreneurs, with extensive ties to other civic, fraternal, and political activities. Leon C. Francis—Cyclops of Klan No. 9, president of the East Bay Club, and vice president of the state White Cross Clan—was a member of the Masons, the American Legion, and later the Republican Party state central committee.[44] Klansman Fred Haase testified as an expert witness for the Thirteenth Avenue Improvement Club in the paving controversy and participated in the recall effort against Commissioner of Streets Baccus, along with Klan No. 9 officers Andrew Brooks, Danver MacGregor, and J. H. MacLafferty Jr. (son of Congressman MacLafferty).[45] Haase was also active in the Nevada Klan, as were Jack Garbutt and C. D. Tudor, who had worked on Francis's 1923 school board campaign. In the 1925 city elections, Garbutt served as a delegate for the Knights of Pythias to the Better Government League, a coalition of civic and improvement clubs that included the East Bay Club.[46]

The most successful Klan politicians were Burton Becker and William Parker, Kailiff (vice president) and Kleopard (lecturer) of Klan No. 9, respectively.[47] Becker was the popular chief of police in Piedmont during the above-mentioned Sidney Dearing affair, and he belonged to the Moose,

Modern Woodmen of America, and several Masonic orders. He was already publicly identified with the Klan in 1922 when he ran for sheriff in the primary against incumbent Frank Barnet, winning more than twenty-three thousand votes or about 34 percent of the total.[48] Parker was a self-made real-estate and insurance salesman in the prosperous Dimond district of East Oakland. Active in the Dimond Progressive Club, he edited a monthly neighborhood newspaper and was first president of the East Oakland Consolidated Clubs, an association of some thirty neighborhood improvement clubs dedicated to "questions of paving, sewage, new park sites, transportation, lighting and other civic improvements."[49]

Notwithstanding its internal divisions, then, the vitality of the Oakland Klan's popular base and the legitimacy of its active leaders helped to sustain the movement's influence. White middle-class residents continued to have grievances against the machine and were increasingly prepared to mobilize around them. The ease with which Klan leaders were able to cross over into the political mainstream underscores the extent to which local civic issues and participation were already framed in ethnic and racial terms. Indeed, the movement's greatest success came in the second half of the decade, with the election of Becker as county sheriff in 1926 and Parker as city commissioner of streets in 1927. Their opportunity for entry into power, however, was to come on a political terrain altered by the rise of another actor, the downtown business elite.

RESHAPING THE POLITICAL TERRAIN: DOWNTOWN AS INSURGENT ELITE

By the mid '20s, the machine was being challenged not only by the Klan but, perhaps more important, by the rising downtown business elite, which viewed the machine's favoritism and inefficiency as barriers to continuing economic development. As discussed in chapter 2, this nascent progrowth coalition began to take shape before World War I, with the organization of the Oakland Chamber of Commerce, the Real Estate Board, and the Rotary Club. After the war, class solidarity hardened in the combined and largely successful anti-union open-shop campaign.[50] Meanwhile, the group's internal social organization advanced with the 1919 founding of the fashionable Athens Athletic Club. By 1921, the club had enrolled fifteen hundred members from the East Bay business and professional community and was the most prestigious private social and cultural organization in the city.[51]

This period marked the rise of Joseph R. Knowland as the preeminent leader of the downtown elite.[52] A staunch conservative and influential regular Republican, Knowland headed the faction that rivaled Mike Kelly's in Alameda County politics.[53] Knowland had been a U.S. Congressman for Oakland from 1904 to 1914, and in 1915 he acquired a controlling interest in the *Oakland Tribune*. Active in the Chamber of Commerce, between 1918 and 1926 he served variously as its vice president, as a member of its board of directors, and as chair or member of its executive, harbor, and naval base committees. In 1925, he assumed the presidency of the Athens Athletic Club and oversaw the opening of its $1.7 million clubhouse in downtown Oakland, not far from his own twenty-story Tribune Tower, completed in 1923.[54] By the mid '20s, the collective power of the downtown elite was visibly embodied in a high-rise construction boom that featured a cluster of imposing new skyscrapers, including the Financial Center building, the Central Bank, the Leamington Hotel, and Capwell's department store.[55]

In the city, this group began to take political initiative with the creation of the Good Government League. In the face of the postwar strike wave, the Chamber of Commerce in early 1920 sponsored a law-and-order campaign to demand a massive increase in police in the industrial district.[56] Subsequently, a group of businessmen began organizing a drive for reform of the police department and for a more "business-like administration" of city government. After an unsuccessful recall effort against several commissioners, the group reconstituted itself as the Good Government League.[57] In the 1921 city council elections, league candidates Frank Colbourn and Albert Carter won upset elections over the machine favorites. Colbourn, a former secretary of the Civil Service Board, took over the Department of Health and Public Safety (including the police), and Carter, a lawyer and former president of the Rotary Club, became Commissioner of Public Works, with responsibility for the Oakland harbor.[58]

The new business reformers began a program to stimulate economic growth and remove control of key economic infrastructures (and sources of patronage) from the corporations and the machine. In 1923, voters passed a measure endorsed by the Chamber of Commerce to create a regional municipal utility (water) district, replacing the private water companies.[59] In 1924, the Chamber organized the Oakland Community Council, composed of the heads of seventeen business, service, and luncheon club organizations, that was dedicated to "the growth and prosperity of Oakland and to cooperation between business and civic interests."[60] On the city council, Commissioner Carter began efforts to revive harbor development, mired for years in political and financial impasse. Backed by the *Tribune*, Carter was elected to Congress in 1924, whereupon the council appointed Leroy Goodrich, president of the Good Government League, to succeed him as Commissioner of Public Works.[61] With support from the Chamber, the Real Estate Board, the Community Council, and the *Tribune*, Goodrich and Carter led a successful 1925 campaign to pass an unprecedented $9.96 million bond issue for the port, to be administered by a temporary board of commissioners that was dominated by the downtown elite.[62] A year later, a small turnout of voters in a special election approved a charter amendment permanently establishing an independent Oakland Board of Port Commissioners.[63]

With the machine's resources under fire, leading Catholic politicians began to move away from Kelly and toward the Knowland faction. Among these were Judge Tyrrell and Dr. John Slavich, a former Grand Knight and State Deputy in the Knights of Columbus and the city physician under Commissioner Colbourn.[64] In 1925, this process dealt a severe blow to Kelly's control of the County Board of Supervisors. Previously, of the five members of the board, Kelly could count at least three who owed their appointment or election to him. But in a critical test of strength between Kelly and Knowland, the board rejected Kelly's choice to replace outgoing district attorney DeCoto. Dismayed by the notorious crime and corruption in his western waterfront industrial district of Emeryville, Supervisor John Mullins, a Kelly loyalist and an Irish Catholic, crossed over to the Republican regulars and voted to name a young assistant, Earl Warren, to the post. Mullins paid for his apostasy: Opposed by both Kelly and the Klan, he was defeated for reelection in 1928. Warren, however, quickly established his reputation as a crusading prosecutor, aggressively pursuing gambling and bootlegging activities as well as bribery in the county bail bonds system.[65]

As the decade progressed, the downtown reformers gradually succeeded in altering the institutional terrain of Oakland politics. Their reforms provided a new administrative framework for managing urban economic growth and undermined the supply of resources traditionally available to the machine. At the same time, their political victories contributed to a self-reinforcing sequence of class formation among the elite, increasing their internal coordination and organizational capacity and broadening their outreach in civil society. Eventually, their successes drew support away from the machine and toward their own agenda, reshaping the alliances among actors in the urban polity.

In the latter half of the '20s, several groups actively contended for space within Oakland politics. In this setting, the multiple paths of group formation and political mobilization converged in two key elections in 1926 and 1927. These events crystallized the issue cleavages between groups, forming a critical juncture in local political development. The triumph of prominent Oakland Klan leaders in these races announced the ascendancy of white middle-class values in the political sphere, while their disastrous failure in office ultimately solidified an alliance of the middle classes and the business elites, producing a transformation of the urban regime.

SHIFTING ALLIANCES AND OPPORTUNITIES:
KELLY AND THE KLAN VERSUS DOWNTOWN

By 1926, the Kelly machine's position had been eroded by four years under an unsympathetic governor and by the rising power of the downtown elite.[66] In desperate need of electoral success, Kelly rallied behind the progressive Republican gubernatorial candidate C. C. Young, whose victory over the incumbent Governor Richardson in the primary opened the way for Kelly's return to power.[67] Meanwhile, in the county, Klansman Burton Becker faced Sheriff Frank Barnet in a rematch of their 1922 contest. In effect, the race between Becker and Barnet epitomized the moral discourses behind the Klan movement, just as the campaign the following year of William Parker for city commissioner expressed its urban spatial and material interests. The political successes of Becker and Parker produced a temporary realignment of local contending actors and forced Kelly to allow the Klan leadership to gain entry into the urban regime.

An ally of Kelly and an officeholder since 1905, Alameda County Sheriff Frank Barnet practically personified the image of a traditional patrimonial-style sheriff, exercising an informal, personal authority to maintain customary social order. As a fellow law enforcement officer recalled,

> Frank Barnet was very liberal. He'd sit down and drink during Prohibition. He was what a lot of people called a regular guy. He didn't think anything of prostitutes and open gambling operating. He believed you needed those! [Interviewer: "That's life, huh?"] Yes. You needed this, you see. It was a common belief that if you close these places up, you'll have a lot of rape cases on your hands. Well, that's what many people thought. . . . Barnet was a very generous sort of person. He was a short, stocky-built man—always wore a big diamond stud and a big diamond ring, and smoked a cigar, and very worldly sort of fella. He just couldn't see anything wrong in the bootlegging business.[68]

In 1925, however, Barnet was implicated in the gruesome death of a young woman named Bessie Ferguson, who allegedly had separately blackmailed several well-known men in the county (including Barnet) into believing that each was the father of her illegitimate child. According to unofficial reports, she was killed in an accident at a party in the home of an Emeryville bootlegger; her body was then dismembered and scattered across the waterfront marshes to hide the evidence of her death. Although no charges were ever filed, the scandal was widely publicized and virtually ended Barnet's political career. Kelly was forced to abandon him and support Becker, who ran as a professional, reformist candidate, receiving endorsements from both the Progressive Republican Club of Alameda and the Christian Citizens' League. In what one newspaper described as "one of the most bitterly fought battles in the history of the East Bay," Becker defeated Barnet by more than thirteen thousand votes in the November election, reportedly winning substantial majorities in Berkeley, Piedmont, and the urban districts of the county, while Barnet was left to rely on his rural south-county support. Upon taking office, Becker immediately appointed fellow Klansmen Francis as county jailor and Parker (who had managed his campaign) as undersheriff.[69]

A few months later, Mayor Davie and Commissioners Baccus and William Moorehead faced reelection in the 1927 city council races. Davie's political fortunes had been slipping for some time, after losing campaigns against Carter for Congress in 1924 and against the port bonds and commission votes. On the council, Commissioners Goodrich and Colbourn had dropped Davie from their coalition with Baccus and Moorehead, and now Colbourn, supported by Knowland and the *Tribune*, was opposing him for mayor. In response, Davie renewed his ties with Kelly and ran against the downtown coalition; once again exploiting his populist outsider stance, he won a clear majority in the mayoral primary.[70]

In the commissioner races, Parker ran as an independent in the primary against Baccus. Campaigning hard on the street paving and sewers issues, Parker's newspaper ads promised to "Get Better Streets—at Less Cost." "The cost of maintaining the streets of Oakland in their present deplorable condition is prohibitive," the ads continued. "The present street administration is inefficient and extravagant. A change is seriously needed in the interests of economy and a better Oakland."[71] Such rhetoric found a sympathetic hearing in many East Oakland neighborhoods. In the newly developed hillside district of Millsmont, dissatisfied residents organized a mass meeting for Mayor Davie and "candidates for commissioner who are opposed to the incumbents," declaring that Baccus, Colbourn, and Moorehead "cannot speak in this district." Meeting organizers complained that the city had grossly overcharged residents for sewer construction while providing inadequate streets, lighting, sidewalks, and police and fire protection. Parker hammered away at Baccus in speeches to neighborhood groups and clubs across East Oakland, denouncing the "slow moving methods of the incumbent," and promising property owners "full value for their money and a pavement that stands the strain of increasing traffic."[72]

In the primary, Parker won the most votes in a field of five candidates, eliminating Baccus and leading runner-up H. T. Hempstead going into the final. Seeing an opportunity to win a new council majority and recapture city patronage, Kelly and Davie backed Parker and challenger Charles Young (no relation to Governor Young) in the runoffs for the two commissioner seats. With support from Kelly and Davie, along with Parker's own base of Klan and neighborhood improvement clubs in East Oakland (including the endorsement of the East Side Consolidated Civic Clubs, of which he was former president), Parker and Young were swept into office.[73]

The elections of Becker and Parker emphasized the extent to which the Klan's political discourses had gained influence over popular opinion in the urban public sphere. The scandal surrounding Bessie Ferguson stirred sentiments on the Klan's touchstone ideological issues of booze, the "honor of women," and the public morals of elected officials. Barnet, who had won re-election easily over Becker in 1922, was overwhelmingly defeated in 1926. At the same time, Parker's campaign hit squarely at the material bases of the system of patronage and the machine's institutional failure to provide the level of services demanded in middle-class neighborhoods.

Yet if the Klan candidates presented themselves as reformers, why then did Kelly endorse Becker and Parker? No doubt they were strange bedfellows, and their alliance in fact proved to be short-lived. Nevertheless, their relationship illustrates clearly the independent causal importance of the political terrain. That is to say, specific political interests and opportunities depend not simply on groups' structural origins but rather on the configuration of relations among them and on the institutional rules of the game. The alliance between Kelly and the Klan would not have existed without the rise of downtown; caught up in his intense intraparty rivalry with Knowland, Kelly badly needed electoral victories, and he had no other viable candidates to support. Moreover, the compromise on both sides fell within the established pattern of factional competition and coalition-making in the regime. Kelly may not have approved of Becker's and Parker's Klan affiliations, but from the machine's point of view they were just another political clique, if not fully under its control then at least to be co-opted or contained. And they appeared to behave like one: Antimachinism was a standard campaign tactic for new office-seekers and helped mobilize the Klan's electoral support, thereby pressuring Kelly to accommodate them.

Once in power, however, the Klan politicians proved to be even more corrupt than their predecessors, with little accountability either to Kelly or to their popular base. On the city council, Parker quickly dispensed with Davie and formed his own majority clique with Young and Commissioner Eugene Sturgis, appointed to replace Goodrich, who resigned in May 1927. Klansmen Haase, Garbutt, and E. Q. Norman were active in Parker's campaign, and after his election Parker hired Garbutt and Norman as "special investigators" to conduct political surveillance on city employees.[74] Garbutt and Norman later became partners with Haase in a street paving business and agreed to pay Parker half a cent per square foot for contracts that specified their patented "vibrolithic" paving process. According to court documents, when Norman offered the paving deal, "Parker said that he was glad Norman had it; that he was not in office for his health; that if Norman and Garbutt expected to lay vibrolithic pavement in the City of Oakland they would have to pay; that he was getting one cent per sq. ft. from the Black Top people; that since Norman and Garbutt had supported him in his campaign and done a lot of work for him around the City Hall he would make it one-half cent per sq. ft. for them." The contracts subsequently awarded under the deal came to more than eight hundred thousand square feet, or one-third of all street paving work in the city.[75]

In the county, Kelly was completely unable to control Becker, who immediately put into place an aggressive system of bribery and extortion from bootlegging and gambling businesses. Sheriff's deputies collected thousands of dollars of protection money from still operators in rural southern Alameda County, and they devised a plan to rationalize the bootlegging industry by arresting smaller and less profitable producers and centralizing both supply and payoffs in a single designated source. Becker's men also arranged with Cromwell Ormsby, the attorney for several Chinese lottery operators, to tip off impending raids in exchange for payments. Ormsby later conspired with Garbutt and Norman in an attempt to influence the Oakland Police Morals Squad, while Garbutt received five thousand dollars from the Mills Novelty Company for the protection of slot machines.[76]

In the 1926 and 1927 elections, Kelly briefly joined forces with the Klan in a populist electoral alliance against the rising power of the downtown elites. The defeat of the incumbents Sheriff Barnet and Commissioner Baccus demonstrated the power of the new middle-class voting constituency and its rejection of the older style of politics in the regime. Members of the Ku Klux Klan played a major role in the mobilization of this group, but upon entry into government the Klan leaders produced no new institutional reorganization or political reform. Rather, Klan politicians simply adopted the prevailing practices of the machine, and without the accumulated checks and balances of its traditional patronage networks, they quickly became even more opportunistic and corrupt. Thus despite their electoral success, the Klan leaders failed to alter the terrain of Oakland politics or to consolidate their position in governing a new regime.

INSTITUTIONALIZING CLASS HEGEMONY:
THE VICTORY OF DOWNTOWN

The crisis of corruption in local politics set off another reactive sequence of mobilization, this time sponsored by the downtown elites. Before the end of 1927, several of Kelly's and Davie's appointments in the Health and Safety Department and city treasurer's office were forced to resign under a cloud of scandal, with the help of exposé coverage in the *Tribune*.[77] Meanwhile, former city commissioner Goodrich and his colleagues in the Lions Club began to explore ways to replace the commission form of government with a city-manager system. In February 1928, the Lions convened a meeting of business, civic, and improvement clubs to launch a new charter reform campaign, and by April the Oakland Council-Manager League was formed, led by local banker and Lions president Harry Harding.[78]

The manager advocates received early support from the members of the Port Commission, who loaned port attorney Markell Baer to help draft a set of amendments to the city charter. The reformers promised to create a more efficient organization of government modeled explicitly on the private corporation, with an executive officer and a board of directors. This projected change would eliminate politics from city administration, attract leading businessmen into public service, and, of course, reduce taxes. By September 1928, the campaign had obtained more than sixteen thousand petition signatures, enough to request a special election on the amendments. The city council, however, denied the petition on procedural grounds, and the issue stalled in litigation for more than a year.[79]

By January 1930, District Attorney Warren had begun earnestly pursuing the graft and corruption in city hall and the sheriff's department, with Knowland's approval.[80] Even so, the Klan's reputation in Oakland at this time was still strong enough that Warren feared Klan members on the Alameda County Grand Jury would refuse to indict their fellow Klansmen.[81] In an effort to win a break in the case, Warren released transcripts of the grand jury investigations to the press, and the resulting publicity led to the swift resignations of Sheriff Becker and Commissioners Parker, Young, and Sturgis. Becker, Parker, Garbutt, Ormsby, and others were eventually indicted, convicted, and sent to prison, and the scandal turned public opinion increasingly against the commission form of government.[82]

The *Tribune* began to editorialize heavily in favor of the manager reform, and with the support of the Lions, the Chamber of Commerce, the Protestant Ministerial Union, and other groups, the Council-Manager League obtained more than thirty-five thousand signatures on a new petition.[83] The new amendments proposed a strong city manager in charge of administration, nine city councillors nominated from districts but elected at-large to four-year terms, and a ceremonial mayor chosen by the councillors from among their ranks. In a final struggle to save the old regime, Mayor Davie and his allies called a freeholders' election to draft a strong mayor-council charter, an effort supported by labor unions, ethnic organizations, and machine-favored businessmen.[84] In the November elections, both the manager amendments and the city hall freeholder slate were victorious. The freeholders submitted their charter in March 1931, but by then the machine had lost the capacity to mobilize its base. Middle-class voters turned out disproportionately to reject the machine's charter and later elected the entire Council-Manager League slate in the first city council elections under the new amendments. The victory of the city manager coalition marked the end of the old machine's dominance in Oakland politics, and the Knowland forces thereafter assumed leading influence over city hall.[85]

CONCLUSION:
THE CONSEQUENCES OF THE KLAN MOVEMENT

The trajectory of the Ku Klux Klan movement in Oakland shows the importance of distinguishing the social bases of collective actors, their institutional political environment, and the mobilization of group identity in civil society. The Oakland Klan represented neither a decadent status backlash nor a vague civic populism. White Protestant middle classes, the social base of the movement, were a rising population in Oakland, concentrated in the rapidly growing suburban areas of the city. Their formation as a group drew on social networks embedded in their own neighborhoods and on norms of racial and ethnic nativism commonly available in urban civil society at the time. These factors allowed the group to distinguish itself from others and provided for a coherent self-consciousness and collective identity. As a social movement organization, the Klan appeared in the midst of this group's ongoing collective rearticulation of the rights and privileges associated with white middle-class identity, its boundaries for membership, and its claims for power.

This was the forward-looking movement of an advancing group, not the backward-looking response of a declining one. Klan political leaders capitalized on middle-class grievances against the ethnic machine, engaging in advocacy on civic issues like prohibition, crime, good government, and adequate city services. Mobilization for civic reform targeted the institutions of rival ethnic group power: the machine, the saloon, and the Catholic Church. Indeed, even protests over ordinary yet indispensable matters like street paving were closely tied to the organization of the patronage regime.

These issues were framed by a dominant political terrain that was already ordered in ethnic and racial terms. Without question, the leaders of the Oakland Klan were white supremacists, as evidenced by their public actions and pronouncements. That the Klan leaders took advantage of urban civic issues to gain popularity, however, is less revealing than that the white middle-class population readily supported known racists in order to achieve their desired reforms.

Similarly, the Klan's demise in Oakland was due neither to the disappearance of its social base nor to the extremism of its ideology; on the contrary, in both of these respects it remained closer to the contemporary middle-class mainstream. Rather, the movement collapsed because it failed to alter the institutional terrain of politics and thereby reconstitute the relations among actors in the urban polity. In the secret fraternal society, the Klan employed an organizational form that was familiar to its followers but also a key source of weakness, susceptible to petty factionalism and corruption. Instead of overthrowing the system of machine politics, the Klan leaders themselves were merely absorbed into it, with disastrous results.

Finally, the Klan politicians were ultimately superseded not by a liberal pluralist coalition but by a conservative business elite. The downtown reformers preempted the movement by both meeting several of its goals (low taxes, "good government," and the suppression of "vice") *and* reconstituting the political terrain, incorporating the Klan's constituency under their own hegemony. White middle-class Protestants transferred their allegiance from the faulty vehicle of the Klan to the more efficient business elite, whose institutional reforms consolidated the alliance of downtown business with large and small property owners into a more stable middle-class regime. The result permanently disrupted the system of patronage links and political leverage between the city government and the ethnic working classes, dissolving the political institutions that supported the maintenance of traditional ethnic group formation. The outcome constituted a major reorientation of the relations between actors in the local state and civil society.

This process highlights an important consequence of the contentious politics of the 1920s; for if the strategic form of the Klan movement failed, its middle-class social base did not do so badly. The business reforms got rid of the machine: City government was no longer a resource for party politicians to distribute ethnic group patronage, and middle-class whites got services and protection for their racially homogeneous neighborhoods. The political struggles of the era achieved an accommodation within the now-dominant sectors of the white population, in a synthesis of class and racial group formation. On the one hand, demands for control over the urban environment helped cement the class alliance between suburban residents and growth-oriented commercial business. On the other, a common commitment to a middle-class culture set the standard for the racial unity between older native-born whites and assimilating European immigrant groups, creating a model of urban social mobility for generations to come. In this way, the outcomes of the Klan movement contributed to the permanent consolidation of a white middle class.

The rise and fall of the Klan movement brought with them the end of popular machine politics and a decline in the salience of ethnicity as a political identity in Oakland. In the next few decades, the boundaries of political community shifted to a terrain more strongly defined in terms of class power. The coalition of businesses and middle classes in the new regime largely excluded the minority and ethnic working-class groups in the city. But the working population of Oakland had hardly disappeared from the urban setting. The decline of previous forms of ethnic incorporation and union organization in the '20s posed anew the problems of class inequality and political solidarity—problems that were to achieve particular urgency in the context of the economic crisis of the '30s.

Figure 1. Aerial view of Oakland looking west, circa 1938. In the foreground lies the Y-shaped Lake Merritt, below the cluster of buildings downtown. To the left, the Oakland Estuary divides the city from the island town of Alameda before flowing into the San Francisco Bay. On the Oakland side are docks, rail yards, and the adjacent working-class neighborhood of West Oakland, while along the western shore, railroad ferry moles reach out into deep water in the bay. From the right, the newly built Bay Bridge extends out to Treasure Island and then on to the city of San Francisco, at the tip of the peninsula that marks the Golden Gate to the Pacific Ocean. (Photograph courtesy of the Oakland Museum of California, *Oakland Tribune* Collection, gift of Alameda Newspaper Group.)

Figure 2. A Southern Pacific steam locomotive at the corner of Seventh Street and Broadway, early 1900s. The railroads dominated public life in Oakland at the start of the twentieth century. By 1911, as many as sixteen hundred trains a day moved through the city. Local and transcontinental lines ran down the center of the city's main commercial streets, with rights-of-way over local vehicular and pedestrian traffic. (Photograph courtesy of the Bancroft Library, University of California, Berkeley; BANC PIC 1905.17500-ALB.)

Figure 3. Workers at the California Cotton Mills in East Oakland, circa 1910. The firm employed up to seven hundred workers, many of them residents of the nearby Portuguese American neighborhood known as Jingletown. Note the bricked-in window bays on the side of the factory, where men, women, and children worked six days per week. One journalist wrote that the noise in the main working rooms "almost deafens you . . . [it is] so great that it is difficult to carry on a conversation." (Photograph courtesy of the Oakland Public Library, Oakland History Room.)

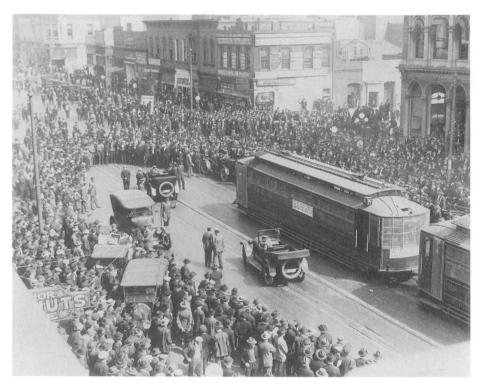

Figure 4. In October 1919, eleven hundred streetcar and ferry operators struck for ten days. The transit company hired armed strikebreakers and drove its streetcars through the assembled crowds, escorted by local police. Seven people were killed in the ensuing violence, and forty seriously injured. The growth of labor organization during and after World War I was met by a concerted anti-union drive by employers that resulted in the virtual destruction of most unions in the 1920s. (Photograph courtesy of the Oakland Museum of California, *Oakland Tribune* Collection, gift of Alameda Newspaper Group.)

Figure 5. Laborers pave a street in a new housing tract in the Laurel neighborhood of East Oakland, mid 1930s. During the previous decade, construction of single-family homes had boomed in the recently annexed foothills east of Lake Merritt, attracting a new middle-class population to the city. Basic urban services like street paving, however, were traditionally prime sources of graft and patronage for the old political machine. (Photograph courtesy of the Oakland Public Library, Oakland History Room.)

Figure 6. Hooded Klan members rally at the Oakland Auditorium, circa 1924. The Klan enrolled at least two thousand members in Oakland and claimed a following of many thousands more. Local Klan leaders gained popularity by capitalizing on middle-class desires for cultural homogeneity and material grievances against the ethnic machine. (Photograph courtesy of the Bancroft Library, University of California, Berkeley; BANC PIC 1998.035-AX.)

Figure 7. Women of the Ku Klux Klan lead three thousand fellow Klan members through downtown Richmond, California, on Independence Day 1924. The Oakland Klan had originally received a permit to march in Oakland, but it was later revoked, forcing their relocation to nearby Richmond. The letters "KIGY" on their sign stand for "Klansmen, I greet you." (Photograph courtesy of the Oakland Museum of California.)

Figure 8. Strange bedfellows: Oakland politicians and their aides celebrate victory in the 1927 city elections. *Front row, from left (seated):* Commissioner-Elect (and Klan leader) William Parker, Mayor John Davie, Commissioner-Elect Charles Young, and Alameda County Republican Party boss Michael Kelly. (Photograph courtesy of the Oakland Public Library, Oakland History Room.)

Figure 9. Aerial view of downtown Oakland, 1930s. The '20s and '30s were the heyday of downtown, whose concentration of high-rise buildings seemed to embody the power of the new commercial elite. At lower right is the twenty-story clock tower of the *Oakland Tribune*; in the center, the dome atop Kahn's department store is visible near the intersection of the main streets of Broadway, Telegraph, and San Pablo Avenues. On the left is the fifteen-story white granite City Hall, crowned by a ninety-one-foot terra-cotta cupola. (Photograph courtesy of the Oakland Public Library, Oakland History Room.)

Figure 10. The Knowland Machine: Members of the Oakland Chamber of Commerce and Mayor Fred Morcom give a sendoff to *Oakland Tribune* publisher Joseph R. Knowland and Harrison Robinson of the Downtown Property Owners Association on October 12, 1932. Knowland and Robinson are leaving for Washington, D.C., to lobby for $62 million in federal financing to build the Bay Bridge. Robinson is in the light buttoned overcoat in the center, front row; Knowland stands next to him in dark suit and glasses. Mayor Morcom is the fourth from left, partially obscured from view. (Photograph courtesy of the Oakland Public Library, Oakland History Room.)

Figure 11. Female workers sort asparagus at an Oakland cannery, circa 1925. Many Italian, Portuguese, and Hispanic women found seasonal employment in local canneries and processing plants. Immigrant and second-generation ethnic workers were to form much of the social base for the revival of labor militancy in the 1930s, organized by the Congress of Industrial Organizations (CIO) unions on the docks and in factories and warehouses. (Photograph courtesy of the Oakland Museum of California.)

Figure 12. Cottrell Laurance (C. L.) Dellums, cofounder and organizer
for the Brotherhood of Sleeping Car Porters and a leading figure in the
West Oakland African American community; pictured here in 1970.
Dellums also fought for racially integrated public housing under the
New Deal and for equal employment opportunity during World War II
and afterward. (Photograph courtesy of the African American Museum
and Library at Oakland [AAMLO].)

Figure 13. Paul Robeson sings "The Star-Spangled Banner" with shipyard workers in a wartime production rally at the Moore Dry Dock in Oakland, September 1942. During the war, tens of thousands of workers migrated to Oakland, seeking jobs in the shipyards and other defense-related industries. Surveys showed that the majority of the new migrants hoped to continue working and settle permanently in the Bay Area after the war. (Photograph courtesy of the Oakland Museum of California, *Oakland Tribune* Collection, gift of Alameda Newspaper Group.)

Figure 14. Female clerks, joined by leaders of local American Federation of Labor (AFL) unions, picket Kahn's department store in downtown Oakland, November 1946. As the war ended and defense production shut down, retail trade emerged as a key sector in the city's postwar economy. Many jobs remained segregated by gender, but women had long worked in retail sales, and they formed a majority of the members in the local AFL clerks' union. (Photograph courtesy of the Oakland Museum of California, *Oakland Tribune* Collection, gift of Alameda Newspaper Group.)

Figure 15. Marchers from the International Association of Machinists parade through the crowd on Broadway past Kahn's, December 3, 1946. Up to twenty thousand people gathered in the downtown streets during a two-and-a-half-day General Strike, officially described by union leaders as a "work holiday." The momentary lifting of norms of social distance allowed for an extraordinary display of popular working-class solidarity, as ordinary men and women claimed the right to urban public space. (Photograph courtesy of the Bancroft Library, University of California, Berkeley; BANC PIC 1959.010 NEG.)

Figure 16. Leaders of the AFL Steering Committee announce the end of the
General Strike, December 5, 1946. *Front row, left to right:* Retail Clerks Local
1265 secretary John Philpott, Al Brown of Teamster Milk Wagon Drivers Local
302 (no relation to Al Brown of the transit workers' union), and George Hunt.
Rear: Building Trades Council business agent Jack Reynolds, Central Labor
Council secretary Robert Ash and counsel James Galliano, and Charles Roe.
(Photograph courtesy of the San Francisco History Center, San Francisco Public
Library.)

Figure 17. "Take the Power out of the Tower" reads the banner on the campaign float of the United Negro Labor Committee, a reference to the political dominance of the *Oakland Tribune*. After the General Strike, local AFL and CIO unions joined in a broad social-democratic coalition to endorse a slate of candidates for the 1947 city council elections. Despite vigorous Red-baiting by the *Tribune*, the slate won four of the five contested seats, one short of a majority on the nine-member council. (Photograph courtesy of the International Longshore and Warehouse Union Library.)

Figure 18. Construction of a section of the Cypress Freeway, February 1955. Land clearance for the freeway cut a huge swath through West Oakland and, along with other transportation and urban renewal projects, destroyed commercial businesses and more than five thousand housing units in the neighborhood. The two-mile-long multilevel highway collapsed in the 1989 Loma Prieta earthquake. (Photograph courtesy of the Oakland Museum of California, *Oakland Tribune* Collection, gift of Alameda Newspaper Group.)

Figure 19. Ralph Williams *(left)* presents a plaque to Maggie
and Wade Johnson, commemorating their fiftieth wedding
anniversary, from the United Taxpayers and Voters Union, a
group founded by Wade Johnson. Williams and the Johnsons
were part of a southern migrant working-class generation who
collectively built much of the postwar black community organization in West Oakland. (Photograph courtesy of the African
American Museum and Library at Oakland [AAMLO].)

Figure 20. Oak Center Neighborhood Association president Lillian Love receives an award from *(left to right)* Oakland Redevelopment Agency commissioner Leo Sorenson, executive director John B. Williams, and commissioner Jack Summerfield. In the early '60s, Love and the OCNA successfully pressured the Redevelopment Agency to halt the demolition of their neighborhood, and Love herself later served on the agency's commission. Williams became perhaps the most influential black public official in Oakland under the administration of Mayor John Reading. (Photograph courtesy of the Oakland Museum of California, *Oakland Tribune* Collection, gift of Alameda Newspaper Group.)

Figure 21. West Oakland resident Luther Smith Sr. speaks at a rally calling for a civilian police review board in Oakland, July 1966. Earlier that year, police allegedly broke into Smith's home and beat him, his two sons, and two white friends in a mistaken raid on the property. Complaints of mistreatment by police—a forceful reminder of their exclusion from white civil society—were among the most acutely felt grievances in the black community. (Photograph by Lynn Phipps.)

Figure 22. Black Panther Party demonstration at the Alameda
County Court House in support of jailed party founder Huey P.
Newton, July 1968. Newton had been charged with the murder of
an Oakland police officer. The Panthers identified themselves with
the growing population of poor, unemployed, marginalized black
"lumpen-proletarians." Their armed surveillance of Oakland police
astonished observers, attracted young recruits, and concentrated
media attention on the group. (Photograph courtesy of the Oakland Museum of California, *Oakland Tribune* Collection, gift
of Alameda Newspaper Group.)

Figure 23. Black Panther Party chair Bobby Seale campaigns door-to-door in Oakland in 1973. Building on their community-based Survival programs, the party organized a systematic voter outreach effort for Seale's campaign for mayor and Elaine Brown's for city councillor. The campaign produced an unprecedented electoral mobilization of local African American working classes and ghetto poor. (Photograph courtesy of the Oakland Museum of California, *Oakland Tribune* Collection, gift of Alameda Newspaper Group.)

Figure 24. Lionel Wilson, first African American mayor of Oakland, speaks before the Oakland Chamber of Commerce, 1977. A political moderate, Wilson had served as a Municipal and Superior Court judge and as chair of the city's Community Action Agency under the federal poverty program. Wilson represented a new black professional middle class that came of age with the rise of the civil rights movement. (Photograph courtesy of the Oakland Public Library, Oakland History Room.)

Figure 25. Downtown seen from West Oakland (Oak Center) in 1991. In the foreground, new town houses line the street across from an older, low-rise housing project. Farther away, the towers of the new Federal Building are under construction in the City Center, beyond the I-980 Grove Street Expressway. (Photograph courtesy of the Oakland Museum of California, *Oakland Tribune* Collection, gift of Alameda Newspaper Group.)

4 Economic Crisis and Class Hegemony

The Rule of Downtown

At the intersection of Telegraph Avenue and Broadway in Oakland, a small statue and fountain mark the corner that bears the name Latham Square. As much as any other street corner in the mid 1930s, Latham Square embodied the heart of commercial downtown Oakland. Here two major streetcar lines converged, one coming from Berkeley along Telegraph and the other running down Broadway from the Oakland hills. Both stopped in front of Kahn's department store, one of the leading retail merchandisers in Alameda County and a nerve center in Oakland for the middle-class urban consumer culture of the first half of the twentieth century.[1] Built in 1912 in the beaux arts style, the seven-story Kahn's building occupied nearly an entire city block at Sixteenth Street between Telegraph and San Pablo Avenues, and featured an elliptical rotunda capped by a distinctive plaster and glass dome. Inside Kahn's, one could find furniture, dry goods, books, and a variety of concession stores selling fashionable clothing, hats, shoes, and perfume, as well as specialty services like hair styling and watch or shoe repair. As one former employee recalled, "It was like a whole town there; they had everything."[2] Outside, the downtown Retail Merchants Association would hang Christmas decorations from the streetlights along Broadway during the holiday shopping season.

The December 4, 1946, issue of the *San Francisco Call-Bulletin* featured a photograph of Latham Square, looking down Broadway toward the estuary.[3] In the picture, a crowd of some five thousand strong is gathered in the square, filling the street from curb to curb underneath the Christmas decorations. Near the camera, a man holds a small child in his arms, while the crowd appears to part in the middle to allow a procession of marchers to come forward, headed by a woman carrying a sign. The people in the street are not shoppers, however; the woman's sign reads "International Association of Machinists," and the marchers are demonstrating as part of a General Strike in the city of Oakland.

Placing ourselves figuratively in Latham Square at these two points in time allows us to ask an analytic question: What caused the change from one historical moment to the other? How did the dominance of a commercial-class culture give way to a mass demonstration of insurgent working-class solidarity? How did shoppers become strikers? The implied causal sequence already underlines the period change from the institutional patterns and ethnic conflicts of the previous decades. Almost immediately after the installation of the new city-manager government, Oakland experienced major structural upheavals, first with the Great Depression and later with World War II. But unlike the '20s, the responses to these changes developed principally along class lines, from within and outside the urban regime.

This chapter examines the shift of social and political conflict to the central axis of class. I begin with a sketch of the structural impacts of the Depression on the Oakland population. Facing economic crisis, the new political elite adopted a developmental strategy and type of governance that I call *business managerialism*. The consolidation of the managerial regime established the primacy of class power in the political arena, embodied in an institutional form that reflected the particular alliance of business and middle-class groups. This alliance marked the boundaries of the dominant political community, indicating which groups were recognized as sharing the mutual right and responsibility to participate in collective self-governance.

The exercise of class power in the regime likewise influenced the organization of groups in civil society. Here, I focus on the paths of formation of three groups: the white middle classes, so recently active in the politics of the '20s; African Americans, by this time the city's largest racial minority; and the ethnic white working classes. The latter, especially, were to form the principal support for the resurgence of a militant, oppositional labor movement, and the articulation of an alternative vision of urban political community.

Despite the rise of working-class militancy, however, the regime effectively maintained its hegemony during the 1930s. To understand why, I look closely at a critical, interactive sequence of events that highlights the competing strategies and alignments among actors in both the movement and the regime. The outcome of these events reveals the limits of the labor movement's formation as a challenging collective actor during the decade. Later, in the post–World War II era, changes in local structural conditions and the political alignments among groups would lead instead to class polarization and, in 1946, a citywide General Strike.

SOCIAL STRUCTURE AND ECONOMIC CRISIS:
THE 1930S

The 1930 charter reform in Oakland took effect just as the city was entering fully into the Great Depression. The urban economic boom times of the '20s abruptly collapsed: Between 1929 and 1933, the number of building permits issued in Oakland declined by 60 percent, while retail sales fell by almost half in the same period. By 1932, as many as 30 percent of the normally employed population were out of work. Faced with its own fiscal crisis, the city government laid off more than a hundred employees and cut wages for laborers by 27 percent. More than fourteen thousand unemployed persons registered at neighborhood fire stations for city relief work, in a program that had jobs for only 250 workers. The Alameda County Welfare Council increased its family welfare caseload by seven times from 1928 to 1932; even so, allowances seldom exceeded forty-five dollars a month, well below the cost of living for a worker with children, and individuals without families rarely received any aid at all. Conditions were such that, in the winter of 1932–1933, a homeless colony of some two hundred men set up camp in a "pipe city" in East Oakland, taking shelter in unused lengths of concrete sewer pipe on an industrial site near the estuary.[4]

As Oakland's economy faltered, so did its population growth. City size increased by only 18,100 or 6 percent between 1930 and 1940, a fall-off from the 31 and 44 percent growth rates (and less than a third of the absolute increases) of the previous two decades.[5] This slowdown, however, concealed significant dislocations within the population. The Depression stimulated historic national patterns of westward migration, particularly to California. In 1940 approximately 877,000 California residents had moved there from out of state in the previous five years, and almost 800,000 more moved from one county or large city to another within the state.[6] In Oakland, 17 percent of the population were such recent migrants, higher than the national average of 12 percent although lower than the rate of 24 percent in the state.

This was, of course, the time of the great so-called "Okie" migration from the central southwestern states to California, but during the Depression the Okies were still mainly agricultural workers and, with the exception of Los Angeles, did not usually settle in large cities. Less than 7 percent of all recent migrants to Oakland in 1940 were from Oklahoma, Arkansas, Texas, or Missouri. Depression-era migrants to Oakland tended to be from within California and were predominantly urban: 82 percent of all new arrivals in Oakland were from urban areas, and 36 percent were from cities with populations over a hundred thousand, including 11 percent from San Francisco.[7]

The effects of economic contraction in Oakland are perhaps best indicated by the city's apparent inability to keep population. Between 1935 and 1940, almost as many people moved *out* of Oakland as came into the city. Total net migration for those years was only 885 people, from a total volume (in- plus outmigration) of 103,663. With a stagnant economy, opportunities in the urban labor market were probably scarce. Migrants were 20 percent of the city's labor force in 1940 but 24 percent of the unemployed, seeking work. Working-class migrants may have found it especially hard to get jobs. Only 17 percent of craftsmen and laborers, 18 percent of operatives, and 17 percent of those doing emergency work were newcomers, compared to 24 percent of professionals and semiprofessionals. Overall, the unemployed (including those seeking work and those engaged in emergency work) in Oakland remained at about 15 percent of the population in the spring of 1940.[8] Thus, while the Depression produced no major increase in or recomposition of the local population, the extent of unemployment threatened its structural economic integration, making access to work itself an urgent and widespread public concern.

The kinds of work that were available reflected the city's historic pattern of industrialization. Although Oakland was relatively more "blue-collar" than the Bay Area as a whole, the entire region had a smaller manufacturing sector than the industrial cities of the North and East. In 1940, only 21 percent of the Bay Area employed population worked in manufacturing, compared with 35 percent in Chicago and 48 percent in Detroit.[9] About half of the male working population in Oakland in 1940 was employed as craftsmen, foremen, operatives, or laborers, but a larger than average share of those were craftsmen and foremen (21 percent compared to 19 percent U.S. non-farm), and fewer were employed as operatives or laborers (18 and 9 percent in Oakland, respectively, compared to 24 and 11 percent nationally). Craftsmen and foremen outnumbered operatives on the railroads, in the shipyards, and in the city's printing, baking, machinery, and metalworking industries. A higher proportion of Oakland men (21 percent compared to 17 percent nationally) also worked in clerical and sales occupations, many of them in the city's important wholesale and retail trade sectors. Working women in Oakland were especially concentrated in these jobs: 42 percent of employed women in Oakland worked in clerical and sales positions, as compared to 30 percent for the United States.[10] Thus, while manufacturing industries like auto making, textile production, and food processing were well established in the city, the Oakland working class had less the character of a large factory proletariat than a variegated mix of the skilled crafts and commercial trade.

THE BUSINESS REGIME:
POLITICS AND URBAN DEVELOPMENT

As economic conditions grew worse in the early '30s, the leaders of the new regime faced a daunting task. The downtown elites had come to power hoping to promote local growth, but the Depression had brought that practically to a standstill. With the collapse of private capital investment, the regime's solution was to turn to the state and federal governments, including the military, to stimulate new urban development. This policy may be observed in the major public-works projects carried out during the decade. The U.S. Department of Reclamation provided $3.9 million for construction of the Broadway Low-Level Tunnel, a 3,200-foot twin-bore highway passage through the Oakland hills that opened up traffic to suburban Contra Costa County. Begun in 1934, the project took three years to build and employed at least eight hundred miners under Oakland-based building contractors Stephen Bechtel and Henry Kaiser. New Deal agencies like the Civilian Conservation Corps, the Works Progress Administration, and the Public Works Administration also arranged for contributions of labor totaling $3 million to projects conserving surplus watershed lands in the East Bay hills, in preparation for their conversion into a system of regional parks.[11]

By far the largest public infrastructure project, however, was the San Francisco–Oakland Bay Bridge, under construction from 1933 to 1936. For years, Oakland elites had lobbied federal War Department officials to win approval of the central bay crossing and to influence its design and siting in order to protect navigation lanes for the Oakland harbor. Final plans called for a suspension bridge from Rincon Hill in San Francisco to Yerba Buena Island and a high cantilevered span on the East Bay side, approaching the shore along the route of the old Key System mole. Construction of the bridge provided thousands of jobs and millions of dollars in contracts for the local economy, including $4.5 million for the East Bay substructure to a firm headed by Kaiser and Bechtel and subcontracts to the Moore shipyard in Oakland to build caissons for the bridge piers. The port of Oakland also saw a 62 percent increase in maritime business in 1935, thanks in part to shipments of concrete, structural steel, and cable for the bridge construction.

Tribune publisher J. R. Knowland was intimately involved in the entire project, serving on the financial and executive committees of the state-appointed San Francisco–Oakland Bay Bridge Advisory Committee. In 1932, Knowland personally traveled with members of the financial advisory committee to Washington, D.C., to negotiate a $62 million loan from the federal Reconstruction Finance Corporation, and he stayed in regular communication with California governor James Rolph Jr., Oakland congressman Albert Carter, and his own son, state assemblyman William F. Knowland, on the status of the financing and the necessary federal and state legislation.[12]

Knowland also used his political connections to help secure the construction of several new U.S. military bases in the East Bay, including the Alameda Naval Air Station and the Oakland Naval Supply Depot. In 1935 the Navy Department selected Knowland's hometown of Alameda, across the estuary from Oakland, as the site of a new air base. Plans for the $15 million project anticipated an annual payroll of $5 million, including a force of six hundred officers, two thousand enlisted men, and five hundred civilian employees. That same year, the navy began negotiations with the Board of Port Commissioners for the acquisition of 390 acres of tidelands in the Oakland middle harbor. In 1936, the navy announced its intention to build on the site a $12 million supply depot for the Pacific Fleet, and the transfer of the land was quickly ratified by Oakland voters. Finally, in January 1941 the War Department took possession of seventy-four acres of port land on the western waterfront for use as an army quartermaster's (supply) depot. In December 1941, the Oakland army base and the naval supply depot were each commissioned into service, within eight days of the bombing of Pearl Harbor.[13]

These projects illustrated an evolving formal organization and functional division of labor within the regime.[14] Major public investments in support of capital accumulation and urban infrastructure were typically organized under autonomous commissions, advisory bodies, or administrative bureaucracies, insulated from electoral politics and linked to the networks of downtown elites that were forged during the '20s. Business leaders themselves often served on these bodies or participated directly in coordinated, quasipublic decision-making, so that we might give the name *business managerialism* to this type of regime. In the city government, executive authority was centralized in the city manager's office, and from 1933 until 1956 this position was held by one man, John Hassler, with only a three-year hiatus from 1943 to 1946 for wartime service. Hassler had been an Oakland banking executive and was a loyal Knowland ally, as was his interim replacement, Charles Schwanenberg, a local department store president.[15]

By contrast, the 1930 charter reform reduced the elected city council to little more than a ceremonial caretaker body, without administrative powers or patronage, and oriented politically to low taxes, tight budgets, and the preservation of public order. While downtown business and political leaders served on the port commission and Bay Bridge advisory committees, city council elections were more likely to attract smaller business entrepreneurs, like grocery store or gift shop owners, or independent sales agents and professionals, who might run for office simply to gain customer publicity.[16] Municipal campaigns quietly devolved into sedate "friends and neighbors" politics among white middle-class homeowners in the neighborhoods, all under a citywide public sphere dominated by Knowland's *Tribune*. The manager charter retained the commission government's nonpartisan, at-large system of voting; but without the lure of patronage, council races became much less competitive, a far cry from the tumultuous Mayor Davie years. The routine informal practice of midterm appointment of successors further discouraged independent political challenges, while the *Tribune*'s endorsements effectively anointed the winning candidates at election time. Voter turnout rates correspondingly fell, and city hall came to be ruled by incumbency: By 1946, the average tenure of the nine councillors was more than eight years, and for the five most senior members it was more than twelve years.[17]

Under Knowland's leadership, the downtown elite consolidated a form of urban governance in the new regime. The elite's ambitious developmental agenda required strong internal business-class unity and public administrative autonomy to protect its political negotiations with state and federal authorities for major infrastructure projects. This strategy dovetailed with the formally democratic but practically demobilized caretaker government representing the city's homeowning and property tax–paying middle class. The division of labor in city government achieved a balance between its allied constituent groups, while virtually excluding from the political community the broad population of working-class, minority, and low-income Oakland residents.

CLASS AND RACE IN CIVIL SOCIETY

By the early 1930s, the boom in residential housing construction had filled in most of the affluent neighborhoods in the lower hills and Montclair, and new property subdivisions were just beginning to reach into higher elevations.[18] At the same time, industrial expansion had spread out along the estuary, attracting working-class settlement near the factories and warehouses around East Fourteenth Street. This pattern of physical development contributed to the emerging class distinction between the "hills" and the "flats" that was to become a familiar part of the civic and cultural topography of Oakland. Within this urban space, the Depression had a powerful impact on all groups, but its social and political effects varied according to their differing paths of formation.

In this section, I follow the trajectories of three principal groups in Oakland civil society: the white middle classes and their racial and class "others," African Americans and the European ethnic working classes. While all endured severe economic dislocation, the white middle classes were now incorporated into the regime and could exercise a relatively privileged withdrawal into their own neighborhoods. After a significant period of growth in the '20s, the small African American community was devastated in the Depression and struggled through a phase of political realignment. The most pivotal group, however, was the ethnic white workers. They would form the base for a resurgence of the union labor movement and the mobilization of a radical class challenge to the urban regime.

The White Middle Class

For white middle-class families, we can catch a glimpse of the meaning of change from a unique longitudinal study of Oakland schoolchildren, begun in the 1930s by the Institute of Child Welfare (later Human Development) at the University of California, and reanalyzed in 1974 by sociologist Glen Elder.[19] In 1931, researchers from the Oakland Growth Study project selected 167 fifth- and sixth-grade students from a section of North Oakland and studied their social and emotional behavior continuously from 1932 to 1939, with periodic reinterviews later through their adult years. Systematic home interviews were also conducted with the children's mothers in 1932, 1934, and 1936, to gather data on socioeconomic background and family and social life. All of the children studied were white, 80 percent were Protestant, and about three-fourths were from intact families headed by native-born parents. Approximately three-fifths of the sample came from middle-class families (27 percent had fathers with professional or managerial occupations, and 36 percent had fathers in white-collar jobs or small businesses), and most of the middle-class respondents were living in or near the more affluent hills area in North Oakland.[20]

In his reanalysis, Elder found that 55 percent of the middle-class families experienced economic "deprivation"; that is to say, between 1929 and 1934 they lost at least 35 percent of their income (a point at which many were forced to dispose of assets). Median income loss for this group was 64 percent, and in just over half the fathers had been out of work for some length of time. Income and job loss were lowest among professionals, of whom a third were deprived and 14 percent unemployed. About half of the fathers in white-collar jobs were deprived, and they also experienced some of the highest unemployment (40 percent). Loss of income was most likely among the self-employed middle class (80 percent), yet more in this group managed to retain their jobs—only 30 percent were unemployed. Elder suggests that these "old middle classes" adapted by working longer hours or employing family members in order to keep their small businesses afloat.[21]

Economic deprivation took its toll on these families, particularly those in the lower middle class, but Elder estimates that most had regained their former status by 1941. For the deprived middle classes, the experience of status loss itself may have been most traumatic, after the prosperity and upward mobility of the '20s. From interview data, Elder found that some families went to extraordinary lengths to maintain appearances with their neighbors and to avoid the social and psychological costs of "coming down in the world." Deprivation was associated with researchers' observations of emotional distress among middle-class mothers, especially when families were forced to move from higher- to lower-status neighborhoods. Unemployment was also strongly associated with reduced associations outside the family among middle-class parents, with heavy drinking by unemployed fathers, and with failure to regain status by 1941.[22]

The results from the Oakland Growth Study offer a small window onto a sample of white families in North Oakland, but for our purposes two things are notable. First, a significant proportion (45 percent) of the middle-class families was *not* deprived even during the depths of the Depression, particularly the professionals, and presumably these families somehow maintained themselves and their social standing. Second, among those that were deprived, the old middle-class entrepreneurs threw themselves into saving family businesses, while the white-collar group either strained their resources to keep from losing face or withdrew from social contacts altogether. Neither response suggests an orientation toward political or collective action. Victorious in the movements of the '20s, white middle classes in Oakland in the '30s either remained integrated within their neighborhoods and social networks or turned inward, to self-employed work, family refuge, or individual discontent.

The shift from public to private civic action is reflected in the contrast between two incidents involving issues central to middle-class neighborhoods: property values and race. In July 1933, members of the Glenview Improvement Club in the lower East Oakland hills mobilized immediately on hearing of the proposed sale of a house on Park Boulevard to an "oriental" buyer. As reported in the club's monthly *Glenview News*, the group met and unanimously affirmed its position as "unalterably opposed to the intermingling of oriental people and white people"; had a copy of the resolution drawn up by its attorney and sent to the owner, the real-estate agent, and the Oakland Real Estate Board; and directed the club president to "take such action as will prevent the sale or occupancy of said premises by people of the oriental race." Two years later, in August 1935, the *Glenview News* noted another "Oriental Problem" with a lease on Randolph Street, this time "Solved in [a] Peaceful Manner." The editor and a committee intervened privately with the owner and lessee to persuade them to cancel the lease, and through a local agent found a white family to move in instead. The editor concluded that "far better results" were obtained than if they had "held indignation meetings and that sort of thing." The newspaper congratulated itself and the club for "forestalling the invasion of our district by Orientals" and asked readers to inform them of "anything that would tend to jeopardize property values in the district."[23]

African Americans

The rise of the white middle class in the '20s brought a hardening of racial boundaries in the city, and black residents who attempted to move into white neighborhoods faced intense hostility. But the Klan and most middle-class whites largely ignored those blacks living in West Oakland, and during the period the latter became the center of an expanding black community. Between 1910 and 1930, the city's African American population more than doubled in size, from 3,055 to 7,503 people, becoming the largest nonwhite group in the city. West Oakland remained a multiracial area, and the still relatively small concentration of blacks may have muted competition between black and white workers—in West Oakland, unlike Chicago or Detroit, no race riots occurred after World War I. Instead, the small but growing black population supported a flowering of indigenous institutions and community formation in the '10s and '20s.[24]

Among these institutions were various black-owned small businesses, churches, and private social-welfare organizations. In addition, several black newspapers were published in Oakland, including the *Western Outlook*, *Western American*, and *California Voice*, while journalist Delilah Beasley's column "Activities among the Negroes" appeared weekly in the *Oakland Tribune* from 1923 until her death in 1934.[25] The Northern California branch of the NAACP was founded in 1915 with its headquarters in Oakland, and by 1919 it reported more than a thousand members throughout the Bay Area. In 1920, a charter was granted to Oakland Division No. 188 of Marcus Garvey's Universal Negro Improvement Association (UNIA), and in 1926 it purchased a building at the corner of Eighth and Chester Streets to house its Liberty Hall. That same year, the Oakland-based Northern Federation of Colored Women's Clubs hosted the biennial convention of the National Association of Colored Women in the Oakland Auditorium, attracting delegates from across the country.[26]

Despite their ideological diversity, these organizations coexisted in the black community, more or less united by values of self-help, liberal tolerance, and racial uplift, and contributing to the development of a distinct local black public sphere. As Lawrence Crouchette, Lonnie Bunch III, and Martha Winnacker explain, "East Bay blacks were as distant from the national black leadership as they were from the local white one. Without the numerical strength to affect the direction of national black organizations, they could afford to welcome the encouragement and strength any black-oriented program offered. They could not afford to feud openly with each other, whatever disagreements they held."[27] The size of the community also limited its potential for mass protest, and in their relations with white society, black leaders relied on their personal ties with white patrons. Historian Joseph Rodriguez writes, "[Oakland] black elites often times formed committees which discussed problems of discrimination with white officials. Confrontation rarely, if ever, took place. Instead, prominent black elites used their personal influence and friendships with city officials to change public policy."[28] Without a broader mobilization, however, by the end of the '20s membership in organizations like the NAACP had dwindled, leaving only a small core of black professionals.[29]

As the Depression took hold, even these groups had difficulty maintaining their resources. Of the several black newspapers that Oakland had supported, only the *California Voice* survived, while the UNIA's Liberty House was ultimately sold to the church of Father Divine.[30] Unemployment hit the black community especially hard: Between 1930 and 1940, the total number of regularly employed black male and female workers declined by 40 percent, from 3,864 to 2,274, even as the total black population grew by nearly a thousand during the same period. Blacks gained only limited access to the jobs provided on the major infrastructure projects and instead were heavily concentrated in relief work: 31 percent of black workers in Oakland were on public emergency work in April 1940, compared to 5 percent of white workers.[31] Overall, the contraction of resources within the community further exacerbated the problem of black dependence on the institutions of the majority white society.

An exception to this pattern was the Brotherhood of Sleeping Car Porters (BSCP) union.[32] Founded nationally by A. Philip Randolph in 1925, the Oakland local was organized in 1926 by Morris "Dad" Moore and C. L. Dellums. Fired from his job as a porter in 1928, Dellums became the full-time business agent for the local and later a vice president of the national union. Standing over six feet tall and a powerful orator, Dellums was an impressive, charismatic figure as he fought with Pullman company officials over working conditions in Oakland and defended local members against the company's spying and harassment. Though not widely supported by the black professional middle class, the Pullman porters' economic and social status made the BSCP union a force in West Oakland.

In 1928, the national BSCP membership voted to authorize a systemwide strike against the Pullman Company. Union leaders expected that this action would trigger federal arbitration under 1926 Railway Labor Act, but the National Board of Mediation refused to intervene. Randolph then met with AFL president William Green, who pleaded for a postponement of the strike, promising AFL cooperation in the campaign. The BSCP officially joined the AFL in 1929, but it took eight more years of struggle before the union finally won a contract from the Pullman Company. During that time, Dellums became a leading activist in the Oakland black community and—along with organizers like Frances Albrier, president of the Ladies' Auxiliary of the Dining Car Cooks and Waiters Local 456—helped turn black political orientations toward the New Deal Democratic Party.[33]

White Working Classes

The crisis of the Depression and the loss of traditional patronage support also gave a new urgency to the grievances of ethnic white workers. Elder reports that 69 percent of the working-class families surveyed in the Oakland Growth Study suffered deprivation, with even higher rates (80 percent) among those with foreign-born parents.[34] Such families were concentrated in the industrial flatland districts that now stretched across the city's entire lowland perimeter. This area began along the city's northern borders with Berkeley and the town of Emeryville, with its foundries, canneries, and popular bars, restaurants, and gambling joints surrounding the minor-league baseball stadium of the Pacific Coast League Oakland Oaks. Within walking distance was the North Oakland Italian American neighborhood of Temescal, and to the south lay the dense older working-class settlements of West Oakland. Industrial development continued along the waterfront periphery around the estuary toward East Oakland, to the cotton mills and canneries at the foot of Twenty-third Avenue and the adjacent Portuguese American community called Jingletown, down the rail lines to the factories and warehouses below the long commercial strip of East Fourteenth Street, up to the Chevrolet plant and workers' houses in Eastmont, and out among the parts suppliers and metal shops near San Leandro. All of these neighborhoods experienced a growing class distance from the more affluent hills, forming a common cultural referent and shaping identities for the American-born descendants of European immigrant groups. As historian

Richard Boyden writes, "Many new ethnics, including Italians, worked in agricultural processing, the local branch assembly plants of Ford and General Motors, and in the engine plants of the East Bay. It was the second generation youth in this work force, particularly the Italians and Portuguese, that provided much of the fire of the new unions in the late Thirties, as they sought to escape the discrimination and poverty endured by their parents."[35]

Many European ethnics also labored as stevedores and freight handlers along the docks and warehouses on the city waterfront. Local activity in shipping, storage, and distribution had grown rapidly with the rise of California agribusiness, the emergence of highway transport, and the reorganization of the port of Oakland, and from 1918 to 1930 seven major marine terminals were opened on the Oakland harbor. Work on the docks was linked economically to the proliferation of both "public" (general-use) warehouses near the waterfront and private in-house storage at places like Albers Brothers Milling Company, which operated a grain elevator at the foot of Seventh Street. Other processing plants in town were located farther inland, often owned by large corporations like the Santa Cruz Packing Company, part of national food chain based in the Midwest, and the California Packing Corporation, called CalPack, one of the world's largest canning and packing firms, known for its products marketed under the Del Monte label.

The destruction of the waterfront unions after World War I left these employers with practically unilateral control in the labor market, and in the depths of the Depression conditions for workers steadily grew worse. By the winter of 1933, shipowners had reduced longshore wages to seventy-five cents an hour, while warehouse workers at the Santa Cruz Packing Company earned a rate of thirty-five to forty-five cents an hour for up to a seventeen-hour day during the busy season. Already known as "hard muscle work," such jobs grew increasingly dangerous as weight loads increased, gang sizes were reduced, and foremen pushed for the "speedup." But perhaps most hated of all was the daily search for work through the "shape-up," the employers' system for hiring casual labor. Workers gathered in the early morning at the dock or warehouse gate, waiting to be picked out by a gang boss—a process rife with favoritism, bribery, and abuse. The strongest or most fortunate might get in with the "star gangs" who got the best jobs and the most work, but others might be hired for only a few hours or not at all. Yet even those on the star gangs might end up working shifts lasting twenty-four hours straight or more, their protests silenced by the constant threat of displacement by other jobless men.[36]

Worker unrest on the docks finally broke out in May 1934, in an eighty-two-day coastwide strike led by Pacific Coast District 38 of the International

Longshoremen's Association (ILA). Oakland teamsters and dockworkers participated in the strike, and BSCP leader Dellums played a central role in persuading black workers not to cross the longshore union's picket lines.[37] In July, the waterfront strike escalated into a citywide General Strike in San Francisco, after two workers were shot and killed by police. The Alameda County Building Trades and Central Labor Councils rallied behind the San Francisco General Strike, and more than seventy East Bay unions called out their members in sympathy, including Key System employees, who shut down streetcar and transbay ferry service. As a result of the Strike, the steamship companies agreed to submit the dispute to arbitration, and the longshore workers were eventually awarded a wage increase, reduced hours, and a jointly operated employer-union hiring hall that eliminated the shape-up.[38]

This landmark victory electrified the Bay Area labor movement, and renewed militancy quickly spread to other groups of workers. By the spring of 1935, the ILA warehouse Local 38–44 had signed its first contracts with the East Bay terminal and public storage facilities. But the fragility of these agreements, and the continued resistance of the employers, convinced the union to embark on a "March Inland" to organize the uptown private storage industry. In October 1936, after more than a year of negotiations, Local 38–44 struck the Bay Area's public warehouses; cold storage plants; grain, flour, and feed mills; and wholesale grocery warehouses. The strike coincided with, and mutually reinforced, the 1936–1937 West Coast maritime strike of workers from the ILA longshore locals, the Sailors' Union of the Pacific, and various marine crafts. On January 5, 1937, after sixty-seven days, the warehouse union won a settlement that included pay raises, a forty-hour week, seniority rights, and a union hiring hall. At the end of the strike, the warehouse Local 38–44 had more than doubled in size, with twenty-two hundred members in Oakland alone.[39]

As a result of these events, the longshore and warehouse workers' union soon became a leading force in the movement of the Committee for Industrial Organization (CIO) on the West Coast. With the participation and support of Communist Party activists, CIO unions in the East Bay moved into the auto, warehouse, maritime, cannery, and public-utility sectors, organizing thousands of unskilled industrial and ethnic minority workers.[40] By the spring of 1937, workers were mobilizing strikes throughout the city. In March, more than two hundred employees at the General Motors–Fisher Body plant in East Oakland staged a one-day sit-down strike to protest the discharge of a United Auto Workers union member. The sit-down sparked a sympathetic action at the nearby Chevrolet plant, altogether involving a total of twenty-five hundred workers.[41] Two days later, approximately fifteen hundred Works Progress Administration employees, led by the local Workers Alliance relief union and the American Federation of Government Employees, walked off their jobs at several parks and public-works projects, demanding wage increases and job security.[42] Meanwhile, some forty female garment workers, mostly Italian, sat down at their tables at the Spirella corset manufacturing company in Emeryville. Their sit-down lasted for six weeks and ended with the company agreeing to recognize the International Ladies' Garment Workers' Union as the collective bargaining representative for the employees.[43]

The rise of the CIO unions showed that native white Protestant craftsmen held no monopoly over the organized working-class movement. Immigrant ethnic and industrial workers eagerly joined the new unions, asserting a class identity and solidarity that extended beyond the workplace and into the community, including crossracial support for New Deal reforms to meet urban needs. This new alternative social-democratic agenda can be seen in the early movement for local public housing. During the Depression, the city as a whole had a shortage of low-income housing, and affordable rental units were scarce, especially for black tenants. Under the 1937 Wagner-Steagall Housing Act, Oakland was eligible to receive federal subsidies for public housing, but the city council refused to adopt the required enabling legislation until pressured to do so by a coalition led by C. L. Dellums, the CIO Labor's Non-Partisan League, and the Oakland League of Women Voters. Dellums later recalled the mobilization in support of public housing:

> So I started to lead demonstrations in city council meetings through Labor's Non-Partisan League, because my strength was in the labor movement and it was where I could get a crowd. City Hall then was looked upon as the jail house, because the jail was on the 13th floor of City Hall and Negroes didn't like to go where the jail is, apparently; it is hard to get them down there. But I knew that in the labor movement I could get an audience so I raised the issue in Labor's Non-Partisan League and that is how we started to go in before the city council to demand that they consider an enabling resolution for low-cost housing and go on record for it.

Their efforts succeeded in getting $5 million in federal funds authorized to build low-income housing projects in Oakland. In 1939, plans were announced for construction of the first two projects, Campbell Village and Peralta Villa, to be located in West Oakland.[44]

Many later critics regarded the introduction of public housing into West Oakland as a prime example of outside government intervention and disruption of the local community. Hundreds of families were uprooted, and scores of older Victorian-era houses were razed and replaced with austere, modern two-story concrete-block apartment complexes. But the neighborhood was already suffering from serious disinvestment, and many houses were in fact overcrowded, illegally subdivided, and deteriorating from age and neglect. Residents complained that the blocks targeted for demolition were not the most dilapidated but rather those with the highest number of black occupants, and that displaced homeowners received appraisals far below their property's value from the business-dominated Oakland Housing Authority. Dellums and others fought again to get fair compensation for homeowners and to ensure racial integration in the projects once they were built. When the first project, Campbell Village, opened in July 1941, black and white tenants were "checkerboarded" in alternating units within each building, thus preserving the prior racial diversity of the neighborhood. Local implementation of public housing remained an object of intense controversy, but for its advocates the policy offered an ideal of low-cost, racially integrated working-class housing, and it represented a hard-won victory against an antagonistic urban regime.[45]

For many, the CIO and its allies signified a radical new departure in industrial relations, an alternative vision of political community, and the promise of a movement for broader urban social change. Yet partly because of the economic structure of the area and the prior establishment of the AFL, the latter remained the larger and stronger union federation, with more than twice the membership of the CIO in Alameda County.[46] In this context, the continued path of working-class mobilization in Oakland would be shaped by the interactions of several actors, including a countermobilization by the political and business elites and a decisive split in the labor movement itself. In the late '30s, a critical sequence of events revealed the competing strategies and alignments of these groups and marked the limits of the labor movement's formation as a collective actor.

THE INTERACTION OF MOVEMENT AND REGIME: MILITANCY VERSUS MACHINE UNIONISM

The Knowland regime met the challenge of labor insurgency with a combination of repression, exclusion, and selective incorporation. The 1934 San Francisco General Strike had provoked a near panic among elites in the East

Bay: Two battalions of National Guard troops with machine guns were called in to patrol the port of Oakland during the Strike, Oakland mayor W. J. Mc-Cracken claimed to have thousands of volunteers signed up as citizen vigilantes, and in the affluent hill suburb of Piedmont (where many shipowners and businessmen lived), local leaders posted armed guards at gas stations and street entrances to the town.[47] For the rest of the decade, the city government maintained an official hostility toward strikes, as Oakland police routinely harassed union (and especially CIO) organizers and enforced constitutionally disputed antipicketing and antileafleting ordinances in an effort to restrain their access to the public sphere.[48]

The threat of unionization also spurred the business community to renewed mobilization as a class actor. The East Bay Industrial Association was revived as the United Employers, Inc., under the sponsorship of first the cannery industry and later the retail merchants. The United Employers organized firms for industrywide collective bargaining, and it eventually helped to create the corporatist "institutionalized labor market" pattern for the Bay Area described by Clark Kerr.[49] But it also aided those employers who chose to maintain an open shop. Among the latter were the downtown merchants, who formed their own Retail Merchants Association, combining twenty-eight of the largest retailers in Alameda County in what became one the most adamantly anti-union of the employer groups.[50]

In addition, the business elites formed strategic alliances with some of the more conservative AFL leaders, in a form of collaboration that might be described as *machine unionism*. One example can be found in the career of James H. Quinn, secretary of the Alameda County Building Trades Council, whose member unions were essential to the construction of the new infrastructure projects. In 1932, Quinn was appointed by the governor to the financial committee of the Bay Bridge Advisory Committee, and in 1933 he was elected to the city council.[51]

In November 1936, Quinn's Building Trades Council offered to undercut wages in order to displace the CIO Mine, Mill, and Smelters union from work on the Broadway Tunnel, and in 1938 he signed an unprecedented two-year blanket agreement with the East Bay Building Advisory Board, covering thirty-six building trades and crafts in Alameda County.[52] A Republican, Quinn depended on his alliance with the Knowland machine for his electoral success, and his campaigns eschewed any militant rhetoric of class solidarity, even in the pages of the *East Bay Labor Journal*, of which he was the editor. In the 1937 city elections, Quinn easily retained his council seat, while the local AFL rejected an independent New Deal slate of pro-labor candidates, all of whom were defeated. In the same election, a union-sponsored initiative to overturn the antipicketing ordinance, similar to one that had recently been victorious in San Francisco, failed by only 477 votes, or less than one percent.[53]

Machine unionism extended into the organization and culture of the labor movement itself, affecting the formation of the working class as a collective actor. This relationship is illustrated particularly in the case of the International Brotherhood of Teamsters (IBT). Teamster economic power derives not so much from their location in a cooperative craft or factory labor process as from their strategic role in moving materials and products among various warehouses, work sites, and stores. In the course of picking up and delivering freight, drivers also experience myriad contacts with workers in other industries. Their ability to shut down the transport of goods often gave the Teamsters a decisive influence in labor disputes—those of other unions as well as their own. This was especially true in Oakland, where the trade sector played a large part in the local economy. With more than two thousand members, the Teamsters Local 70 was regarded as the most powerful union in the East Bay.[54]

Yet labor solidarity was a chronic problem for the Teamsters. The union was frequently pulled into other workers' labor struggles, sometimes in conflict with the contractual claims of its own employers. Moreover, the teaming "craft" was neither spatially concentrated in a single work site nor strongly bounded by skill, making it difficult to unite all the workers in its labor market. The drayage industry further included many small employers, blurring the lines between bosses who might be former teamsters and drivers who aspired to start their own businesses. As a result, the union was vulnerable to strong-arm leaders, who sometimes colluded with employers in order to control hiring, enforce contracts, and maintain power.[55]

Dave Beck, the Seattle-based West Coast organizer (and later vice president) of the IBT, typified this kind of labor leader. Beck had risen swiftly in the Teamsters in the mid '30s, as a result of his successful campaigns to organize over-the-highway drivers along the Pacific Coast. His counterpart and ally in Oakland was Charles Real, secretary-treasurer of Local 70 and a leading figure in the local and state AFL. Real had been an officer in Local 70 since 1926, and he was described by fellow union leaders as "a good union man in the early days." Following his involvement in a notorious 1934 taxicab strike, however, he was indicted and tried for conspiracy in the murder of a strikebreaker. The trial ended in a hung jury, and Real was never retried. Other union leaders suspected that a deal had been made with District Attorney Warren's office; in any case, Real subsequently became a conservative business unionist, a prominent Republican, and a strong supporter of the Knowland machine.[56]

At the same time, rank-and-file Teamster members in the East Bay preserved a militant tradition of honoring picket lines, born of the hard years of the open-shop era of the '20s. Indeed, Oakland Teamsters had supported the longshore workers in 1934 and remained sympathetic to the warehouse union's March Inland through most of 1936. This grassroots solidarity culture was best represented by Teamster Cliff Lester, elected president of Local 70 in 1935. Lester had grown up in a strong union family: His father was a charter member of Local 70, and his brothers Roy and Vic had played an important part in the leadership of the Bartenders Union, Local 52. A former amateur boxer and onetime operator of a small hamburger diner on Second Street near the warehouse district, Lester was a popular figure in the union and in the West Oakland community. The tension between Lester's popular militancy and Real's machine unionism reflected the contradictory class culture of the Teamsters, between values of tough, combative, courageous solidarity on the one hand, and conservative, apolitical, and sometimes violent and corrupt control on the other.[57]

A DISSONANT REPERTOIRE:
THE SPLIT OF THE AFL AND CIO

The relations among these actors were to determine the paths of local working-class organization over the next decade. In early 1937, as part of its March Inland, ILA Local 38–44 began organizing warehouse workers at six East Bay plants of the California Conserving Company and the California Packing Corporation. In March, after negotiations had failed, the union voted to strike and was joined by the cannery workers' AFL Federal Union 20099. Both unions sought and were granted official sanction for the strike by the Alameda County Central Labor Council, thereby obliging fellow AFL unions to honor their picket lines.

Conflicts within the national labor federation were already high following the expulsion of the CIO unions from the AFL in November 1936. In the Teamsters, leaders in the International hierarchy had become increasingly alarmed by the militancy and influence of the West Coast ILA among warehouse workers. In February 1937, at the request of Beck and IBT president Daniel Tobin, the national AFL executive council granted jurisdiction over inland warehouses to the Teamsters. A few weeks later, Real and other

Teamster officials met with J. Paul St. Sure, the attorney for the canners' association, to discuss mutual cooperation in displacing the ILA-supported unions in the canneries. On April 5, AFL president Green notified the Central Labor Council of the jurisdictional decision; and Real, following directions from Tobin and Beck, ordered Local 70 drivers to cross the strikers' picket lines. Four days later, an estimated one thousand warehouse and cannery workers marched en masse to a Local 70 membership meeting to plead their case to the Teamster rank and file. ILA leader Harry Bridges was allowed to address the meeting, and with support from Local 70 president Lester, Teamster members voted by a margin of five to one to defy their international union and respect the strikers' pickets.

"Nobody, not even [AFL] President Green, has the right to order men to become strikebreakers," Lester was reported to have said. "We don't want any part in the fight between the teamsters international and the ILA."[58] The following week, IBT president Tobin summarily placed Local 70 in receivership. An IBT representative, Joseph Casey, took over administration of the union; Real was retained as secretary-treasurer and trustee, and Lester and others were replaced as officers and as delegates to the Central Labor Council. The council, however—outraged at what it saw as AFL and IBT attempts to break an ongoing, sanctioned strike—refused to seat the appointed officers. Tobin then sent a wire to the council demanding that the new delegates be seated, but a motion to comply was defeated in the council by a vote of eighty-four to fifty. On April 26, AFL president Green sent an ultimatum to the council, and when the members again refused to comply, AFL organizer Rowland Watson revoked the charter of the Alameda County Central Labor Council.

Seventy-one council members immediately formed a Charter Restoration Committee, but to no avail. Officials of the AFL quickly set up a new, reformed Central Labor Council, and all locals sympathetic to the CIO or organized by it were expelled. The official sanction for the warehouse and cannery workers' strike was withdrawn, the striking cannery workers' federal union charter was rescinded, and a new union was chartered in its place. Real promptly obtained wage increases for Local 70 members from the trucking employers, and in June, Casey ordered drivers to cross the picket lines at the canneries. Working-class solidarity broke down, as AFL and CIO union members fought each other in violent clashes on the streets of Oakland. Later that summer, the purged CIO locals formed their own Industrial Council, the Pacific Coast district of the ILA was issued a CIO charter as the International Longshoremen's and Warehousemen's Union (ILWU), and Bridges was named West Coast director of the CIO. The split within the Bay Area labor movement was complete.[59]

In Oakland, the effects of this struggle were felt as early as the following year. The reorganization of the Central Labor Council allowed Casey and Real to carry out their purge of Local 70, and the new face of the reshuffled Teamsters leadership was displayed in the defeat of a 1938 Retail Clerks Union strike. During the Depression, the downtown merchants who dominated the urban regime also enjoyed considerable power over their own employees, who worked long hours for low pay. Retail clerks earned less than sixteen dollars for a forty-eight-hour week, while larger stores kept a "ready room," not unlike the shape-up on the docks, where extra workers might wait unpaid for hours in hopes of receiving a day's hire if the stores were busy.

When the ILWU began organizing among its members' stockroom and warehouse employees, the Retail Merchants Association quickly offered to enlist the AFL Clerks Union as a passive partner in a wage-fixing cartel among the retail stores. The Central Labor Council initially endorsed the plan, but dissident union leaders and members rejected the agreement and voted to strike at Whitthorne and Swan's, a department store. The strike was defeated when Real ordered Local 70 members to cross the clerks' picket lines, after he allegedly received five thousand dollars from the merchants association for making a radio broadcast condemning the strike.[60]

The outcome of the clerks' strike set the pattern in the Oakland retail industry for the next decade. For practical purposes, the Clerks Union local was destroyed, and it would not fully recover until 1946. Real consolidated his control over Teamster Local 70 and proved his loyalty to the regime and his willingness to cross other unions' picket lines. Finally, the Retail Merchants Association proceeded anyway with its cartel, and thereafter adopted an "all or none" stance against the clerks, forbidding its member stores to negotiate individually with the union and threatening expulsion to any member who signed a separate labor contract. A confidential merchants association source was later quoted as saying, "The [merchants association] membership regards the conduct and demands of the [clerks'] union as unreasonable. And if they ever become reasonable, we'll find some other reason for having nothing to do with the Clerks Union."[61]

CONCLUSION:
MOVEMENT DIVISION AND REGIME STABILITY

The results of the cannery workers' and retail clerks' strikes demonstrate the effects of a reactive sequence of interactions on working-class formation in Oakland. No single event in the sequence was fully determining, but each intervening step conditioned the resources and alternatives available to actors in subsequent events. Together, the successive, related strike defeats in the key local cannery and retail sectors blunted the thrust of labor insurgency and helped cut short the mobilization of a challenging working-class collective actor. In addition, the split between the AFL and CIO unions strengthened the employers' leverage and fractured the possibilities for a wider expression of labor solidarity in the public sphere. This divided working-class identity was symbolically enacted in the organization of the 1937 Labor Day parade: At the insistence of the AFL, the Oakland City Council denied permission for the CIO unions to join the AFL procession, and instead issued permits for separate morning and afternoon parades for the two federations.[62]

Thus the organizational trenches of class conflict were dug in the '30s. The economic crisis of the Depression created an opening for the return of working-class protest, in the Bay Area and across the nation. In Oakland, the CIO unions brought thousands of new ethnic and industrial workers into the labor movement, but they also developed an enduring rivalry with the older and larger AFL. Local employers exploited this division and successfully contained labor militancy through their alliance with the machine unionism of James Quinn and Charles Real. Meanwhile, the city government, immune from any electoral challenge, maintained its repressive stance toward public strikes and organizing activity.

These sequences of events contradict any simple cumulative or internal model of the formation of the working class as a collective actor. The resurgence of labor mobilization in Oakland occurred only after the "break" in the movement during the '20s, and the initiative shifted from the older craft unions toward the ethnic industrial workers organized by the CIO. But the rivalry between the AFL and CIO was not simply a conflict between industrial and craft unionism, nor was it a struggle purely internal to the labor movement. After all, rank-and-file teamster drivers were not so distant from longshore and warehouse workers, and the former had even supported the latter in the early to mid '30s. Rather, movement actors' choices were conditioned by the set of opportunities and alliances within the polity as a whole, between a strategy of popular class solidarity on the one hand and one of machine unionism on the other.

Despite the new insurgency, then, the working-class challenge in Oakland reached its limits at this juncture. Radical unionism was effectively quarantined, while the regime maintained its hegemony—not by its ideological legitimacy, but through the fragmentation and demobilization of conflict in the public sphere. Indeed, many of these same actors were to appear again in 1946. With the change in structural conditions and political alignments after World War II, however, their interactions then would result in class polarization and a citywide General Strike.

5 Working-Class Collective Agency

The General Strike and Labor Insurgency

In cities across the United States, working-class protest had returned during the 1930s. In Oakland, however, such protest was mostly contained, unable to break through the hegemony of the Knowland regime. The conservative coalition in city government remained securely in power, as did the economic leadership of the downtown elite. By 1938, the Bay Bridge and the Broadway Tunnel had been completed and military base development was under way. Although the Depression was hardly over, Oakland businesses were already looking forward to a future of metropolitan expansion into the suburban and rural areas of Alameda County.[1]

Within a few years, however, the status quo was to change drastically with the outbreak of World War II. The structural impacts of economic and military mobilization on Oakland were enormous. Tens of thousands of new workers migrated into the city, transforming the composition, organization, and alignment of groups in urban civil society and politics. After the war, formerly dominant patterns of hegemony broke down, giving way to a pattern of increasing class polarization. Late in 1946, a strike of predominantly female department store clerks led to a showdown between the AFL unions and the business elites, and to a conflict that exploded into the citywide Oakland General Strike.

The General Strike itself opened up a new period of movement challenge in the city, as local union leaders attempted to mobilize popular class interests in the political arena. In the municipal elections of 1947, they were partially successful in organizing a social-democratic coalition of groups against the managerial regime. Nevertheless, their efforts encountered significant institutional barriers in the pursuit of an alternative model of urban development. The popular coalition would ultimately fall apart in a key controversy over urban housing policy, in ways that foreshadowed the alignment of groups in the subsequent period of the '50s and '60s.

STRUCTURAL CHANGE AND CLASS FORMATION: THE REMAKING OF THE WORKING CLASS

The Impact of Migration

World War II brought a mass exodus of young people into the armed services and an even larger wave of population influx, as the Bay Area quickly converted to a center of war industry, specializing particularly in shipbuilding. Manufacturing employment in Oakland rose by 166 percent from December 1941 to a peak in August 1943, and one Oakland shipyard alone employed as many as thirty-five thousand workers.[2] In addition, Oakland served as a major supply and distribution center for the Pacific theater of operations, stimulating production for defense-related needs in food processing, textiles, machine parts, paints, and other manufactured goods. By the latter half of 1943, government prime and subcontracts exclusive of shipbuilding exceeded $7.8 million in Alameda County. Finally, thousands of civilians found employment on the new military bases in the area. Overall, the percentage of unemployed in Oakland (those seeking work and those on emergency work) fell from 15 percent in March 1940 to less than 2 percent in April 1944.[3]

The city's population grew by 14 percent, or 43,182 people, between 1940 and the spring of 1944. The war industries attracted migrants from across the country, and by 1944 more than 22 percent of Oakland residents had lived in the city less than four years. The majority of these new residents came from out of state, many directly from rural backgrounds, including large numbers of black and white workers from the central southwestern states. Almost one-fifth of all wartime migrants to the Bay Area were from Oklahoma, Arkansas, Texas, or Louisiana, and 16 percent of war migrants to Oakland had lived on farms four years earlier—more than three times the proportion among late Depression-era migrants.[4] In 1940, the number of foreign-born whites still exceeded the number of nonwhites in the city by about three to one. During the war, the African American population more than tripled in size, going from less than 3 percent of the city total in 1940 to almost 10 percent in 1945.[5]

Wartime labor shortages also affected the position of female workers. The number of employed women in Oakland nearly doubled from 1940 to 1944, raising the share of women in the city's employed population from 27 percent to 35 percent. Women entered manufacturing in unprecedented numbers: By one estimate, as many as seven thousand women were employed in one Oakland shipyard in 1943.[6] Growth in the Bay Area's important trade sector, however, meant that female employment in wholesale and retail trade kept pace. Unlike other cities with major concentrations of war production, manufacturing never surpassed trade and services as the principal sector employing Bay Area women.

Such rapid structural changes brought new pressures to bear on urban civil society. In contrast to the flow of migrants into and out of Oakland during the '30s, war migrants tended to be settlers, seeking a permanent stake in the local community. Most war migrants to the Bay Area were members of families: 71 percent were either married adults with a spouse present, or children under the age of fifteen—about the same ratio as the nonmigrant population.[7] Moreover, much of the new migration was "one-way." The Okies had fled economic catastrophe in their home states, while southern black migrants had little incentive to return to the racial apartheid of the South. Several surveys reported that migrants, women, and black workers all hoped to remain in the Bay Area and continue working in their jobs after the war.[8]

All of these groups came together in urban space. One immediate problem was housing, as residential vacancies in Oakland fell from an already low 2 percent in April 1941 to 0.8 percent in April 1942, finally reaching an astounding 0.06 percent in September 1942. Whole families crowded into one-room apartments, or shared living quarters with relatives, or simply slept in their cars or on the streets. In West Oakland, population density increased fourfold from 1940 to 1945.[9] One longtime resident recalled seeing a daily stream of migrants arriving at the Southern Pacific's Sixteenth Street Station: "It was like a parade. You just couldn't believe that many people would come in, and some didn't even have any luggage, they would come with boxes, with three or four children with no place to stay."[10] The need for shelter overwhelmed the capacity of the private housing market, and led to government intervention through the provision of federally financed public housing.

Oakland had not yet completed construction of its second New Deal–era housing project, Peralta Villa in West Oakland, when the war emergency converted all public housing to the defense effort. Peralta Villa and a third project, Lockwood Gardens in East Oakland, were promptly reassigned to war workers, but thereafter the Oakland Housing Authority refused to build any more permanent projects that might compete with the postwar private construction industry. Instead, federal funds were used to build temporary housing for migrant war workers under the federal Lanham Act of 1940. These legally subcode, barrackslike structures were located on surplus land in the shoreline flats, near the shipyards, military bases, and industrial areas and apart from established residential neighborhoods. Moreover, unlike the checkerboard integration of Campbell Village, in these projects blacks and whites were separated in different buildings or segregated entirely in different complexes. By the end of the war, Oakland operated three permanent and eleven temporary projects, of which four had mixed racial occupancy, seven were all-white, and three were all-black. All three of the black projects (and a fourth nearly all-black one) were located in West Oakland, and all of the white projects were located in or near East Oakland. As historian Marilynn Johnson points out, local implementation of wartime public housing created a separate zone of migrant temporary settlement along the city's industrial margin and accelerated the racial concentration of African Americans in West Oakland.[11]

The isolation of migrant and minority residential areas contrasted with the sudden mingling of groups in the shared space of downtown. Before the war, the downtown commercial district had already developed as the center of the city's public life, with dozens of restaurants and movie houses, large department stores, and retail specialty shops. With the wartime boom, the area became packed with a bustling twenty-four-hour street scene. Theaters and cafes stayed open all night to accommodate the swing shift, and dance halls, taverns, and other amusements sprang up to appeal to war workers with disposable income. Older Oakland residents were shocked at the unruly crowds and the seeming breakdown of moral order, yet for many workers the experience was a liberating release from established social barriers. As Johnson writes, "Contemporary accounts noted the presence of wandering pedestrians at all hours, either window shopping or just taking in the city environment. 'My husband and I often walk the downtown streets after dinner just for the pure joy of the movement all around us,' explained one Oakland newcomer."[12] The loosening of rules governing social space also brought out competition and tensions between groups. In May 1944, a race riot erupted after black patrons were turned away from a sold-out Cab Calloway show at the Oakland Auditorium. Fighting broke out on a crowded streetcar after the show and spread rapidly to include two thousand black and white servicemen and civilians.[13]

The Labor Movement

Different groups also encountered one another in the workplace. There, labor unions were one of the few mass organizations to incorporate new residents quickly, albeit in often highly ambivalent ways. Thousands of migrant workers, many of them previously excluded by race, gender, or skill, suddenly became new union members during the war.[14] In the war industries, "maintenance of membership" agreements automatically enrolled employees into existing unions, and AFL and CIO membership in Alameda County more than doubled from the late Depression years.[15] Some local unions actively sought these workers' participation in their organizations, others were indifferent, and many vigorously resisted them. The boilermakers' union, representing more than two-thirds of all West Coast shipyard workers, froze its officers in their positions for the duration of the war and suspended all membership meetings for two years. Black members of the union were forced to join segregated auxiliary locals, with no voting rights, business agents, or grievance protections, and with reduced insurance benefits.[16]

Faced with racial exclusion, black workers organized to gain equal access to employment and union representation. Nationally, BSCP president A. Philip Randolph's call for a march on Washington in the spring of 1941 pressured President Franklin D. Roosevelt into signing Executive Order 8802, which banned discrimination by defense contractors and established a federal Fair Employment Practices Committee. In Oakland, prewar black activists like C. L. Dellums and Frances Albrier played important roles in the fight for fair employment, forging some of the first political links between the older black community organizations and the new black working class. In 1943, Albrier herself became the first black woman hired as a welder at the Kaiser shipyards in nearby Richmond.[17]

These efforts used federal and state administrative and judicial means to eliminate racial restrictions and achieve equal rights in the union and on the job. At the same time, with support from white workers and the local Communist Party, black workers at Kaiser formed the United Negro Labor Committee, to advance their struggles within the International Brotherhood of Boilermakers. In Oakland's Moore dry dock, black shipfitter Ray Thompson founded the East Bay Shipyard Workers' Committee against Discrimination, and with similar interracial backing it claimed a membership of five thousand at its peak.[18]

Most AFL craft unions had long excluded racial minority and female workers by custom or rule, but certain locals in Oakland attempted to include new groups. In the shipyards, the AFL laborers' union, Shipwrights Local 1149, and Painters Local 1175 as well as the East Bay CIO "Steel" Machinists Local 1304, accepted black workers without delay. The Steamfitters Local 590 encouraged the organization of female but not black members, while the dissident Boilermakers Local 681 (burners and welders) submitted to its 1944 international convention a resolution supported by petitions signed by six thousand workers from all Bay Area shipyards, asking for an end to the policy of discrimination. Outside the yards, CIO unions like the ILWU had generally better records against racial discrimination, as did the AFL Carpenters Local 36. Though only a marginal presence in the shipyards, the CIO also reached out to new workers through activities addressing civic concerns like housing, postwar employment, race relations, and more.[19]

As it absorbed new members, the labor movement itself began to change. By the mid 40s a more militant, liberal, and politically oriented leadership began to gain power in the local AFL, opening the door to cooperation with the area's CIO unions, despite official disapproval from the national AFL hierarchy. Among the new leaders were Jack Reynolds, who succeeded James Quinn as business representative for the Alameda County Building Trades Council, and Robert Ash, secretary of Teamster Garage Employees Local 78. Reynolds was a controversial figure; in 1944 he was sentenced to probation after pleading guilty and testifying to his role in a bootlegging operation. Nevertheless, he and Ash—a liberal white southerner originally from Texas—led the AFL unions into greater participation in the Democratic Party. In 1937, Ash had helped organize the predominantly black Local 78, after the machinists' automotive local refused membership to the African American workers. In 1943, on his second try, Ash was elected secretary of the Alameda County AFL Central Labor Council. That same year, Reynolds served as chair of the newly formed United Labor's Legislative Committee, which included officers from the local AFL, CIO, and Railroad Brotherhood unions. Together with the CIO's Political Action Committee, the legislative committee helped to register voters in 1944 and contributed to Democratic challenger George Miller's victory over incumbent Republican (and longtime Knowland friend) Albert Carter in the Sixth Congressional District.[20]

In March 1945 the legislative committee held an unprecedented joint meeting of the AFL, CIO, and Building Trades Councils, attracting 250 delegates. The group voted unanimously to support the formation of the United for Oakland Committee (UOC), a political coalition seeking to challenge the Knowland machine in the upcoming city council elections. The UOC endorsed a slate of candidates that included Central Labor Council secretary Ash, and its platform called for a program of industrial expansion and job creation; improved transit, schools, and health services; housing development; and establishment of a civic unity committee to address racial and labor issues. Though opposed by Knowland allies Charles Real and James

Quinn, on Election Day the UOC challengers reportedly received majorities in the working-class flatlands of West and East Oakland, but were defeated citywide in a very light (28 percent) turnout.[21]

The 1945 UOC campaign signaled an important organizational shift in the local labor movement, in conjunction with its new membership. And although the unions were not yet able to mobilize a mass political challenge, ordinary workers in Oakland could and did show signs of militant class solidarity, particularly in defense of individual workers or unions against perceived attacks by employers. In the shipyards, ethnographer Katherine Archibald observed, "If a clear-cut dispute occurred between management and a group of employees, and the newspapers blazed with headlines condemning the workmen, the membership of the union under attack customarily rallied around its standards; with amazing rapidity a sprawling, disunited cluster became almost an integrated group."[22] During the war, Oakland itself had become a "sprawling cluster," drawing in a vast new working population and undermining the political foundations of the established regime. In the postwar period, structural and conjunctural forces were to push local actors toward a public class confrontation, leading ultimately to a citywide General Strike.

The Structural Fault Line

The end of the war left Oakland and the nation as a whole in a state of considerable uncertainty and social flux. For many, military demobilization and the prospect of economic reconversion brought renewed fears of rising unemployment and a new era of depression. Union leaders openly anticipated a repeat of the post–World War I open-shop and wage-cutting drive on the part of employers. These economic tensions were reflected in the largest strike wave in American history, involving some 4.5 million workers throughout 1946.[23]

With its heavy concentration of defense industries, Oakland underwent a drastic restructuring. In the first three months of 1945 alone, the shipbuilding industry lost more than four thousand jobs in Alameda County. Manufacturing employment in the city fell by 70 percent from August 1945 to February 1946, recovered briefly for a few months, then fell again to below prewar levels by November 1946. Meanwhile, federal price decontrols spurred a rapid wave of inflation, wiping out the wage gains for which many workers had struck that spring. In San Francisco, the Consumer Price Index rose 19.7 percent from August 1945 to November 1946, while the average retail price of food went up 40 percent in the same period.[24]

Locally, such pressures built up in a historic structural context. The Bay

Area working class was shaped by a peculiarly stratified labor market: Blue-collar employment for men had always included a higher proportion of skilled crafts, and both the war and reconversion reinforced this trend. Among female workers, the clerical and sales sectors employed by far the largest share, and in the postwar period fully half of all female workers were in these fields.[25] During the war, female employment actually surpassed male employment in clerical and sales jobs; by 1947, 57 percent of workers in these jobs were women.

These sectors dominated the local postwar economy. In the short run, overall unemployment in the Bay Area stayed comparatively low, as building construction, trade, and services expanded to meet the needs of the increased population.[26] Retail trade was especially important, employing more workers in Alameda County than the wholesale trade and construction sectors combined. The number of department store employees alone nearly equaled all workers in the auto industry or in metal fabricating. Department store employers were also big: Eight firms in the county had more than one hundred employees each, and four had more than five hundred.[27]

As a field, retail trade employed large numbers of men and women, yet typically in different types of firms. Shoe store employees were usually male, and clothing and accessory stores were also frequently gender-typed. Department store clerks were traditionally female: In 1940, 76 percent of the clerical and sales workers in general merchandise and variety stores in Oakland were women.[28] Without challenging the boundaries of these gender-segmented labor markets, the AFL clerks' union crossed over them and brought male and female workers into the same organization.

Female retail clerks also bridged class and gender identities in unusual ways. Though considered to be white-collar, store clerks often came from blue-collar families, with husbands or kin who might be union members. These women also generally thought of themselves as permanent workers: In a survey of Bay Area working women, 70 percent of those employed in retail and wholesale trade in 1945 said they planned to continue working after the war, most in the same industry. Indeed, during the war, women had become a majority of the membership of the Oakland retail clerks' union.[29]

These patterns came together to set the stage for a class confrontation. In the Bay Area, skilled crafts and clerical and sales were the leading sectors, respectively, of the male and female working class. Spurred by the mass layoffs at the end of the war, the fears of an imminent open-shop drive by the employers, and rivalry with the CIO, the local AFL was moved to organize workers beyond its traditional base. In Oakland, this drive centered

on the large group of female retail clerks, concentrated in the member stores
of the downtown Retail Merchants Association.

THE GENERAL STRIKE

The Path to Confrontation:
The Kahn's and Hastings Strike

When the Department and Specialty Store Employees Union Local 1265 began its campaign in 1946 to organize retail clerks in the East Bay, then, its
efforts carried a special significance. Early victories in shoe stores and a five-
and-dime chain encouraged the union to take on the big retailers once again.
By the fall of 1946, the union had recruited a majority of workers at two
downtown sites: Kahn's, a large department store, and Hastings, a men's
store. This move brought the union up against its old adversary, the Retail
Merchants Association, which again took a unified position against recognition of the union by individual stores. In late October, the employees at
the two stores voted to strike.[30]

AFL union leaders in Oakland immediately saw the strike as a bellwether
of postwar labor relations. On November 1, the *East Bay Labor Journal* announced, "We have or have not a labor movement in Alameda County. The
Kahn's strike will be the test. If Kahn's management is successful, you and
your union may be next." Two weeks later, after the Republican Party sweep
in the national elections, the tone became even more urgent. "The Open
Shop Drive Is On and Labor Must Get Out and Fight," read the headline of
the paper's lead editorial. "Right here in Oakland we have a strike that could
lead to an open shop drive against all of labor. . . . Get out and fight for the
Clerks' Union and protect your own neck and your own union." The *Journal* referred explicitly to the unions' experiences in the '20s, and to the profits
the stores had made under wartime prices. Individual unions also passed the
word along to their members. The Draftsmen's Union distributed a letter
warning of an "all-out war on the part of organized business to completely
destroy your Union and all others, and to reduce your wages to a depression level. The employers are attempting to repeat history and are using the
Kahn's and Hastings strike to break the labor movement and weaken the
Unions as they did after the close of World War One."[31]

The Kahn's and Hastings strike quickly developed into a public showdown between the downtown business elites and the AFL unions in Alameda
County, and each side marshaled its allies. The merchants association united
solidly behind the struck stores, providing material and financial aid to the

stores' management, donating advertising space in the *Tribune*, and running its own ads attacking the union and the strike.[32] On the other side, the Central Labor Council promoted its views on radio shows and in the *East Bay Labor Journal*, while union picketers took advantage of the stores' location in the heart of the busy downtown district to seek public sympathy and discourage customers and nonstriking employees from entering the stores. The council also appointed a special negotiating committee composed of leaders of several major local unions and obtained the support of the Teamsters. Local 70 drivers refused to transport goods to or from the struck stores, which soon ran low on inventory and faced a serious loss of business during the Christmas shopping season.

The business leaders then turned to the city government. On Thursday, November 28, a meeting was held in the office of the district attorney in downtown Oakland. Reportedly in attendance were the counsel for the Retail Merchants Association, the head of the United Employers, executives from Kahn's and other leading downtown retailers, the publishers of the *Oakland Tribune* and the *Oakland Post-Enquirer*, the head of the Central Bank, the district attorney, the Oakland police chief, the county sheriff, and other unidentified individuals.[33] The participants at this meeting (and in subsequent ones, as we will see) illustrate the powerful informal unity that existed among the members of the economic elite, as well as their personal involvement in the control of the managerial regime. The store officials announced their intention to move half a million dollars worth of merchandise into the struck stores using a nonunion trucking firm from Los Angeles, and with the consent of all present, the chief of police agreed to provide security for the event.

Union leaders later received word of the plan, and about midnight that Saturday night approximately seventy special pickets, many of them business agents and officials from other local unions, surrounded the stores. Within hours, the police arrived and began to cordon off all streets in the adjacent six-block area, using billy clubs to disperse the picketers and tow trucks to haul away their parked cars. By sunrise, some 250 policemen were on duty at the scene, equipped with shotguns and tear gas. Strikers and union leaders were forced to watch from behind police lines while dozens of police squad cars and motorcycles escorted two separate convoys of strikebreaking trucks, allowing them to complete their deliveries to the stores.

Class Action in Urban Public Space

The response to the police action was immediate. Shortly before 7:00 A.M., the first Sunday-morning streetcar came down on its route along Broadway. When police ordered it to pass through the cordon, business agent Al Brown of the carmen's union jumped on board and convinced the driver to stop. Declaring the police barrier to be a picket line, Brown announced that he would refuse to cross it, and then physically removed the control mechanism from the car. All streetcar and bus traffic through the area was soon halted as other drivers similarly abandoned their runs and joined the crowd. For the rest of the day, a growing number of strikers and onlookers gathered in the center of downtown as outraged unionists hurriedly met and, led by Teamsters Local 70, demanded action. The following day, as pickets continued to mill around the struck stores, the local AFL union leaders voted almost unanimously for a general strike. On Tuesday morning, an estimated hundred thousand AFL members from 142 unions walked off their jobs, and CIO members, though not called out, honored AFL picket lines. (Water, gas, and electric public utilities, organized by CIO unions, remained in service.)[34]

Several of the Oakland strike leaders had participated in the San Francisco General Strike of 1934, and the experience influenced their actions in 1946. Recalling the inflammatory local press coverage during the San Francisco Strike, the Oakland leaders shut down all major newspapers in the city and prevented the delivery of the San Francisco dailies into Oakland. In addition, the Central Labor Council called for striking workers not to stay home but to come downtown for mass rallies and picketing. Crowds estimated at between five thousand and twenty thousand people assembled downtown through the duration of the Strike, and several unions turned their members out for special demonstrations and marches around the streets near the stores.

Observers described the scene on the streets as a "carnival-like atmosphere." The unions officially referred to the Strike as a "holiday," strikers and sympathizers sang and danced to guitars or music played from union loudspeakers, and a few pickets even showed up on roller skates. The strikers acted out their own form of political theater: According to the *San Francisco Call-Bulletin*, on the first day, "About 500 unionists, marching four abreast, staged a 'parade' in front of the City Hall, chanting 'hail, hail, the gang's all here.'" Another journalist complained of heavy absenteeism at Oakland Technical High School, and of "young high school girls with their jeans rolled up above their bobby socks and saddle shoes and their white shirt tails fluttering in the breeze." And a *San Francisco Chronicle* reporter wrote, "Convinced that old Saint Nick wasn't unfair to anyone, milling pickets in front of a downtown Oakland department store opened a path for the kids to see Santa in the display window."[35]

The picketers were overwhelmingly white and male, union members from the Teamsters, Boilermakers, Machinists, Transit Workers, and Sailors, many of them war veterans wearing their military jackets with insignia still attached. Yet newspaper photographs show them demonstrating alongside white women and men of color, as well as scenes of interracial couples dancing in the streets. The strikers themselves were keenly aware of the public representation of the strike. Knowing that photographs might be used either in biased newspaper accounts or in court actions against pickets, strikers assaulted several photojournalists and destroyed their cameras or film.[36]

Some fistfights broke out as strikers confronted police and individuals attempting to enter the stores, but union picket captains kept order and exhorted people to remain nonviolent. The emergent celebration of working-class identity in the city center defied the cultural definition of downtown as a place of commercial consumption and the regime's political control of urban space. A Teamster member later remembered, "Strangers met in the middle of the night on the picket line and you would think they'd known each other all their lives." Another eyewitness recalled, "The participants were making history, knew it, and were having fun.... Never before or since had Oakland been so alive and happy for the majority of the population. It was a town of law and order. In that city of over a quarter million, strangers passed each other on the street and did not have fear, but the opposite."[37]

Unexpectedly, a strike of retail store clerks had mushroomed into an insurgent challenge to the urban regime as a whole. Union rhetoric was unequivocal in its analysis of local political power: The *East Bay Labor Journal* denounced the "nine 'Charlie McCarthys' forming the City Council," declaring that "Oakland Police Act as Strikebreakers for 'Big Business' to Smash Organized Labor," and, "Big Business, not satisfied to pull the dummy strings at the city hall, now also own the city streets."[38] On Tuesday evening, despite drizzling rain and the shutdown of all public transportation, twenty thousand people showed up at the Oakland Auditorium to hear union leaders condemn city government and support the clerks' strike. Central Labor Council secretary Ash later recalled, "All I would have had to say with the way that crowd reacted [at the rally] was just 'Let's knock the baloney off— let's go down and take the City Hall apart,' and I don't think we'd have lost a thousand people. I think they'd have taken that City Hall apart, brick by brick."[39] The unions' distrust of city government was visibly substantiated two days later, on Thursday, December 5, when authorities again antagonized the crowds by evacuating nonstriking employees stranded in Kahn's through a double cordon of police officers, directly from the store into the city hall, located barely a hundred yards away.

The massive show of militancy seemed to catch all sides by surprise, and both business and union leaders immediately sought negotiations to end the General Strike.[40] Although Mayor Herbert Beach publicly condemned the Strike and promised to take control of events, in reality both the mayor and the city council abdicated what little authority they had; by one report neither the mayor nor the council was even given any advance notice of the police action on Sunday.[41] Union representatives met instead with the city manager at the Athens Athletic Club, along with a "citizen's committee" composed largely of the same men present at the previous meeting in the district attorney's office. As the talks got under way, the local union officials experienced mounting pressure from their international leadership to end the Strike. On the second day, IBT vice president Dave Beck released a public declaration calling the General Strike "nothing but a revolution" and adding, "It isn't labor tactics. It's revolutionary tactics."[42] He ordered Teamster members to go back to work, and with that the employers broke off negotiations. Worried about alienating public opinion, the unions then settled with the city manager that the police would no longer be used to break legal picket lines, and each party issued separate statements. The AFL unions officially ended the Strike on Thursday morning, December 5, and a CIO mass meeting, set for that evening to decide whether to join the Strike, was never held.

The Outcome of the General Strike

The abrupt ending of the General Strike begs the question: Why did the local AFL unions call it off? On the streets it had been stunningly effective, largely peaceful, and self-disciplined, and union leaders had received verbal assurances from (now governor) Earl Warren that the national guard would not be sent in. Oakland labor leaders had resisted pressure from their international unions before, of course, and it was not entirely clear that Local 70 drivers would actually obey Beck's order to return to work.[43] In any case, the entry of the CIO locals would have brought out another thirty thousand workers and could have shut down the public utilities, effectively paralyzing the city. Indeed, according to rumors, the entire city council was allegedly prepared to resign if the Strike lasted one more day.

We should not underestimate the degree of risk and uncertainty inherent in moments of collective action. The Central Labor Council leaders had been informed that criminal indictments would be filed against them if they continued the Strike; yet they had also been told that the police chief refused a verbal order from the city manager to use force to remove the crowds, and a written order was never handed down.[44] Even at the height of the events, however, the union leaders were constrained by the inheritance of their organizational repertoire. The legacy of interunion rivalry, the pressure from the IBT and AFL hierarchies, and the limits of their own perceived legitimacy all made a spontaneous alliance with the CIO an unlikely prospect. For the Strike leaders, such action would have jeopardized the resources that they had for a set of possibilities that they did not know or control, notwithstanding their popular support. As council secretary Ash explained, "We knew we were going to have enough problems fighting with Beck and [IBT president Daniel] Tobin and [AFL president] Bill Green and others, just with a big squabble like this, especially if we were going to call any kind of general stoppage of work, without making it worse by even thinking of discussing anything with the CIO."[45]

Instead, the Central Labor Council leaders approached the General Strike from a conventional AFL ideology of economic voluntarism and autonomy from state interference. From the outset, the Strike was framed as a protest; the unions made no attempt to operate vital city functions under their own authority. On the contrary, against the charges of "revolution," union spokespersons justified the Strike as a conservative restoration of civil liberties and economic order. In a radio address broadcast on December 3, the unions' attorney, James Galliano, declared,

> A.F. of L. labor, always conservative, was convinced it had no alternative but to sanction the [General Strike]. . . . We want stable labor relations established. We want labor disputes settled amicably. We want a city government to represent all the people and not to violate constitutional rights, state laws and local ordinances, and to put on shows in order to assist employers in using professional strikebreakers. This general walk out is a protest to this breakdown of city government and to the irresponsible employer leadership that has forced such a situation.

Galliano invoked an image of an Oakland political community able to take care of its own affairs through adherence to rules of fair play. "We find no fault with ordinary non-union hauling, except that we would like to see them unionized, but there are such concerns in every community," he continued. "But the unions cannot accept the importing of professional strikebreakers from the southern part of California. We have always settled our labor disputes within our own backyard."[46]

If the local AFL remained bound to its economic voluntarism, however, the alternative was by no means simply a spontaneous mass revolt. Had the AFL Central Labor Council not supported the clerks in their challenge to the retail merchants and then called the General Strike against the actions of the police, working-class protest in Oakland might not otherwise have found the collective expression that it did—by itself, the CIO was not similarly positioned to conduct a citywide mobilization. Nonetheless, the voluntarist approach placed the unions in the role of bargaining with the regime as they might with an employer; and without the support of the Teamsters, the unions lacked the economic clout to compel the merchants association to settle the Kahn's and Hastings dispute.

Unable to reach a public settlement with the stores in the General Strike, the AFL unions accepted the city's promise of police neutrality and returned to the status quo ante in the clerks' strike. Their decision revealed a crucial limit of AFL unionism: The principle of economic voluntarism, if normally sufficient for the Teamsters or the skilled crafts, gave no advantage to the striking female clerks, who would remain out for at least five more months. Exhausted from a long and bitter strike, they finally consented to what even secretary Ash acknowledged was a "bum agreement." The rest of the merchants association members succeeded in blocking the clerks' campaign, and in general the department store sector in Oakland subsequently resisted unionization for many years.[47]

The downtown elites' dominance of city government had isolated the regime from the working-class population, but it also provided few existing institutional mechanisms for the unions to apply political pressure or guarantee a settlement. Though undoubtedly correct in their low estimation of the incumbent mayor and city council, the unions were instead obliged to put their faith in the personal authority of City Manager Hassler as the negotiating representative for the regime.[48] Partly as a result, in the immediate aftermath of the strike there seems to have been confusion on all sides about what had been decided. Having conceded the huge display of protest, the regime nevertheless maintained its steep institutional closure, backed by a solid business-class unity. On Friday, December 6, three days after the union rally, more than twelve hundred local businessmen attended a mass meeting of their own, called by the United Employers at the Oakland Auditorium, where they gave the city manager a unanimous vote of confidence.[49] Hassler quickly began to backtrack on his promises to the unions, and within two weeks police were escorting strikebreaking employees back into the stores. By then, the momentum of the General Strike had passed, and a union threat to renew it never materialized.

ORGANIZING A COUNTERREGIME: THE CITY COUNCIL, 1947–1951

Despite its immediate outcome, the ending of the General Strike in no way spelled the end of labor insurgency in Oakland. The mobilization galvanized the militant leadership in the Central Labor Council and strengthened their opposition to machine unionism within the labor movement. Council leaders openly and bitterly denounced Teamster chief Real and his belated efforts to broker the clerks' strike, even though Real happened to be president of the California Federation of Labor at the time. The Strike also reinforced traditions of militancy among the AFL unions' rank-and-file membership, raising the confidence of ordinary workers in their capacity for collective action and heightening the respect of the CIO unions for the AFL. Finally, the sheer size of the event had an impact on popular consciousness, crystallizing discontent with the city government. According to Robert Ash, "Four months after the General Strike, at the opening of the baseball season in Oakland they had the Oakland motorcycle drill team lead the dignitaries into the ball park. They were not all trade unionists in that ball park, but I never heard anybody get booed so loudly and hard as those cops did that day."[50]

As the limits of the initial settlement became clear, the unions again came together to form a political alliance in preparation for the city elections the following spring. Spurred by the United Brotherhood of Carpenters Local 36, the Central Labor Council joined with the CIO, the Building Trades Council, and the Railroad Brotherhoods in March 1947 to organize a Joint Labor Committee to Combat Anti-Labor Legislation as a vehicle for cooperative political mobilization.[51] The committee later joined with disaffected business and real-estate interests in North and East Oakland in an electoral coalition called the Oakland Voters' League (OVL).[52] In the 1947 city council elections, the OVL endorsed a slate of five candidates: Vernon Lantz, an oil company chemist; Raymond Pease, a railroad engineer; Ben Goldfarb, an insurance agent; Scott Weakley, a radio announcer; and attorney Joseph Smith. The incumbent councillors in the race included Mayor Beach and Dr. John Slavich, both of whom had served on the council for sixteen years, since the passage of the council-manager charter. Other incumbents included Frank Shattuck, George Peters, and Henry Haler, in office for twelve, ten, and six years, respectively.

Reaching out to small businesses and homeowners, the OVL campaign centered on inequities in the city's tax structure that favored downtown property holders over those in the outlying areas.[53] In addition, the league's platform called for the immediate expenditure of $15 million in bonds already approved for streets, parks, playgrounds, and other city improvements; "immediate open hearings" on transportation needs; city planning for new industry and full employment; election of a board of freeholders to reform the city charter; planning for a "full program" of housing including support

for rent control and "low-cost, low-rent, no-discrimination municipal housing"; and, not least, "impartial statesmanship in business-labor relations."[54]

Tax issues and traffic management attracted the support of small merchants, many of whom had profited from wartime population growth and
the increase in consumer demand but now faced congested streets and shortages of parking and transit services. One of these was William Clausen, a
hardware store owner and president of the Elmhurst Merchants' Association.[55] Clausen was heir to a long line of small-business political mobilization in East Oakland, ranging from the independent progressive T. F. Marshall in the 1910 commission charter reform, to the aggressive middle-class
populism of Klansman William Parker, to the neighborhood particularism
of retail grocers James DePaoli and Walter Jacobsen, who had been elected
to the city council in the '30s. The contrasting politics of these figures highlights the volatility of this group and the importance of its specific alliances
within the conjunctural context. In the immediate postwar period, Clausen
and other "uptown" small businessmen felt equally excluded from the
Knowland regime and were prepared to join with their residential neighbors, customers, and the unions in a popular social-democratic coalition
against the downtown elite.

In the primaries, the OVL slate shocked the old guard, winning plurali-
ties in all five races and prompting a runoff with the incumbents, who each
placed second. Alarmed by the upset, the incumbents hired a San Francisco
public-relations firm, Eric Cullenward and Associates, which had recently
managed the successful reelection of J. R. Knowland's son, William, to the
U.S. Senate. Cullenward arranged to set up an Oakland "citizens' committee" to conduct a vigorous Red-baiting campaign, aided by the *Tribune:*
"Oakland Picked as Testing Ground in Effort to Secure Communistic Control," read one of the paper's lead editorials. The *Tribune* ran repeated articles attacking the personal backgrounds of the OVL candidates and their
"communist" and "left-wing" support, and printed a full-page Oakland Citizens' Committee advertisement charging communist conspiracy, with a car-
toon figure of a burglar, labeled "Oakland Commies," entering the home of
a sleeping Oakland resident. Elements of anti-Semitism also entered into
the campaign: A local magazine described one OVL fund-raiser as attended
by "new, strange characters prowling around with monikers that sounded
like a roster of Dave Dubinski's [sic] gang in New York's East Side," and another as a "high sounding group muster[ing] a round dozen men and
women, nearly all of whom could speak English, though mostly with a gut-
tural accent."[56]

For its part, the labor movement organized a tremendous effort to get out the vote. The Joint Labor Committee staged a mass rally on April 3, attracting ten thousand unionists to hear the OVL candidates at the Oakland Auditorium. The ILWU Local 6 alone raised $14,000, while the militant AFL Draftsmen's Local 89 and the United Negro Labor Committee canvassed voters in West Oakland, and striking CIO cannery workers took time off from their picket line for precinct work. On the eve of the runoff, the OVL held a mass torchlight parade of some five hundred cars through the streets of Oakland. A highlight of the parade was a float built by the United Negro Labor Committee, featuring the mock-burial of a casket tagged "The Machine," and a sign depicting black and white gloved fists smashing into the *Tribune* tower, over the slogan "Take the Power out of the Tower."[57]

The municipal campaign drew on the working-class solidarity aroused by the General Strike, while shifting mobilization into a different institutional arena. Unlike the demonstration of mass protest, the election called for a remaking of alliances in a multiclass, interracial, and joint union coalition against the urban regime. The outcome represented another pivotal juncture, and a test of the influence of insurgent class awareness in the public sphere. Confronted with the choice, Oakland citizens rejected the *Tribune*'s anticommunist rhetoric and rallied to the OVL cause. The runoff elections marked a peak of popular electoral participation, with a record turnout of 66 percent of registered voters, up from 45 percent in the primary and from only 28 percent in the 1945 city elections.

Yet the campaign fell short of achieving a major reconstitution of the political terrain. Within the labor movement, the Joint Labor Committee threatened the position of the Teamsters' Real and the Knowland-backed incumbents he supported. Hoping to deal a crippling blow to Ash and the other militant Central Labor Council leaders, Real used the Joint Labor Committee's collaboration with the CIO as a pretext for pulling the ten thousand members in all thirteen locals of the Teamsters' Joint Council out of the Central Labor Council. The council was rescued by the immediate affiliation of the Building Trades Council, with its twenty-five locals and sixteen thousand members. Nevertheless, it was forced to downplay its participation in the united labor front just as the campaign was gathering its full momentum.[58]

In the final tally, four of the five OVL candidates won election, by margins of at least 5 percent. The fifth candidate, Ben Goldfarb, lost by one percent, or just over a thousand votes. His defeat was attributed variously to anti-Semitism, prejudice against his "foreign-sounding name," and an irregularity in the order of his name on the ballot. Whatever the reasons, the OVL slate was left without a majority on the new city council. City Manager Hassler remained in office and was able to use his administrative authority to outmaneuver the inexperienced councillors. Although the OVL representatives succeeded in getting one of their own, Smith, named as mayor, they later fell to disagreements among themselves and failed to move much of their political agenda.[59]

The Institutional Limits of Reform

With the impasse on the city council, the popular electoral unity began to fall apart. Angered by persistently unequal property taxes, in late 1948 William Clausen launched a recall campaign against the entire city council, including the OVL members. Forming his own group called the East Oakland Tax Protest Association, Clausen's agitation began to split off small business and homeowners from the OVL coalition. By January 1949, Clausen had renamed his group the League for Better Government, and as the recall campaign faltered he shifted his focus to charter reform, which had been promised by the OVL councillors but was now opposed by three of them. Charter reform drew the interest of union leaders, themselves frustrated with the council's inaction and increasingly divided by local rivalries and by the growing tide of anticommunism. The CIO Industrial Council remained behind the OVL, but Central Labor Council secretary Ash, Building Trades head Jack Reynolds, and the United Auto Workers Local 76 all backed a petition for a freeholders' election to draft a new charter. The petition drive failed to reach the necessary minimum of twenty-six thousand valid signatures, and the city council declined to call a freeholders' election on its own, but the controversy further weakened the already fractured progressive coalition.[60]

The decisive blow, however, came on the issue of public housing. In 1946, the Oakland Housing Authority had estimated that at least twenty-three thousand new housing units were needed to accommodate families then living in temporary units or doubled up with others, and in the postwar years housing shortages would remain a pressing problem, as thousands of war veterans and southern black and white migrants continued to settle in the city. Facing discrimination in the private housing market, racial minority families in particular relied disproportionally on public housing: In July 1947, nonwhites accounted for better than 40 percent of all families in temporary and low-income public-housing units, and approximately 11 percent of all nonwhite families were living in some form of public housing.[61]

By the spring of 1949, the OVL coalition had already lost city council votes on rent control and on a civil rights ordinance to establish a local Fair Employment Practices Commission. In July 1949, Councillor Vernon Lantz passed away, leaving three remaining OVL representatives. At the end of July, City Planning Engineer John Marr submitted a report to the city council titled "Urban Redevelopment in Oakland" for adoption into the city's master plan. In it, Marr recommended that a 5.5-square-mile area surrounding downtown, including all of West Oakland north to Thirty-second Street and the "East of the Lake" district as far as Fourteenth Avenue, be declared blighted and slated for renewal. The report also called for the creation of a city redevelopment agency, and initiation of planning and site selection for private-enterprise redevelopment projects. Finally, the report urged city officials to apply to the federal Housing and Home Finance Agency for at least three thousand units of subsidized public housing.[62]

The Marr report presented an ambitious program for the social and spatial reconstruction of Oakland. Unlike later designs for urban renewal, the plan was seen as part of a New Deal tradition of social reform and was endorsed by leaders from the AFL Central Labor Council, the Building Trades Council, the CIO, and the NAACP. Moreover, the proposal embodied a broad, challenging, alternative vision for the development of the urban community. During the war, workers from various backgrounds had come together in the urban spaces of the shipyards and downtown, but they typically went home to spatially separate neighborhoods. A policy to build low-cost, racially integrated housing in the heart of Oakland, and thus anchor a diverse working-class population in the city center, held significant implications for both democratic social provision and the future path of working-class formation.

On the other side, leaders of the Apartment House Owners Association, the Associated Improvement Clubs, and the Associated Home Builders of Alameda County all spoke out strongly against the public-housing plan. With the support of the National Association of Real Estate Boards, several of these groups had come together in 1948 to form a branch of the statewide Committee for Home Protection, and they succeeded in passing a non-binding referendum against public housing. In a series of public hearings, these groups now brought intense pressure against the housing proposal. The Oakland Planning Commission and the city council quickly backed away from the sweeping land clearance plans of the Marr report, but in September the three OVL councillors led a five to four vote to authorize the construction of three thousand units of public housing on federally owned or vacant property.[63]

The council's decision to proceed with public housing touched off a new wave of polarization in Oakland politics and led directly to the downfall of the progressive coalition. Under the auspices of the Committee for Home

Protection, landlord and developer groups mobilized a recall campaign against OVL councillors Raymond Pease, Joseph Smith, and Scott Weakley. Aided once again by the Cullenward agency, opponents attacked public housing as "socialistic," organizing aggressively among middle-class white homeowners and black homeowners in West Oakland who feared the loss of their property. By early 1950, the campaign had gathered enough signatures to place the recall before the voters. The ballot asked first for a yes or no on the recall of each councillor, and then a vote for candidates to fill the vacated seat, if necessary (recalled councillors could run for their own seats). Taking advantage of their campaign momentum, the home protection committee recruited a slate of candidates to challenge the incumbents. Against Councillors Pease, Smith, and Weakley the committee endorsed, respectively, Howard Rilea Jr., a white West Oakland homeowner and president of the West Oakland Improvement Association; Myrtle Goodwin, an active member of the Apartment House Owners Association; and East Oakland merchant and Better Government League president William Clausen.[64]

The unions rallied in defense of the OVL councillors, but they now faced an antagonistic bloc of real-estate interests, homeowners, and Clausen's antitax, small-business support. After a campaign said to be "rocked with bitter accusations from both sides," 41 percent of Oakland voters turned out for a special election on February 28, 1950. Councillors Smith and Pease survived the recall, but in a result that City Clerk Charles Don said was the "closest in Oakland history," Councillor Weakley lost by only five votes out of more than seventy-five thousand cast. In a runoff held two weeks later, Clausen defeated Weakley by a margin of 5 percent. The following year, Smith and Pease lost to committee-endorsed candidates in the regular 1951 municipal elections, and the new city government quietly rescinded the program of public housing.[65]

By 1950, the period of labor-led challenge in local politics was over. From the start, the efforts to build a social-democratic counterregime were constrained by the institutional limits on the power of the city council. And as the '40s came to a close, the labor movement itself was increasingly divided and could no longer sustain an insurgent popular coalition. In the campaign against public housing, local real-estate, landlord, and construction groups mobilized substantial resources and appealed to small business and white and black homeowners against the progressive city councillors. Their success in the recall election reconfigured the dominant set of interests and alliances in the urban regime and prepared the way for a more conservative agenda for urban development in Oakland.

CONCLUSION:
CLASS CONFLICT AND COLLECTIVE ACTION

Between 1930 and 1950, political contention in Oakland revolved around a central axis of class conflict, following a path from the emergence and containment of labor militancy in the '30s to the polarization and regime challenge of the '40s. In the '30s, the economic dislocation of the Depression weakened conventional forms of labor discipline and allowed a resurgence of working-class collective action. Nevertheless, the Knowland regime sustained its hegemony through its organization of relations in both state and society: promoting unity among the business elites, consolidating institutional power in local government, and intervening in the labor movement itself through the alliance with machine unionism. By contrast, the rapid industrialization and urbanization during World War II upset this balance of power. The elites remained internally cohesive but were now politically distant from the new mass working population and its claims for membership in the urban community. With the growth of the unions during the war, previous regime alignments broke down, as seen particularly in the conflict between the downtown merchants and the newly militant AFL Central Labor Council.

The struggle at Kahn's and Hastings sparked a reactive sequence of polarization, concentrating public attention on the most powerful class actors in the Oakland polity. The AFL unions supported the clerks' strike as a first line of defense against what they believed was an open-shop drive that threatened their very existence. Likewise, the Retail Merchants Association was determined to resist the labor movement and maintain its control over the key retail industry in Oakland. Both sides were well organized and were committed to a struggle from which they could not back down. In the face of this conflict, the local political institutions clearly failed to integrate the groups contending within the community. Removed from electoral influence, the city government had long since lost touch with the populace, and in the police actions it had proved its subservience to the business elites. The AFL unions, themselves representing a specific social and economic base, were able to rally wide support for their protest. Tens of thousands of working people in Oakland—migrants, veterans, members of ethnic minorities, and survivors of economic Depression and war—all came forward to claim their membership in the urban community.

In the General Strike, the unions overcame the regime's use of force and successfully defended their movement against an elite counterattack—a substantial victory in comparison to the post–World War I period. For the clerks, however, the outcome was a different story: Their struggle began not as a defensive effort by an established actor, but as a drive for recognition by workers in a previously nonunion sector. The difference highlights the historical stakes for the path of working-class formation. The clerks' union represented a large category of female workers who had not yet been fully accepted into the local labor movement. On the one hand, their mobilization offered the unions the prospect of expanding their social base and strengthening class organization in the local working population; and on the other, it marked a test of the unions' commitment toward their new members and of their collective identity as a movement.

The limits of solidarity were tested again in the 1947 elections. The General Strike pushed class conflict to the center of public awareness, but the inconclusive settlement showed both the weakness of the AFL unions' traditional repertoire and the continuing closure of local political institutions to working-class concerns. In the municipal campaign, the Oakland labor movement again displayed a remarkable organizational unity, notwithstanding the obstructions of the national AFL hierarchy and Charles Real. Popular class consciousness remained strong, and the OVL coalition won a surprising show of support against the Red-scare tactics of the regime.

The shift to institutional politics, however, confronted union leaders with the difficult task of realizing an expanded vision of political community. Within a short time, anticommunist factional battles had badly split the labor movement itself, diminishing its capacity to forge a broad interracial and popular class unity. And on their own, the AFL unions were unlikely to lead a radical reconstruction of working-class identity. Despite the liberalism of the Central Labor Council, the unions that had played the largest part in the General Strike, including the Teamsters, the Transit Workers, the Machinists, and the Sailors, were themselves among the most racially exclusionary in the East Bay.[66] With the purge of the left, leadership in the East Bay labor movement turned more conspicuously to the forces of machine unionism, whose corruption could no longer be denied. In 1950, the Teamsters' Charles Real was charged with misconduct and finally ousted from office after an audit of Local 70's books revealed a shortage of more than a hundred thousand dollars. Similarly, the Building Trades' Jack Reynolds was indicted on federal bribery and conspiracy charges the following year.[67]

As industrial relations in the workplace came more and more to be governed by federal and state law, local police and authorities became less central to the regulation of labor disputes. The unions dug in for collective bargaining with employers in the sectors already organized, and their political orientation shifted to higher levels of government. Yet the consequences of the struggles of the previous decades continued to affect the trajectory of local working-class formation. Without a movement toward an urban-based, interracial working-class unity (or a public policy to reinforce the same), white workers turned to the model of white middle-class suburbanization established in the '20s. Relations between white working and lower middle classes reverted to a conservative alliance based on traditional channels of small business as an avenue of blue-collar social mobility, as typified in the trucking industry and in the building trades. Even there, however, the impact of AFL unionism remained evident in the East Bay. An extraordinary example was in the restaurant industry, where as late as 1970, an alliance of culinary workers' unions held contracts with nearly five hundred small, independent or locally owned restaurants and taverns in Alameda County, regulating the labor market through a union hiring hall.[68]

In the postwar prosperity of the '50s and '60s, European American ethnic workers followed in the paths of white middle-class formation through higher levels of income and consumption, small-business opportunity, and the growth of suburban home-ownership. This reconfiguration of the shape of civil society was premised on continuing forms of racial exclusion in labor markets, housing, and local politics. As one African American labor and civil rights activist remarked, in the old South, blacks could be cooks and waiters but couldn't eat in public restaurants, while in the Bay Area, "you could eat in the cafeteria but you couldn't work."[69] Such institutionalized patterns of racial discrimination soon came to dominate and redefine the urban political terrain. With the growing outward mobility of white working and middle classes, Oakland elites would attempt to reconstitute their regime in a new prodevelopment agenda aimed at maintaining the metropolitan centrality of downtown. That agenda would come increasingly into conflict with the rising black population concentrated in the city center and lead to a new period of social movement challenge in Oakland in the '60s.

6 Reconstituting the Urban Regime

Redevelopment and the Central City

In 1950, there was little indication that white Oaklanders in general were very concerned about the growing number of black residents living in the city. Although African Americans made up more than 12 percent of the total population, they were largely confined to West Oakland; black settlement remained almost nonexistent through most of central and east Oakland above East Fourteenth Street. Nor was there much in public affairs to remind whites of the presence of their fellow citizens. The defeat of the housing program temporarily halted planning for urban renewal, and local politics returned to its former quietude. As white residents turned to the individual pursuit of private prosperity, business boosters sought to present Oakland as an "all-American city." Well into the '60s, the *Oakland Tribune* made it an editorial policy never to use the words *slum* or *ghetto* to describe any neighborhoods in Oakland.[1]

But in the '50s and '60s, the growing inequality of racialized groups would become the central focus of conflict and once again transform the terrain of politics in Oakland. This chapter begins with the structural change in the city's racial composition, and in particular the growth of the African American population and its concentration in the city center. I then review the elites' efforts to reconstruct a developmental regime oriented toward regional expansion and maintaining the hegemony of downtown. The project of redevelopment would bring major alterations in local land-use patterns in transportation, economic infrastructure, and housing and provoke racial and class conflicts that appeared first in the early experiences of urban renewal in West Oakland.

The conflicts that emerged in the process of redevelopment eventually reverberated across the field of urban civil society. With the displacement of the black population and its expansion into formerly all-white areas, race relations became more volatile in neighborhoods throughout the Oakland flats. Faced with problems of "delinquency" and "racial transition," city officials created new administrative programs and layers of bureaucracy in order to manage social problems and reassert public authority. These "reforms from above" later served as a model for, and shaped local implementation of, the urban social programs of the Great Society.

By the '60s, black residents found themselves the targets of regime interventions aimed at both urban restructuring and social control. In response, black movement activists began to organize within the venue of the new urban bureaucratic agencies. More than the restricted channels of the formally democratic city government, these agencies were to become a key site for the negotiation of emerging group conflicts. Before long, however, the limits of this form of bureaucratic political incorporation would become apparent, and African Americans would explore other means to achieve black power.

POPULATION CHANGE AND RACIAL CONCENTRATION

Before World War II, African Americans had accounted for less than 3 percent of Oakland's population. During and after the war, however, the black population grew rapidly, as many wartime migrants settled permanently and others moved into the city. By 1960, more than 22 percent of Oakland residents were African American.[2] With increasing size came greater spatial concentration, as white reaction to black inmigration produced a "Chicago effect" of intensified racial segregation in housing. In 1940, 60 percent of the black population had lived in census tracts located in West Oakland; in 1950, despite more than a fivefold increase in size, 80 percent lived in the same area. As white families fled the old neighborhood, West Oakland rapidly converted into a virtually all-black ghetto. In 1938, West Oakland's McClymonds High School enrolled 648 white and 115 black students. Ten years later, 797 black students attended, but only 50 whites remained.[3]

Racial segregation was reinforced by a discriminatory pattern of police violence, which effectively constituted a form of official social control in the ghetto. In 1950, spurred by protests from the Communist Party-affiliated East Bay Civil Rights Congress, the California State Assembly's Interim Committee on Crime and Corrections held investigative hearings on racial discrimination by the Oakland police department. The committee heard charges of racial harassment and beatings of black citizens, including the fa-

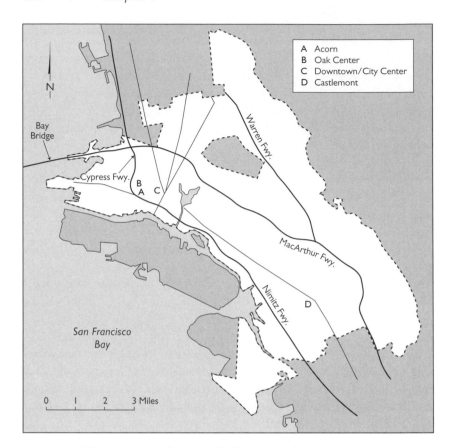

Map 3. Oakland, 1960s: highways and urban renewal.

tal shooting of an unarmed black man by an Oakland policeman in 1949. C. L. Dellums, chair of the Alameda County NAACP, told the committee that the police department ignored black citizens' complaints, and concluded, "Generally Negroes regard the police as their natural enemies." The Rev. Harold Geistweit echoed this view, noting that blacks "feel they can get no justice from the police."[4]

Meanwhile, the area that black migrants inherited in West Oakland was itself becoming spatially more separate from the rest of the city. The opening of the Bay Bridge in 1936 had spelled the abrupt end of the auto ferries from the foot of Seventh Street, and a few years later the Southern Pacific removed its local train service from the same route. Although the military bases continued to be important to the local economy, mechanization at the port and the decline of rail travel reduced traffic on the adjacent streets and employment opportunities at the neighborhood's traditional economic anchors. Finally, the completion of the elevated Cypress Freeway in 1958 cut a huge concrete swath through the middle of the entire neighborhood, displacing hundreds of residents and isolating its westernmost section (see map 3).[5]

Nevertheless, wartime and postwar black migrants adapted to their surroundings and brought a new commitment and vitality to their urban environment. As William Brown Jr. observes, "From a depression-impoverished community of less than 9,000, headed by a tiny professional elite . . . [the black population] had suddenly expanded within ten years to nearly forty eight thousand, most of whom had managed to secure and retain employment at a wide range of incomes."[6] Despite disproportionally high jobless rates after the war, black workers gradually regained their position in the industrial labor market, particularly in manufacturing. By 1960, the blue-collar sector—craftsmen and foremen, operatives and laborers—employed proportionally more African American men than any other sector.[7] The arrival of a mass black working class revived and transformed the institutions of the preexisting black community. Taylor Memorial Methodist Church in West Oakland grew from 150 members in 1940 to more than a thousand in 1954, while Seventh Street emerged as a black commercial and popular cultural district, with small businesses, restaurants, clubs, and entertainment venues that attracted nationally known performers.[8]

At the same time, economic and population growth contributed to the rise of a new black middle class, symbolized by the 1954 founding of the Men of Tomorrow, a civic service club of black business, professional, and religious leaders. Among the founders of the Men of Tomorrow were Kenneth Smith of the Bay Area Urban League and George Vaughns, a leading attorney and president of the Trans-Bay Federal Savings and Loan Association, a black financial institution. By 1961, several prominent Oakland black citizens had served as chair of the club, including attorney Clinton White of the NAACP—Oakland Branch, Evelio Grillo of the East Bay Democratic Club, and educator Dr. Norvel Smith.[9] A network of black law firms also gave a start to a younger generation of black political figures, including Tom Berkley, publisher of the *Oakland Post*, NAACP activist Donald McCullum, and attorney and later judge Lionel Wilson. In the '60s, all of them were to play a role in the political mobilization of the black community and in efforts to contest its exclusion from the urban regime.

REDESIGNING THE URBAN AGENDA:
THE METROPOLITAN CITY

As the period of working-class challenge in the '40s passed, elites in Oakland resumed their leadership under new conditions. Not least important was the expansion of *Oakland Tribune* publisher Joseph R. Knowland's political horizons and power. In 1945, California's senior U.S. senator, Hiram Johnson, passed away near the end of his fifth term in office. To fill Johnson's seat, Governor Earl Warren appointed Knowland's son, William, who was then stationed in Europe on military service. Senator Knowland won reelection as an incumbent in 1946, and in 1953 he was chosen as Senate majority leader for the Republican Party. The elder Knowland and his *Tribune* increasingly turned their attention from local to national and world politics, as J. R. Knowland entertained notions of making his son the president of the United States.[10]

Oakland business leaders also widened their horizons as the Bay Area economy boomed in the postwar decades. Before the war, the Chamber of Commerce had established the Metropolitan Oakland Area Program to encourage industrial development in newer areas in southern Alameda County. But manufacturing interests were never a primary actor in the Knowland regime; many large local factories were branch plants of national corporations based elsewhere, and even the globally diversified Kaiser Industries group kept mainly administrative headquarters in Oakland. As economic growth spread to the suburban periphery, downtown commercial elites again took the lead, attempting to maintain the city's centrality in the East Bay through the organization of a new prodevelopment political regime.

Much of their effort lay in the introduction of regional planning, particularly in transportation. Hoping to resist the dominance of San Francisco, Oakland elites wanted regional transportation to include central destinations in downtown Oakland. In 1950, downtown businessmen Edgar Buttner (an electrical contractor) and R. W. Breuner (a furniture merchant) helped found the Oakland Central Business District Association to promote transit, highway construction, and parking facilities for the city center. That same year, State Senator Arthur Breed Jr. of Alameda, a close ally of the Knowlands, sponsored a bill in the state legislature creating the Bay Area Rapid Transit Commission to develop plans for a regional rapid rail transit system. Buttner and Breuner were named to the commission, along with Sherwood Swan, a department store owner and former Oakland city planning commissioner. Swan and Breed also played a major role in the creation of the Alameda–Contra Costa Transit District, which reorganized local surface (bus) transit in the East Bay, replacing the old Key System. In 1956, Breed authored the enabling legislation that established the Bay Area Rapid Transit District (BARTD), encompassing Alameda, Contra Costa, and San Francisco counties; and Swan later served on the new BARTD board of directors.[11]

In 1954, executives from Kaiser Industries, Bank of America, Wells Fargo, Sears Roebuck, the East Bay Homebuilders Association, and the Oakland Real Estate Board came together to form the Oakland Citizens' Committee for Urban Renewal (OCCUR). OCCUR promoted the creation in 1956 of an official Oakland Redevelopment Agency and was designated as the agency's official citizens' participation body. Within a few years, the Redevelopment Agency began its first major slum-clearance campaign with the Acorn Project in West Oakland. By the mid '60s, policies of wholesale demolition would wreak havoc on black neighborhoods around the city center. Altogether, between 1960 and 1966 more than 7,000 housing units in Oakland were destroyed by urban renewal, freeway and BART construction, and other governmental action, and in West Oakland alone almost 5,100 units were removed, resulting in a net outmigration from the neighborhood of about 14,000 residents.[12]

Meanwhile, the port of Oakland embarked on an era of technological modernization with the opening of its first mechanized container ship terminal in 1962. That same year, voters in Oakland and in Alameda County approved their share of $792 million in BARTD bonds to build the rapid transit system. In June 1965, the port and BARTD made an arrangement to grant the latter an easement to route a subway tube along Seventh Street through the former Southern Pacific ferry mole. In return, the BARTD agreed to dike 140 acres of adjoining shallow water and fill the enclosure with rock, sand, and gravel from its subway excavations through downtown Oakland. On this giant landfill peninsula at the foot of Seventh Street, the port planned to build a $35 million container terminal, expanding its capacity by as much as 80 percent. Groundbreaking for the project began in September 1965, and by 1968 the first part of the Seventh Street Terminal was opened to container shipping.[13]

Finally, led by Edgar Kaiser (son of Henry Kaiser) and Steven Bechtel, the Chamber of Commerce produced in 1960 a planning study for a new major-league stadium and sports arena. The following year, the Chamber sponsored the formation of a nonprofit corporation, the Oakland–Alameda County Coliseum, Inc., with Chamber president Robert Nahas as president and Edgar Kaiser, William Knowland, and construction firm owner George Loorz as board members. The coliseum corporation negotiated an elaborate lease-purchase agreement with local authorities, in which the corporation would finance construction and operation of the facility in return for annual payments from the city and county, allowing project sponsors to avoid seeking voter approval for a public bond issue. The $25 million stadium and sports arena were built on a 105-acre site near the Eastshore (Nimitz) Freeway, on land donated to the city by the port after the latter had arranged a swap of parcels near the area with the East Bay Municipal Utilities District. Ground was broken in May 1964, and the new Oakland–Alameda County Coliseum opened on September 18, 1966, a year ahead of its scheduled completion date.[14]

These ambitious redevelopment activities took shape through the organization of new, politically insulated, elite-dominated bureaucracies, continuing a pattern that dated back to the creation of the Board of Port Commissioners in the '20s. The proliferation of such bodies, however, gradually exceeded the informal, personal relations of elite political and institutional coordination under the former managerial regime. In 1958, as a stepping-stone for his anticipated future presidential candidacy, William Knowland made a disastrous decision to run for governor of California. His candidacy forced the popular Republican incumbent governor, Goodwin Knight Jr., to give up his office and run instead for Knowland's senate seat—a tactic that alienated voters and split the state Republican Party. Knowland further provoked strong labor opposition by linking his campaign to an anti-union statewide right-to-work proposition. In November, Knowland, Knight, the proposition, and much of the Republican slate were all defeated, and Knowland's political career was finished. He returned to Oakland to join his father at the *Tribune*, where they remained a powerful force in local politics, but neither again exercised the kind of personal preeminence that had once united the urban regime.[15]

Despite their increasing fragmentation, the new developmental bureaucracies preserved the regime's traditional separation of major economic functions from the formal democratic arena of the city council. In 1951, voters approved a charter amendment to allow direct election of the mayor, though it continued to be a part-time, low-salary job, like the councillor positions. Council stability was reinforced by the long-standing practice of midterm appointment of successors: Between 1953 and 1969, nine councillors and one mayor were originally appointed, all of whom won their ensuing elections, while overall, 85 percent of incumbent candidates in council elections were returned to office.[16] Unlike the developmental agencies, the city council remained a bastion of low-tax, minimal-government conservatism. Nominated from districts but elected at-large, councillors regarded the city's property taxpayers as their principal constituency, whose priorities superseded even their own districts' service needs. In order to reduce political opposition, elected city officials normally avoided new expenditures and actively sought to limit or disperse public awareness of and interest in city business.[17]

Behind the city council's fiscal conservatism lay a white middle-class voting electorate, much of which resided in neighborhoods that spanned the foothills of central East Oakland. This area was known locally as the "Bible Belt" for its high concentration of Protestant churches, a legacy of the Protestant middle-class formation of the '20s. Observers described it as politically conservative, with an older, settled population, "composed mostly of small business owners, teachers, Boy Scout leaders, [and] PTA members" oriented toward private or neighborhood concerns of home, family, church, and school. Above the foothills lived more affluent whites, whose distinct social and political status was underlined by the 1961 opening of the Skyline High School. Previously, attendance areas for Oakland's high schools had been drawn in broadly parallel strips reaching from the flatlands to hills. Skyline's boundaries stretched for ten miles across the entire hills area, thereby creating an exclusive wealthy white high school separate from the flatlands schools below.[18]

Within their respective institutional arenas, both the conservative and the growth-oriented factions coexisted in the urban regime. The social and spatial practices of these groups, however, soon led them down conflicting paths. The downtown elite's agenda called for major land-use restructuring in order to reclaim the city center, now surrounded by a growing concentration of African Americans. As redevelopment began to get under way, the regime's political unity would start to break down in the conflict of class and racial interests emerging from the implementation of urban renewal.

THE POLITICS OF RACE AND CLASS:
URBAN RENEWAL

The Acorn Project and Public Housing

In 1959, the city council unanimously approved a General Neighborhood Renewal Plan (GNRP) calling for extensive urban renewal of a 250-block area of West Oakland. The plan designated five redevelopment areas, the first of which was the Acorn Project, a mixed residential and industrial use plan for one of the poorest parts of the city. The Acorn site covered about fifty blocks flanking the Nimitz Freeway between Union and Brush Streets, from Tenth Street south to the Southern Pacific railroad tracks. This included a part of Seventh Street, once considered the commercial heart of black West

Oakland, yet described in the GNRP as "largely marginal in operation, suffering generally from a movement of 'buying power' out of the area." The existing population of Acorn was 78 percent black, 20 percent Mexican American, and 2 percent white or other. Nearly half of the households were dependent on some form of welfare, pension, or social security.[19]

The Redevelopment Agency estimated that at least five hundred low-income families displaced from Acorn (and from construction of a huge new post office facility adjacent to the project) would be unable to afford private replacement housing in the city. The statewide passage of Proposition 10 in 1950 now required a local voter referendum to permit construction of public housing, but Oakland still had unused federal credits for 506 units that were authorized before the law went into effect. On October 1, 1959, the Oakland Housing Authority (OHA) requested approval from the city council for construction of the new units. Among those in favor of the proposal were Rev. H. Solomon Hill of the NAACP and Grillo of the Men of Tomorrow; support also came from Lamar Childers of the Alameda Building Trades Council, as well as the Oakland Council of Churches and the League of Women Voters. Opposed were John Hennessey of the Associated Home Builders of the East Bay, a leader of the 1950 recall campaign, and representatives of the Apartment House Owners Association and the Oakland Real Estate Board. Unable to agree on the proposal, the city council authorized a committee, led by Kaiser executive (and OCCUR chair) Norris Nash, to study the need for public housing. On November 4, this committee reported that no additional public-housing units were needed for the Acorn project.[20]

In response, Redevelopment Agency board member Reverend E. W. J. Schmitt charged that the study was a "power play." "As I see it," he said, "it revolves around the desire of a particular part of the community to oppose public housing at any cost. The real estate lobby has got control of the citizens' committee on this point." The committee report claimed that normal vacancies in existing OHA facilities would be sufficient to house families displaced by renewal, but OHA commission chair John Kronenberg stated that this would preclude accommodating low-income families from other parts of the city. Committee member Childers stressed that the report did not address overall or future needs for public housing, and he urged the council to determine the total community need for low- and middle-income housing. The council then asked Councillor Howard Rilea Jr., a seventy-six-year-old white West Oaklander active in the 1950 recall election, to appoint a committee to survey citywide needs.[21]

Rilea named a committee chaired by Hennessey of the Associated Home

Builders.[22] Notably absent from the committee were any representatives from the NAACP, which protested to federal officials to delay approval of the Redevelopment Agency's relocation plan. Reverend Hill of the NAACP said that the plan did not have enough safeguards to ensure rehousing for displaced minority families, and he doubted that the plan's estimates of private rental vacancies open to blacks were accurate. At this time, Oakland had 1,515 temporary housing units in emergency projects built for defense workers during World War II. These units were mostly substandard, in poor condition, and slated for demolition. In an effort to minimize new construction, the Hennessey committee proposed to renovate 450 of these temporary units for relocation use, and to build 100 new three- and four-bedroom units for large families.[23]

City Councillor (and former City Planning Commission chair) John Houlihan seized on this proposal, arguing that it showed that a total of 550 units were needed after all. At a meeting on January 20, 1960, the city council voted to grant the OHA's original request for 506 new units, but not before a tense confrontation between Reverend Hill and Councillor Robert Osborne over what the *Tribune* described as the latter's "racial tirade." Criticizing the NAACP for its role in the public debate, Osborne said, "I believe there is a direct affinity between public housing and public welfare," and he suggested that unwed minority-group mothers were a disproportionate burden on the county budget. Reverend Hill replied, "Erase 150 years of slavery. Erase 80 years of low wages, segregation, and having doors slammed in our faces. Then you might find some moral reason for condemning instead of helping. But don't continue to push these people into a vicious circle and then blame them for being there."[24] After Hill's comments, Osborne got up and walked out of the meeting.

The debate over public housing for Acorn gave an early indication of the emerging conflict of racial and class interests in the urban regime. The business elites in OCCUR and the ORA wanted urban renewal, regardless of whether this required public housing, while the building trades supported both in the hope of generating new jobs. The NAACP endorsed urban renewal, but wanted public housing because it did not believe low-income black families faced equal opportunity in the private housing market. For many whites, however, public housing was already identified with a racialized image of the black poor, as Councillor Osborne's remarks suggest. Nonetheless, black leaders took advantage of the opportunity to ally with the business elites and the building trades unions to win a partial victory over those interests—white homeowners, small property taxpayers, and real-estate and homebuilding firms—that had defeated public housing in 1950.

This was an important turning point, yet the victory was only partial: The 506 new units were offset by the elimination of 1,382 temporary units, so that by 1966 Oakland still had only 1,422 permanent public-housing units. By that time, the City Planning Commission estimated that more than 20,000 households in Oakland were eligible for public housing.[25]

The settlement of the public-housing issue left many questions unanswered, and in particular the problems of relocation and racial integration in the city's private housing market. On October 12, 1961, the Redevelopment Agency held its first hearing with the residents of the Acorn Project area. More than five hundred people attended and heard the agency's acting executive director, Arthur Hoff, explain that Acorn was to be a total clearance project, with the old housing replaced by moderate-cost units likely to be too expensive for the current residents. According to the *Tribune*, the residents "made it known emphatically that they [did] not want to be moved from their homes." Nevertheless, "after listening to thirty speakers for about three hours, the Agency voted unanimously to [approve] the program." The agency agreed to three demands from the NAACP's Clinton White: first, to urge appointment of a committee to assure housing for minorities; second, to develop residential sites suitable for current residents; and third, to set a time schedule for allowing residents to find decent housing. Reverend Robert Hill of Taylor Memorial Methodist Church articulated the key problem: "If you're [the Redevelopment Agency] not able to relocate these people at a price they can afford to pay, how can you assume they will be housed in other areas when there is a resistance on the part of the community against Negroes moving into certain areas?"[26]

On November 21, 1961, a crowd of 250 people jammed the city council chambers as the council voted seven to one to give final authorization for the Acorn Project (Councillor Rilea cast the only no vote). Attorney Donald McCullum of the NAACP said his group offered "qualified approval" of the project but would oppose Acorn "unless this city will provide leadership to create a climate of opportunity for open housing without regard to race, creed or color."[27] Demolition of all residential properties in Acorn began in earnest in late summer of 1962. In May of that year, however, two lone protesters appeared in front of the Acorn site office on Seventh Street, calling for Acorn homes to be rehabilitated, not razed.[28] Wade Johnson, a sixty-eight-year-old retired Pullman porter and property owner in the Acorn area, and David Lawrence, a fifty-eight-year-old homeowner and small landlord in the neighborhood, passed out leaflets saying, "Be proud of West Oakland. Retain your ownership in this property. Let us unite our forces and fight to save our property." Johnson was president of an organization he had founded called the United Taxpayers and Voters Union, and in June he and thirteen other residents filed suit in federal court to halt the redevelopment, complaining that there was no plan to provide residents with at least equal housing "on a racially integrated basis." The suit was later dismissed, after the court ruled that the Redevelopment Agency was providing housing in physically better condition than that previously occupied by most Acorn residents. The court did not address the issue of de facto racial segregation in relocation housing.[29]

In the controversy over Acorn, black middle-class leaders showed their willingness to confront the regime on behalf of the black community. Committed to an integrationist agenda, this leadership supported renewal as a way to overcome ghettoization and help meet the needs of the black poor. By mobilizing first for public and then for open housing, their actions gained a foothold in the urban renewal process and partially overcame the resistance of the city council. These victories, however, raised further questions about the fate of the black community in West Oakland and about racial integration in the city as a whole. By and large, the black middle-class leadership did not live in Acorn, and many black residents who did live there did not want to move. The quixotic protests of Johnson and the United Taxpayers and Voters Union foreshadowed a very different form of mobilization in the next West Oakland renewal project, Oak Center.

Oak Center and the Defense of Neighborhood

The second renewal project planned for West Oakland, Oak Center, was a fifty-block residential area immediately north of Acorn, extending roughly from Tenth Street to Eighteenth Street between Cypress and Brush Streets. This neighborhood was somewhat better off than Acorn had been, with a higher percentage of homeowners occupying many substantial old Victorian houses. The Redevelopment Agency had promised to preserve as many of these homes as possible, with an estimated 20 percent of properties eligible for rehabilitation rather than clearance.

With the progress of Acorn, however, city leaders began to take a more aggressive stance on urban renewal. Especially critical of Oak Center conservation plans was former city councillor Houlihan, now the mayor, who objected that rehabilitation would only result in "re-housing" current residents within the same area.[30] The mayor's sentiments were echoed by Redevelopment Agency executive director Thomas Bell, who took office in April 1962. Bell wanted to eliminate the "band of depressed area" around the central business district, as a priority over neighborhood renewal. Supported by OCCUR, Bell favored action on the Corridor project, located in a twenty-eight-block area lying directly between the downtown business district and the Acorn and Oak Center projects in West Oakland. Unlike the earlier two projects, the Corridor was slated for total clearance and redevelopment with semiluxury apartment buildings. On May 17, 1962, the Redevelopment Agency voted to scrap plans for the remaining three West Oakland areas scheduled to follow after Acorn and Oak Center, eliminating 150 acres of the original GNRP, in order to shift focus to the downtown Corridor.[31]

In the meantime, Bell speeded up demolition of entire blocks of buildings in Acorn.[32] The massive destruction occurring only a short distance from their own houses frightened many Oak Center homeowners, and in June 1963 a group of them formed the Oak Center Neighborhood Association (OCNA). The first chair of the OCNA was Lillian Love, a black homeowner whose father had fought unsuccessfully in 1938 against displacement for the construction of the Peralta Villa public housing project. Love and the OCNA mobilized quickly to prevent the clearance of Oak Center, and their first mass meeting on July 1 at McClymonds High School drew more than three hundred people.[33]

In March 1964, the OCNA sent a letter to Redevelopment Agency chair Kenneth Smith charging that director Bell had misled residents and was deliberately delaying progress so as to implement a total clearance plan for Oak Center. In response, Bell blamed "too strict" federal rules for rehabilitation that he said could force demolition of most of the buildings in Oak Center. Bell's remarks brought an angry reply from Robert McCabe, regional director of the federal Urban Renewal Administration. McCabe accused Bell of "subterfuge" in telling residents that Oak Center houses could be saved while adopting rehabilitation standards that would make that impossible, and then blaming the federal government. With potential funding for future downtown renewal projects at stake, McCabe, Mayor Houlihan, and members of OCCUR held a series of unannounced emergency meetings, after which Bell and his assistant director, Hoff, abruptly resigned.[34]

Bell's resignation was a stunning victory for Love and the OCNA. Almost immediately, federal officials relaxed standards of rehabilitation for Oak Center homeowners to make them technically and economically more feasible. On September 1, 1964, John B. Williams, a black former redevelopment official from Cleveland, Ohio, took over as executive director of the Redevelopment Agency. The following February, Williams announced a policy that would allow nearly three-fourths of Oak Center residential structures to be rehabilitated rather than razed. Williams said the agency would work with an advisory committee of OCNA members to survey the condition of dwellings in Oak Center, and named Wade Johnson, George Vaughns, Charles Goady, and Reverend R. A. G. Foster to the group, along with chairperson Love. Finally, in October 1966, Mayor John Reading appointed Lillian Love to the board of the Oakland Redevelopment Agency.[35]

The mobilization in defense of Oak Center formed a clear contrast to the experience in Acorn. The Oak Center Neighborhood Association was an indigenous organization of established homeowners and longtime residents in West Oakland. No similar indigenous organization developed among the poorer and more transient Acorn residents; black community mobilization in that case was led by middle-class professionals oriented beyond the renewal area. The OCNA leaders were not outside professionals, but neither were they the black poor, and they personally distinguished themselves sharply from the lower-income tenants in the neighborhood. Having witnessed the destruction of Acorn, they demanded not better housing elsewhere but economic stability and protection for the homes they already owned. Through their organization and sophisticated use of strategic allies in the federal government, they compelled the regime to incorporate their interests as middle-class property owners in a majority black neighborhood. As such, they negotiated their own political alliances with the Redevelopment Agency under Williams and with the mayor in city hall.

The Oak Center protest highlighted several features in the emerging formation of the black community as a collective actor. The emphasis on the defense of neighborhood and the role of indigenous organization within majority black areas prefigured future political mobilization in West Oakland, as in the War on Poverty and Model Cities programs. Similarly, the use of federal government policy and allies was to become an familiar part of the movement's tactical repertoire. Finally, leaders and organizations within the ghetto would increasingly claim their independent right to speak for themselves and for the black community.

At the same time, the loss of housing in West Oakland and the demands for an end to racial segregation pointed to the spread of the black population to other parts of the city. The prospect of integration, or what often became simply "racial transition," forced white Oaklanders to confront the issue of "race relations" in civil society. But the city's formal democratic institutions offered only weak and exclusionary channels for mediating conflicts between groups, while urban policy-making was effectively concentrated in bureaucratic arenas like the city manager's office and the autonomous agencies. Within the regime, then, the initial response to racial social change came not through a process of electoral incorporation or political bargaining, but from public administrative authorities responsible for social control.

REFORM FROM ABOVE:
RACIAL TRANSITION AND SOCIAL ORDER

As the black population continued to grow, it could no longer be contained within the old West Oakland ghetto, and began to move into the flatland areas of North and East Oakland. With this spatial expansion, city officials became concerned with problems of racial group conflict, especially among youth and in the public schools. In 1957, the chief of police reported that his department was sending fifteen police cars every day to North Oakland's Technical High School, as racial disturbances between black and white teenagers spilled over across the neighborhood.[36] That year, City Manager Wayne Thompson organized the Associated Agencies, a program to coordinate the efforts of welfare, school, and law-enforcement agencies in the control of juvenile delinquency. At Thompson's urging, administrators from the public schools, the county probation department, the city police and recreation departments, and the state youth authority met regularly to share information and coordinate policy, and joint committees of frontline service professionals were formed to handle specific cases in the neighborhoods. Although the Associated Agencies remained a voluntary program with no formal jurisdiction over its member agencies, the combination of executive cooperation and neighborhood-based deployment aimed at strengthening the local government's capacity to maintain its authority amid a changing city population.[37]

Thompson and the agency executives developed their program without the involvement or support of the city council, which was generally uninterested in neighborhood social programs and unwilling to spend city money on them.[38] By the early '60s, however, the Associated Agencies had attracted the attention of national civic and policy experts, including the staff of the Ford Foundation, who were looking to support innovative efforts by public and private organizations to address urban social problems. After preliminary contacts with foundation officials, Thompson persuaded local business elites to form a citizens' committee, composed of influential figures in white economic and civic circles along with black middle-class leaders, to sponsor a grant application to Ford.[39] With this groundwork, Oakland became the first city to receive funding under Ford's new Gray Areas program.

In December 1961, one month after the city council voted final approval of the Acorn project, the Ford Foundation announced a $2 million grant for the Oakland Interagency Project (OIP), a program designed to coordinate social services in the Castlemont district of East Oakland, in order to keep it from becoming a "negro ghetto."[40] The proposal to Ford attributed the problems of "transitional areas" like Castlemont to the departure of long-time white middle-class residents and their replacement by lower-income blacks, resulting in "social disorganization" among new residents unfamiliar with the neighborhood or with one another. The OIP programs focused on the education and socialization of unassimilated "newcomers"—a euphemism for postwar black migrants from the rural South—in order to integrate them into the life of the community.[41] In its first year, the Ford Foundation funded eight projects sponsored by established public and private agencies and provided $750,000 for a development fund to generate new program initiatives.[42]

Evelio Grillo, coordinator of the Associated Agencies and author of the grant proposal to Ford, was named OIP project director. Like the Associated Agencies, the OIP depended on the voluntary cooperation of its members; responsibility for planning and implementing projects remained with the autonomous agency heads composing its executive committee.[43] Moreover, the city council refused to raise taxes or authorize any new city funds for the OIP, or to establish it as a permanent city department or agency, leaving the project as a special program under the aegis of the city manager's office.[44]

The Ford grant called for a citizens' advisory committee, appointed by the city manager with the concurrence of the executive committee, to oversee program expenditures and progress. Hoping to lend prestige to the project, City Manager Thompson appointed a blue-ribbon group of members to this committee, including Philip Ennis of the Retail Merchants Association, businessman Edgar Buttner, shipping executive Peter Howard, and Municipal Court judge Lionel Wilson, among others.[45] As with the initial citizens' committee, however, no representatives from local unions or from the Castlemont neighborhood were included on the advisory committee, which in any case exercised little oversight over the agency heads on the executive committee. Thompson and others were later surprised to learn that when Castlemont residents first received news of the program, they reacted strongly against the entire project, protesting that their neighborhood was not a slum and demanding that the city return the money to Ford.[46]

In fact, subsequent research cast doubt on many of the project's assumptions. Studies by the County Health Department and by the University of California's Survey Research Center showed that "newcomers" were a minority of Castlemont residents, and that most of them had moved there from a previous address within the city or county. Blacks composed no more than half of those moving into the area, and of those moving from elsewhere in the county, they had higher median incomes than whites. Black households in Castlemont were also found to have a larger percentage of male heads, and more black adult women were married and living with their spouses than their white counterparts. In short, black Castlemont residents did not fit the image of poor, rural, or disoriented migrants from the South, but more strongly suggested a population of striving, intact working-class families moving up and out of West Oakland.[47]

The problems of Castlemont derived less from individuals' social disorganization than from mobile groups challenging racial and class boundaries in a changing neighborhood. And if the failure to "assimilate" was not the underlying problem, neither was administrative coordination the simple answer. Tests of project effectiveness found that while several of the programs had increased communication and cooperation among agency personnel, most had only weak or indiscernible impacts on the residents' experiences in the areas of public health and school-age education.[48] As one critic observed, the program "assumed the existence of a homogeneous moral and political community and contrived to 'help' the newcomer to fit in."[49] Agency authorities took the role of representatives of the public interest and treated residents as "clients" rather than as citizens or participants in their own right. Yet the residents of Castlemont did not appear to be moved by the regime's efforts to integrate them under the model of bureaucratic social control.

The Associated Agencies and the OIP emerged from an alliance of white and black professional, governmental, and private bureaucratic elites, brought together by problems of racial transition and the local government's desire to control conflict within its territory. Project planning and management were carried on in isolation from both the elected city councillors, who were ideologically opposed to the programs, and the area residents, the actual targets of social intervention. Project director Grillo operated within the framework of existing agency autonomy, relying on his own personal relations of trust to manage consensus among the department heads.

This approach, however, produced little stimulus for change, and in a March 1963 project review, Ford officials expressed dismay at the lack of new program development. Subsequently, Grillo resigned and was replaced in September 1963 by Dr. Norvel Smith. Where Grillo had been reluctant to go beyond established agency prerogatives, Smith aggressively sought funding for new programs to use as leverage to encourage change in institutional practices. Under Smith, the OIP accelerated the process of new program development and broadened participation in project design to involve "leading citizens and selected consultants," though this group did not yet include the affected target populations.[50]

On January 8, 1964, President Lyndon B. Johnson declared war on poverty. Drawing on its experience in the Gray Areas projects, the Ford Foundation played a major role in the design of the new federal antipoverty legislation. With the example of the OIP already in place, Oakland leaders were able to get a fast start on obtaining funds from the federal poverty program. Nevertheless, the contradictory local politics of race and class would continue to dominate the attempts to build the Great Society under the urban regime.

POLITICAL OPPORTUNITIES AND COLLECTIVE ACTORS: THE WAR ON POVERTY

Constituting Community Action: The Oakland Economic Development Council

In 1964, Oakland was one of only a few cities in the nation to be designated as a depressed area under the federal Area Redevelopment Act.[51] Its unemployment rate of 8 percent in 1960 was roughly twice the national average, though in the older industrial flatlands the official jobless rate ran closer to 14 percent. In these low-income areas lived some 150,000 people, including more than three-quarters of the city's black population and more than half the Spanish-surnamed population. These flatland neighborhoods—more than half of whose residents were defined as poor—became the focus for the new poverty program and were divided into target areas in North Oakland, West Oakland, Fruitvale, and East Oakland.[52]

In April 1964, Dr. Smith and the OIP executive committee began planning for a comprehensive antipoverty program for Oakland. Project staff and committee members met with public and private agencies, academic consultants, and leaders of minority group organizations, and in May, Mayor Houlihan appointed members of these groups along with business, labor, and civic organization leaders to an Anti-Poverty Planning Advisory Committee.[53] By the time Congress passed the Economic Opportunity Act in October, Oakland was prepared to submit its proposal to the federal Office of Economic Opportunity (OEO), with projects for education, job training and placement, and related support services.

The OIP was quickly merged into the city's federally mandated Community Action Program and was transformed into the new Department of Human Relations (DHR), with Dr. Smith as director, although still under the authority of the city manager. The citizens' advisory committee was enlarged to become the Oakland Economic Development Council (OEDC), but its relations with the agency executives were now reversed. The advisory committee under the OIP had served mainly to legitimize the project and ratify policies adopted by the agency heads in the executive committee. Now the OEDC was the policy-making body, as the city's official Community Action Agency under the OEO. Exactly which members of the community were empowered to shape such policy, however, would become one of the deepest issues of conflict in the poverty program.

In December 1964, Mayor Houlihan appointed twenty-five members to the new OEDC, including six representatives of business, two from labor unions, six minority group leaders, four religious leaders, two private agency representatives, two school board members, and two political figures, with himself as chair. Nine of the twenty-five appointees were African American, two were Mexican American, and one was a woman.[54] This council held its first meeting on December 23, 1964, and approved an application to the OEO for approximately $800,000, leaving review of specific programs for a later date. Part of the application called for the creation of neighborhood-based multiservice centers to provide legal, health, family counseling, and consumer education services. The OEDC also accepted a proposal to create Target Area Advisory Committees (TAACs), staffed by DHR field service coordinators in the multiservice centers, to provide "grassroots liaison" between neighborhood residents and the poverty program.[55]

The speed with which the OIP was transformed into the OEDC meant that major decisions on first-year program design and funding were made well before the TAACs were even seated. As a result, the OEDC initially reproduced the elite bias of the OIP: No more than three of the original appointees actually lived in the target areas, and none met poverty-level income guidelines.[56] At its second meeting on February 3, 1965, African American members Don McCullum and Clinton White moved to have the OEDC choose its own officers, and Judge Wilson, now on the Superior Court, was elected as chair. The replacement of Mayor Houlihan with Judge Wilson marked the accession of middle-class black professionals to the leadership of Oakland's poverty program. Having won the OEDC away from the mayor, however, the black professionals also wanted to protect it from the city council. The OEDC's duties and responsibilities, including policy making and approval of funds, were spelled out in a resolution voted by the city council on February 9, 1965. The language of the resolution, however, left unclear the city council's veto power over OEDC programs, and tensions persisted between the interests embodied in the two political arenas.[57]

As black middle-class professionals took control over the OEDC, they adopted a strategy of using federal programs to expand opportunities for the black population and facilitate their own political entry into the new institutional forms of the regime. To carry out this strategy, however, they needed to mobilize and retain the support of the black community. This highlighted an emerging problem of collective political identity within the community, and black residents in the ghetto flatlands would eventually split with the black professionals over the direction and control of the poverty program.

Ghetto Mobilization and Community Control

The organization of the TAACs began in February 1965. The composition of the committees in their first year varied somewhat across the target areas. Women outnumbered men on all committees except West Oakland, though men were usually in positions of leadership. In East, North, and West Oakland the membership was approximately 85 percent black, while the Fruitvale committee included a mix of Mexican Americans, blacks, Asian Americans, and whites. Low-income members ranged from less than 10 percent of the membership in East Oakland and about a quarter in West Oakland and Fruitvale to slightly less than half in North Oakland. Liberal white Protestant clergymen held leadership roles in North and West Oakland and in Fruitvale, home of the East Oakland Parish, an advocacy group of white ministers, students, and residents.[58]

As the TAACs became more active, differences arose between them and the at-large members of the OEDC board. The latter saw the OEDC as a citywide coalition, bringing together major institutions and groups concerned with economic and social development. For the black professionals like Dr. Smith and Judge Wilson, such a coalition offered an opportunity to educate elites about social problems, negotiate concessions from public officials, reform institutional practices, and improve services to the poor. They felt that the inclusion of established organizations with large poor or minority constituencies, like churches and the NAACP, was enough to meet citizen participation requirements, and while they saw the target area residents as an important element of the coalition, they considered them only one of many, and certainly the group with the fewest resources necessary to achieve change.[59]

For their part, members of the TAACs held a different view of their role and of the best strategy for fighting poverty. They had much less faith in established institutions and believed that what the poor needed most were direct, immediate benefits—like jobs, legal aid, and child care—not technical assistance, information referral, or even education programs (such as Head Start) aimed exclusively at future generations. Following traditions of self-help within the black community, they preferred programs that they could run on their own. Concerned about their ability to hold the more educated and professional at-large OEDC members accountable, they believed that they understood their own needs better and that they should properly control the poverty program.[60]

These contrasting points of view illustrate the competing conceptions of collective identity and legitimate authority held by the two groups. The black professionals defended their leadership of the poverty program, despite their higher incomes and residence outside the target areas, by invoking their personal origins and memories of growing up in the ghetto, and they justified their strategy of negotiation by stressing the limited resources of the OEO program. They questioned the target area leaders' own representativeness and accountability, and were especially critical of those they labeled "social workers"—namely, white clergy and students—whose claim to legitimacy rested on their marginal status as unattached intellectuals.

The TAAC members, by contrast, felt distinct class differences from the OEDC leaders, even if they themselves were not the poorest residents in their communities. They criticized service programs that gave money to established institutions and professional salaries when area residents were in need of jobs and income. They based their own claims to authenticity on their everyday experience and knowledge of the neighborhood, and regarded the white activists as useful allies who were working for the residents. Thus, each side articulated different visions of the racial and class boundaries implicit in the definition of the "community."

These differences set the target area representatives increasingly at odds with the black middle-class professionals on the OEDC board. The black professionals' strategy of coalition and negotiation would be undermined if the OEDC became dominated by only one group, even if it was the group the council was intended to serve. Nevertheless, the black professionals were willing to make concessions to the TAACs, in order to preserve their bargaining position as representatives for the poor.[61] In March 1965, the OEDC agreed that two delegates be elected from each of the target areas to the OEDC board, in addition to the at-large members already appointed by the mayor; and in August, Dr. Smith proposed that the OEDC executive committee be enlarged from seven to eleven members by the addition of one representative from each of the TAACs.[62]

The TAACs, however, continued to seek authority over programs in their areas. In May, the Ford Foundation expressed a willingness to renew its grant to Oakland, with a special interest in self-help programs run by neighborhood groups. When the OEDC announced that $600,000 in new Ford funds would be assigned to this purpose, the committees eagerly took advantage of the chance to start their own programs.[63] Members of TAACs from North and West Oakland even formed an organization called the Corporation of the Poor, to provide staff support and leadership training to target area residents independently of the DHR.[64] The Corporation of the Poor received $10,000 from the OEDC for a series of leadership retreats, and while it did not develop into a permanent staff arm for the TAACs, it signaled the growing political and organizational development within the target neighborhoods.

In the TAACs ghetto residents had found a means through which to organize for political power. As they began to mobilize, they demanded the right to oversee the activities of public and private agencies in their neighborhoods, and later to plan and carry out their own programs. By extending opportunities to previously unrepresented groups, however, activists also confronted the question of their own legitimacy. The search for authentic collective identity—who is really poor, who is really black?—plagued the movement as it attempted to expand participation in the local political community. These questions soon led to a struggle for control of the OEDC itself.

Collective Identity: Who Speaks for the Community?

Although the TAACs had won the right to organize their own programs, the two sides continued to disagree on funding priorities and authority within the OEDC. The issue of target area representation emerged toward the end of 1965. Led by the Fruitvale Area Advisory Committee, the TAACs began meeting among themselves to draft a set of demands. They agreed to demand 51 percent control of the OEDC board and executive committee by elected TAAC representatives, as well as the right to review and approve decisions regarding programs, staff, funding requests, and reports sent to the OEO. They also demanded that requirements for staff jobs be defined so as not to exclude residents without formal education or professional training. These demands elevated the conflict from adequate representation to effective control over the OEDC.

In January 1966, members from the North Oakland, West Oakland, and Fruitvale committees formed a Target Area Coordinating Committee to press for reorganization of the OEDC. At a program review meeting on March 12, they introduced a resolution calling for an expansion of the OEDC to sixty members, with eight representatives from each of the target areas. The motion was defeated, and when Judge Wilson refused to allow the target area representatives to read a statement, seven of the nine present walked out of the meeting. After the walkout, the dissident representatives released a statement signed by eight advisory committee OEDC members and three advisory committee chairs, announcing their intention to make a formal request to the federal OEO to recognize the TAACs and their coordinating committee as the official Oakland Community Action Program agency.

Judge Wilson appealed to the Western Regional OEO office, but its reply was inconclusive.[65] The OEDC then appointed a special committee, headed by at-large member Don McCullum, to come up with a solution. Reporting on April 23, McCullum's committee recommended that 51 percent of the OEDC members be elected target area representatives, and that 75 percent of all TAAC members and their OEDC delegates be required to meet low-income criteria. The committee also urged that the TAACs take responsibility for community organizing and have final approval over any indigenous self-help program limited to their area, and that TAACs participate in the personnel decisions of delegate agencies for neighborhood and professional employees. Finally, it called for creation of a fifth advisory committee, for Spanish-speaking Mexican Americans, that would be housed in existing service centers in all four areas but have its own staff. These proposals were adopted by the OEDC on May 25. Target area elections were held later that year, and on January 25, 1967, twenty TAAC representatives took their seats on the new thirty-nine-member OEDC board.[66]

Two years after the creation of the OEDC, residents of poor neighborhoods had won majority control over Oakland's poverty program. These changes led to a strategic shift within the OEDC, from the leveraged support of established agencies to a preference for locally generated self-help projects. As neighborhood residents increased their involvement, the white ministers of the East Oakland Parish soon lost their political justification and influence, and the four original TAACs became virtually all black.[67] The black professionals conceded program changes in order to retain their leadership roles on the OEDC board, while the target area representatives, satisfied with formal democratic control over OEDC decisions, were compelled to reach out to the black poor.[68]

CONCLUSION:
THE LIMITS OF BUREAUCRATIC HEGEMONY

Like many American cities, Oakland experienced substantial structural changes in its population and economy in the post–World War II era. These changes generated patterns of concentrated group inequality in the urban center. In order to preserve the metropolitan dominance of downtown, elites in Oakland pursued a series of major developmental projects in transportation, economic infrastructure, and housing, organized through a proliferation of semiautonomous bureaucratic agencies. As redevelopment forced the redistribution of groups in the urban space, conflicts among progrowth elites, conservative white homeowners, and inner-city minority residents emerged in public disputes over policies of urban renewal. In the struggles over Acorn and Oak Center, the growing black community began to mobilize as a collective actor and contest its exclusion from the local political community.

The bureaucratic model of the redevelopment regime was replicated in the origins of the social welfare programs. The Associated Agencies and the OIP were led by liberal professionals and agency administrators concerned with the control of urban social problems, including racial transition and growing poverty. As the scope of intervention expanded in the OIP and with the OEDC, the definition of the relations between state and society also changed. "Citizen participation" moved gradually from a conventional regime coalition of elite notables and established interests to a phase in which black middle-class professionals used their intermediary position to consolidate their function as spokespersons for the black community. The mobilization of poor and working-class residents in the poverty program, in turn, forced the black professionals to concede an autonomous role to the target area residents, who had previously been excluded from social program planning.

The trajectory of the poverty program in Oakland reflects the changing relationship between social groups and political institutions in the process of mobilization. With changes in form came changes in content. The agency bureaucrats' early emphasis on the assimilation of the minority poor shifted to the black professionals' strategy of leveraged reform of established institutions, and finally to the target area residents' demand for community control. After 1966, the TAACs grew in size and turned inward, focusing on program creation and self-help services in their own neighborhoods. Thus the poverty program became a locus of grassroots political organization in poor black and Latino neighborhoods, subsidized by federal funds, within the framework of the bureaucratic regime.

Meanwhile, the institutional conservatism of the city council, its lack of resources, and its barriers to entry all deflected attention away from the arena of municipal electoral politics. Regular city government remained committed to lower taxes, minimal intervention, and budgetary restraint, providing few opportunities for the political incorporation of new groups. As one black activist commented, "Why bother with the city? It has nothing to offer."[69] Instead, black mobilization was channeled toward the separate arena of externally funded bureaucratic urban programs. These offered better prospects for winning concrete gains and political leverage, and black movement organizers quickly took advantage of them in the Redevelopment Agency and in the poverty programs.

The price of this orientation was the movement's greater dependence on outside allies and resources, as well as the continued insulation of local political institutions from electoral challenge. The result was a relative stalemate in Oakland politics, as contending interests remained fixed within their respective institutional arenas. Indeed, the stability of the regime rested precisely on its segmentation, which encouraged the containment of black protest to programs specifically limited to the ghetto.

The limits of this arrangement were soon to become clear. While offering marginal benefits, the bureaucratic programs did little to alter black exclusion from urban housing and labor markets, or to undo the discriminatory protection of white civil society. When black mobilization challenged these boundaries, it faced powerful resistance from more entrenched regime interests, as was shortly to be demonstrated in struggles over ghetto unemployment and community relations with police. As the '60s wore on, these struggles led to growing racial polarization and a crisis for the urban regime.

7 Bureaucratic Insulation and Racial Conflict

The Challenge of Black Power

By the mid '60s, black activists in Oakland had gained an institutional footing in the federal urban programs. Nevertheless, they still faced the more difficult task of altering the substantive relations among groups in the city. Despite the political opportunities offered by federal programs and money, movement leaders continued to face opposition from more powerful, competing local interests, whose resistance effectively stymied efforts for reform. The regime's refusal to compromise illustrated its failure to absorb the movement challenge and signaled a growing crisis of the urban political community. At the same time, the movement's inability to win more significant concessions transformed the conditions of mobilization, encouraging the use of more radical tactics and the rise of the ideology of black power. Together, these events would contribute to the polarization of groups in the urban polity along the central axis of race.

In this chapter, I begin by reviewing the failures of bureaucratic reform in two crucial areas: unemployment and relations between the police and the community. The former reflected the structural exclusion of minority poor workers from the urban economy, while the latter ignited black grievances over the coercive enforcement of a racialized civic order. Attempts to redress these problems repeatedly ran up against the institutionalized relations among actors in the urban regime. The failure of reform in these areas led directly to the formal separation of the Oakland Economic Development Council (OEDC) from the city government and formed the context for the emergence in Oakland of the Black Panther Party.

For the black movement, demands for equal rights and self-determination found their most unified political expression in the negotiations for the design of the Model Cities program in West Oakland. In the wake of that campaign, I argue, the search for black power would divide into three basic

145

paths: bureaucratic alliance, as represented in the Oakland Redevelopment Agency; bureaucratic opposition, typified by the now-autonomous OEDC, Inc.; and independent party organization, embodied in the Black Panther Party for Self-Defense. The latter reached its peak in the 1973 mayoral campaign of party leader Bobby Seale, which produced an unprecedented electoral mobilization of the black ghetto poor. In each case, however, the weakness of the urban political community created difficult choices for movement actors—dilemmas that foreshadowed the form of relations in the subsequent remaking of the regime.

THE FAILURE OF ECONOMIC INCORPORATION: UNEMPLOYMENT AND THE BLACK POOR

For inner-city minority residents, one of the most pressing structural problems was unemployment. In Oakland, unskilled and semiskilled blue-collar jobs were rapidly disappearing: Between 1958 and 1966, the city lost more than nine thousand manufacturing jobs. Regional industrial expansion shifted to newer areas in southern Alameda County, epitomized by General Motors's relocation of its East Oakland plant in 1964 to the recently incorporated suburban town of Fremont. With economic growth moving to the urban periphery, ghetto residents appeared to be permanently shut off from the prosperity that surrounded them. In 1966, unemployment in the Oakland flats averaged 12.9 percent, and rates for youth were perhaps two to three times higher.[1] Remarkably, such jobless rates persisted in the city at the time that it was serving as a major military port during the height of the escalation of the Vietnam War. In 1968, federal defense expenditures in Oakland (including military and civilian payroll, along with prime contract awards to Oakland contractors) exceeded $391 million—roughly four times the amount spent on all nondefense federal programs.[2]

The Private Sector:
Job Training versus Racial Discrimination

The first concerted effort to reduce unemployment in Oakland during this period came from an alliance of business, labor, minority groups, and state government. In 1962, a group of local businessmen, concerned about property tax rates "linked, in the opinions of some, to the large numbers of Negro welfare recipients," began meeting to discuss possible solutions. With the help of minority civic leaders, labor unions, and Oakland Interagency Project (OIP) staff, they developed a proposal for a community-based outreach, placement, and training program, which became known as the Oakland Adult Minority Employment Project (OAMEP). A key part of the program was the creation of an advisory committee, with members from business, minority groups, and organized labor, to encourage private employers and local unions to make jobs and apprenticeships available. Jointly funded by the Ford Foundation and the U.S. Department of Labor, and staffed by California State Employment Service professionals located in target-area neighborhood service centers, the OAMEP got under way in late 1964.[3]

By 1965, a variety of federally financed jobs programs were in operation in the city. The Department of Labor provided funds for positions in its On-the-Job Training program and a Neighborhood Youth Corps (aimed at high-school dropouts), while the OAMEP sponsored training courses under the 1962 federal Manpower Development and Training Act (MDTA), and the OEDC distributed Office of Economic Opportunity (OEO) money for summer work projects for youth run by the Department of Human Relations (DHR) and the Central Labor Council. In November 1965, Dr. Norvel Smith of the DHR announced a proposal to develop an independent vocational school for OAMEP and other job trainees, and in April 1966 the East Bay Skills Center opened in a former factory building in North Oakland.[4]

The Skills Center, however, immediately sparked conflicts among the members of the OAMEP coalition. Although plans called for training to be based on a survey of skill needs in the East Bay labor market, the unions charged that the State Employment Service chose lower-skilled occupations already in labor surplus, and that the short-term training offered undercut union apprenticeship standards. Of course, many unions had long denied nonwhite workers access to apprenticeship, but Central Labor Council leaders argued that they could not pressure their member organizations to integrate or to support the program if it threatened to bypass a basic mechanism of craft union labor-market power. Funding cutbacks further limited Skills Center courses, and in May 1966, the council members collectively resigned from the OAMEP advisory committee.[5]

The unions feared an expanded labor supply without an increase in demand, pointing to the program's failure to generate new jobs. From its inception, the employer members of the OAMEP advisory committee were supposed to use their influence to "open new doors" and encourage their peers to hire unemployed minorities. But employers were unwilling to commit to specific goals, and a 1967 study of the program found little effort made to persuade businesses to alter their customary practices.[6] Between September 1964 and January 1966, 6,518 job seekers were registered at the neighborhood centers, of whom less than 12 percent were placed in permanent jobs lasting more than three days. Most jobs offered through the project were the same type of low-skill, low-wage, short-term labor traditionally available to minority workers, yet few applicants actually received additional training: Through March 1967, only 9 percent of male and 5 percent of female applicants had been referred to MDTA courses. By that date, less than one percent of all project applicants had been referred to training, completed the classes they started, and obtained a training-related job.[7]

Public Policy:
Administrative Coordination versus Political Conflict

Prospects for employment gains might have seemed brighter on public-works projects, but even there the outcomes were similar. The construction of the huge Bay Area Rapid Transit system, the largest project, promised to employ up to eight thousand workers, even as it threatened to displace residents near its West Oakland elevated line. In early 1966, a coalition of civil rights, neighborhood, and black church leaders known as Justice on Bay Area Rapid Transit (JOBART) became active in the East Bay, demanding relocation assistance and jobs for unemployed minority workers. JOBART leaders confronted BART at public hearings and staged a march and rally of more than a thousand people at Lake Merritt in June 1966. In response, BART officials called a temporary halt to evictions and promised to study employment problems, but they refused to negotiate directly with JOBART. The following January, BART did adopt an affirmative action plan, under the direction of the federal government's Office of Contract Compliance, and by June 1967 minorities made up 30 percent of the workers on BART. But most of these were laborers, few apprentices had been hired, and only nine of 178 office staff employees were nonwhite.[8]

The unwillingness of established regime actors to support minority employment limited the impact of the various jobs programs, despite the increasing scale of federal aid. In April 1966, the federal Economic Development Administration announced a $23 million package of aid to public-works projects in Oakland, in a massive showcase effort to stimulate hiring of minority poor. The package included $10 million to the port of Oakland for improvements to the Seventh Street marine terminal, and another $10 million for a joint agreement between the port and Oakland-based World Airways, Inc., to build a maintenance hangar at the Oakland airport, expected to employ more than a thousand workers. By late 1968, however, neither project had begun construction, the estimated costs for the aircraft hangar had increased by more than $4 million, and no concrete plans for minority employment were in place.[9]

Federal and local officials expressed frustration in their efforts to hold the port and World Airways accountable, but the latter were frankly more concerned with capital improvements than with minority hiring. As one port administrator remarked, "Our people felt the federal government was going a little too far in telling us how to run our business." Yet in 1968 the port employed no minority persons in professional jobs, while the number of minority employees at World Airways actually *declined* from 1967 to 1968, even as the company's total workforce rose by 10 percent.[10]

Some critics blamed these outcomes on the bureaucratic complexity of the new programs, or on the lack of administrative coordination among federal, state, and city agencies. Such comments overlooked the *political* conflicts of interest among groups where minority employment was concerned. On this score, local elected officials proved no better at managing relations in the regime. In February 1966, Mayor John Houlihan abruptly resigned amid charges of embezzlement related to his private law practice. The city council then appointed one of its own members, small businessman John Reading, to be the new mayor. In October, Mayor Reading announced plans to form a new Manpower Commission, funded by the federal Economic Development Administration, to consolidate the advisory committees of the various existing job programs. The mayor hoped to centralize employment efforts as a way of uniting the dominant regime actors behind a renewed agenda of economic growth.

Emphasizing an elite coalition with business and industry, Mayor Reading questioned whether neighborhood residents, regardless of their "good intentions," could help in what he described as "a technical administrative problem."[11] When the Department of Labor announced in February 1967 that Oakland had been selected to participate in the Comprehensive Employment Program (CEP)—a crash program involving five federal agencies, intended to employ twenty-five hundred hard-core jobless by the summer— the mayor assumed his Manpower Commission would have authority over the program. He was later outraged to learn that federal rules required the local Community Action Agency (that is, the OEDC) to be the prime sponsor for the CEP.[12]

Reading accused the OEDC of being "stacked" with minority group leaders, and defended his approach. "Employment must come from business and industry," he argued. "Therefore, business and industry must have more representation."[13] The mayor's insistence forced top officials from the Labor Department and the OEO to come to Oakland and personally work out a compromise. The federal officials granted Mayor Reading's request that $1.5 million of CEP money be earmarked for the East Bay Skills Center, but gave the OEDC formal authority over CEP administration and funds. Meanwhile, a joint subcommittee would prepare projects for review by both the Manpower Commission and the OEDC before they received final approval by the city council. In practice, the projects approved by the joint subcommittee included significant participation and management by target area residents, and the mayor lost his bid for control of the CEP.[14]

Mayor Reading had hoped to use his office to broker the interests of employers and other actors in the Oakland labor market. But major local economic-development functions were already insulated in the port, the BART, and other bureaucratic agencies, and he lacked the authority to unite these functions or to center the regime under his own political direction. In the private sector, attempts to build voluntary alliances between challenging and regime groups, as in the OAMEP, also failed to create a binding institutional framework able to keep important decision-makers accountable. The federal programs offered substantial resources, but they could not by themselves reorient the relations among groups in the urban polity. As a consequence, unskilled minority workers remained disproportionately excluded from the primary paths of local economic development, and the population of economically marginalized black poor continued to grow. By 1970 (a recessionary year), black joblessness in the target areas exceeded 20 percent, while the rates for black youth were over 48 percent.[15]

RESISTANCE TO REFORM: THE OEDC VERSUS THE CITY COUNCIL

Local resistance to reform was also powerfully demonstrated in the area of police-community relations. For many black residents, perhaps no grievance was more acutely felt than the belief that they were subject to discriminatory and violent treatment by police. The problem was underlined by a highly publicized incident in April 1966, when Oakland police were accused of beating black West Oakland resident Luther Smith Sr., his two sons, and two white friends in his own home, in a mistaken raid on the property. The next month, the California state advisory committee to the U.S. Commission on Civil Rights held an open hearing in Oakland and received "numerous allegations of police intimidation and excessive use of force against Negroes and Mexican Americans." Racial disparities added to the mistrust minority residents felt toward the nearly all-white police force: In 1966, only sixteen out of 617 members of the Oakland Police Department were black, and only four were Mexican American.[16]

Throughout the black community, activists perceived an urgent need to do something about the problem of police brutality. The Oakland branch of the NAACP had previously tried to convince the city council to establish a police review board, but without success. In February 1966, the OEDC approved a proposal for a Police Affairs Committee, to be formed as a nonprofit organization that would hear citizens' complaints and provide assistance in using established channels to those with seemingly justifiable cases.[17]

The proposal immediately turned into a test of authority between the city council and the OEDC. As the official Community Action Agency for Oakland, the OEDC was recognized by the OEO and by the Ford Foundation as the proper policy-making body and recipient of anti-poverty funds. But the administration for the poverty program was housed in the DHR under the city manager's office, a legacy of its origins in the OIP, and federal and foundation grants were received in a trust fund under the custody of the city auditor-controller. Thus the city council appeared to retain veto power over expenditures recommended by the OEDC.[18]

The situation was complicated by recent changes in the city administration. Liberal city manager Wayne Thompson, the founder of the Associated Agencies and the OIP, retired and was replaced in January 1966 by Jerome Keithley. In his career as manager, Thompson had been an enthusiastic organizational entrepreneur who enjoyed close personal relationships with some of Oakland's leading business elites. Keithley, a former city manager for suburban Palo Alto, was a professional administrator much less sympathetic to social programs, who developed stronger ties with members of the city council.[19] These differences involved more than just personality, as Keithley's tenure heralded a political change in the relationship of the city government and the poverty program.

On March 3, City Councillor and Vice Mayor Fred Maggiora told the press that the city council had already stated its opposition to a police review board, and said, "We are the policy-making body. . . . [The OEDC] are acting as if they were running the city." A few days later, the *Oakland Tribune* reported that Judge Wilson expressed "'serious reservations' about continuing as [OEDC] chairman if the city council became 'another organization that we are going to have to fight.'"[20] Seeking to mediate the conflict, recently appointed Mayor Reading urged the formation of a joint city/OEDC committee to explore alternative proposals. The mayor favored the establishment of a human relations commission or a general ombudsman's office, and he persuaded the city council to ask the city manager for a review of existing grievance procedures.

In April, the OEDC authorized a committee to negotiate with the city over the police affairs committee proposal.[21] Shortly afterward, the president of the Oakland police officers association announced that his members would refuse to cooperate with any review board and would sue to avoid participation. The Ford Foundation sent notice of the proposal's eligibility for funding in late June, and over the summer, the OEDC committee continued to negotiate with the city manager and police department officials. In August, the OEDC formally requested release of the Ford funds, but City Manager Keithley refused, claiming that the city council had already adopted a policy opposing any type of police review board. Talks dragged on for several more months, until finally, on February 7, 1967, Keithley prepared to report to the city council on all efforts to "review procedure for handling public grievances." By a six to three vote, the city council declined even to hear the report.[22]

The dispute over the police affairs committee showed the power and determination of entrenched interests on the city council to resist minority group demands. This, along with the struggles over the CEP, convinced the OEDC leaders to explore their legal option to separate from the city and incorporate as a nonprofit organization. In June 1967, DHR executive director Dr. Smith announced his resignation, to become deputy director of the OEO's Western Regional Office. A joint OEDC-Ford-city review committee was set up to screen candidates for his job, and in August it submitted a list of three to City Manager Keithley. When Keithley refused to appoint the committee's first choice, it was the last straw. OEDC board members voted on August 23 to sever their relationship with the city, and on January 1, 1968, the OEDC was officially reconstituted as the Oakland Economic Development Council, Inc. (OEDCI), contracting directly with the federal government as the Community Action Agency for the Oakland poverty program.[23]

THE CRISIS OF POLITICAL COMMUNITY

By the mid '60s, local governing institutions in Oakland were rapidly losing their ability to coordinate the competing interests in the urban polity. In 1966, *Oakland Tribune* publisher Joseph R. Knowland, the dominant figure of midcentury Oakland politics, passed away at ninety-two years of age. His son, William, took over as editor and publisher of the *Tribune*, but the era in which his father had once exercised close personal direction over the city's affairs had passed. No other actors seemed able or willing to fill the breach: Mayor Reading's efforts to centralize a business-led growth coalition were ineffective, while the conservative city council remained intransigent, refusing to pass a fair housing ordinance, refusing to approve the police review board, and hostile even to the mayor's own Manpower Commission. Black activists gained organizational resources through the federal programs but had little bargaining power to compel a broader institutional transformation of the regime. Meanwhile, urban redevelopment proceeded apace, but typically under autonomous or regional agencies like the Oakland Redevelopment Agency, the coliseum corporation, the port, or the BARTD.[24]

The political impasse overlaid deep divisions in urban civil society. If black ghetto dwellers often saw the police as an antagonistic force, white Oaklanders frequently supported police control of perceived threats emanating from the ghetto. Conservative whites remained a significant social and political presence, especially in the hills and the Bible Belt area in the central foothills of East Oakland. In November 1966, 55 percent of voters in the East Oakland Fifteenth Assembly District precincts rejected a local proposition to allow twenty-five hundred units of scattered-site public housing, even as the proposal passed with a 52 percent majority citywide. In much of the flatland area, however, white residents were increasingly abandoning the city altogether. Between 1960 and 1970, a net 56,611 whites migrated out of Oakland, representing a loss of more than 20 percent of the white population. Meanwhile, a small but growing number of younger whites, disaffected by the war in Vietnam, began turning to the new left and countercultural movements. The shift was signaled in October 1965 when some fifteen thousand antiwar protesters, marching from Berkeley down Telegraph Avenue toward the U.S. Army induction center in West Oakland, were turned back at the city line by a wall of Oakland police.[25]

Inside the black community, important divisions also remained. Judge Wilson, Dr. Smith, and other OEDC leaders personified the new black professional-administrative stratum, and its embrace of the Democratic Party and the Great Society. A significant segment of the old black middle class, however, remained tied to local business elites and the Republican Party. These included attorney and Men of Tomorrow founder George Vaughns, real-estate broker C. J. Patterson, *California Voice* publisher E. A. Daly, utility company representative Charles Goady, and Housing Authority manager Barney Hilburn, appointed in 1958 as the first black member of the Oakland School Board.[26] Other black "firsts" in city government were also political moderates who originally gained office by appointment, including City Councillor Joshua Rose, selected in 1964 to represent a district outside the black West Oakland ghetto; and attorney and *Oakland Post* newspaper publisher Tom Berkley, a maverick Democrat appointed to the Board of Port

Commissioners in 1969.[27] As mass uprisings began to break out in Watts and across urban America, these groups faced a growing crisis of confidence in their leadership of the black community. This sentiment was captured in the theme of the 1967 conference retreat of the Men of Tomorrow, titled "The Dilemma of the Negro Middle Class in the Black Revolution."[28]

The Radical Turn:
The Emergence of the Black Panther Party

Many observers believed that Oakland, too, might soon go up in flames, but no major riot ever occurred. With the promise of millions of dollars of federal aid, neighborhood activists worked hard to keep order in the streets.[29] By mid-decade, though, the black movement in Oakland still had not come together as a unified collective actor. On the contrary, the year 1966 saw a series of strategic organizing failures, including an abortive school boycott, the inconclusive JOBART protests, an unsuccessful attempt to bring nationally known community organizer Saul Alinsky to Oakland, the short-lived Corporation of the Poor, and the defeat of the police affairs committee. The following spring, three OEDC target area leaders ran for office in the municipal election, but none came close to overcoming the institutional barriers to electoral victory in Oakland.

As the anticipated progress of the movement stalled, more radical actors came to the fore. Late in 1966, two employees of the North Oakland Neighborhood Anti-Poverty Center sat down in a back office room and drafted a ten-point program for a group they called the Black Panther Party for Self-Defense. Huey Newton, a twenty-four-year-old former junior college student and the son of wartime migrant parents, and Bobby Seale, a twenty-nine-year-old U.S. Air Force veteran, opened the first storefront office of the Black Panther Party on January 1, 1967. Inspired by the writings of Malcolm X and Frantz Fanon, the Panthers identified themselves with the growing population of poor, marginal, or criminalized black "lumpen-proletarians," reaching out to unemployed black adults and youth, an increasing number of whom now had recent military experience in the Vietnam War.[30]

The Panthers astonished ghetto residents and gained swift attention by conducting armed surveillance patrols against brutality by Oakland police. In February, they were joined by journalist and former prison convict Eldridge Cleaver, who brought additional media contacts and exposure to the group. In May 1967 (three months after the Oakland City Council had refused to discuss the police affairs committee), the Panthers staged a public-relations coup by marching on the state capitol in Sacramento with loaded shotguns and rifles to oppose a bill to ban the open carrying of weapons. No one was hurt, but the incident galvanized awareness of the party as a black paramilitary force in the inner city.[31]

Young black men and women rushed to join the Panthers, whose initial strength was based less on their internal organization than on the symbolic power of their direct confrontation of the police. The symbolic challenge quickly became real: In the early morning hours of September 28, 1967, in West Oakland, two police officers stopped an automobile carrying Newton and Panther member Gene McKinney. Within minutes, the incident erupted into a shootout that left officer John Frey dead and Newton seriously wounded. Newton was arrested for murder, and over the next year, his trial became the center of a highly public Panther agitation for his release, with repeated demonstrations by Panther members and supporters on the steps of the Alameda County Courthouse in downtown Oakland.[32]

The publicity generated by these actions helped make the Panthers a standard-bearer for the new ideology of black power, underscored by the appearance of top leaders of the national Student Non-violent Coordinating Committee before six thousand people at a "Free Huey" rally on February 17, 1968, at the Oakland Auditorium. Unlike other black radical groups, however, the Panthers rejected cultural nationalism in favor of what they called "revolutionary nationalism," including both a critique of capitalism and the acceptance of aid and alliances from the white new left. By early 1968, the Panthers had formed an ad hoc coalition with the recently organized California Peace and Freedom Party, which nominated Cleaver as its candidate for president, the still-imprisoned Newton for the East Bay Seventh Congressional District, and Seale for the state Assembly.[33]

The appearance of the Black Panther Party announced a radical turn in the trajectory of black protest. What had begun to occur elsewhere as spontaneous rioting or disorder took the form of an organized political actor with the Panthers. Their armed refusal to accept the boundaries of a racialized civil order gave voice to deeply held grievances in the black community, while their dramatic presence brought the issue of racial inequality of power forcibly into the public sphere.

The Spaces of Division

By the second half of the '60s, different groups in Oakland seemed to inhabit almost entirely separate worlds—a social distance that found material expression in the progress of the city's physical renewal. On the one hand, the regime's redevelopment activity continued to remake the public face of the city. The coliseum opened in September 1966, and by the next year it housed successful major league football and baseball franchises, providing national media recognition of Oakland and a focus of civic identity. In 1967, the Redevelopment Agency and the city council agreed to provide land near Lake Merritt to the Peralta Community College District as a home for its new downtown campus. The $21 million project was located across the street from the Oakland Auditorium and the 7.7-acre site of the new $6 million Oakland Museum of California, already under construction.[34]

Meanwhile, city officials learned they could receive credits for local expenditures on BART and freeway construction when applying for federal urban renewal aid. The Planning Commission promptly issued a study for a new Central Business District Plan, endorsed by the Central Business District Association, the Retail Merchants Association, the Oakland Real Estate Board, and OCCUR. The Redevelopment Agency's Corridor project was redrawn to include the downtown BART stations, and in June 1967, the city council approved an application to transfer the previous $3.8 million Corridor grant to a high-rise development project called City Center, concentrating on a three-block area around the corner of Fourteenth Street and Broadway in the core of downtown.[35]

On the other hand, these major development projects far overshadowed the efforts at neighborhood renewal in the black community. By 1966, the vacant Acorn residential site had "grown thick and deep in grass," three years after most of its buildings were razed.[36] More than a year earlier, the Redevelopment Agency had selected the black-owned Beneficial Development Group as developer for Acorn housing, but the city council demanded extra financial assurances before approving Beneficial's application.[37] Further delays were caused by the Federal Housing Administration (FHA)'s reluctance to guarantee the $7 million construction loan for moderate-income housing in a ghetto area, and later by the withdrawal of the building contractor over differences in cost estimates with the FHA. Beneficial secured another contractor, but construction did not begin until January 1968. For more than five years, thirty-four acres of land lay empty in the heart of West Oakland.[38]

West Oakland remained the most depressed area in the city, a vivid reminder of those left behind by the urban regime. A third of its residents lived below the federal poverty level, compared to a rate of about 13 percent citywide. Although racial concentration was relatively stable, with nonwhites constituting about 70 percent of the residents, the neighborhood had lost a quarter of its population between 1960 and 1966.[39] As development in the adjacent port and downtown areas boomed, West Oaklanders watched their neighborhood fall more deeply into decline.

Speaking before a U.S. Senate subcommittee in May 1967, Mayor Reading criticized the federal antipoverty programs as "divisive and disruptive.... There is no city agency to serve 'the rich' or to represent 'whites,'" the mayor said. "Charges have been made that we used to have a 'white power structure' made up of a wealthy elite, but that does not justify setting up a whole new government, for example, of poor Negroes."[40] In West Oakland, many black citizens were beginning to believe otherwise. Their demands for both black power and community control would come together in the negotiations for the design of the Model Cities program.

BLACK POWER AND COMMUNITY CONTROL: THE MODEL CITIES

In January 1966, President Lyndon Johnson proposed to Congress the Demonstration Cities and Metropolitan Development Act, later known as the Model Cities. The legislation was intended to combine urban physical renewal and social-service delivery in a comprehensive approach to the full range of ghetto problems, including housing, jobs, health, education, and others. These goals were to be accomplished through "the most effective and economical concentration and coordination of Federal, State, and local public and private efforts," in designated Model Neighborhood Areas.[41] While several federal agencies would participate, the program was placed under the Department of Housing and Urban Development (HUD), the agency that administered federal urban renewal funds.

Aware of the protests that its urban renewal activities had provoked, HUD wanted to increase the involvement of neighborhood residents in planning for Model Cities, but at the same time leave final authority firmly in the hands of local government. Program guidelines allowed the local City Demonstration Agency to be the city itself, which placed administrative responsibility with the chief executive officer—in the case of Oakland, the city manager. The statute called for "widespread citizen participation," but unlike the OEO the Model Cities program did not prescribe any detailed formula for representation. Rather, within certain limits the exact form of citizen participation was left to the parties themselves.[42]

Representing the Ghetto: The West Oakland Planning Committee

Although the Model Cities did not become law until November, the Oakland Redevelopment Agency quickly prepared a preliminary proposal, which the city sent to HUD in February 1966. In October, City Manager

Keithley appointed a task force of city and county agency representatives, including Dr. Smith of the OEDC and DHR, to draft a formal application. This task force began meeting in December, but once again, as with the original Ford and OEO applications, no representatives from the affected target areas were included. Pressured by a federal deadline, members of the task force assumed that OEDC involvement satisfied requirements for citizen participation in the application phase. In February and March 1967, the OEDC began meeting with neighborhood residents to discuss the proposal, at which time the latter voiced their objections at being left out of the application planning process. Two target area representatives were hastily added to the task force, but by this time the process was nearly complete. On April 20, 1967, the city council approved the application and forwarded it to HUD.[43]

Seven months passed before HUD gave conditional approval of a $200,000 planning grant to Oakland in November 1967. During this time, relations between the OEDC and the city continued to deteriorate, leading to their eventual separation. In the fall, the OEDC hired Percy Moore, a black political activist and former ILWU union official in San Francisco, to replace Dr. Smith as executive director. Parting from the strategy of Smith and other black professionals on the OEDC, Moore endorsed a more militant black nationalism, stressing political action over service delivery and calling for direct confrontation between the neighborhoods and city hall.[44]

Among the conditions HUD required for its approval was the clarification of citizen participation in the local program. The regional HUD office scheduled a meeting with city officials to discuss this and other matters on November 28, 1967; but HUD immediately received complaints that the city had refused to invite either the residents or OEDC director Moore to attend. Nearly fifty residents showed up at the meeting anyway, demanding that the federal government guarantee neighborhood participation and control over the program. Officials from HUD reiterated that the city retained final administrative authority, and City Manager Keithley asked Moore to have the OEDC take the lead in developing a participation plan that would be satisfactory to the residents.[45] Within twenty-four hours, organizers held a mass meeting attended by some one hundred residents of West Oakland. Moore spoke at the meeting and appealed to black racial unity, declaring that the Model Cities program "should be controlled by black people for the benefit of black people."[46] He urged the formation of a new, independent West Oakland Planning Committee (WOPC) as the participatory body for the Model Cities, in place of the OEDC's West Oakland Advisory Committee. According to political scientist Judith May's detailed ethnography of the events, Moore and others believed the advisory committee was too narrowly based and constrained by its institutional ties to the OEDC. Seeking a wider political foundation, they constituted the WOPC as a delegate assembly: Any group of at least ten members operating partially or totally in West Oakland could become a member by submitting the names of two representatives. By December, delegates from sixty-five organizations were present, including churches, political groups, block clubs, and others. Within a year, more than 160 member groups had joined, ranging from the West End Nursery to the Black Panther Party.

The membership of the WOPC reflected the major socioeconomic divisions within the West Oakland community. The largest faction centered on West Oakland Advisory Committee leaders Ralph Williams and Booker Emery. Both in their fifties, Williams and Emery belonged to the generation of blacks who had migrated to Oakland during World War II. Veteran community activists, they and others like them represented a black working-class population striving for upward mobility despite their low occupational status and lack of formal education. Another grouping formed around the Peter Maurin Neighborhood House, a Catholic social-service agency, and included residents from a slum area cut off from the rest of the neighborhood by the Cypress Freeway. Generally poorer and less sophisticated than the other committee members, they organized themselves into the Western End Model Cities Organization with the help of volunteers from outside the neighborhood. More concerned with immediate needs than political autonomy, this group was able to use its access to outside private aid to challenge the West Oakland Advisory Committee's attempts to control resources in their area. The third major faction was represented by the black middle-class homeowners in the Oak Center Neighborhood Association (OCNA), who had already won significant political clout in their battles over urban renewal. Never an advocate for poor tenants, the OCNA leadership had built alliances with the Redevelopment Agency and the mayor, and shared their goals of promoting an integrated, middle-class neighborhood in the central city.[47]

The WOPC delegates met again in December and elected an executive committee with Ralph Williams as chair. In addition, OEDC director Moore paid the salary for a young activist, Paul Cobb, to be a WOPC staffer. The WOPC formally declared its independence from the OEDC on December 14.[48] It then turned to its relationship with the city and its role as the participation body for the Model Cities program.

Negotiating the Terms of Community: The Model Cities Program

The WOPC's opening proposal to the city outlined a participation structure for Model Cities planning. It began with a series of study committees that would receive input from various sources and report to the WOPC executive committee, which would prepare the reports for review by the full WOPC prior to direct submission to the city council. The WOPC executive committee would hire the project director and supervise its own staff, and it requested $92,000 from the planning grant for this purpose. Finally, the WOPC demanded veto power, equal to the city council's, over federal program expenditures in the Model Cities area. In this way, the proposal substituted the WOPC executive committee for the city manager's role and established the WOPC as the peer of the city council and the official voice of the West Oakland community.[49]

In January 1968, City Manager Keithley sent his formal reply. His plan merged the city's task force and the WOPC executive committee into a steering committee, which would receive study-committee proposals and prepare them for review first by the city manager and then by the city council. The WOPC would select West Oakland members on the study and steering committees and have 51 percent control of the steering committee, which would oversee project staff. In turn, the city manager would supervise and select the project director from a list of candidates nominated by a five-member screening committee. This gave the WOPC control over the steering committee but removed final approval of plans from the full WOPC and reinserted the city manager between the steering committee and the city council.[50]

As May argues, the two proposals embodied sharply different visions of the relationship between citizens and the local state. The WOPC version assumed that the existing city government did not adequately represent West Oakland; hence, the WOPC would function as a kind of "second government" for the neighborhood with its own democratic procedures, organization, and legitimacy, apart from the city council or the city manager's administration. For the first time, black community participation would be independent from the model of bureaucratic incorporation; urban policy was to be the outcome of negotiations between two separately constituted public bodies, or what May describes as a "dual sovereignty." The city manager correctly perceived this attempt to bypass his authority, so his counterproposal restored his administrative control. It offered instead to grant the WOPC predominant influence within a program that would remain under his jurisdiction and be subordinate, not equal, to the city council.

These disagreements led to a series of often acrimonious negotiations, which lasted for several months. By March 15, the parties had agreed to a format including the study committees, a 51 percent WOPC majority on the joint steering committee, a $92,000 share of the planning grant for WOPC staff, and a WOPC veto of steering committee proposals prior to submission to the city council.[51] Substantial differences remained, however, over the authority of the city manager, and in particular his power to select and supervise the project director. These issues proved so intractable that City Manager Kiethley withdrew from the process and turned them over to direct talks between the WOPC and the city council.

In the meantime, the WOPC sought clarification from the city and from HUD about whether its veto covered only Model Cities program grants or included *all* federally funded programs and agencies in the neighborhood. The implications of this demand were momentous: Oakland expected to receive perhaps $4 to $5 million annually in Model Cities funds, compared to the nearly $100 million the federal government was spending on various nondefense, categorical programs and services throughout the city, including local security, justice, and fiscal operations. If the broader veto were recognized, it would transform the WOPC from a participant in a bureaucratic decision-making process to a legitimate political entity able to govern its own territory and bargain with all other levels of the state; or, in the words of one observer, a "state within a state."[52]

The mayor and city council met with the WOPC on April 2 and agreed to compromise on issues regarding the city manager, while the question of the veto was left for a meeting with federal officials on April 10.[53] On April 4, however, the nation was shocked by news of the assassination of the Rev. Dr. Martin Luther King Jr. in Memphis, Tennessee. As violent protest broke out in cities across the country, WOPC leaders worked desperately to maintain peace, but two days later, Black Panther members and Oakland police engaged in a ninety-minute shootout in West Oakland. Two police officers and two Panthers were wounded, and teenage Panther member Bobby Hutton was shot and killed by police as he and Panther leader Cleaver were attempting to surrender.

The following week, WOPC leaders met with a range of federal and local agency officials regarding the extent of the veto. At stake were millions of federal dollars in aid for local law enforcement and for major public works like BART and the port. According to an OEO representative, the WOPC especially wanted to "stop federal money from going to the Oakland Police Department because of a bitter and profound distrust of the Oakland Police Department for alleged police brutality."[54] The federal officials indicated at least a willingness to respect neighborhood views even if statutory limits prevented a formal veto, and that was enough for the WOPC to demand city council approval of their veto over all federal programs operating in the Model Cities area. At a heated session on April 15, the city council ratified the April 2 agreements but ignored the veto demand, and a week later it sent its revised proposal to the WOPC, after deleting the downtown City Center project and port-owned lands from the Model Neighborhood boundaries.[55]

Meanwhile, racial tensions on the city's streets crystallized in a protest against the Oakland police. An ad hoc Blacks for Justice Committee organized a boycott of the downtown Housewives Market, where many West Oaklanders shopped, and threatened to extend it to all the members of the Retail Merchants Association. In response, the *Tribune* ran full-page advertisements every day for a week, denouncing the boycott as "extortion" and featuring a picture of a white-gloved hand holding a revolver aimed at the reader. The mayor defended the police department and condemned the boycott leaders, while *Tribune* publisher Knowland reportedly toured the Housewives Market himself to show his support.[56]

The boycott ended after several weeks without a public settlement, and the city made no further concessions on the Model Cities. The city council and the WOPC met again on July 1. The WOPC agreed to negotiate separately with the port, but restated its demand to include the City Center project. Councillor Joshua Rose made a motion for inclusion, which failed for want of a second. Angered, the WOPC leaders walked out of the meeting, but their options were running out. On July 15, the WOPC agreed to drop the City Center from the Model Neighborhood boundaries. A month later, the full WOPC ratified the Model Cities agreement with the city, at a desultory, poorly attended meeting in West Oakland. When the city council unanimously approved the revised Model Cities application at a meeting on August 27, no West Oakland residents were in attendance.[57]

The controversy over the Model Cities program was the culmination of a decade of political struggle in Oakland. The attempt to build an autonomous second government in West Oakland showed both the depth of racial polarization and the limits of bureaucratic reform. In the WOPC, black residents built a vehicle for mobilizing the ghetto community as a collective actor. Without authority or leverage over crucial urban economic functions, however, the exercise of community control ultimately allowed the city government to insulate itself once again from popular demands. Although the WOPC gained resources, for practical purposes the responsibility for change was merely exiled to the neighborhood. As local Model Cities director Maurice Dawson later said, "I was in effect given an invisible rope and told 'Go hang yourself, because city hall is not going to give any support to the program.'" Finally, the Model Cities, like the OEDCI, relied on federal money and authority, and hence was vulnerable to the change in national political administrations after 1968. By 1974, the federal Model Cities initiative was terminated, and, after little more than five years, the Oakland program was phased out of existence.[58]

BUREAUCRATIC ENFRANCHISEMENT AND POLITICAL DEMOBILIZATION: THE PATHS TO BLACK INCORPORATION

The campaign for the Model Cities program was the most unified political mobilization of the Oakland black community to date, and its ending marked a turning point for the movement. In its aftermath, local organizing for black power took three main paths: bureaucratic alliance, led by the example of the Redevelopment Agency; bureaucratic opposition, symbolized by the OEDCI; and independent party organization—the Black Panther Party. Each path offered a different strategy and relationship with the urban political community, and each would meet with varying experiences of success.

Bureaucratic Alliance: The Redevelopment Agency

Bureaucratic reform was perhaps most successful in the Redevelopment Agency under executive director John Williams, which took an early lead in the implementation of affirmative action. In Acorn, 46 percent of construction workers were minorities by the time the project was completed in 1969, and in January 1972 the agency claimed a 62 percent minority employment ratio on all demolition, construction, and rehabilitation work in the previous year.[59] Between 1970 and 1974, $10 million in urban renewal building contracts went to minority firms, with another $10 million to joint ventures between white- and black-owned companies.[60] The agency also fostered cooperative partnerships between black developers and community institutions in West Oakland. The black-owned Trans-Bay Engineers, Inc., served as prime contractor for the $1.3 million West Oakland Health Center, funded by the federal Economic Development Administration and opened in Acorn in 1969, and it also built the new Martin Luther King Jr. Elementary School in Oak Center, completed in 1971. In Oak Center, Taylor Memorial Methodist and Beth Eden Baptist Church each sponsored new housing developments, as did the General and Specialty Contractors Association (GSCA), a consortium of black homebuilders, whose $1.3 million, seventy-nine-unit low- to moderate-income project opened in 1972.[61]

Redevelopment provided resources for organization building within the ghetto, along with opportunities for negotiating relations with other urban actors. The Acorn housing project was sponsored and owned by the Alameda County Building Trades Council, which also took part with the GSCA and the OCNA in the federally funded PREP program, providing preapprenticeship training on housing rehabilitation jobs in Oak Center to unskilled minority residents. In 1969, the nonprofit Kaiser Urban Corporation, together with five West Oakland organizations, formed More Oakland Residential Housing, Inc. (MORHI), to develop a 12.5-acre, $9 million complex of 126 town house and 341 high-rise condominiums next to Acorn housing.[62] Finally, the downtown City Center project included developer commitments to 50 percent minority employment on project supervisory and property-management staff, joint marketing with black real-estate brokers, and 5 percent equity for a local economic development corporation created by the developer with nine minority leader co-investors. Construction of the first City Center office building was co-ventured by a national contractor and Trans-Bay Engineers, Inc., and by 1974 the Redevelopment Agency reported that 66 percent of City Center construction work-hours were performed by minorities, and 49 percent by Oakland residents.[63]

Bureaucratic Opposition: The OEDCI

The success of the bureaucratic incorporation strategy in the Redevelopment Agency contrasted sharply with the fate of the OEDCI. Under executive director Moore, the OEDCI shifted its emphasis from service provision to political advocacy, and it centralized control of its staff to strengthen its ability to mobilize pressure against local political institutions. This evoked an increasingly hostile reaction from city hall and from Republican administrations in the state and federal governments. In 1969, the city council twice delayed release of OEO and Ford Foundation funds pending audits of OEDCI records, while Mayor Reading used his appointments to the OEDCI board to try to muster the votes to fire Moore. Repeated investigations of Moore and of OEDCI finances by regional OEO and state authorities kept the program's future in constant doubt.[64]

Citing his power under the federal statute, Governor Ronald Reagan vetoed $234,800 in OEO funds for the East Oakland–Fruitvale Planning Committee, an OEDCI delegate agency, in October 1969. The following June,

Reagan issued a conditional veto of the entire $1.9 million 1970 operational grant for the OEDCI, to ensure that OEO-mandated organizational changes were enforced. The OEDCI acceded to the changes, including limits on protest activity by staff members and an expansion of its board, adding twelve at-large seats, four of them to be appointed by the mayor. In August, however, the regional OEO again froze the 1970 funds, claiming insufficient representation of nonblack minority and white poor in OEDCI decision-making. The OEO finally released the money in October, after court-ordered negotiations with the OEDCI.[65] Moore managed to outmaneuver the numerous attempts to remove him as director, but his confrontational stance alienated many older black leaders on the poverty program board. Judge Wilson resigned as OEDCI chair in November 1969, while West Oakland Advisory Committee members Ralph Williams and Booker Emery and OCNA president Lillian Love backed Mayor Reading in the latter's ongoing public battles with Moore.[66]

Notwithstanding the conflicts within the OEDCI, black activists extended the strategy of bureaucratic protest to other local agencies. In 1969, neighborhood leaders filed a complaint with HUD, charging that the business-dominated Oakland Citizens' Committee for Urban Renewal (OCCUR) excluded poor and minority residents from the urban renewal citizen-participation process. To the surprise of many, HUD agreed, and OCCUR was reorganized with a new cochair and a more representative twenty-one-member elected board of directors.[67] Such actions often drew their leadership from the Oakland Black Caucus, a local grouping of civil rights activists that included Moore, Paul Cobb, Don McCullum, Dr. Smith, attorney John George, and others. Described by one member as "a launching pad for attacks on an agency, starting affirmative action law suits and organizing an economic boycott," the Black Caucus pressed for fair hiring in the police department and at the Oakland Museum of California.[68] In May 1969, it succeeded in preventing the installation of the Oakland School Board's choice for a new superintendent, after a highly publicized protest at a school board meeting that led to misdemeanor and felony charges against several caucus members, including OEDCI director Moore.[69]

Protests against individual bureaucracies, however, did not in themselves add up to a larger popular mobilization, and the Black Caucus was unable to present itself as a united political voice for the black community as a whole. Meanwhile, local electoral mobilization continued to produce lackluster results. In 1969, East Oakland–Fruitvale Planning Committee chair Lawrence Joyner was soundly defeated in his bid to unseat Mayor Reading, while three other incumbent councillors ran unopposed.[70] In 1970, Black Caucus members aided Berkeley City Councillor Ronald Dellums (nephew of C. L. Dellums) in his successful race for the Seventh U.S. Congressional District seat, covering liberal South Berkeley and the North Oakland flats. Almost immediately afterward, however, leaders of the caucus and the OEDCI split over plans for the 1971 Oakland city elections. Supported by Moore's West Oakland rivals Ralph Williams and Booker Emery, caucus cochair Paul Cobb announced his candidacy for the West Oakland Third District City Council seat, and in January he joined a liberal, citywide "Oakland Coalition" slate of challengers to the incumbents. Moore and his allies, in turn, backed OEDCI staffer Stephen Brooks for councillor-at-large and circulated a ballot initiative to allocate 2 percent of the city's annual budget permanently to the OEDCI.[71]

Moore's stance drew a barrage of criticism from city and state officials, and on February 17, 1971, Governor Reagan vetoed the OEO's $1.6 million 1971 program grant to the OEDCI. A week later, the Oakland City Council passed a resolution asking the federal government to uphold the veto and to transfer control of $3.5 million in Department of Labor funds from the OEDCI to the city. Moore blasted the city councillors and, in defiance of federal guidelines, publicly vowed to have OEDCI staff campaign against them in the upcoming elections. On April 13, national OEO director Frank Carlucci upheld Governor Reagan's veto, effectively terminating the OEDCI's official status as the city's Community Action Agency.[72] The following week, Brooks, Cobb, and all nonwhite Oakland Coalition challengers for the city council were defeated in the April 20 municipal primary. The coalition slate gained majorities in the flatland precincts, but the turnout was not enough to overcome the incumbents' margin in the hills, despite the efforts of Cobb and others to distance themselves from Moore. In the May 18 final election, the OEDCI's ballot measure lost by more than twenty-one thousand votes. Three days later, the OEDCI ceased its operation of the poverty program in Oakland.[73]

With the beginning of a new decade, relations between the black community and the urban regime were becoming more clearly defined. In the Redevelopment Agency and in OCCUR, black business leaders, professionals, and neighborhood organizations found success using federal leverage to gain resources in exchange for cooperation with urban renewal. In other local bureaucracies like the city manager's office and the school district, however, black movement actors were more often outsiders, and faced greater resistance in extracting concessions from conservative, white-dominated administrations. Finally, both of these experiences contrasted with the regime's hostility toward mobilization in the poverty programs, whether focused on community control as in the Model Cities program or on political protest like the OEDCI. Although black actors gained resources and power in such programs, they remained vulnerable to limits on federal protections for movement activity.

The sheer multiplicity of bureaucratic arenas further divided the focus of mobilization, inhibiting organizational unity and making it harder to overcome barriers to electoral challenge. Indeed, in Oakland black entry into political office occurred first at higher levels of government, where concentrations of black voters in state legislative and U.S. Congressional districts made access easier than in the at-large elections for the city council. Yet even Ron Dellums's 1970 congressional victory relied on a coalition of blacks and the white liberal left, a group often shunned by more conservative interests in the black community. By the end of 1971, the OEDCI was dead and the Black Caucus was in disarray; neither could act as the catalyst for black mobilization in Oakland politics. But another actor was again becoming an independent political force, challenging for power and reaching out to the black poor: the Black Panther Party. In the 1973 city elections, the party pushed the black movement from an emphasis on targeting urban bureaucracies to one addressed to the Oakland polity as a whole.

THE RETURN OF THE REPRESSED: THE BLACK PANTHERS

At the start of the 1970s, the Black Panther Party hardly seemed to be in any position to lead a mass electoral mobilization. In September 1968, Huey Newton was found guilty of voluntary manslaughter in the death of Officer John Frey and sentenced to two to fifteen years in prison. Supporters were buoyed that Newton had escaped the death penalty, but in November of that year Eldridge Cleaver fled the country to avoid returning to jail for his involvement in the April 6, 1968, shootout with Oakland police. Federal and local police harassment and infiltration further disrupted the organization, and from 1969 to 1971 the party experienced a series of deadly struggles with police, with rival groups like the Los Angeles–based US organization, and internally with opposing factions associated with Newton and Cleaver. In March 1969, Bobby Seale was arrested for his role in the protests at the 1968 Democratic Party convention in Chicago, and two months later he was charged with ordering the murder of Panther member and suspected police informant Alex Rackley in New Haven, Connecticut. The charges against Seale in both cases were eventually dismissed, but the costs of these and dozens of other arrests and trials of members drained the party's resources. By the summer of 1970, in Newton's own assessment, the Black Panther Party was in a "shambles."[74]

Nevertheless, opinion polls showed that the Panthers had earned the respect of many African Americans for their militant resistance to racial injustice. In May 1970, the California Appeals Court reversed Newton's manslaughter conviction, and in August a crowd of ten thousand people gathered at the Alameda County Courthouse to greet him on his release.[75] Over the next year, Newton moved to rebuild the organization, developing its community "Survival" programs and recalling members from other chapters to create a "base of operations" in Oakland. By 1972, the Survival programs included free distributions of food and shoes, a free health-care clinic and screenings for sickle cell anemia, a Panther school for children, and free transportation for visitation of prisoners in California jails.[76]

These programs required resources, which the Panthers gained from book publishing, lecture fees, and donations from wealthy patrons. In addition, the Panthers used force to extract payments from drug dealers, pimps, and other illegal enterprises in the ghetto—a legacy of the party's links with its criminalized lumpen social base. As a nationalist movement, the party also sought to expand its influence in the black community, demanding that above-ground black small businesses also contribute to the Survival programs. Many did, but liquor store owner Bill Boyette, president of the California State Package Store and Tavern Owners Association, refused to cooperate on the Panthers' terms. Newton ordered a boycott and picket of Boyette's store on Grove Street that lasted for six months, while Boyette rallied support from an Ad Hoc Committee to Preserve Black Business in Oakland that enlisted some two hundred professionals and small business owners, the Interdenominational Ministerial Alliance, and members of the NAACP. Finally, in January 1972, Congressman Ron Dellums mediated a settlement in which Boyette and other businesses agreed to give to an independent charitable foundation that would donate to a range of organizations in addition to the Panthers. The boycott ended, but the conflict marked a repudiation by black businesses of the Panthers' bid for hegemony within the black community.[77]

Nonetheless, the Panthers continued to organize within the ghetto. On May 13, 1972, a year before the election, the party announced the candidacies of Seale for mayor and Elaine Brown for city councillor, at a rally of four thousand people in West Oakland. That August, ten party members ran for election to the West Oakland Model Cities board, winning six of the eighteen open seats.[78] Over the next ten months, Seale and Brown campaigned tirelessly in the flatland neighborhoods, riding city buses, standing outside workplaces and shopping centers, and speaking before small groups and religious congregations, trying to reach a larger audience. Running apart from the political mainstream, the Panthers relied on their own disciplined party cadre as well as young volunteers who engaged in door-to-door canvassing, phone banking, and voter registration. By the time of the city primary in April 1973, the Panthers claimed to have registered almost thirty-five thousand new voters.[79]

Brown later wrote, "Working black people were joining our constituent *lumpen*, as the so-called black middle class became more than a smattering of Survival Program supporters. Our campaign was one all of them could openly support." The Panther platform called for a radical redistributional agenda, including a 5 percent capital gains tax on transfers of income property and the property of large corporations, a one percent tax on intangible stocks and bonds, increased rental charges and fees at the Coliseum and city golf courses, and a residency requirement for police and firefighters, three-quarters of whom were said to live outside the city. Revenues from these and other changes were expected to help pay for development of a $4 million "multi-ethnic international trade and cultural center," and for $5 million in increased health, child care, and senior citizen services.[80]

Brown ran for the city council Second District seat against incumbent black moderate Joshua Rose, while Seale's main opponents in the primary were Mayor Reading and two other challengers: attorney John Sutter, a liberal white city councillor and the sole Oakland Coalition candidate elected in 1971; and black businessman Otho Green, owner of a successful job training and management consulting firm. Described as the "establishment" black candidate, Green was a participant in the Ad Hoc Committee to Preserve Black Business in Oakland, and was endorsed by the Black Caucus, the Interdenominational Ministerial Alliance, the Baptist Ministers' Union, and Democratic Party state legislators. Many black activists in Oakland backed Green, believing that Seale had no chance against an inevitable white backlash. Mayor Reading, in turn, exploited white fears, campaigning against Seale and spending a total of $163,000 on the race, with large contributions from donors like Steven Bechtel, Edgar Kaiser, World Airways, and the Southern Pacific.[81]

On primary day, the Panthers defied skeptics as Brown received thirty-four thousand votes or 33 percent of the total in losing to Rose. Seale won twenty-one thousand votes or 19 percent, second behind Reading but ahead of Green—enough votes to force a runoff on May 15. In the final, 71 percent of registered voters in Oakland cast ballots, the largest turnout for a regular municipal election in the city's history. Seale doubled his primary total to forty-three thousand votes, running strongly in the flatlands and winning 158 of 436 city precincts. That was no match, however, for the out-pouring for Reading in the hills; with turnouts in some areas as high as 85 percent, the mayor received more than seventy-seven thousand votes and a winning majority of 64 percent.[82]

Seale's loss disappointed his supporters, but the Panthers had succeeded in mobilizing a poor black electorate that neither Green nor any previous candidate had reached, and they demonstrated the disaffection with the regime that remained among the mass of the city's black population. Within a year, however, the Panthers' own internal organization began to fall apart, as the Survival programs were eclipsed by Newton's deepening drug ad-dictions and the party's violent underground activity. Newton arbitrarily expelled Seale and many other original party members, and he soon faced new criminal charges for the murder of a prostitute and the beating of a tai-lor. In August 1974, Newton jumped bail and fled to Cuba, leaving Brown as head of the party organization.

Brown maintained the Survival programs and ran for city councillor again in 1975, this time gaining 41 percent of the vote with support from liberal Democrats and middle-class black leaders including Green. In July 1977 Newton returned to face trial in Oakland, and although he avoided convic-tion on major charges, his volatile behavior and addictions grew worse, and thereafter the Black Panther Party rapidly disintegrated. Months before his return, however, the various black political factions joined with white lib-erals, labor unions, and Democratic Party politicians to back Judge Wilson in the 1977 mayoral election. With more than a hundred thousand dollars in campaign funds and grassroots outreach by the Black Panthers and other volunteers, Wilson defeated conservative white businessman David Tucker to become the first black mayor of Oakland. Black popular insurgency, how-ever, had already peaked: Even in his historic breakthrough victory, Wilson's winning total was more than a thousand votes less than the total Seale had received in losing in 1973.[83]

CONCLUSION:
THE ROOTS OF THE BLACK URBAN REGIME

Black political succession in Oakland followed a long and hard road. As Ru-fus Browning, Dale Rogers Marshall, and David Tabb have argued, regime change might have been expected to occur much sooner, based on the size of the black population and the percentage of Democratic Party voter registration in the city.[84] Browning, Marshall, and Tabb blame the intensity of protest in Oakland for the failure to form a moderate biracial electoral coalition, but the actors allied in the old regime were extraordinarily resistant to any substantive reform, as we have seen. Major private and public employers were not particularly interested in hiring the unemployed black poor, and unions were unwilling to risk their position in the local labor market. On the issue of community relations with the police, the city council refused even to acknowledge any problem. Despite the availability of federal money and resources, entrenched local actors—not movement radicals or federal bureaucrats—effectively stymied pressures for reform.

The ongoing frustrations and mistrust between black leaders and city authorities led to the move toward community control. But the racial separatism implicit in that demand was less of a radical departure than it might seem. The insulated bureaucratic character of the regime already amounted to practically separate governments for white and black residents, Mayor Reading's assertions to the contrary notwithstanding. The interests of white business elites and middle-class homeowners were well ensconced in regional economic development bodies like the port and the BART and in the city council, while black residents were disproportionately subjected as clients to the regulatory power of the various social-service and criminal justice agencies. In the Model Cities negotiations, black activists attempted to turn this arrangement on its head, using their administrative authority under the federal program to establish a bargaining relationship with city hall. In the end, however, the city refused to deal with the WOPC, removing the port and the City Center from the project area boundaries and letting the program face the problems of the neighborhood on its own.

In the aftermath of the Model Cities negotiations, organizing for black power split into three directions. Radical nonviolent protest continued in the OEDCI and the Black Caucus, but it remained confined within the framework of the bureaucratic regime. Unable to spark or unite a larger mobilization, it lost much of its political leverage through changes in federal policy, and it came under increasing counterattack from state and local authorities. By 1972, the Black Panther Party had recovered sufficiently from government harassment and its own factional divisions, and had concentrated its resources in Oakland. Its grassroots electoral campaign reached thousands of poor and working-class blacks, bringing their voting power for the first time into the city's political arena. But the party never resolved the ambivalence of its own identity as both an armed nationalist resistance movement and a community-based human rights organization. Without the support of the black middle class, the Panthers never gained hegemony within the black community, and the nationalist project faltered. Despite the efforts of some leaders, after its electoral challenge the party failed to reconstitute itself on a new institutional political terrain. With Newton's descent into drug addiction, the Survival programs gradually declined, and the armed section fell into criminal violence against the party's own members.

As much as any other path, then, black power in Oakland followed the example of bureaucratic incorporation demonstrated by the Redevelopment Agency under John Williams.[85] Even before Wilson's mayoral election, Williams's strategies of alliance building and economic partnership had indicated the role that black community actors were to play in the remaking of the urban regime. A political moderate, Mayor Wilson acted as a mediator between groups, keeping his independence from the Black Caucus and drawing on his experience as the chair of the OEDC and his connections to the Oakland elite as a Superior Court judge. By the 1980s, Lionel Wilson's Oakland would come to exemplify the successes, and the limits, of the black urban movement in many American cities.[86]

8 From Social Movements to Social Change

Oakland and Twentieth-Century Urban America

Consider these sequences of events: Ku Klux Klan leaders victorious in local politics in the late '20s, only to be driven from office in a celebrated scandal just a few years later. One hundred thousand AFL union members on strike in 1946, followed by two bitterly contested municipal elections in 1947 and 1950. Shootouts between Black Panther Party members and police in the '60s, and Bobby Seale's surprising mayoral campaign in 1973, amid a long march toward racial equality for the urban black community. In the short span of about fifty years, the city of Oakland experienced at least three dramatic and radically different periods of mobilization, each of which was accompanied by widespread polarization and a crisis in the urban polity. Whatever the reasons for their discontinuity, one would think these events would be etched in the city's history, remembered as formative moments in its political development.

At roughly the same time as the third period, in the '60s and '70s, a team of political scientists from the nearby University of California campus in Berkeley undertook a major study of Oakland politics, known as the Oakland Project. Under the direction of Professor Aaron Wildavsky, individual researchers spent approximately two years working part-time with a variety of city agencies. Yet Wildavsky and his colleagues claimed to find scarcely any traces of popular mobilization, commenting instead on the "'non-group, non-political' nature of Oakland's social environment."[1] "Oakland as a city does not exist; it is a collection of neighborhoods without community," wrote project member Arnold Meltsner in 1971. "The usual grand drama of political scientists, the electoral battles for office, the conflict of interests and groups, and the disparities between men [sic] who seek power and men who have it is muted in a melange of separate public arenas and private concerns."[2]

Could this possibly be the same city? What about all the events of collective action that have been described here, those that had gone before and those that were still happening even at the time? I do not believe that the Oakland Project investigators were simply myopic, nor were they alone in their view. A few years later, political scientist Paul Peterson asserted that *all* local urban politics were essentially "issueless" and "groupless," while sociologist Paul Starr, contemplating the decline of urban protest activity in the '70s, wondered what had become of the "dozens of 'mass mobilizations' and ghetto riots of the 1960s that left so light a trace on the body politic."[3] Was each movement really so invisible or irrelevant? How could such episodes of intense conflict occur and then be so difficult to discern?

At the beginning of this book, I asked what explained the historical discontinuity separating the three social movements in Oakland. In this concluding chapter, I return to this question, as a problem for sociology and for American urban political history. In the first section, I recap the actors and events in Oakland, highlighting the relationship of social movements and urban political community. I argue that it is precisely the weakness or fragmentation of urban civil society that constrains movements from engaging other actors, leading them back to institutional politics and resulting in discontinuity. I consider the implications of this case study for contemporary social movement theory, and its comparative value for understanding race, class, and urban development in other American cities in the twentieth century. Finally, I reflect on changes in Oakland and in the nation since the 1980s, and on their significance for concerns about community and politics in the United States today.

COLLECTIVE ACTORS AND THE STRUGGLE FOR COMMUNITY

The theoretical framework guiding this study emphasizes three dimensions: socioeconomic structure, political institutions, and civil society. In this framework, structural forces produce systemic inequalities and the social bases of groups, allowing us to track the fate of broad categories of persons across periods of institutional change. Similarly, the politics of urban regimes links the institutions of the local state with its constituent groups, shaping the interests and opportunities in the polity, as well as its boundaries of inclusion and exclusion. Finally, group formation and collective identity emerge from stratified relations of association in civil society, grounded in the "micromobilization contexts," "submerged networks," and everyday interactions found in workplaces, neighborhoods, and other social spaces.[4]

Collective actors form out of sequences of development across all three dimensions. Within a particular structural context, groups are constituted as collective agents in historical conjunctures that register their internal formation and their relation to one another. In Oakland, the system of public franchises at the turn of the century gave birth to a powerful corporate elite, directing large enterprises that employed an immigrant working class on the railroads, waterworks, and transit companies. The latter built up group solidarity through institutions like the ethnic neighborhood, the saloon, and the Catholic Church. At the same time, urban economic growth permitted the rise of a downtown merchant class and its commercial associations, along with a new white middle class, brought together in its own neighborhood clubs, homeowners groups, and secret fraternal societies. The proliferation of these ties in East Oakland and other areas formed the medium for the development of social movement actors, including the Ku Klux Klan.

Meanwhile, organized labor moved from its origins in craft labor market segments through its defeat in the '20s to its reconstitution in the '30s and '40s. Unions provided a vehicle for myriad groups of workers to act collectively and gain resources and a degree of control over their work, on the job and in the urban economy. Finally, black migration during and after World War II stimulated the corresponding increase and transformation of the social infrastructure in the black community. In the '50s and '60s, a generation of black middle-class leadership grew out of their association in groups like Men of Tomorrow, black law firms, and the traditional civil rights organizations, while black ghetto residents organized in neighborhood associations in West Oakland and elsewhere.

Collective actors, however, are not simply the products of their historical context. They are also *producers* who exercise historical agency in at least two ways. First, elite actors build regimes. Through self-reinforcing relations of formal and informal coordination, regimes forge exclusive links between the state and civil society, facilitating the pursuit of urban economic projects and sustaining their member groups' continued formation as actors. Under the patronage regime, the franchise corporations dominated the city's development and regulated their labor force with the aid of political brokers in the ethnic machine. The managerial regime achieved a commercial-class alliance of large and small business, middle-class consumers, and residential property owners, removing the executive direction of local economic functions from democratic politics while assuring social and material standards in white suburban neighborhoods. In the postwar period, the redevelopment regime attempted to re-create this alliance through regional metropolitanism with downtown as its core, incorporating white workers in the pattern of middle-class suburbanization and containing the rising black population through bureaucratic agencies of social control.

Successful regimes coordinate action and reproduce themselves and their members' interests, but they also sharply limit the opportunities for substantive political participation. Outside the regime's boundaries, subordinate and excluded groups must develop their own resources and identities on the multilayered field of civil society. These processes sometimes take shape as urban social movements, a second mode of historical agency. The trajectories of challenging group formation "collide" with the principles of organization embedded in regimes, thereby defining the historical stakes involved in moments of collective action. Following the path of Protestant middle-class reformers, the Klan in the '20s attacked the institutions of ethnic working-class formation—the machine, the saloon, and the Catholic Church—while the downtown merchants declared their independence from the old corporate elite, renouncing patronage for a more aggressive business discipline. Dispossessed of their ethnic niches with the death of the old machine, workers pressed toward class solidarity in the '30s and '40s, mobilizing against the coercive authority of the new economic elite. In the '60s, African Americans fought against racially discriminatory housing and labor markets, enforced by public bureaucracies and the repressive powers of the police.

These challenges became meaningful because they either occurred alongside or provoked conjunctural crises that interfered with the regime's mechanisms of reproduction.[5] The reformism of the '20s threatened the machine by depriving it of resources essential for patronage. Perhaps not so surprisingly, Mike Kelly was more willing to compromise with the Klan, as long as they acted like a traditional political faction, than with his true rivals, the business reformers and J. R. Knowland. In the '30s, the insurgent CIO unions challenged the employers' unilateral control of the local economy, and in the postwar era the AFL Central Labor Council clashed with the downtown elite's dominance of city government. Later, the growing concentration of the African American poor collided with both the commercial redevelopment of the city center and the homogeneity of adjacent white neighborhoods. Local public-welfare agencies at first tried to manage the problems of racial transition, while conservative interests in the city council supported police enforcement of the racial status quo. In the federal urban renewal and poverty programs, black protest gradually circumvented and politicized the institutions of bureaucratic social control, undermining the regime unity of downtown business and white residents.

In each case, challenging actors articulated alternative visions of urban politics and development. The Klan sought to impose a culturally and racially homogeneous polity, reflecting an idealized image of the suburban neighborhoods where its supporters lived. The resurgent labor movement appealed to workers across ethnic lines and backed social-democratic policies like public housing, both before and after the war. The black movement advanced goals of civil rights and equal opportunity in jobs and housing regardless of race. In their respective sequences of mobilization, we can trace key events that identify the crossroads where these challenges were engaged in public space. The victories of Klansmen Burton Becker and William Parker in the elections of 1926 and 1927 affirmed the power of their constituency and the popular support for their issues, notwithstanding the Klan's own internal failings. The strikes of the warehouse and cannery workers in 1936 and the clerks in 1937 tested the organizational limits of class unity in the labor movement, just as the General Strike in 1946 and the election of 1947 showed its capacity for solidarity. Urban economic and social programs furnished the institutional venues where black resistance to racial discrimination gained public attention, while the negotiations over the police review board and the Model Cities program charted the path toward racial polarization, foreshadowing the uprisings of the Black Panther Party in the streets and at the ballot box.

In these moments of struggle, movements make strong claims for alternative imaginings of urban political community, conceptions that go beyond the exclusive linkages between state and civil society organized in the regime. Challengers do not (and cannot) simply compete for the limited political space within the regime but must go outside it, to deprivatize and disrupt established relations of power, expand the public arena, and create new space for political action. In their electoral campaigns, Becker and Parker drew on an active middle-class civic sphere that had developed apart from and opposed to the limited hierarchy of group access and privilege in the ethnic machine. The Klan leaders' subsequent failure in office occurred precisely because they embraced the old rules of machine politics, allowing the downtown reformers to steal their political fire and absorb their middle-class support. In the '30s, the managerial regime effectively suppressed labor insurgency by incorporating selected "machine union" leaders into its narrow governing circle. By the '40s, however, these ties had little meaning for the masses of workers brought together during the war, who rallied behind the newly militant AFL Central Labor Council leaders in their battle against the business elite. And as African Americans became an ever larger proportion of the local population, black organizers sidestepped the closed arena of the city council for the political opportunities presented by the federal programs, breaking through the redevelopment regime's administrative insulation to make racial inequality a compelling general public concern.

In these events, we might say that challenging actors make not only themselves but also the stage on which they must act. The disruption of the exclusionary spaces of established power is a precondition for the strategic pursuit of movement goals. Hence, for social movements the logic of historical agency is *different* than it is for actors in normal politics, relying instead on reactive sequences of disorder and reconfiguration. The entry of challenging groups into the polity is never simply assimilative, but rather calls into question the content of the political community.

Objectively, the images of community that challengers invoke are *prospective*, not retrospective, regardless of the rhetoric that movement actors themselves use. The vitality of the Klan movement sprang from a new, rising white middle class, centered in recently settled East Oakland. There, the Klan appeared as a progressive force fighting for a new institutional order, against the values of the older community in West Oakland. In the General Strike, Central Labor Council lawyer James Galliano may have insisted that Oakland unions and employers had "always settled our labor disputes within our own backyard," but in fact whatever stable labor relations existed were of recent origin, and certainly did not include the open-shop era of the '20s. Finally, the postwar migrant black generation and their children looked forward to a future of racial equality in their adopted home, not backward to a racist past, whether in the South or on the margins of prewar Oakland society.

These attempts to reconstitute political community are key to understanding the problem of discontinuity. Movement challenges create critical choice points where actors try to bridge conjunctural processes of group formation and institutional development in a common public space. But this common political space is highly fragile, and all too often the center does not hold: More powerful actors simply withdraw, relations of power are reprivatized, and there is not enough civic solidarity to the keep the actors onstage or in dialogue with one another. The difficulty of maintaining political engagement drives movement organizers to seek permanent gains through institutional means. This leads challengers back to those who possess institutional resources, and to the political terrain of regime making. In the end, the process contributes to the demobilization of collective action and the diminution of the public sphere.

Thus, the Klan's vigilantism conspicuously failed to impose on the Oakland polity a cultural morality that even its own leaders could not uphold. If the issues in the 1926 and 1927 elections conveyed the image of community that white middle classes wanted, however, then ultimately that is much of what they got: Following the downtown merchants, they succeeded in eliminating the machine and gaining protection for their homogeneous suburban lifestyle. If the Protestant reformers could not change the character of West Oakland, white homeowners could still withdraw to the security of their own neighborhoods, and in so doing they set the norm of residential social mobility for the groups that followed.

The radical labor movement did not succeed in establishing urban social democracy in Oakland. As the street solidarity of the General Strike passed into the coalition politics of the Oakland Voters' League and then the institutional constraints of the city council, the opportunities to build a path of biracial urban working-class formation were splintered and dispersed. The 1950 recall election marked the decisive break in the popular class alliance. Unable to lead a broader shift in public policy, the unions consolidated their base in the private economic arena of collective bargaining with employers. Meanwhile, control over the pattern of urban growth shifted to the emerging metropolitan alliance of downtown businesses, regional economic and political elites, suburban housing developers, and middle-class residents.

Under the redevelopment regime, African Americans were initially viewed as a "social problem" to be regulated by expanded layers of bureaucratic administration. In their mobilizations against urban renewal, unemployment, discrimination, and poverty, black Oaklanders rejected their status as bureaucratic clients and sought recognition as citizens with an equal voice in local political life. Even the West Oakland Planning Committee's radical demands for ghetto community control, as Judith May argues, presupposed a bargaining relationship with the city government and an identification with the growth of the city as a whole.[6] But black activists likewise faced an inability to compel other actors to confront racial inequality or maintain their loyalty to the city. The flight of both investment capital and white residents left the subsequent black mayoral administrations searching for resources in whatever partnerships they could find.

From moments of intense collective action and public engagement, Oakland's political community reverted to the "melange of separate public arenas and private concerns" that make up the normal politics that Arnold Meltsner saw. Fragmented by enduring structural inequalities and uneven paths of institutional development, urban civil society proved too weak to keep opposing groups present together in a shared public sphere. Without a strong citywide civic community to recognize or adjudicate their claims, movement actors turned to institutional political channels. The memory of past junctures was preserved, if at all, in particular organizational contexts, within unions, community groups, or networks of activists, but not as part of a broader political culture.

Institutionalization, however, was itself no guarantee of permanent group incorporation. All dominant coalitions were ultimately mortal; mechanisms of regime reproduction failed as place-based elites fell apart, moved elsewhere, or lost their linkages with wider economic and political structures. Political power did not ensure group longevity in the polity: The franchise corporations lost their monopolies, ethnic group loyalties faded, the downtown merchants became isolated in the '40s and eventually disintegrated in the '70s, white middle classes moved out of East Oakland to the farther suburbs. Urban development projects carried the seeds of their own destruction by reinforcing or aggravating conflicts between member and challenger groups.

These conflicts highlight the limits of both urban civil society *and* the local state. In each period, regime stability rested on the *nonparticipation* of most groups in the polity. The hegemony of the dominant elites was based more on the practical difficulty of forging alternatives than on any strong civic consensus—hence the repeated outbreak of polarization. The outcomes of struggle reveal no evolutionary progression or assimilative dynamic between movements, no simple compartmentalization of ethnicity in the '20s, class in the '40s, and race in the '60s. Instead, we see the successive mobilization and demobilization of identities expressing recurrent class, racial, and group tensions that appear in different combinations throughout the era. Defeated in the '20s, the labor movement rebounded in the '30s; invisible to most whites in 1950, race became the central axis of conflict in the '60s.

Finally, discontinuity shows that political boundaries and identities are not fixed. As tensions between structural and conjunctural paths continue to occur, new or reconfigured identities appear, from groups affected by other dimensions of exclusion. Social movement actors are crucial to these processes of political innovation, mobilizing collective actors in new and different ways and transforming the terrain between the polity and society. The narrative analytic framework captures these multiple paths of formation without either reifying actors as organic, suprahistorical cultural subjects or reducing them to a single attribute of class, race, or other structural category.

OAKLAND AND AMERICAN URBAN POLITICAL HISTORY

Not every city in America was like Oakland. Elsewhere, the exact lineup of actors varied, polarization was perhaps less pronounced, movements had more or less success. But the theoretical model I have applied here provides criteria for a comparative analysis with urban contexts in other parts of the United States. Again, the model emphasizes, first, the socioeconomic structural makeup of the urban setting, its composition and internal stratification, and its relation to larger spatial and temporal structures. Oakland had its own unique patterns of industrial development and population flows; for example, manufacturing never reached the concentration found in many northeastern or midwestern cities, and the mass migration of African Americans occurred primarily after 1940. These patterns affected the social bases of groups and hence the conditions for collective action: The CIO remained a smaller force in the local labor movement, black protest was sharply limited before World War II. Attention to social structure not only helps explain the context for mobilization, it also crucially underscores the fate of contending groups even after a cycle of protest has subsided. As we have seen, while the Klan as an organization may have failed, this by no means spelled the end of its white middle-class base.

Second, the framework highlights the links among formal political institutions, informal governing coalitions, and policies of urban development. Regime building in Oakland shared several features with other cities in the region. In her study of eight large southwestern cities, Amy Bridges found that, along with business and real-estate interests, white middle classes were a core constituency of reform coalitions, favoring restricted electoral participation, low taxes, "frugal and sparing" government, and economic growth.[7] Like Oakland, many of these cities experimented with commission charters prior to their adoption of city-manager systems, and in Phoenix, San Diego, and Albuquerque, middle-class homeowners also successfully resisted the introduction of low-income or public housing. But a crucial mechanism of regime reproduction for Bridges's cities—territorial annexation of new subdivisions—was unavailable in Oakland, which was effectively landlocked after 1909. Unable simply to extend the city's periphery and anchored in the city center, postwar elites in Oakland pursued more disruptive policies of land-use restructuring in downtown urban renewal.

Machine politics also lasted longer in many northern and midwestern cities, managing class relations and racial transition in different ways. In New York and Chicago, as John Mollenkopf and William Grimshaw each have demonstrated, black political insurgency was divided by a legacy of partial incorporation into systems of ethnic patronage.[8] But, as Steven Erie argues, such patronage was hardly democratic; machines themselves remained hierarchical and exclusionary, constrained by limited resources and their own supporters' changing demands.[9] Those that survived after World War II ultimately embraced white homeowners and redeveloping elites, as in Chicago—where, Arnold Hirsch has shown, the Daley machine accommodated both groups by relocating displaced black residents in massive high-rise projects built within the confines of the ghetto.[10]

In the South, other institutional arrangements prevailed. In Clarence Stone's Atlanta, a strong corporate elite negotiated an accord with moderate leaders of the growing black community to preserve control of the city. Black voters supported a 1951 annexation plan that kept the wealthy white northern suburbs within city limits while adding undeveloped territory for black residential expansion on the south and west sides. Local government took the lead in opening the area to black settlement with new public-housing projects, thereby diverting black population growth away from the central business district and from white neighborhoods. The system offered benefits for black contractors, financial institutions, and entrepreneurs, and it solidified an informal understanding between white and black business leaders as participants in the urban regime.[11]

The paths of group formation in civil society form the third analytical dimension in this study. Everywhere, ethnicity declined for European American groups, as new immigration fell off and middle and then working classes left behind the cultural institutions embedded in their old neighborhoods. The change involved a reconstruction of racial and class identity for groups and for urban areas. The rise of East Oakland as a suburban "white" middle-class area in the '20s contributed to disinvestment in ethnically mixed West Oakland, well before the mass influx of African Americans in the '40s. These urban outcomes affected the paths of working-class formation as well. In the workplace, Oakland workers organized strong, militant unions, achieving greater power than in many other Sunbelt cities. They did not, however, succeed in implementing a form of social-democratic community development—unlike for example New York, with its tradition of union-sponsored cooperative housing described by Joshua Freeman. In this way, Oakland more closely resembled the experience of Detroit—where, as Thomas Sugrue shows, even the powerful United Auto Workers union could not overcome white homeowners' resistance to public housing and racial integration.[12]

The comparative dimensions of socioeconomic structure, political institutions, and civil society are important not as objective variables but as contexts for historical sequences of actor formation and interaction. In cities across America, movement actors emerged and confronted established forms of power, contesting the terms and spaces of political community. The outcomes of these interactions were forged in critical junctures that varied in different locales. Yet in Oakland as elsewhere, local conflicts developed from common structural tensions of urban class and racial inequality.

OAKLAND SINCE 1980:
THE RISE AND FALL OF THE BLACK REGIME

These tensions have continued to define the paths of Oakland politics. The election of Lionel Wilson as mayor in 1977 ushered in an era of what political scientist Adolph Reed has called the black urban regime.[13] Under Wilson, minorities were named to key positions in city government, and by 1980 a majority of the members on the port, planning, and civil service commissions were black, Hispanic, or Asian American. In 1980, voters passed a charter amendment establishing district elections for city councillors, and within three years black candidates had won five of nine council seats.[14]

Electoral entry led to substantive changes in public policy. Mayor Wilson negotiated a compromise with the police department that established a citizens' review board, addressing a long-standing grievance within the black community. He strengthened affirmative action in city hiring, and by 1986, 39 percent of Oakland police officers were minorities, and 23 percent were black. In 1979, the city revised its bidding system to allow greater opportunities for minority businesses, and within three years minority vendors had increased their share of city purchases from 6 to 22 percent. By 1993, African Americans made up more than 40 percent of city government employees, up from only 15 percent in 1969, and roughly at parity with their share of the 1990 voting-age population.[15]

Once in office, however, the Wilson administration looked out on a changed local economic and political landscape. By the '70s, the pillars of the old downtown elite had collapsed. Henry Kaiser retired from Oakland years earlier and then passed away in 1967, and within a decade his Kaiser Industries was broken up and control passed into the hands of outside interests. Under William Knowland, the *Oakland Tribune* had suffered a steady decline, as subscribers and advertisers increasingly moved to the suburbs. Plagued by failures in politics, business, and his personal life, Knowland committed suicide in 1974, and a few years later the *Tribune* was sold to a Phoenix-based corporation and then absorbed by a national chain. Executives from the Oakland-based Clorox Corporation and Safeway Stores inherited the mantle of local business leadership, but they had neither the political resources nor the inclination to play the part that the former elites once had.[16]

As the older business elite fell away, so did much of the conservative white middle class. The flight to the suburbs continued: Between 1970 and 1990 Oakland's white population declined absolutely by more than ninety thousand people.[17] Nevertheless, the surrounding sea of suburban conservatism remained a powerful force in Oakland politics. In June 1978, California voters passed Proposition 13, which radically limited the ability of city governments to raise property taxes. In its first year Proposition 13 cut the city's resources by more than $14 million, causing service reductions, closures of facilities, and layoffs of city employees.[18] The fiscal constraints imposed on local governments made any substantive redistributional agenda more difficult and reinforced public dependence on private investment in the city.

Seeking new development, Mayor Wilson allied himself with white business interests and embraced the downtown City Center renewal project, hoping to transfer resources to the black community through the strategy of minority equity participation pioneered by Oakland Redevelopment Agency chief John Williams. At the same time, the mayor renounced many of his white liberal allies and deemphasized electoral mobilization in the ghetto, relying instead on the power of his incumbency to win two more four-year terms.[19] The regime's development strategy was hampered, however, by the reluctance of its intended coalition partners, and in particular by the virtual disappearance of the once-powerful downtown retail sector. By the '80s, major retail stores were rapidly leaving the central city for the suburban malls: In 1977, Oakland's central business district could still boast seven department stores; ten years later, there were only four across the entire city.[20]

The administration managed to see through the completion of a new hotel and convention hall in the City Center, but an adjacent shopping mall was scrapped when Macy's and other prospective tenants declined to participate, and the project was reduced to a more modest plaza of small shops and restaurants. Later, the Bechtel Corporation withdrew from a plan to build a pair of high-rises in the area, and further delays occurred as developers balked at requirements for 8 percent equity stakes for minority groups.[21] Other ambitious designs for downtown also failed to materialize. In 1985, the city contracted with the Rouse Company for a colossal $350 million regional retail center, with office buildings, residences, and a multilevel mall anchored by as many as five department stores. Again the developers were unable to secure tenants, and the deal broke down amid demands for a massive public subsidy. Finally, in 1984 the former Kahn's department store, symbol of downtown's commercial grandeur and site of the historic 1946 General Strike, at last closed its doors, after several ownership changes. Developer Myron Zimmerman took over the structure and spent $30 million of a projected $55 million for renovations before ultimately going bankrupt. For years afterward, the still-unfinished building lay boarded-up and vacant in the heart of downtown Oakland.[22]

As the city searched for new investors, at least one developer admitted that big retailers had to be convinced that Oakland's racial composition was not a "stumbling block" to its market potential.[23] In a further reversal of the growth politics of the '60s, in 1982 Al Davis, the owner of the Oakland Raiders professional football team, abandoned the Oakland–Alameda County Coliseum and relocated the team to Los Angeles. The city spent millions of dollars in unsuccessful litigation to prevent the move, and in 1989, Mayor Wilson backed a proposal to lure the Raiders back with a generous expenditure of public funds. Strong disapproval from Oakland citizens scuttled the plan, however, and the following year, after twelve years in office, Wilson lost his bid for a fourth mayoral term in the 1990 primary election.[24]

Wilson was defeated by Elihu Harris, a twelve-year veteran state legislator and member of the black political elite. Like Wilson, Mayor Harris also pursued efforts to attract downtown development. Oakland leaders used their political clout to win construction of several major government office buildings, including the $191 million, twin-tower Federal Building, initiated under Wilson and opened in 1993; and a $97 million, twenty-two-story state administrative complex named for Harris himself. The concentration of government agencies helped sustain the city's economy, as 30 percent of all public-sector employment in Alameda County (including federal, state, and county workers) was located in Oakland, together providing more than thirty-five thousand jobs.[25]

Yet private capital remained resistant, and average vacancy rates in downtown Oakland hovered around 15 percent through the mid '90s. In 1995, the city embarked on a plan to develop an entertainment district near the old Fox Theater on Telegraph Avenue, but two years later the city council voted to kill the project when the developers asked the city to pay $35 million of the estimated $83 million cost.[26] The city government was not alone in its disappointments: The port of Oakland also ventured into real-estate development, spending $100 million on a waterfront complex of retail, office space, and restaurants known as Jack London Square. Completed in 1990, much of the project's ninety-eight thousand square feet of retail space initially went unoccupied, costing the port $200,000 a month when it first opened.[27]

Despite these setbacks, the black urban regime succeeded in opening up the city's political institutions, creating a space for the flourishing of a black middle class. From 1970 to 1990, the number of black professionals and managers in Oakland more than tripled in size, rising from 11 percent to 23 percent of the black employed population.[28] By 1983, Mayor Wilson governed alongside a black majority on both the city council and the school board, and black professionals served as city manager, city attorney, city clerk, city planning director, and director of economic development. That year, the transformation of Oakland's civic sphere was epitomized when Robert Maynard, the African American editor and publisher at the *Oakland Tribune*, purchased the newspaper once owned by J. R. Knowland.[29]

For poor and working-class blacks, however, the regime had fewer resources to offer. Opportunities in Oakland's blue-collar economy continued to shrink: Between 1981 and 1988, the city lost a combined twelve thousand jobs in its traditional manufacturing, transportation, communications, and utility industries. Unemployment stood at 9.5 percent in Oakland in 1990, but for black workers the rate was 14.5 percent, and in areas like West Oakland it ran closer to 20 percent. Nearly 23 percent of black families in the city lived below the poverty line in 1989, approximately the same percentage as ten years earlier. And according to a 1992 report, *every* census tract in East Oakland (and many in North and West Oakland) was designated by the U.S. Department of Health and Human Services as medically underserved, based on the prevalence of poverty, infant mortality rates, and the shortage of primary-care physicians.[30]

These conditions left low-income black neighborhoods especially vulnerable to the rising epidemic of drugs and crime, and notorious gang lords like Felix Mitchell emerged as powerful figures in the ghetto. Mitchell's 69 Mob operated out of the San Antonio public housing project on Sixty-ninth Avenue in East Oakland, netting as much as twenty thousand dollars a day in heroin and cocaine sales. Mitchell was only thirty-two when he was stabbed to death in prison in 1986; his funeral in Oakland featured a horse-drawn hearse carrying his bronze casket, followed by a three-block-long cortege of Rolls Royces, Cadillacs, and other vehicles, in a gaudy parade through the city's streets.[31] After Mitchell's demise, other gangs rose quickly to take his place, among them Milton "Mickey" Moore's Family and Harvey Whisenton's Funktown organization. Black youths were swept into the lucrative drug business and criminal subculture; members of Funktown were as young as fifteen years old, and even younger juveniles participated as small dealers, lookouts, or runners. Already in 1983 Oakland had witnessed more than 100 murders annually, but the violence escalated as the crack epidemic spread and the drug trade became more chaotic, driving the homicide rate to 175 per year in 1992, an average of one killing nearly every other day in a city of less than 375,000 people.[32] The plague of drugs and violence was devastating to ghetto communities and overwhelmed much of the legacy of radical political mobilization from the '60s. That contrast was brutally acted out on the morning of August 22, 1989, when Black Panther Party founder Huey Newton, long addicted to crack cocaine, was finally shot and killed by a petty drug dealer in a dispute on the streets of West Oakland.[33]

Although low-income neighborhoods bore the brunt of crime, it added to what downtown interests politely called Oakland's "image problem"— namely, its perception as a dangerous black city. In fact, with the arrival of the '90s boom economy, the number of homicides dropped steadily after 1992, reaching a thirty-year low in the city by 1999.[34] Meanwhile, other signs of structural change were also beginning to appear. The number of white residents continued to decline through the '80s, but black population growth slowed as well, as many black families also began to move to the suburbs.[35] In their place came an influx of new immigrant groups from Asia and Latin America. The proportion of Oakland residents identified as Asian/Pacific Islander and Hispanic or Latino jumped from approximately 8 and 9 percent, respectively, in 1980, to nearly 16 and 22 percent in 2000. The effects of these trends could be seen in the public schools: In 1990, 31 percent of Oakland School District students spoke a primary language other than English. By the end of the '90s, the student population in the district was approximately half black, one-quarter Latino, 17 percent Asian, and 6 percent white.[36] Oakland schools had struggled for years with a lack of resources, administrative problems, and debates over curriculum, but now the groups involved were no longer simply black and white.

As it entered its second decade, the Oakland black urban regime endured another series of immediate crises. In October 1989, the Loma Prieta earthquake shook the Bay Area, causing extensive damage in Oakland and other cities. In West Oakland the elevated Cypress Freeway, a monument of postwar urban planning, collapsed, killing 42 people. The quake also destroyed more than a thousand housing units in the city and fractured many older buildings downtown, halting development plans and requiring seismic repairs for City Hall, the Tribune Tower, and Kahn's, among others. In 1991, a wildfire broke out in the Berkeley-Oakland Hills, and for three days the fire burned, killing twenty-five people and destroying more than thirty-eight hundred houses and apartments.[37] Finally, beginning in 1993, the federal government announced it would close most of its military bases in the Bay Area, including the Alameda Naval Air Station, the Naval Supply Center, the Oakland Naval Hospital, and the Oakland Army Base. Projected impacts of these closures in Oakland included the loss of more than twelve thousand military and six thousand civilian jobs.[38]

The regime faced each of these challenges in turn, yet altogether it appeared to lose focus. Oakland seemed to be falling behind the economic prosperity of the region, its importance as a central city eclipsed by the fast-growing suburbs. The change was underscored in 1992 when *Oakland Tribune* owner Robert Maynard, in failing health, sold the financially strapped newspaper to the suburban-based Alameda Newspaper Group.[39] Anxious to regain the spotlight, Oakland leaders seized on a chance to bring the Raiders football team back to Oakland. In 1995, city and county officials approved a $225 million bond issue to pay for improvements to the Coliseum stadium, including construction of 125 luxury box suites and two private clubs, as well as $63 million in cash guarantees and loans to the Raiders. Public officials expected to finance the deal without raising taxes, through the sale of personal seat licenses that gave fans the right to purchase season tickets for a period of ten years. But the arrangement proved to be a fiscal disaster: Sales of tickets and seat licenses (which cost from $250 to $4,000) lagged, while corporate buyers failed to put up money for the luxury suites. By 1997, taxpayers were left facing annual public subsidies of $15 million to $20 million to cover the shortfall, with no easy solution in sight.[40]

The regime's difficulties came to a head in 1998. When Mayor Harris declined to run for a third term, no fewer than five black candidates mounted legitimate campaigns, revealing the fragmentation within the African American political community. In 1998, however, all other mayoral hopefuls stood in the shadow of Edmund G. "Jerry" Brown. The former California governor and three-time presidential candidate had moved to Oakland in 1994, setting up in a loft apartment near Jack London Square and entering into local issues with his We the People foundation. Despite his unorthodox political reputation, Brown's mayoral campaign was surprisingly low-key, centered on neighborhood visits, house meetings, and vague promises of better schools, less crime, and more economic growth. Elsewhere, black mayors had already given way to white successors, but in Oakland Brown won support from both black and white voters. Older residents remembered the liberal civil rights and social-democratic policies of his father, former governor "Pat" Brown, while black political leaders recalled Jerry Brown's own record as governor, including his appointment of black judges like Clinton White, Don McCullum, Allen Broussard, and others. Many Oakland residents were ready for change, wanting an end to the failed development schemes, the neglect of the neighborhoods, and the frustrations in the schools. Brown easily used his celebrity status to focus media attention and gain recognition for the city, promising to be the "voice of Oakland" in a reinvigorated urban public sphere.[41]

In the June 2 primary, Brown beat all of the other candidates combined, winning election outright with a 59 percent majority, sweeping every precinct in the city except two and rolling up totals of 42 to 57 percent in the black flatland districts.[42] Riding the wave of his popularity, Brown immediately pushed through a series of landmark political reforms of Oakland government. Even before the primary vote, he sponsored a strong-mayor charter-reform petition for the November ballot. Similar initiatives had lost under Mayors Wilson and Harris, but Brown's version won by a landslide, making the mayor's office an executive position with sole administrative authority over the city manager.[43]

Once in office, Brown moved swiftly to name a new police chief and a majority of the members of the Port Commission.[44] He also formed a special education task force that proposed replacing the independently elected school board with mayoral appointees and cast the tie-breaking vote on the city council to place a compromise measure on the ballot, allowing him to select three members in addition to the seven elected officers on the board. Despite opposition from the incumbent school board, the teachers' union, and the NAACP, voters narrowly passed the measure in March 2000, with support concentrated in majority white neighborhoods in the Oakland hills.[45]

Brown's victory as mayor marked the end of the black political regime of the '80s and '90s in Oakland. By June 1999, only two black representatives remained on the eight-member city council and the then seven-member school board.[46] If Brown's political reforms have changed the organization of local government, however, they have not in themselves succeeded in constituting a new regime. Perhaps the most controversial part of Brown's agenda is his "10K" program, intended to boost downtown development by attracting ten thousand new residents to live within the area. Setting a target of 6,600 new housing units within four years, Brown offered Oakland as a haven to private developers fleeing overbuilt conditions in San Francisco and promised to expedite approval for market-rate apartments and condominiums built without city subsidies or requirements for affordable housing. In October 1999, the city announced plans for 610 new market-rate units, ranging in price from $155,000 to $316,000, in four projects, including a 12-story condo complex on the site of the old Housewives Market and a 22-story luxury apartment building on Lake Merritt.[47] In February 2000, the city began negotiations for its largest project, a $500 million design to build 2,000 new apartments and condos on 14 acres across eight parcels between Telegraph and San Pablo Avenues below Twenty-first Street. By January 2001, 113 new downtown housing units had been completed under Brown's administration, with another 1,119 under construction and some 3,000 more in the planning process.[48]

Brown's policy shift came as the Bay Area's Internet and technology boom made Oakland increasingly attractive for commercial real-estate investors. By 1999, rehabilitation efforts were again under way at Kahn's (now renamed the Rotunda Building) and the Tribune Tower, aided by more than $13 million in city-funded grants and loans.[49] The following year, construction started on a new twenty-story office building near City Center, and plans were announced for a twenty-six-story office and residential tower at Broadway and Seventeenth Street.[50] In addition, the city council approved the sale of land for a 214-room downtown hotel, to be built in the renovated old Key System building on Broadway. Meanwhile, the port also announced a five-year, $200 million expansion of its Jack London Square area, to include a new hotel, retail spaces, and other attractions.[51]

Promotional statements for the 10K initiative invoked the memory of former Redevelopment Agency director John Williams, yet the program still more recalled the early '60s Corridor project under Williams's predecessor, Thomas Bell. City officials admitted that 10K was meant to attract new residents from the suburbs, not provide homes for the moderate-income hotel or service employees who worked downtown. At market rates, an estimated 80 percent of existing Oakland households would not be able to afford a two-bedroom unit in the new developments, yet few provisions were made to include more affordable units.[52] According to a city study, two out of five Oakland families had already been experiencing problems with housing costs when rents across the city suddenly soared. Average Oakland apartment rents increased by 65 percent from 1995 to 2000, with a one-year jump of between 17 and 32 percent in 1999 alone.[53] Complaints to the Oakland Housing and Residential Rent and Relocation Board in 2000 were three times the level they were in 1996, and even established nonprofit service agencies found themselves priced out of newly expensive office space downtown.[54]

The rapid changes in the real-estate market stirred widespread fears of gentrification and displacement of working-class and minority residents. As one local labor leader said, "Orinda [a wealthy white suburb in Contra Costa County] invaded Oakland." Indeed, for the first time in fifty years, the 2000 census showed an absolute increase in the city's white population.[55] Although some of Brown's longtime supporters were surprised by his neoliberal, prodeveloper stance, he merely replied, "In capitalism, capital counts, and as Mayor, I can't repeal that law."[56] But city government policies did affect the shape of the community, and as much as any other issue, the housing crisis provoked the question: Who belongs in Oakland?

Across the city, there were many groups prepared to answer that question. Despite structural and institutional change, Oakland remained heir to a rich and multilayered tradition of popular organization in civil society. In West Oakland, the legacy of community mobilization was renewed in the wake of the 1989 earthquake. Led by some of the same individuals who were active in the '60s, residents successfully mobilized to force the state to relocate the Cypress Freeway along disused rail lines away from the residential neighborhood, opening up a wide boulevard now renamed Mandela Parkway. While the area remains poverty-stricken and vulnerable to gentrification, West Oakland residents have been determined to shape the neighborhood's future, intervening in the public planning process for the reuse of the strategically located site of the former Oakland Army Base.[57]

In East Oakland, the Allen Temple Baptist Church has long served as an institutional anchor, from its home at Eighty-fifth Avenue and A Street in Elmhurst. Led by the Reverend Dr. J. Alfred Smith Sr., the church has grown to more than five thousand members, forming a bridge between its loyal middle-class black congregants who live in the hills or suburbs and the surrounding low-income black community. In the '70s, Smith worked with Black Panther Party members to organize voter registration for Lionel Wilson, and in 1981 he was elected to a term on the school board. Since then, Allen Temple has sponsored several federally subsidized housing developments in East Oakland for elderly, disabled, and HIV-positive residents, and it operates a credit union in the neighborhood. The church also provides an array of educational, social, and cultural services, including job counseling and legal assistance, a prison ministry, and cultural, arts, and youth programs. In line with changes in the area, it has recently added a Hispanic ministry and offers Spanish language courses to its English-speaking members.[58]

Latinos have become the largest ethnic group in the Fruitvale neighborhood, accounting for more than half the population in 2000.[59] Here, the Unity Council (founded in 1964 as the Spanish Speaking Unity Council) took the lead on several projects. In 1992 the council began working with concerned residents over a proposed parking structure at the local Bay Area Rapid Transit station. With the cooperation of the city and the BART, the group developed an alternative, integrated "transit village" plan, combining increased mass transit access with affordable housing, senior and child care centers, and a health clinic. In addition, the council has worked to help small businesses revive the local commercial district along East Fourteenth

Street, now renamed International Boulevard. In 1997, the council and other groups joined with the city and with planners from the University of California at Berkeley to explore the creation of a waterfront park and recreation area on a nine-acre site along the estuary known as Union Point. The collaborative process included multilingual outreach to solicit community participation in setting the goals and design for the project.[60]

Like the other flatland neighborhoods, the San Antonio district east of Lake Merritt has experienced economic and physical decline; at the same time, it exhibits a highly diverse ethnic makeup, in particular a growing immigrant Asian population. To confront the area's multiple needs, in 1995 the San Antonio Community Development Corporation convened a series of public meetings to produce a Lower San Antonio Neighborhood Plan, in partnership with the East Bay Asian Local Development Corporation (EBALDC). A nonprofit community development organization founded in 1975, EBALDC has developed more than five hundred units of affordable housing, as well as retail, office, and child care facilities. In San Antonio, the group helped organize an Eastlake Merchants Association and worked to bring local churches, community groups, and ethnic associations together with job training, child care, and other service agencies.[61]

These groups have brought new approaches to the kinds of activities typically pursued by community development corporations, such as affordable housing and neighborhood commercial revitalization. Additionally, Oakland has important citywide, cross-ethnic networks that carry community organization into protest and the political arena. Founded in the '70s, Oakland Community Organizations (OCO), affiliated with the national Pacific Institute for Community Organization, is a church-based coalition with more than a dozen member congregations in East, West, and North Oakland. Historically based among more stable working- and lower-middle-class residents, OCO has organized successfully on classic bread-and-butter community issues of schools, crime, and urban blight.[62] In 1979, a group of activists formed the Oakland-based Center for Third World Organizing, now also a national network, to train minority organizers to work in communities of color. The center functions as a nexus for a range of activities, but its major project in Oakland is the People United for a Better Oakland (known as PUEBLO), started in 1989. Unlike OCO, PUEBLO is a secular, membership organization, and it reaches out to often poorer, less integrated residents, focusing more explicitly on issues of racial inequality. It has won citywide campaigns on public health and police-community relations in the ghetto.[63] In 2002, it led a victorious drive for a ballot referendum establishing "just cause" protections against unfair evictions for Oakland tenants.[64]

Then there is the labor movement. In 1952, the AFL Central Labor and Building Trades Councils together claimed more than 135,000 members in Alameda County, but by the mid '90s, that figure had been eroded by half. The simple decline of numbers, however, masked substantial changes within the union movement. The '60s and the '70s, especially, saw the rise of public-sector unionism. Oakland city workers held their first representation elections in 1972, and in 1976, a major turning point came when thirty-five hundred Alameda County employees in three local unions struck for forty-nine days. The strike was the longest countywide public-sector strike to that time, and it helped to establish public-employee unionization permanently in the East Bay.[65]

As service and clerical jobs continued to replace manufacturing, labor mobilization grew among workers in more spatially anchored and locally organized employers like city and county governments, large hospital complexes, tourist destination hotels, citywide janitorial contractor associations, and state-subsidized nursing homes and home health care services. In health care, unions like the Health Care Workers Local 250 and the independent California Nurses Association emerged as militant organizations in the public and private sectors. In a strong showing of labor solidarity, in 1992, Local 250, the nurses, and three other unions struck for several weeks at Summit Hospital in defense of their right to respect one another's picket lines. In 1997, seven thousand home health care workers affiliated with the Service Employees International Union won a first contract with Alameda County, under new state legislation recognizing their collective bargaining rights.[66]

These organizing efforts drew more minority and female workers into unions, gradually changing the face of the labor movement and, ultimately, even its leadership: By 1999, two women—one black, one white—served as president and executive secretary of the Alameda County Central Labor Council. Other local unions have also crossed traditional institutional boundaries, linking workplace issues with wider community concerns. In 1996, Oakland public-school teachers struck for four and a half weeks, the longest teachers' strike in the city's history. The teachers' union rallied support from parents around demands for class size reductions, and an estimated 70 percent of students honored the strike.[67] In the Bay Area, the building trades have remained a vital segment of the local labor movement, thanks in part to the booming construction industry. In 1999, the Alameda County Building Trades Council negotiated a multiyear project labor agreement with the port of Oakland, mandating that half of the work hours on its planned $400 million seaport expansion go to local area hires, including provisions for training local residents as apprentices. Finally, the Hotel Employees and Restaurant Employees Local 2850 joined with the Association of Community Organizations for Reform Now (ACORN) to sponsor a living-wage ordinance that was passed by the city council in 1998; and it supported the East Bay Alliance for a Sustainable Economy in its successful efforts for similar measures covering the port.[68]

These brief narrative threads convey only a part of the depth and diversity of organization in Oakland's civil society. Yet they illustrate both the resilience of mobilization and its overall fragmentation across the urban public sphere. As one study put it, Oakland has a plurality of crises, and a plurality of competing agendas.[69] In their claims for social justice and community, however, all groups contended in one way or another with the neoliberal development regime promoted by Mayor Brown. As it has been historically, the struggle over the shape and content of political community remains a central axis of conflict in Oakland.

SOCIAL MOVEMENTS AND AMERICAN DEMOCRACY

Such struggles also pose difficult choices for contemporary American democracy. As citizens, we must ask ourselves if we really want a more inclusive and participatory practice of public politics. In 1969, Daniel Patrick Moynihan—then a former assistant secretary of the Department of Labor, and later a U.S. senator from New York—published a bitter indictment of the federal poverty program that he himself had played a part in creating. In *Maximum Feasible Misunderstanding,* Moynihan expressed deep skepticism toward the "quest for community" he saw motivating the War on Poverty. He blasted the Community Action Program's requirement for participation of the poor and defended the political stability upheld by traditional urban machines and other institutions, suggesting that the rapid incorporation of excluded groups had caused only confusion and disorder. "It may be that the poor are never 'ready' to assume power in an advanced society," Moynihan wrote; "the exercise of power in an effective manner is an ability acquired through apprenticeship and seasoning." He wondered whether "much of the discontent evident in Negro communities in the summer of 1967 was stirred by community action workers" and warned, "We may discover to our sorrow that 'participatory democracy' can mean an end to both participation and democracy."[70]

In the wake of the popular mobilizations of the '60s, other critics evinced similar views. Political scientist Samuel Huntington complained of an "excess of democracy" and argued that Americans must accept limits on their exercise of rights in the polity. In 1975, Huntington wrote, "In the past, every democratic society has had a marginal population, of greater or lesser size, which has not actively participated in politics. In itself, this marginality is inherently undemocratic, but it has also been one of the factors which has enabled democracy to function effectively."[71]

Moynihan's and Huntington's remarks are consistent with what I have called here the cyclical disorder theory of social movements. Insofar as it assumes that legitimate, rational values and interests are already incorporated into the polity, noninstitutional politics or protest is portrayed as irrational collective behavior, symptomatic of ideological extremism or "creedal passions," stirred up by opportunistic political entrepreneurs. A significant level of political apathy is therefore desirable, especially among lower-status groups, in order to preserve institutional stability and social order.[72]

These ideas fit uneasily with the values of liberal assimilationism and civic engagement, yet over the past twenty-five years American political culture has changed in ways that have undermined the latter two normative and interpretive traditions. Older models of pluralist accommodation presupposed the structural and institutional conditions of the modern American welfare state, yet many of its basic political settlements have now been radically altered or reversed, transforming relations in the economy, the state, and civil society. In particular, the last few decades of the twentieth century saw a dramatic deinstitutionalization of the position of labor, a relative impasse in the progress toward racial equality, and renewed attempts to regulate or exclude immigrant groups.

Beginning especially in the '70s, the postwar system of industrial relations rapidly disintegrated, as indicated by the extraordinary decline of unions: From a peak of 38 percent of the labor force in 1954, private-sector union membership in the United States had fallen to less than 10 percent by 1999, a level not seen since before the New Deal.[73] Nor is this simply a result of changes in economic structure or in worker attitudes.[74] American businesses have turned away from their institutional compromise with organized labor in the workplace, and now they adamantly resist unions in both the traditional core and emerging economic sectors, using elaborate legal and, commonly, illegal means. National Labor Relations Board (NLRB) data show that in 1990 the number of unfair labor practice charges filed was more than five times higher than in 1955, despite a nearly equal number of certification elections,[75] and in recent years as many as 28 percent of employers involved in NLRB elections were found to have unlawfully discharged employees for union activity.[76] Coupled with the shift of new investment and technology to nonunion sectors and production sites, this reflects a broad-based stance among employers to avoid collective bargaining and exclude unions from their decision-making altogether.[77]

The decline of unionization has coincided with changes in the standing of American workers. Despite economic growth, the '80s and '90s saw an absolute decline in real earnings for the majority of workers and a dramatic increase in earnings inequality.[78] From 1979 to 1995, real hourly wages fell for the bottom 60 percent of wage earners, with the greatest losses seen among the lowest-paid workers. Many families compensated by working longer hours or having additional family members work, but even so, median family income remained stagnant through most of the '90s, recovering to 1989 levels only in 1997.[79] Traditional forms of social protection in the private labor market have also eroded: In 1979, 71 percent of private-sector workers had employer-provided health insurance and 48 percent had employer-provided pensions; by 1993, only 64 and 45 percent, respectively, were covered. Reduced earnings have been accompanied by rapidly rising income inequality. In 1982, the top 10 percent of the workforce received compensation equal to 4.5 times that of the bottom 10 percent; by 1996, that ratio had increased to 5.5 times as much.[80] For male workers, studies attribute 20 percent or more of the overall increase in wage inequality directly to declining unionization.[81]

Unionized workers are not alone in facing challenges to their place in American society. For African Americans as a group, the years since the civil rights movement have produced an ambivalent pattern of political and economic incorporation. By the '90s, three to four times as many blacks held congressional and state legislative office as in 1970, and black mayors governed in many of the nation's major cities. But the number of black representatives fell well short of the proportion of blacks in the voting-age population, especially in the South, and white reluctance to vote for black candidates limited black electoral success largely to districts with a black or a racial-minority majority.[82] In the cities, black mayoral administrations have produced tangible gains in local affirmative action and in the reduction of police violence, but have often lacked the fiscal or political capacity to meet the scale of urban needs, and in places like New York, Chicago, and Philadelphia, black incumbents were succeeded by more conservative white mayors.[83]

The results for black economic integration have been no less mixed. Indisputably, affirmative action policies have increased opportunities not only for black managers and professionals but also for black workers in industry, the skilled trades, civil service, and other jobs.[84] At the same time, by itself affirmative action has neither eliminated racial disparities nor overcome rising inequality within the black population. Despite the growth of a black middle class, median black family income in 1995 was no more than 61 percent of that for white families—almost unchanged from its level of 59 percent in 1967.[85] Black unemployment rates have persistently averaged more than twice those for whites, while poverty rates are typically three times higher.[86]

These disparities have remained constant since the '70s, and according to demographer Reynolds Farley, "No currently operating economic or political trend will narrow black-white differences, either in the short or long run."[87] On the contrary, recent years have seen aggressive campaigns to eliminate government programs perceived to benefit blacks, including successful initiatives against affirmative action in California and Washington State, and the passage of the 1996 Personal Responsibility and Work Opportunity Reconciliation Act (welfare reform), which abolished the federal Aid to Families with Dependent Children program, popularly identified with the black poor.[88]

Finally, disputes over the content and control of American ethnic and cultural identity have reentered the national consciousness. Since 1965, rising numbers of immigrants, particularly from Asia and Latin America, have begun to transform the racial and ethnic composition of the U.S. population. This trend has been met with increasing pressure for restrictions on entry and on the rights of immigrants themselves, in what historian George Sanchez calls "a resurgence of a nativism unparalleled in this country since the 1920s."[89] The 1996 welfare reform imposed new limits on federal benefits for both legal and illegal immigrants, and in California, the state with the highest proportion of foreign-born residents (24 percent), voters in 1994 passed Proposition 187 by a three to two margin. Although many of its provisions were later ruled unconstitutional, Proposition 187 would have denied public education and health care services to undocumented aliens and to their U.S.-born children. Californians also passed Proposition 63 in 1986, making English the state's official language, and Proposition 227 in 1998, eliminating bilingual education and mandating English-only instruction in the public schools.[90]

In these initiatives we can see a revival of controversies over the definition of national identity, the rights of citizenship, and the boundaries to membership in the polity. The events since September 11, 2001, have exacerbated these conflicts, with heightened fears for security, an upsurge of wartime nationalism, rising hostility toward foreigners, and pressures for the suppression of ethnic difference.[91] Yet the historical evidence reminds us that mobilization from the right is hardly unusual in American politics, and indeed it has significantly influenced the development of our civic culture. Nor are such movements essentially backward-looking or defensive; on the contrary, they have also been associated with conditions of economic growth and upward political and social mobility for specific groups.

THE FUTURE OF COMMUNITY?

These considerations form a counterpoint to the recent debates over civic engagement. As I have tried to show in this book, the analysis of collective actors must be grounded in the three dimensions of civil society, institutional politics, and socioeconomic structure. This approach emphasizes not only the forms of mobilization but also their content: the trajectories of group formation, and their relation to dominant political forces and structures of inequality. With this framework, we may also gain a perspective on the prospects for emerging relations between social movements and political community.

By the early '90s, the protest cycle of the '60s and '70s seemed ever more distant from the contemporary scene. Just as movements for democracy were arising in all parts of the world, popular political participation in the United States appeared to reach an alarming new low. Surveys showed that public trust in politics and government had fallen below even those levels recorded during the Watergate scandals of the 1970s, while turnout in the 1996 national election amounted to only 49 percent of the voting-age population, the smallest proportion since 1924.[92]

Conservative critics were quick to blame "big government" for the apparent decline in civic attachment, depicting a zero-sum opposition between a remote bureaucratic state and an ideal view of supposedly more authentic, primary, and organic relationships in civil society. In this view, federal programs fail because they displace indigenous self-help networks and lack a moral anchor in the consensus of the community. In line with social capitalist theory, efforts at reform must instead aim to rebuild networks and restore initiative and responsibility at the local level. In practice, these ideas have already been widely implemented through the devolution of fiscal and social policy obligations onto state, local, and private voluntary actors.[93]

The conservative ideal, however, abstracts the image of local community from the historical contexts of socioeconomic structure and institutional power. As the examination of Oakland amply shows, civil society in the United States bears little resemblance to any simple model of free association and organic community. Rather, it is a deeply fragmented and uneven terrain, divided by race, class, and other forms of structural inequality. These divisions existed prior to the expansion of the welfare state, and they will likely endure beyond its recent retrenchment. Promoting individuals' social capital is unlikely to compensate for these conditions, and may instead provide greater opportunities for discrimination or withdrawal into private social worlds, within job markets, in neighborhoods and suburbs, or in separate cultural realms.[94]

Similarly, local politics is far from inherently more democratic, as we have seen. Regime institutions are typically exclusive, conflicts persist outside the regime's boundaries, and groups' rights and responsibilities to one another are themselves the object of dispute. Dependent on property taxes, city governments are powerfully constrained to seek economic development and avoid expensive commitments to high-needs, low-resource populations. Attempts to devolve or expel these responsibilities further onto civic voluntarism can only diminish the scope of an already truncated public sphere.

What then lies ahead for urban political community? Some scholars have argued that contemporary citizen action no longer really depends on active local grassroots organizations or dense city environments. The proliferation of professional advocacy groups, Washington-based lobbies, direct mail services, legal defense funds, and Internet e-mail lists all seems to testify to the continual inventiveness of American civil society. These types of association employ new forms of communication and operate on a wider geographic and political scale. Movements today may simply take a different form, and participation may not have declined so much as adapted to institutional change.[95]

Political scientist Theda Skocpol agrees that the forms of civic association in the United States have changed, but she denies the contrast with a lost ideal of autonomous local community. She stresses the role of translocal and national elites in creating and sustaining traditional voluntary organizations like the Veterans of Foreign Wars, the Parent-Teacher Association, or the American Legion. Such groups have historically reflected the form and scope of national political institutions and were often themselves built from centralized resources and initiative.[96]

In the current period, however, Skocpol contends, elites have abandoned their former role as sponsors and mobilizers of popular civic action. Where political actors once maintained far-reaching leadership networks through national federations of locally rooted membership associations, these have been replaced by the newer and more expensive marketing and media technologies. As a result, elites have lost touch with the manifold public spaces of civil society, withdrawing instead into narrow professional circles centered in the nation's political, financial, and media capitals.[97]

Skocpol's argument effectively counters both the conservative romance for civic localism and the liberal confidence in movement professionalization. Yet her analysis parallels the conceptual split between the local and the larger world. Elites may well have stronger ties to national and even global networks than to their own adjacent urban communities. But global forces are not new, and they pervade all levels of urban life, entering into the constitution of local groups. Experiences of immigration, cultural interaction, economic restructuring, and marshaling for war have crisscrossed our cities for the past century. The urban is not merely the target or object of external forces, but the field where they intersect in concrete historical junctures.

The effects of structural and institutional change reverberate through the workplaces, neighborhoods, and everyday scenes of urban public life. As I have argued here, traditional theoretical models of assimilation and group incorporation can no longer be taken for granted. Civic and political participation in the United States is highly skewed in favor of the more advantaged, as Sidney Verba, Kay Lehman Schlozman, and Henry Brady have shown.[98] This is not simply a function of individuals' norms and values, but is strongly related to the possession of resources and to patterns of recruitment; or, as we might say, to the structural bases of groups and their political opportunities. Any substantial increase in democratic participation would have to go beyond the limits of normal politics and engage groups currently outside the system. These groups are disproportionally concentrated in the city. To understand the prospects for their mobilization, then, we will need a map of the urban terrain.

Today, the goal of a more inclusive American democracy faces formidable barriers. Over the past generation, our society has become increasingly unequal, with the reduction of the welfare state and the return of unregulated market power. If there is to be a successful challenge to these conditions, it will likely require the construction of new forms of collective identity and public politics. Throughout our history, social movements have been a crucial source of such cultural and political innovation. For Americans, the achievement of a democratic political community remains an unfinished task. In the fragmented spaces of our civil society, solidarity must be continually reinvented.

Telling Stories about Actors and Events

The argument in this book relies on a narrative analytic method to explain social movements and their outcomes. Consequently, I take seriously not just the behavioral forms and processes of collective action but also historically specific collective *actors*. Nevertheless, critical problems can arise in using this approach. In this methodological appendix, I identify some of the dangers of representing groups and movements as collective actors. I then lay out an alternative framework to ground an actor-oriented, event-based narrative analysis of historical causality and collective agency.

MOVEMENTS AS ACTORS: COLLECTIVE BIOGRAPHY

Perhaps the most traditional or familiar model of collective actors is one that might be described as *collective biography*. As a paradigmatic example, we may take E. P. Thompson's famous study of the working-class movement in early-nineteenth-century England, *The Making of the English Working Class*.[1] For Thompson, the working class is not simply an economic category but a "social and cultural formation" whose defining element is class *consciousness*—the articulation of a collective identity of interest by diverse groups of workers, for themselves and against other classes. Class consciousness is the product of a long-term process of social and cultural development, and is embodied in popular customs, values, organizations, and institutional forms.

A similar approach can be found in the American sociological genre of urban community studies. A classic case is St. Clair Drake and Horace Cayton's *Black Metropolis*, an ethnography of the black South Side of Chicago in the 1930s and '40s. Significantly, Drake and Cayton divide their book into two parts: Volume 1 describes the structural segregation of the black population, while volume 2 shows the indigenous formation of social and cultural institutions that make up the African American community, or what they call "Bronzeville."[2] In both of these examples, the historical development of group consciousness or culture resembles a "biographical" account of the growth of a collective subject.

The strength of these approaches lies in their concern with agency, with the self-organization of groups and movements, and with the ways people construct their own sense of collective identity and interest. At the same time, the model has several important drawbacks. First, it presumes the continuous development of a class or community over time, as a basis for social action. Yet in the case of Oakland, for instance, we find a series of "breaks" or radical reconstructions of the social and political terrain. The historical cast of characters does not remain stable; instead, qualitatively different actors emerge from different social origins and with different collective identities.

Analyzing these multiple and often overlapping relations is difficult so long as we define any single group or movement as our narrative central subject.[3] From its own point of view, each movement revolves around a core axis of social stratification, group formation, and identity, in which alternative formations often appear as marginal or separate phenomena, subplots or deviations from the primary narrative path.[4] Thus, either race *or* class *or* ethnicity serves as the central organizing principle, at the expense of showing how these processes may occur simultaneously or interact with one another.

Second, the biographical metaphor implies that once formed, groups persist as independent, organic entities, much like mature adult persons. Despite the emphasis on social construction, there is a tendency to treat collective actors like individual actors writ large. Assuming the durability of actors, however, runs the risk of reifying or essentializing group culture. The result parallels what Paul Gilroy has called "ethnic absolutism," in which culture becomes "a fixed property of social groups, rather than a relational field in which they encounter one another and live out social, historical relationships."[5]

Finally, the method of collective biography is often motivated by a desire to understand subaltern groups as active subjects. By focusing on *internal* processes of social and cultural formation, however, it elides the issue of objective historical agency. Without a sustained relation to social structure or politics, the lack of overt consciousness of or mobilization around class or race could be taken to mean that such categories were unimportant or had ceased to exist in social life.[6] Even if the process of self-formation did produce a conscious, mobilized group, what then would it be empowered to do? In response to structural forces, groups might well develop autonomous social institutions or subcultures of resistance, but it is not always clear how these in turn might produce wider social change.

These problems suggest trying a different approach. The challenge is to overcome reification without sacrificing agency, to show that collective actors are socially constructed but also observe how in some situations they may become causal forces in their own right.[7] I propose to take up this task by reconsidering here the spatial and temporal grounds for representing historical agents. Clarifying these terms will help us to articulate a set of formal guidelines, consistent with our substantive sociological concepts, for organizing a narrative account of actors and events.

ACTORS ON A MOVING STAGE: A MODEL OF AGENCY

My first step is to reconcile the problem of competing narrative streams by shifting the narrative central subject from the point of view of each movement to the point of view of the city. The city is not a fixed entity but a historical context, the reflexive site and product of the social and spatial practices of multiple groups and actors. This shift highlights what sociologist Margaret Somers calls the "relational setting of action" or the "patterned matrix of institutional relationships among cultural, economic, social and political practices."[8] The local configuration of such relationships affects the patterns of association in civil society, the availability of political opportunities, and the forms of participation in the public sphere.

Focusing on the city provides a spatial center for tracking the development of and interactions among various collective actors. The identities of the actors are derived not from any essential categories or attributes, but, as Somers says, from their "places in the multiple relationships in which they are embedded." Within a concrete historical setting, the interactions among diverse groups make possible a narrative analysis of what political scientist Judith Garber calls the "plural heroes" arising out of a multilayered urban public sphere.[9] Nevertheless, any attempt to make actors into narrative historical characters risks falling back into a conceptual reification. To avoid this problem, I draw from the work of political scientist William Sewell Jr. in order to disaggregate the processes of actor formation and situate collective agency within the temporal flow of events.

Borrowing from the great French historian Fernand Braudel, Sewell argues that causal forces in history are located in different temporal orders or scales. In Braudel's terms, structural time, or the *longue durée*, is the time of centuries, of long-lasting material, social, or cultural forms that change very slowly. Conjunctural time embodies shorter-term but still relatively stable relations, as for example economic or generational cycles lasting decades. Finally, eventful time is "the time of the chronicle and the journalist," the everyday flow of emergent events. For Braudel, eventful time is merely an ephemeral surface masking deeper structural rhythms, but for Sewell, it holds the potential for historical agency, "where the actions of human subjects can reconfigure pre-existing structures and conjunctures."[10]

As Sewell suggests, we need not adhere to a strict Braudelian metric to take advantage of this approach. So, in my study of Oakland, broad economic and political structures of capitalist development and American constitutional sovereignty remain largely continuous throughout the period as a whole, punctuated by moments of rapid localized economic or demographic change. Against this background, institutional processes of political regime-building and group formation take place in conjunctural time, roughly marking the borders of our three cases.[11] In turn, specific collective actions like strikes, demonstrations, and other forms of insurgency occur at the level of events.

Sorting causality into temporal registers helps us to distinguish formally between context and action. Structural and conjunctural conditions establish the context for historical actors, not so much as objective determinants but as slower-moving causal streams that set boundaries on more transitory sequences of events within them.[12] Normal sequences of events are path-dependent; positive feedback or causal "lock-in" mechanisms (like structural interdependence, vested interests, or cultural ritual) reproduce persistent outcomes, at least until subsequent choice points turn things onto other paths.[13] Historical change thus follows a pattern of "trajectories and transitions"—causal regularities along the stable paths that we call periods and turning points that mark the differences or changes between periods.[14]

The logic of social causality, therefore, can change from one period to another, as the institutional rules governing social relations and action are transformed by events. In Oakland, for example, we see the primary terrain of political conflict shift from ethnicity to class to race. From this perspective, moments of transition become critical, for it is especially in those turning points that actors can exercise independent causal agency and challenge the prevailing "rules of the game." This framework gives us a standard for assessing the impact of events of collective action, to the extent that they succeed in reconfiguring their structural and conjunctural contexts.

How do events transform their context? Sewell suggests that one way is by constituting new groups of actors or empowering existing groups in new ways.[15] How then do actors make history through events? On this question, conventional theories of path dependency fall short, allowing agency only at contingent turning points, in contrast to the otherwise highly determined paths. In normal periods, the autonomy of actors fades into the causal context, while the crucial turning points appear as fortuitous accidents or the effects of exogenous shocks. Moreover, the mere zigzag of trajectories and transitions loses its bearings in longer-term structural and conjunctural streams, so it does not tell us what is really at stake in each change.

We might begin to address this problem by reframing period changes as a process of "reiterated problem-solving," as sociologist Jeffrey Haydu has proposed.[16] In this view, structural conditions generate recurrent problems that are solved by alternative sets of arrangements in successive periods, and solutions worked out at earlier conjunctures become part of the context for changes at later points. In Oakland, persistent structural inequalities among groups continually posed the problem of creating and maintaining a political community. At different times, various actors prevailed in defining and institutionalizing their preferred solutions, without ever eliminating the recurrent problem of inequality.

We can refine this concept further by recognizing at least two types of paths or event sequences. Scholars James Mahoney and Kathleen Thelen have distinguished positive feedback or "self-reinforcing" sequences, which include mechanisms supporting the formation and long-term reproduction of institutional patterns, from nonreinforcing or "reactive" sequences—chains of temporally ordered and causally connected events that can transform or reverse earlier paths.[17] Established relations of political power tend to be self-reinforcing, as in the construction of urban regimes; dominant actors exploit their institutional and systemic advantages and defend their solutions as the norm for the polity as a whole. Patterns of group formation can also show self-reinforcing effects, as in the cumulative concentration of resources, social networks, and cultural orientations within groups in civil society.

By contrast, cycles of collective action more closely resemble reactive sequences, in which events trigger subsequent changes through a series of linked interactions among contending actors. Such reactive sequences can be broken down into their intervening steps, revealing key choice points where actors face opposing alternatives and must decide their future. Indeed, challengers try to *make* events into turning points, to reconfigure settled arrangements in new and more favorable ways.

This approach puts agency at the center, in stable periods as well as in times of flux. Elite and emerging actors contend with one other to challenge or uphold existing solutions, and moments of transition can arise endogenously from crises or breakdowns of a particular order. Actors constituted from different structural origins and embodying different norms "interact and collide," in a process not unlike what political scientists Karen Orren and Stephen Skowrenek have dubbed "intercurrence."[18] The intersection of structural, conjunctural, and eventful causal streams can produce critical junctures that increase the space for political action, provide opportunities for innovation, and endow some actors with the resources and orientation to "seize the day."[19]

This is where events matter. Challenging movements are "mobilizations that confront organized opposition in attempting to change the social structure, prevailing fundamental policies, and/or balance of power among groups."[20] Social movements introduce choice points between the reproduction of the dominant order and the movement's alternative future. Individual events of collective action become significant as part of reactive sequences of interactions between challengers and more powerful actors. The consequences of these interactions (whether intended or unintended) can be measured by their impact on the ongoing processes of group- and actor-formation, political institution-making, and structural social inequality.

Together, these formal guidelines give us the grounds for telling a story of actors and events that is consistent with the substantive analytic concepts introduced in chapter 1. Accordingly, I begin by taking the city as my narrative center or relational setting. Broad structural forces affect the social bases and composition of those groups brought together in urban space. Within this context, conjunctural patterns of institutional development define the terms of conflict for each period. On the one hand, elites organize political regimes, each with its own mode of coordination, boundaries of inclusion and exclusion, and unifying project. On the other hand, multiple streams of group- and movement-formation emerge, sometimes in opposition, on the terrain of urban civil society.

Normally, structural and conjunctural conditions both enable and constrain actors' capacity to shape events. At certain times, however, the collision of different sequences of development may bring about a critical juncture, in which actors openly confront one another in the public sphere. In such moments, historical analysis must be able to show how normal institutional mechanisms of order have failed, the opposing paths that actors represent, and the alternative arrangements concretely available to them. We can then better evaluate the interactions among actors in these events, and their outcomes for the political community.

This framework allows us to engage in a disciplined narrative analysis of the "thick" case history without falling into an empiricist "storytelling." It resolves the multiplicity of different actors by taking the city or relational setting as its narrative center, and it avoids reification by situating agency in the temporal flow of events. Actors are socially constructed and embedded in their structural and conjunctural context, but their encounter with one another opens up strategic choice points and the possibility of change. Elites and challengers rise and fall in these events, and new or rearticulated identities appear from the manifold spaces of civil society. The concepts drawn from political sociology, neo-institutionalism, and social movement theory provide the causal mechanisms for understanding the relations among structurally unequal groups, conjunctural processes of institutionalization, and mobilization in collective action. It remains for us to discover the world that the actors have made, and its consequences.

Notes

CHAPTER 1. NO THERE THERE

1. *Oakland Post-Enquirer,* May 6, 1922; *San Francisco Examiner,* May 7, 1922.

2. Seymour M. Lipset and Earl Raab, *The Politics of Unreason: Right-Wing Extremism in America, 1790–1970* (New York: Harper & Row, 1970), p. 21.

3. *Knights of the Ku Klux Klan, Inc., v. Leon C. Francis et al.,* case file no. 81245, Civil Division, California Superior Court, Alameda County, 1925; *Knights of the Ku Klux Klan, Inc., v. East Bay Club of Alameda County,* case file no. 82470, Civil Division, California Superior Court, Alameda County, 1925; *San Francisco Chronicle,* August 12, 1924; *Oakland Tribune,* August 24, 1925.

4. Commonwealth Club of California, *The Population of California* (San Francisco: Parker, 1946), pp. 105–120, 169; U.S. Bureau of the Census, *Special Reports,* Series CA-3, no. 3: *Characteristics of the Population, Labor Force, Families and Housing, San Francisco Bay Congested Area: April, 1944* (Washington, D.C.: GPO, 1944), pp. 7, 14; idem, *Special Census of Oakland, California: October 9, 1945* (Washington, D.C.: GPO, 1946).

5. Joel Seidman, *American Labor from Defense to Reconversion* (Chicago: University of Chicago Press, 1953).

6. Marilynn Johnson, "Mobilizing the Homefront: Labor and Politics in Oakland, 1941–1951," in *Working People of California,* ed. Daniel Cornford (Berkeley: University of California Press, 1995), pp. 344–368; *Oakland Tribune,* July 21, 1949; *San Francisco Chronicle,* February 27 and 18 and March 2 and 5, 1950.

7. U.S. Bureau of the Census, *1970 Census of the Population, Supplementary Report: Negro Population in Selected Places and Selected Counties* (Washington, D.C.: GPO, 1971), p. 5. Oakland City Planning Department, *West Oakland: A 701 Subarea Report* (Oakland: City Planning Department, 701 Division, May 1969).

8. Ralph Kramer, *Participation of the Poor: Comparative Community Case Studies in the War on Poverty* (Englewood Cliffs, N.J.: Prentice-Hall, 1969).

9. J. David Greenstone and Paul Peterson, *Race and Authority in Urban Pol-*

itics: Community Participation and the War on Poverty (New York: Russell Sage Foundation, 1973).

10. Bobby Seale, *Seize the Time* (New York: Vintage, 1968); Gilbert Moore, *Rage* (New York: Carroll and Graf, 1993 [orig. 1971]), p. 193.

11. Rod Bush, *The New Black Vote: Politics and Power in Four American Cities* (San Francisco: Synthesis, 1984), pp. 323–324.

12. For review essays, see Leonard Moore, "Historical Interpretations of the 1920's Klan: The Traditional View and the Populist Revision," *Journal of Social History* 24 (Winter 1990): 341–357; and Stanley Coben, "Ordinary White Protestants: The KKK of the 1920s," *Journal of Social History* 28 (Fall 1994): 157–165.

13. George Lipsitz, *Class and Culture in Cold War America: "A Rainbow at Midnight"* (New York: Praeger, 1981).

14. Aldon Morris, "A Retrospective on the Civil Rights Movement: Political and Intellectual Landmarks," *Annual Review of Sociology* 25 (1999): 517–539.

15. John Mollenkopf, *The Contested City* (Princeton, N.J.: Princeton University Press, 1983), p. 11.

16. Other political theorists have called for a similarly explicit tripartite approach. See Margaret Somers, "Citizenship and the Place of the Public Sphere: Law, Community, and Political Culture in the Transition to Democracy," *American Sociological Review* 58 (October 1993): 587–620; Jean Cohen, "Interpreting the Notion of Civil Society," in *Toward a Global Civil Society,* ed. Michael Walzer (Providence, R.I.: Berghahn Books, 1995), pp. 35–40; Mustafa Emirbayer and Mimi Sheller, "Studying Publics in History," *Comparative and Historical Sociology* 11, no. 1 (Fall 1998): 5–6; Iris Marion Young, "State, Civil Society and Social Justice," in *Democracy's Value,* ed. Ian Shapiro and Casiano Hacker-Cordon (Cambridge: Cambridge University Press, 1999), pp. 141–162.

17. Robert Dahl, *Who Governs?* (New Haven, Conn.: Yale University Press, 1961); S. M. Lipset, *Political Man* (New York: Doubleday, 1960); David Truman, *The Governmental Process* (New York: Knopf, 1953). See also David Held, *Political Theory and the Modern State* (Cambridge: Polity Press, 1989), pp. 57–58.

18. Although cultural and institutional forces were acknowledged, for traditional political sociologists the most important structural force was undoubtedly the economy. See Reinhard Bendix and Seymour Martin Lipset, "Political Sociology," *Current Sociology* 6 (1957): 79–99.

19. Charles Tilly, *Durable Inequality* (Berkeley: University of California Press, 1998).

20. Roger Friedland and Robert Alford, "Bringing Society back In: Symbols, Practices, and Institutional Contradictions," in *The New Institutionalism in Organizational Analysis,* ed. Walter W. Powell and Paul DiMaggio (Chicago: University of Chicago Press, 1991), pp. 232–263.

21. Doreen Massey, *Spatial Divisions of Labor: Social Structures and the Geography of Production* (London: Macmillan, 1984); Alan Warde, "Spatial Change, Politics and the Division of Labor," in *Social Relations and Spatial Structures,* ed. D. Gregory and J. Urry (London: Macmillan, 1985), pp. 190–212.

22. Roger Waldinger, *Still the Promised City: African Americans and New Immigrants in Post-Industrial New York* (Cambridge, Mass.: Harvard University Press, 1996).

23. Douglas Massey and Nancy Denton, *American Apartheid* (Cambridge, Mass.: Harvard University Press, 1993).

24. Paul DiMaggio and Walter W. Powell, "Introduction," in *The New Institutionalism in Organizational Analysis*, ed. Walter W. Powell and Paul DiMaggio (Chicago: University of Chicago Press, 1991); James G. March and Johan P. Olsen, *Rediscovering Institutions: The Organizational Basis of Politics* (New York: Free Press, 1989); Theda Skocpol, "Bringing the State back In: Strategies of Analysis on Current Research," in *Bringing the State back In*, ed. Peter Evans, Dietrich Rueschemeyer, and Theda Skocpol (Cambridge: Cambridge University Press, 1985), pp. 3–37.

25. Theda Skocpol, "A Society without a 'State'? Political Organization, Social Conflict, and Welfare Provision in the United States," *Journal of Public Policy* 7, no. 4 (1987): 349–371. Among the ways the state used to shape the political terrain are its repressive powers of social control; its "infrastructural" activity, including the selective promotion and extraction of resources from the economy and population under its authority; its administrative ability to formulate and carry out policy; and its regulation of the channels through which groups claim access to the state. See J. Craig Jenkins, "Social Movements, Political Representation, and the State: An Agenda and Comparative Framework," in *The Politics of Social Protest*, ed. J. Craig Jenkins and Bert Klandermans (Minneapolis: University of Minnesota Press, 1995), pp. 14–38.

26. Stephen Elkin, "Twentieth Century Urban Regimes," *Journal of Urban Affairs* 7, no. 2 (1985): 11–28; Clarence Stone, *Regime Politics: Governing Atlanta, 1946–1988* (Lawrence: University Press of Kansas, 1989).

27. See also the model of institutional power in Hanspeter Kriesi, "The Political Opportunity Structure of New Social Movements: Its Impact on Their Mobilization," in *The Politics of Social Protest*, ed. J. Craig Jenkins and Bert Klandermans (Minneapolis: University of Minnesota Press, 1995), pp. 167–198.

28. Clarence Stone, "Urban Regimes and the Capacity to Govern: A Political Economy Approach," *Journal of Urban Affairs* 15, no. 1 (1993): 1–28.

29. Idem, *Regime Politics*, p. 229. Gerry Stoker adds, "A regime once established is a powerful force in urban politics. Opponents 'have to go along to get along' or face the daunting task of building an effective counter-regime"; Stoker, "Regime Theory and Urban Politics," in *Theories of Urban Politics*, ed. David Judge, Gerry Stoker, and Harold Wolman (Thousand Oaks, Calif.: Sage, 1995), p. 65.

30. Doug McAdam, *Political Process and the Development of Black Insurgency* (Chicago: University of Chicago Press, 1982); Roberta Ash Garner and Mayer Zald, "The Political Economy of Social Movement Sectors," in *Social Movements in an Organizational Society*, ed. Mayer Zald and John D. McCarthy (New Brunswick, N.J.: Transaction, 1987). pp. 293–317.

31. Manuel Castells, *The City and the Grassroots: A Cross-Cultural The-*

ory of Urban Social Movements (Berkeley: University of California Press, 1983), p. 294; John Logan and Harvey Molotch, *Urban Fortunes* (Berkeley: University of California Press, 1987), p. 20.

32. Nancy Fraser, "Rethinking the Public Sphere: A Contribution to the Critique of Actually Existing Democracy," in *Habermas and the Public Sphere,* ed. Craig Calhoun (Cambridge, Mass.: MIT Press, 1992), pp. 109–142; Jean Cohen, "Does Voluntary Association Make Democracy Work?" in *Diversity and Its Discontents,* ed. Neil Smelser and Jeffrey Alexander (Princeton, N.J.: Princeton University Press, 1999), pp. 263–291. Contemporary theorizing about the "public sphere" is inspired, of course, by Jürgen Habermas, *Structural Transformation of the Public Sphere* (Cambridge, Mass.: MIT Press, 1989).

33. Doug McAdam, "Micromobilization Contexts and Recruitment to Activism," *International Social Movement Research* 1 (1988): 125–154; John McCarthy, "Constraints and Opportunities in Adopting, Adapting and Inventing," in *Comparative Perspectives on Social Movements,* ed. Doug McAdam, John McCarthy, and Mayer Zald (Cambridge: Cambridge University Press, 1996), pp. 141–151; Hanspeter Kriesi and Dominique Wisler, "The Impact of Social Movements on Political Institutions: A Comparison of the Introduction of Direct Legislation in Switzerland and the United States," in *How Social Movements Matter,* ed. Marco Guigni, Doug McAdam and Charles Tilly (Minneapolis: University of Minnesota Press, 1999), p. 60; Richard Wood, "Religious Culture and Political Action," *Sociological Theory* 17, no. 3 (November 1999): 307–332.

34. Fraser, "Rethinking the Public Sphere," p. 125, and Geoff Eley, "Nations, Publics, and Political Cultures: Placing Habermas in the Nineteenth Century," in *Habermas and the Public Sphere,* ed. Craig Calhoun (Cambridge, Mass.: MIT Press, 1992), pp. 289–339; Doug McAdam and Ronelle Paulsen, "Specifying the Relationship between Social Ties and Activism," *American Journal of Sociology* 99 (1993): 640–667; Aldon Morris, "Political Consciousness and Collective Action," in *Frontiers in Social Movement Theory,* ed. Aldon Morris and Carol Mueller (New Haven, Conn.: Yale University Press, 1992), pp. 351–373.

35. Ira Katznelson, *City Trenches: Urban Politics and the Patterning of Class in the United States* (Chicago: University of Chicago Press, 1981).

36. See, for example, Ira Katznelson and Aristide Zolberg, eds., *Working Class Formation* (Princeton, N.J.: Princeton University Press, 1986); Kim Voss, "Labor Organization and Class Alliance: Industries, Communities and the Knights of Labor," *Theory and Society* 17 (1988): 329–364; Eric Arnesen, *Waterfront Workers of New Orleans: Race, Class and Politics, 1863–1923* (Oxford: Oxford University Press, 1990).

37. Young, "State, Civil Society, and Social Justice"; Alejandro Portes and Patricia Landolt, "The Downside of Social Capital," *The American Prospect* 7, no. 26 (May–June 1996): 18–21, 94.

38. Mayer Zald and John D. McCarthy, "Social Movement Industries: Conflict and Cooperation among SMOs," in *Social Movements in an Organizational Society,* ed. Mayer Zald and John D. McCarthy (New Brunswick, N.J.: Transaction, 1987), pp. 161–180; Ruud Koopmans, "The Dynamics of Protest

Waves: West Germany, 1965 to 1989," *American Sociological Review* 58 (October 1993): 637–658; Charles Tilly, "Repertoires of Contention in America and Britain, 1750–1830," in *The Dynamics of Social Movements*, ed. Mayer Zald and John McCarthy (Cambridge, Mass.: Winthrop, 1979), pp. 126–155, and idem, "How to Detect, Describe, and Explain Repertoires of Contention," Working Paper 150 (New York: Center for Studies of Social Change, New School for Social Research, 1992); Elisabeth Clemens, "Organizational Repertoires and Institutional Change: Women's Groups and the Transformation of U.S. Politics, 1890–1920," *American Journal of Sociology* 98, no. 4 (January 1993): 755–798.

39. Aldon Morris, *The Origins of the Civil Rights Movement* (New York: Free Press, 1984); McAdam, *Political Process*, pp. 124–145.

40. David Snow et al., "Frame Alignment Processes, Micromobilization, and Movement Participation," *American Sociological Review* 51 (1986): 464–481; David Snow and Robert Benford, "Master Frames and Cycles of Protest," and Verta Taylor and Nancy Whittier, "Collective Identity in Social Movement Communities: Lesbian Feminist Mobilization," both in *Frontiers in Social Movement Theory*, ed. Aldon Morris and Carol Mueller (New Haven, Conn.: Yale University Press, 1992), pp. 133–155 and 104–129, respectively.

41. Michael Walzer, *Spheres of Justice* (New York: Basic Books, 1983), p. 60; Elizabeth Frazer, *The Problems of Communitarian Politics* (Oxford: Oxford University Press, 1999), pp. 203–210.

42. Dahl, *Who Governs?* pp. 34–36; Gabriel Almond and Sidney Verba, *The Civic Culture* (Princeton, N.J.: Princeton University Press, 1963).

43. Lipset and Raab, *The Politics of Unreason*, p. 114. See also John Higham, *Strangers in the Land* (New York: Atheneum, 1971 [orig. 1955]), pp. 276–294; Richard Hofstadter, *The Age of Reform: From Bryan to FDR* (New York: Knopf, 1977 [orig. 1955]), p. 291; George Mowry and Blaine Brownell, *The Urban Nation: 1920–1980*, rev. ed. (New York: Hill and Wang, 1981); David Burner, *The Politics of Provincialism* (New York: Knopf, 1968), pp. 42–28, 74–102; Arnold Rice, *The Ku Klux Klan in American Politics* (New York: Haskell House, 1972).

44. Arthur Schlesinger Jr., *The Age of Roosevelt: The Politics of Upheaval* (Boston: Houghton-Mifflin, 1960); Samuel Lubell, *The Future of American Politics*, 3d ed. (New York: Harper & Row, 1965); Robert Dahl, *Pluralist Democracy in the United States: Conflict and Consent* (Chicago: Rand McNally, 1967), pp. 430–450; Lipset, *Political Man*, pp. 92–93.

45. Nathan Glazer and Daniel Moynihan, *Beyond the Melting Pot: The Negroes, Puerto Ricans, Jews, Italians, and Irish of New York*, 2d ed. (Cambridge, Mass.: MIT Press, 1970); Stephen Thernstrom and Abigail Thernstrom, *America in Black and White* (New York: Simon and Schuster, 1997).

46. Leonard Moore, *Citizen Klansmen* (Chapel Hill: University of North Carolina Press, 1991); Christopher Cocoltchos, "The Invisible Empire and the Search for the Orderly Community," and Shawn Lay, "Imperial Outpost on the Border: El Paso's Frontier Klan No. 100," in *The Invisible Empire in the West*, ed. Shawn Lay (Urbana: University of Illinois Press, 1992), pp. 97–120 and 67–95, respectively; William Jenkins, *Steel Valley Klan: The Ku Klux Klan in Ohio's*

Mahoning Valley (Kent, Ohio: Kent State University Press, 1990); Nancy MacLean, *Behind the Mask of Chivalry* (Oxford: Oxford University Press, 1994); Kathleen Blee, *Women of the Klan: Racism and Gender in the 1920s* (Berkeley: University of California Press, 1991); Robert Goldberg, *Hooded Empire: The Ku Klux Klan in Colorado* (Urbana: University of Illinois Press, 1981); Kenneth Wald, "The Visible Empire: The Ku Klux Klan as an Electoral Movement," *Journal of Interdisciplinary History* 11, no. 2 (Autumn 1980): 217–234.

47. Sheldon Danziger and Peter Danziger, *America Unequal* (Cambridge, Mass.: Harvard University Press, 1995); Richard Freeman, *The New Inequality* (Boston: Beacon Press, 1999); Massey and Denton, *American Apartheid;* William J. Wilson, *The Declining Significance of Race,* 2d ed. (Chicago: University of Chicago Press, 1980).

48. Nelson Lichtenstein and Howell John Harris, eds., *Industrial Democracy in America: The Ambiguous Promise* (Cambridge: Cambridge University Press, 1993); Christopher Tomlins, *The State and the Unions: Labor Relations, Law, and the Organized Labor Movement in America, 1880–1960* (Cambridge: Cambridge University Press, 1985); Michael Goldfield, *The Decline of Organized Labor in the United States* (Chicago: University of Chicago Press, 1987), pp. 26–38.

49. Landmark acts like the NLRA, the 1935 Social Security Act, and the 1937 Fair Labor Standards Act all excluded agricultural labor and domestic service, where three-quarters of all African American workers were still concentrated during the '30s. Jill Quadagno, *The Color of Welfare* (Oxford: Oxford University Press, 1994); G. William Domhoff, *The Power Elite and the State* (New York: Aldine de Gruyter, 1990).

50. Arnold Hirsch, *Making the Second Ghetto* (Cambridge: Cambridge University Press, 1983); Thomas Sugrue, *The Origins of the Urban Crisis: Race and Inequality in Detroit* (Princeton, N.J.: Princeton University Press, 1996).

51. Cedric Herring and Sharon Collins, "Retreat from Equal Opportunity? The Case for Affirmative Action," in *The Bubbling Cauldron: Race, Ethnicity, and the Urban Crisis,* ed. Michael Peter Smith and Joe R. Feagin (Minneapolis: University of Minnesota Press, 1995), pp. 163–181.

52. Samuel P. Huntington, *American Politics: The Promise of Disharmony* (Cambridge, Mass.: Harvard University Press, 1981), p. 147.

53. James Morone, *The Democratic Wish: Popular Participation and the Limits of American Government* (New Haven, Conn.: Yale University Press, 1990).

54. Arthur Schlesinger Jr., *The Disuniting of America* (New York: W. W. Norton, 1992); Frederick Siegel, *The Future Once Happened Here: New York, D.C., L.A., and the Fate of America's Big Cities* (New York: Free Press, 1997).

55. Doug McAdam, Sidney Tarrow, and Charles Tilly, *Dynamics of Contention* (Cambridge: Cambridge University Press, 2001), pp. 65–67.

56. Stephen Craig, "The Angry Voter: Politics and Popular Discontent in the 1990s," in *Broken Contract? Changing Relationships between Americans and Their Government,* ed. Stephen Craig (Boulder, Colo.: Westview Press, 1996),

pp. 46–66; Stephen Nichols, David Kimball, and Paul A. Beck, "Voter Turnout in the 1996 Election: Resuming a Downward Spiral?" in *Reelection 1996: How Americans Voted*, ed. Herbert Weisberg and Janet Box-Steffensmeier (Chappaqua, N.Y.: Chatham House, 1999), pp. 23–44.

57. Robert Putnam, "The Strange Disappearance of Civic America," *The American Prospect* 7, no. 24 (Winter 1996): 34–48. See also idem, "Bowling Alone: America's Declining Social Capital," *Journal of Democracy* 6, no. 1 (January 1995): 66.

58. Idem, *Bowling Alone: The Collapse and Revival of American Community* (New York: Simon and Schuster, 2000).

59. Cohen, "Does Voluntary Association Make Democracy Work?"; Theda Skocpol and Morris Fiorina, "Making Sense of the Civic Engagement Debate," in *Civic Engagement in American Democracy*, ed. Theda Skocpol and Morris Fiorina (Washington, D.C.: Brookings Institution, 1999), pp. 13–14.

60. Stephen Samuel Smith and Jessica Kulynich, "It May Be Social, but Why Is It Capital? The Social Construction of Social Capital and the Politics of Language," *Politics and Society* 30, no. 1 (March 2002): 149–186; Dietrich Rueschemeyer, Evelyn Huber Stephens, and John Stephens, *Capitalist Development and Democracy* (Oxford: Polity Press, 1992).

61. Christopher Beem, *The Necessity of Politics* (Chicago: University of Chicago Press, 1999), pp. 170–172.

62. Max Weber, "'Objectivity' in Social Science and Social Policy," in his *The Methodology of the Social Sciences*, trans. and ed. E. A. Shils and H. A. Finch (New York: Free Press, 1949), pp. 49–112.

63. Charles Ragin, *The Comparative Method* (Berkeley: University of California Press, 1987), pp. 3, 31; Tilly, *Durable Inequality*, p. 7; see also John Walton, *Western Times and Water Wars* (Berkeley: University of California Press, 1992), p. 2; and Arthur Stinchcombe, *Theoretical Methods in Social History* (New York: Academic Press, 1978), pp. 21–22.

64. Walton, *Western Times and Water Wars*, p. 7; Jeffrey Haydu, "Making Use of the Past: Time Periods as Cases to Compare and as Sequences of Problem Solving," *American Journal of Sociology* 102, no. 2 (September 1998): 339–371.

65. Ragin, *The Comparative Method*, p. 49; Michael Burawoy, "Two Methods in Search of Science: Skocpol versus Trotsky," *Theory and Society* 18 (1989): 759–805; Haydu, "Making Use of the Past," p. 348.

66. Andrew Abbott, "From Causes to Events: Notes on Narrative Positivism," *Sociological Methods and Research* 20, no. 4 (May 1992): 428–455; idem, "What Do Cases Do? Some Notes on Activity in Sociological Analysis," in *What Is a Case?* ed. Charles Ragin and Howard S. Becker (Cambridge: Cambridge University Press, 1992), pp. 53–82; Ragin, *The Comparative Method*, pp. 59ff.

67. Larry Griffin, "Narrative, Event-Structure Analysis, and Causal Interpretation in Historical Sociology," *American Journal of Sociology* 98 (March

1993): 1094–1133. See also Abbott, "What Do Cases Do?" pp. 62–63; Jill Quadagno and Stan Knapp, "Have Historical Sociologists Forsaken Theory?" *Sociological Methods and Research* 20, no. 4 (May 1992): 481–507.

68. Susan Fainstein and Norman Fainstein, "Economic Change, National Policy, and the System of Cities," in *Restructuring the City*, ed. Susan Fainstein, 2d ed. (New York: Longmans, 1985), pp. 1–26.

CHAPTER 2. CORPORATE POWER
AND ETHNIC PATRONAGE

1. David Weber, *Oakland: Hub of the West* (Tulsa: Continental Heritage Press, 1981), pp. 17, 59; Ruth Hendricks Willard, *Alameda County, California Crossroads* (Northridge, Calif.: Windsor Publications, 1988), pp. 30–33, 58; Beth Bagwell, *Oakland: Story of a City* (Oakland: Oakland Heritage Alliance, 1994 [orig. 1982]), p. 126.

2. Mel Scott, *The San Francisco Bay Area: A Metropolis in Perspective* (Berkeley: University of California Press, 1959), pp. 33–34; Weber, *Oakland: Hub of the West*, pp. 42–44.

3. William Deverell, *Railroad Crossing: Californians and the Railroad, 1850–1910* (Berkeley: University of California Press, 1994), pp. 22–23; Scott, *The San Francisco Bay Area*, p. 48; Weber, *Oakland: Hub of the West*, p. 61; Bagwell, *Oakland: Story of a City*, p. 51; Willard, *Alameda County*, pp. 35–37.

4. Bagwell *Oakland: Story of a City*, p. 59; Scott, *The San Francisco Bay Area*, p. 59; Weber, *Oakland: Hub of the West*, p. 92.

5. Peter Conmy, *The Beginnings of Oakland, California, A.U.C.* (Oakland: Oakland Public Library, 1961), p. 45. Ward numbers and boundaries are as of approximately 1900. See R. S. Masters, R. C. Smith and W. E. Winters, *An Historical Review of the East Bay Exchange* (San Francisco: Pacific Telephone and Telegraph, 1927); *Map of the City of Oakland* (Oakland: J/ H. MacDonald, 1900), in the collection of the Earth Sciences and Map Library, University of California, Berkeley.

6. John Dykstra, "A History of the Physical Development of the City of Oakland: The Formative Years, 1850–1930" (master's thesis, University of California, Berkeley, 1967), pp. 187–193, 217–218; E. T. H. Bunje, "Oakland Industries, 1848–1938" (Oakland: Works Progress Administration, 1939); Edgar Hinkel and William McCann, *Oakland, 1852–1938: Some Phases of the Social, Political, and Economic History of Oakland, California* (Oakland: Works Progress Administration, 1939), p. 887; California Department of Transportation, *Historic Property Survey Report: For the Proposed I-880 Reconstruction Project*, vol. 4: *Historic Architecture Survey Report* (San Francisco: CALTRANS District 4, 1990), part 7, C-4.

7. Bagwell, *Oakland: Story of a City*, pp. 175–179; Dallas Smythe, "An Economic History of Local and Interurban Transportation in the East Bay Cities with Particular Reference to the Properties Developed by F. M. Smith" (Ph.D. diss., University of California, Berkeley, 1939), pp. 130–132; U.S. Bureau of the

Census, *Census of the Population: 1950,* vol. 2: *Characteristics of the Population,* part 5: *California* (Washington, D.C.: GPO, 1952).

8. Roger Waldinger, "When the Melting Pot Boils Over: The Irish, Jews, Blacks, and Koreans of New York," in *The Bubbling Cauldron,* ed. M. P. Smith and J. R. Feagin (Minneapolis: University of Minnesota Press, 1995), pp. 265–281; Suzanne Model, "The Ethnic Niche and the Structure of Opportunity: Immigrants and Minorities in New York City," in *The 'Underclass' Debate: Views from History,* ed. Michael Katz (Princeton, N.J.: Princeton University Press, 1993), pp. 161–193.

9. Mary Praetzellis, ed., *West Oakland: A Place to Start From,* Research Design and Treatment Plan: Cypress I-880 Replacement Project, vol. 1: *Historical Archaeology* (Oakland: CALTRANS District 4, 1994), pp. 83, 115–118; Robert Knight, *Industrial Relations in the San Francisco Bay Area, 1900–1918* (Berkeley: University of California Press, 1960), p. 42.

10. Tim Hallinan, "The Portuguese of California" (master's thesis, University of California, Berkeley, 1964), pp. 36–37.

11. Delores Nason McBroome, *Parallel Communities: African Americans in California's East Bay, 1850–1963* (New York: Garland, 1993), pp. 33, 67; Lawrence Crouchette, Lonnie Bunch III, and Martha K. Winnacker, *Visions toward Tomorrow: A History of the East Bay Afro-American Community 1852–1977* (Oakland: Northern California Center for Afro-American History and Life, 1989), pp. 9–10; Eric Brown, "Black Ghetto Formation in Oakland, 1852–1965," *Research in Community Sociology* 8 (1998): 255–274. According to one estimate, in 1930 the Pullman Company and the Southern Pacific Railroad together accounted for 60 percent of the income of the Oakland black population: William Brown Jr., "Class Aspects of Residential Development and Choice in the Oakland Black Community" (Ph.D. diss., University of California, Berkeley, 1970), pp. 82–83.

12. Bagwell, *Oakland: Story of a City,* pp. 85–89; L. Eve Armentrout Ma with Jeong Huei Ma, *The Chinese of Oakland* (Oakland: Chinese History Research Committee, 1982).

13. Howard Chudacoff, *The Evolution of American Urban Society* (Englewood Cliffs, N.J.: Prentice-Hall, 1975), pp. 84–85; Bradford Luckingham, *The Urban Southwest* (El Paso: Texas Western Press, 1982).

14. Judith V. May, "Progressives and the Poor" (MS, Institute of Governmental Studies Library, University of California, Berkeley, 1970), p. 2; Steven Blutza, "Oakland's Commission and Council-Manager Plans—Causes and Consequences" (Ph.D. diss., University of California, Berkeley, 1978), pp. 13–14; Hinkel and McCann, *Oakland, 1852–1938,* p. 29 ("fountain of franchises").

15. Joseph E. Baker, ed., *Past and Present of Alameda County, California,* 2 vols. (Chicago: S. J. Clarke, 1914), vol. 1, p. 237; Hinkel and McCann, *Oakland, 1852–1938,* p. 638; May, "Progressives and the Poor," p. 18.

16. Kenneth Jackson, *Crabgrass Frontier: The Suburbanization of the United States* (New York: Oxford University Press, 1985), p. 121; Hinkel and McCann, *Oakland, 1852–1938,* pp. 30–34; Smythe, "An Economic History of Local and Interurban Transportation."

17. California Department of Transportation, *Historic Property Survey Report: For the Proposed I-880 Reconstruction Project,* vol. 3: *Historic Resources Inventory* (San Francisco: CALTRANS District 4, 1990), pp. 10–18, 26–31; May, "Progressives and the Poor," pp. 30–31, 37; George Mowry, *The California Progressives* (Chicago: Quadrangle Books, 1963 [orig. 1951]), p. 10.

18. May, "Progressives and the Poor," pp. 2, 10; Blutza, "Oakland's Commission and Council-Manager Plans," pp. 7–14.

19. John F. Mullins, "How Earl Warren Became District Attorney," an oral history conducted 1963, in *Perspectives on the Alameda County District Attorney's Office,* Regional Oral History Office, Bancroft Library, University of California, Berkeley, 1972, pp. 2–8; Hiram Johnson to Major Archibald Johnson, July 13, 1931, and Hiram Johnson to Hiram Johnson Jr., January 15, 1933, in *The Diary Letters of Hiram Johnson, 1917–1945,* ed. Robert E. Burke (New York: Garland, 1983); Baker, ed., *Past and Present of Alameda County,* vol. 2, p. 369; *Oakland Tribune,* November 20, 1940; *Oakland Post-Enquirer,* November 20, 1940; *East Bay Labor Journal,* September 2, 1932.

20. May, "Progressives and the Poor," pp. 49–50.

21. In 1926, Republican voter registrants in Alameda County outnumbered Democrats by more than five to one; *Oakland Tribune,* October 9, 1926. On Republican Party machines, see Steven Erie, *Rainbow's End: Irish Americans and the Dilemmas of Urban Machine Politics, 1840–1985* (Berkeley: University of California Press, 1988), p. 229. In 1923, it was estimated there were more than five hundred state and federal jobs in the county; *Observer,* August 12, 1923.

22. *Observer,* June 9 and October 27, 1928; William Denahy, *The Irish in West Oakland,* an oral history conducted 1982, Neighborhood History Project, Oakland History Room, Oakland Public Library, Oakland, p. 6; Mullins oral history, pp. 23–24. For working-class job seekers in the police and fire departments, the machine could obtain a passing grade in medical examinations by referral to friendly doctors; tape-recorded interview with Donald Mockel, conducted 1981, Neighborhood History Project, Oakland History Room, Oakland Public Library, Oakland. Conversely, the railroads used health exams as a way of blacklisting undesired employees; Praetzellis, ed., *West Oakland,* p. 84.

23. Martin Shefter, "Trade Unions and Political Machines: The Organization and Disorganization of the American Working Class in the Late Nineteenth Century," in *Working Class Formation,* ed. Ira Katznelson and Aristide Zolberg (Princeton, N.J.: Princeton University Press, 1986), pp. 197–276.

24. Consider Jack London's account of his experience of joblessness as a youth in Oakland:

> Times were hard. Work of any sort was difficult to get. And work of any sort was what I had to take, for I was still an unskilled laborer. . . . I failed to find a job at anything. I had my name down in five employment bureaus. I advertised in three newspapers. I sought the few friends I knew who might be able to get me work, but they were either uninterested or unable to find anything for me. . . . Yet I was

a bargain in the labor market. I was twenty-two years old, weighed one hundred and sixty five pounds stripped, every pound of which was excellent for toil.

Jack London, "John Barleycorn," in *The Collected Jack London*, ed. Steven Kasdin (New York: Barnes & Noble, 1992), pp. 632–633.

25. Denahy oral history.

26. Oakland Police Department, *Oakland Police Department History—1919* (Oakland: Police Department, 1985?), part 2, p. 36.

27. Madelon Powers, *Faces along the Bar: Lore and Order in the Working-man's Saloon, 1870–1920* (Chicago: University of Chicago Press, 1998).

28. London, "John Barleycorn," pp. 578, 603–604.

29. Denahy oral history, pp. 12–14.

30. California Department of Transportation, *Historic Property Survey Report*, vol. 3, pp. 41–46.

31. Mockel, tape-recorded interview.

32. Ibid.

33. Robert Merton, *Social Theory and Social Structure*, rev. ed. (New York: Free Press, 1968 [orig. 1949]), pp. 125–136; Robert Dahl, *Who Governs? Democracy and Power in an American City* (New Haven, Conn.: Yale University Press, 1961), pp. 32–34; Samuel P. Hays, *The Response to Industrialism 1885–1914* (Chicago: University of Chicago Press, 1957).

34. California Department of Transportation, *Historic Property Survey Report*, vol. 3, p. 40 (both quotes).

35. Ibid., vol. 3, p. 41.

36. Praetzellis, ed., *West Oakland*, p. 83.

37. Mockel, tape-recorded interview.

38. "New Industrial Ventures Being Developed in East Oakland," *Oakland Enquirer*, January 7, 1902.

39. "Thirteenth Biennial Report of the California Bureau of Statistics Reveals Oakland's 'Prosperity,'" *The World*, January 30, 1909; Elizabeth Reis, "Cannery Row: The AFL, the IWW, and Bay Area Italian Cannery Workers," *California History* 64, no. 3 (Summer 1985): 175–191.

40. Erie, *Rainbow's End*, p. 13.

41. McBroome, *Parallel Communities*, p. 40; James Fisher, "A History of the Political and Social Development of the Black Community in California, 1850–1950" (Ph.D. diss., State University of New York, Stony Brook, 1972), p. 207.

42. "Must Restore Discipline," *The Civic Reporter and Oakland Review*, May 17, 1916; *Observer*, October 27, 1928.

43. May, "Progressives and the Poor," p. 22; Smythe, "An Economic History of Local and Interurban Transportation," pp. 123–123; "Gouging the Public," *Western Appeal*, December 7, 1921; California Department of Transportation, *Historic Property Survey Report: For the Proposed I-880 Reconstruction Project* (San Francisco: CALTRANS District 4, 1990), vol. 1, appendix A: "Archaeological Survey Report," p. 10; Praetzellis, ed., *West Oakland*, p. 165.

44. Praetzellis, ed., *West Oakland*, pp. 121, 161–169.

45. Philip McArdle, "The Police Scandal of 1919," Oakland Police Department, *Oakland Police Department History—1919*, part 3.

46. Ma with Ma, *The Chinese of Oakland*, pp. 26–27.

47. Alexander Saxton, *The Indispensable Enemy: Labor and the Anti-Chinese Movement in California* (Berkeley: University of California Press, 1971); Gladys Waldron, "Antiforeign Movements in California, 1919–1929" (Ph.D. diss., University of California, Berkeley, 1956).

48. Praetzellis, ed., *West Oakland*, pp. 71–81.

49. Ibid., pp. 82–86; Knight, *Industrial Relations*, pp. 253–254.

50. Ira Cross, *A History of the Labor Movement in California* (Berkeley: University of California Press, 1974), pp. 229–231; Knight, *Industrial Relations*, pp. 43–45, 177, 208–209, 250, 375–377.

51. Saxton, *The Indispensable Enemy*, p. 269.

52. U.S. Bureau of the Census, *Fourteenth Census of the United States, 1920: Population*, vol. 4: *Occupations* (Washington, D.C.: GPO, 1923), pp. 186–194, 1185–1188; Knight, *Industrial Relations*, p. 267.

53. Blutza, "Oakland's Commission and Council-Manager Plans," p. 29; Knight, *Industrial Relations*, p. 128. The Union Labor Party did succeed in electing at least one of its own, unionist John Forrest, as city commissioner in 1911.

54. *Socialist Voice*, March 9, 1907; *Tri-City Labor Review*, September 22, 1916; Ralph Shaffer, "Radicalism in California, 1869–1929" (Ph.D. diss., University of California, Berkeley, 1962); "Lethargic Labor Is Responsible: Failure to Defeat Ordinance at Tuesday's Election May Awaken Slackers," *Tri-City Labor Review*, May 13, 1917.

55. Knight, *Industrial Relations*, pp. 128, 262; Michael Rogin, "Nonpartisanship and the Group Interest," in *Power and Community*, ed. Philip Green and Sanford Levinson (New York: Pantheon, 1970), pp. 112–141.

56. Knight, *Industrial Relations*, p. 262.

57. Ibid., p. 241.

58. Austin Lewis, "The Municipal Campaign," *The World* [Oakland], February 27, 1909.

59. Hinkel and McCann, *Oakland, 1852–1938*, pp. 107–109; DeWitt Jones, ed., *Port of Oakland* (Oakland: State Emergency Relief Administration, 1934), pp. 92–93.

60. Smythe, "An Economic History of Local and Interurban Transportation," pp. 149–189; Jones, ed., *Port of Oakland*, p. 79.

61. Founding members of the Chamber included Mayor Frank Mott (former treasurer of the Board of Trade and director of Security Bank and Trust, with business interests in hardware and real estate), W. J. Laymance (real estate), Frank Bilger (construction), Frederick Kahn and H. C. Capwell (department stores, the latter also president of Security Bank and Trust), Theodore Gier (head of a wine company, founder of the Board of Trade, Merchants' Exchange, and founder and director of Security Bank and Trust), W. W. Garthwaite (bank-

ing), and W. E. Dargie (publisher of the *Oakland Tribune*). Blutza, "Oakland's Commission and Council-Manager Plans," pp. 45–65; Hinkel and McCann, *Oakland, 1852–1938*, p. 157.

62. Charter members of the Real Estate Board included W. J. Laymance (founding member of the Chamber of Commerce), A. H. Breed (city auditor), F. Bruce Maiden, Wickham Havens, Walter Liemert, and R. J. Montgomery, among others; Hinkel and McCann, *Oakland, 1852–1938*, pp. 223, 762.

63. Bilger was a founding member of the Chamber of Commerce in 1905, its vice president in 1906, and its president in 1907. That same year he organized the Harbor Bank. In 1905, he had managed Frank Mott's first mayoral campaign. Other charter members of the Rotary included vice president H. C. Capwell (see above), treasurer C. J. Heeseman and director Frank A. Leach Jr. (both founding members of the Chamber of Commerce), Naph Greenfelder (chairman of the Harbor League), and R. J. Montgomery (charter member of the Real Estate Board). Jones, ed., *Port of Oakland*, p. 95; Rotary Club of Oakland, "Rotarily Yours: A History of the Rotary Club of Oakland" (booklet produced in Oakland, 1969); Hinkel and McCann, *Oakland, 1852–1938*, pp. 157, 223.

64. Bagwell, *Oakland: Story of a City*, p. 182; Blutza, "Oakland's Commission and Council-Manager Plans," pp. 7–10.

65. Blutza, "Oakland's Commission and Council-Manager Plans," pp. 33–35; May, "Progressives and the Poor," pp. 44–50.

66. Dykstra, "A History of the Physical Development of the City of Oakland," pp. 146–153; Blutza, "Oakland's Commission and Council-Manager Plans," pp. 42ff., 102–108; Judith V. May, "Struggle for Authority: A Comparison of Four Social Change Programs in Oakland, California" (Ph.D. diss., University of California, Berkeley, 1973), p. 61; U.S. Bureau of the Census, *Thirteenth Census of the United States: Reports by States, Supplement for California* (Washington, D.C.: GPO, 1913), p. 574.

67. Blutza, "Oakland's Commission and Council-Manager Plans," pp. 110–183.

68. "Oakland's New City Charter," *The World*, June 3, 1910.

69. Blutza, "Oakland's Commission and Council-Manager Plans," pp. 208–209; *Observer*, January 29, 1921; *Alameda County Union Labor Record*, March 9, 1923.

70. Davie had served a brief term as mayor, elected on the Populist ticket, from 1895 to 1897. *Observer*, March 17, 1923; May, "Progressives and the Poor," pp. 36–40; Bagwell, *Oakland: Story of a City*, p. 206.

71. Blutza, "Oakland's Commission and Council-Manager Plans," p. 211. In 1916, F. M. Smith attempted a comeback by proposing to develop the harbor in the Key Route basin. The city granted him the franchise, but Smith was unable to secure financing. In 1918, the city agreed to subsidize development of a new shipping terminal, which opened in 1920, but it too was soon tied up in litigation. Jones, ed., *Port of Oakland*, p. 143.

72. *Observer*, February 5 and April 30, 1921, and March 17, 1923; see also

May, "Progressives and the Poor," pp. 55–56; Blutza, "Oakland's Commission and Council-Manager Plans," pp. 210–212; G. A. Cummings and E. S. Pladwell, *Oakland: A History* (Oakland: Grant Miller Mortuaries, 1942), pp. 91–93.

73. William Lunch, "Oakland Revisited: Stability and Change in an American City" (MS, Environmental Design Library, University of California, Berkeley, 1970), p. 31; *San Francisco Examiner,* February 1, 1916, quoted in Oakland City Planning Department, *Oakland Cultural Heritage Survey,* vol. 32: *West Oakland Survey, Oak Center Redevelopment Area* (Oakland: City Planning Department, 1992), p. 8; Bunje, "Oakland Industries, 1848–1938," pp. 75–85.

74. Knight, *Industrial Relations,* pp. 338–341, 360–363.

75. Ibid., pp. 336, 357; Reis, "Cannery Row," p. 183; *Tri-City Labor Review,* July 26 and August 16, 1918, and April 16, 1920.

76. Knight, *Industrial Relations,* pp. 358–361.

77. Ibid., pp. 319, 358–359.

78. *Tri-City Labor Review,* October 10, 1919; Oakland Police Department, *Oakland Police Department History—1919,* part 3, pp. 38–39.

79. David Selvin, *A Terrible Anger* (Detroit: Wayne State University Press, 1996), pp. 28–30; Richard Boyden, "The San Francisco Machinists and the National War Labor Board," in *American Labor in the Era of World War II,* ed. Sally Miller and Daniel Cornford (Westport, Conn.: Praeger, 1995), pp. 105–119.

80. Cross, *A History of the Labor Movement in California,* pp. 251–255; David Selvin, *Sky Full of Storm,* rev. ed. (San Francisco: California Historical Society, 1975), pp. 39–44; J. Paul St. Sure, *Some Comments on Employer Organizations and Collective Bargaining in Northern California since 1934,* an oral history conducted 1957, Institute for Industrial Relations, University of California, Berkeley, 1957, pp. 63–64; Oakland Chamber of Commerce, "Industrial Oakland" (1923; Oakland Public Library, Oakland).

81. Cross, *A History of the Labor Movement in California,* p. 253; *Alameda County Union Labor Record,* April 9, 1926.

CHAPTER 3. THE MAKING OF A WHITE MIDDLE CLASS

1. Leonard Moore, "Historical Interpretations of the 1920's Klan: The Traditional View and the Populist Revision," *Journal of Social History* 24 (Winter 1990): 341–357. See also idem, *Citizen Klansmen: The Ku Klux Klan in Indiana, 1921–1928* (Chapel Hill: University of North Carolina Press, 1991); and Shawn Lay, ed., *The Invisible Empire in the West* (Urbana: University of Illinois Press, 1992).

2. U.S. Bureau of the Census, *Abstract of the Thirteenth Census of the United States, 1910* (Washington, D.C.: GPO, 1913), p. 95; idem, *Abstract of Fourteenth Census of the United States, 1920* (Washington, D.C.: GPO, 1923), p. 109; idem, *Abstract of Fifteenth Census of the United States, 1930* (Washington, D.C.: GPO, 1933), p. 100.

3. Idem, *Census of Religious Bodies, 1916,* part 1: *Summary and General Tables* (Washington, D.C.: GPO, 1919), p. 126; idem, *Census of Religious Bod-*

ies, 1926, vol. 1: *Summary and Detailed Tables* (Washington., D.C.: GPO, 1930), p. 496.

4. Idem, *Fourteenth Census of the United States, 1920: Population*, vol. 4: *Occupations* (Washington, D.C.: GPO, 1923), pp. 1185–1188; idem, *Fifteenth Census of the United States, 1930: Population*, vol. 4: *Occupations* (Washington, D.C.: GPO, 1933), pp. 202–216; idem, *Fifteenth Census of the United States: 1930: Population*, vol. 6: *Families* (Washington, D.C.: GPO, 1933), p. 57.

5. *Plat of Maxwell Park:* owned and recorded by John P. Maxwell, Conner and Milner, selling agents, East Oakland, California, 1910; and *Map of Central Terrace*, Mutual Realty Company, Oakland, California, 1915 (both in the collection of the Earth Sciences and Map Library, University of California, Berkeley, California).

6. Delores Nason McBroome, *Parallel Communities: African Americans in California's East Bay, 1850–1963* (New York: Garland, 1993), pp. 39, 48; Beth Bagwell, *Oakland: Story of a City* (Oakland: Oakland Heritage Alliance, 1994 [orig. 1982]), pp. 204–206. According to William Brown Jr., North Oakland above Thirty-sixth Street remained free of black settlement until well after 1940; Brown, "Class Aspects of Residential Development and Choice in the Oakland Black Community" (Ph.D. diss., University of California, Berkeley, 1970), p. 106.

7. E. A. Daly, "Alameda County Political Leader and Journalist," an oral history conducted 1971, in *Perspectives on the Alameda County District Attorney's Office*, Regional Oral History Office, Bancroft Library, University of California, Berkeley, 1972, p. 10; "U.S. to Probe 'Friendly' Warning to Negro Woman," *Oakland Times*, July 23, 1926.

8. *Oakland Tribune*, October 5, 1926; *Oakland Daily Record*, February 20 and May 19, 1925; *Western American*, October 26, 1926.

9. U.S. Bureau of the Census, *Fifteenth Census of the United States, 1930: Population* (Washington, D.C.: GPO, 1921), vol. 3, part 1, pp. 278, 287.

10. *The Crusader* [Oakland], November 1921, 2.

11. Fred Hunter, "Oakland Has Started the Second Largest School Building Campaign in the United States," *Oakland Tribune Yearbook* (Oakland: Tribune Publishing Company, 1920), p. 98.

12. *Oakland Tribune Yearbook* (Oakland: Tribune Publishing Company, 1921), p. 117.

13. James Timberlake, *Prohibition and the Progressive Movement, 1900–1920* (Cambridge, Mass.: Harvard University Press, 1963).

14. Oakland City Clerk, *Elections 1852 to the Present* (Oakland: Office of the City Clerk, n.d.), p. 18; Steven Blutza, "Oakland's Commission and Council-Manager Plans—Causes and Consequences" (Ph.D. diss., University of California, Berkeley, 1978), pp. 185–186.

15. "Police Charge Principal Interferes," *Oakland Enquirer*, March 12, 1921.

16. Marchant was president of the federation, and Howard chaired its executive committee. "Alameda County Federation Stands for Good Government," Alameda County Politics and Government Pamphlet File, Bancroft Library, Uni-

versity of California, Berkeley (emphases in original); *Polk's Oakland City Directory* (Oakland: R. L. Polk, 1918).

17. Harry Lafler, "Oakland and Eastbay Cities Maintain Proud Rank of Pacific Coast Industrial Center," *Oakland Tribune Yearbook* (Oakland: Tribune Publishing Company, 1925), p. 10; John Dykstra, "A History of the Physical Development of the City of Oakland: The Formative Years, 1850–1930" (master's thesis, University of California, Berkeley, 1967), pp. 227–230; David Weber, *Oakland: Hub of the West* (Tulsa: Continental Heritage Press, 1981), p. 130; U.S. Bureau of the Census, *Fourteenth Census of the United States, 1920,* vol. 1: *Population,* p. 353; idem, *Seventeenth Census of the United States, 1950: Population,* vol. 2, part 5: *California* (Washington, D.C.: GPO, 1952), pp. 5–13.

18. *Observer* [Oakland], December 2, 1922.

19. *Oakland Post-Enquirer,* April 24, 1924; *San Francisco Examiner,* April 25, 1924; *Oakland Daily Record,* December 16, 1924, and January 1 and 12, 1925; Earl Warren, *The Memoirs of Earl Warren* (New York: Doubleday, 1977), p. 88; *Oakland Post-Enquirer,* May 15, 1926; *Oakland Times,* May 14, 1926.

20. *Oakland Daily Record,* May 2, 1925; *Oakland Tribune,* October 27, 1930; Joseph Baker, *Past and Present of Alameda County, California* (Chicago: S. J. Clarke, 1914), vol. 2, p. 19; Blutza, "Oakland's Commission and Council-Manager Plans," p. 53.

21. *Oakland Daily Record,* June 20 and October 1 and 8, 1925.

22. *Oakland Daily Record,* December 18, 1924, and February 4 and 7, 1925; Oakland City Clerk, 1925 election files, City Clerk's Office, Oakland.

23. *Observer,* April 2, 1921; *Western Appeal,* April 22, 1922.

24. *Oakland Daily Record,* July 30 and 31, August 1, 6, 18, 19, and 20, and September 9 and 18, 1925.

25. *San Francisco Chronicle,* August 12, 1921, and May 11 and 15, 1922.

26. *San Francisco Chronicle,* March 4 and 12, 1922.

27. *Knights of the Ku Klux Klan, Inc., v. Leon C. Francis et al.,* case file no. 81118; *Knights of the Ku Klux Klan, Inc., v. Leon C. Francis et al.,* case file no. 82491; and *W. F. Courtney et al. v. John L. McVey et al.,* case file no. 82948, all from the Civil Division, California Superior Court, Alameda County, 1925; also *Eli J. Coon et al. v. Fidelity and Deposit Company of Maryland, Inc.,* case file no. 101707, Civil Division, California Superior Court, Alameda County, 1928; *Eli J. Coon et al. v. H. Sephton et al.,* case file no. 107549, Civil Division, California Superior Court, Alameda County, 1929; *California v. Parker et al.,* case file no. 11369, Criminal Division, California Superior Court, Alameda County, 1930; *Polk's Oakland City Directory* (Oakland: R. L. Polk, 1924, 1925, 1929, 1930); *Oakland Daily Record,* January 17, 1925.

28. East Oakland is defined here as the pre-1910 charter Seventh Ward, including the annexed territories east of Lake Merritt. North Oakland comprises the old First Ward bordering on the Berkeley line, including Rockridge. West Oakland includes the Second, Third, Fourth, and Sixth Wards, from the western waterfront to downtown and from Thirty-sixth Street to the estuary. Blutza, "Oakland's Commission and Council-Manager Plans," pp. 502–504; *Map*

of the City of Oakland (Oakland: J. H. MacDonald, 1900), in the collection of the Earth Sciences and Map Library, University of California, Berkeley.

29. See Moore, "Historical Interpretations of the 1920's Klan"; and the essays in Lay, ed., *The Invisible Empire in the West.*

30. Kenneth Jackson, *The Ku Klux Klan in the City, 1915–1930* (New York: Oxford University Press, 1967), p. 190; *Oakland Tribune,* May 9 and 25, 1922.

31. David Chalmers, *Hooded Americanism: The First Century of the Ku Klux Klan, 1865–1965* (New York: Doubleday, 1965), p. 122.

32. *Observer,* September 9, October 21 and 28, and November 4, 1922.

33. Unprocessed political pamphlet, Bancroft Library, University of California, Berkeley; emphases in original.

34. See also Alexander Saxton, *The Rise and Fall of the White Republic* (London: Verso, 1990); David Montejano, *Anglos and Mexicans in the Making of Texas, 1836–1986* (Austin: University of Texas Press, 1987).

35. Oscar Jahnsen, *Enforcing the Law against Gambling, Bootlegging, Graft, Fraud, and Subversion,* an oral history conducted 1970, Regional Oral History Office, Bancroft Library, University of California, Berkeley, 1976, pp. 36–37.

36. Arnest and Francis were also both endorsed by the Redwood Improvement Association, a neighborhood group in East Oakland; Oakland and Alameda County Political Scrapbooks, 1910–1930, vol. 3, Oakland History Room, Oakland Public Library, Oakland.

37. *Knights of the Ku Klux Klan, Inc., v. East Bay Club of Alameda County et al.,* case file no. 82470, Civil Division, California Superior Court, Alameda County, 1925; Oakland City Clerk, *Elections 1852 to the Present,* p. 32.

38. *Knights of the Ku Klux Klan, Inc., v. Leon C. Francis et al.;* case file no. 81245, Civil Division, California Superior Court, Alameda County, 1925; *Oakland Post-Enquirer,* June 19 and 23, 1924; *San Francisco Chronicle,* July 5, 1924.

39. *Ku Klux Klan v. Francis et al.; Coon et al. v. Sephton et al.*

40. *San Francisco Chronicle,* August 12, 1924.

41. *Ku Klux Klan v. Francis et al.; Ku Klux Klan v. East Bay Club.*

42. *Oakland Tribune,* August 24, 1925.

43. *Oakland Daily Record,* January 24 and May 19, 1925.

44. *Ku Klux Klan v. East Bay Club;* Frank C. Merritt, *History of Alameda County* (Chicago: S. J Clarke, 1928), pp. 102–103.

45. The younger MacLafferty was chaplain of Klan No. 9 and of the East Bay Club until May 18, 1925. Brooks was appointed secretary of Klan No. 9 in 1925, while MacGregor served on the executive committee and as chair of the auditing committee. Both men acted as verification deputies for the petition drive. *Oakland Daily Record,* December 17, 1924, January 17 and 22 and February 25, 1925; *Ku Klux Klan v. East Bay Club; Courtney et al. v. McVey et al.; Coon et al. v. Sephton et al.;* 1925 election files, Office of the City Clerk, Oakland.

46. *Ku Klux Klan v. East Bay Club;* 1923 election files, Office of the City Clerk, Oakland; *Oakland Daily Record,* April 18 and 20, 1925. In 1925 the Better Government League endorsed H. T. Hempstead and F. F. Morse against the downtown candidates Leroy Goodrich and Frank Colbourn.

47. *Oakland Tribune,* December 4, 1924.

48. Merritt, *History of Alameda County,* pp. 218–221; *Observer,* July 15 and 29, 1922; *Oakland Tribune,* August 30, 1922; *Oakland Post-Enquirer,* September 1, 1922.

49. Merritt, *History of Alameda County,* pp. 517–518. *Dimond News,* March 23, 1923, and January 29, 1926; *Oakland Daily Record,* July 20, 1925.

50. *Observer,* June 19 and November 27, 1920; Ira Cross, *A History of the Labor Movement in California* (Berkeley: University of California Press, 1974 [orig. 1935]), pp. 252–254.

51. The first board of directors of the club included department store owners Frederick Kahn and H. C. Capwell (the latter also president of Security Bank and Trust); automobile manufacturers Norman De Vaux and R. C. Durant; Chamber of Commerce president Joseph King; J. F. Carlston, president of the Central National Bank; Arthur Moore, vice president of the Oakland Bank; J. R. Millar, general manager of the California Cotton Mills; Max Horwinski, president of the Rotary Club; and others; "Oakland Clubs and Societies—Athens Athletic Club," vertical files, Oakland History Room, Oakland Public Library, Oakland.

52. For years Oakland business elites had pursued reform through unsuccessful efforts to consolidate East Bay city and county governments in a "Greater Oakland," their final attempt being defeated at the polls in November 1921 and February 1922. The defeat of county consolidation marked the ascendancy of Knowland, who almost alone among Oakland businessmen had opposed the plan. Blutza, "Oakland's Commission and Council-Manager Plans," pp. 218–219; *Observer,* October 8 and 15, 1921; Edgar Hinkel and William McCann, *Oakland, 1852–1938: Some Phases of the Social, Political, and Economic History of Oakland, California* (Oakland: Works Progress Administration, 1939), pp. 768–769; John Gothberg, "The Local Influence of J. R. Knowland's *Oakland Tribune,*" *Journalism Quarterly* 43, no. 3 (Autumn 1968): 487–495; William Lunch, "Oakland Revisited: Stability and Change in an American City" (MS, Environmental Design Library, University of California, 1970), pp. 38–39, 53.

53. Daly oral history, pp. 23–25; John F. Mullins, "How Earl Warren Became District Attorney," an oral history conducted 1963, in *Perspectives on the Alameda County District Attorney's Office,* Regional Oral History Office, Bancroft Library, University of California, Berkeley, 1972; courtesy of the Bancroft Library.

54. In 1926 Knowland and his sons William and J. Russell Jr. became the first three paid-up lifetime members of the Athens Athletic Club; "Clubs and Societies, Athens Athletic Club"; *Oakland Tribune Yearbook* (Oakland: Tribune Publishing Company, 1924), p. 4.

55. Dykstra, "A History of the Physical Development," pp. 230–231; *Oakland Tribune Yearbook* (Oakland: Tribune Publishing Company, 1926), p. 27.

56. *Oakland Tribune,* March 16 and 17, 1920; *Observer,* March 20 and April 3, 1920.

57. Leaders of the recall campaign included contractors T. D. Sexton, W. E.

Whalin (president of the Building Contractors Association), and R. W. Littlefield (past master of the Scottish Rite Masons and active in the Elks and Lions Clubs), Herman Johnson (manager of the Otis Elevator Company and president of the Rotary Club), attorney and former tax collector Clinton Dodge, and insurance broker and campaign chair L. C. Fraser. All of the above except Fraser served on the executive committee of the Good Government League, along with J. Cal Ewing, baseball club owner and founding member of the Athens Athletic Club; Allen Hibbard of the Laymance Insurance Agency; and league president Leroy Goodrich, manager of a book publishing company, president of the Lions Club, and chair of the Chamber of Commerce's city interests committee in 1920. Goodrich, Johnson, and Dodge were also active in the Chamber's law-and-order campaign, while Fraser and Hibbard later served on the board of the Athens Athletic Club building corporation; *Observer,* May 5, 1920; "Oakland Council," "Oakland Chamber of Commerce," and "Oakland Clubs and Societies: Athens Athletic Club," vertical files, Oakland History Room, Oakland Public Library, Oakland; *Polk's Oakland Directory,* 1921; *Oakland Tribune Yearbook* (Oakland: Tribune Publishing Company, 1922), p. 100, (1923), p. 98, and (1924), p. 75.

58. Carter and Colbourn were supported by Mayor Davie, who had temporarily split with Kelly. By 1924, however, Davie in turn had split with them, and the league commissioners allied with Commissioner of Streets Baccus to form a new majority clique on the council; *Oakland Daily Record,* March 2, 1925.

59. Hinkel and McCann, *Oakland, 1852–1938,* p. 175; "Oakland, Chamber of Commerce, 1909–1929," vertical files, Oakland History Room, Oakland Public Library, Oakland; *Oakland Tribune,* April 11, 1923.

60. The initial officers and members of the Community Council included President O. H. Fisher, who was also president of the Chamber of Commerce; Vice Presidents R. S. Milligan of the Lions Club and Willard White of the Real Estate Board; and members Warren Williams of the Rotary Club, Sherwood Swan of the Downtown Association, Bestor Robinson of the American Legion, and others. The council's activities focused particularly on generating public support for bond issues for urban infrastructure, including the county hospital, the estuary tube (the tunnel bore that now contains the underwater roadway between Oakland and the island of Alameda), street lighting, schools, and harbor development; "Civic Clubs Play Large Part in Oakland's Growth," *Oakland Tribune Yearbook* (Oakland: Tribune Publishing Company, 1925), p. 61.

61. Dykstra, "A History of the Physical Development," p. 203; *Observer,* August 30, 1924. Goodrich remained active in the Chamber of Commerce, serving as director and finance committee chair in 1922, vice president and director in 1923, and harbor committee member in 1924; "Oakland, Chamber of Commerce 1909–1929" files, Oakland History Room, Oakland Public Library, Oakland; *Oakland Daily Record,* February 21, 1925.

62. *Oakland Daily Record,* September 25 and October 3 and 5, 1925; "Real Estate in Oakland Is on a Sound Foundation," *Oakland Tribune Yearbook* (Oakland: Tribune Publishing Company, 1925), p. 129. Under the bond issue and the

charter amendment, board members were appointed by Public Works Commissioner Goodrich, not Mayor Davie, as on other city commissions. Not surprisingly, Mayor Davie vigorously, and unsuccessfully, opposed both. By contrast, Kelly supported both, because they did not affect county government and the machine stood to gain from millions of dollars in new contracts; Blutza, "Oakland's Commission and Council-Manager Plans," pp. 221–225; Lunch, "Oakland Revisited," pp. 39, 53.

63. Goodrich's original appointments to the port board included, as chair, fellow Good Government League activist Roscoe D. Jones, who was also a former chair of the Civil Service Commission, head of the citizens committee advocating the regional utility district, and Chamber of Commerce harbor committee member in 1923 and water committee chair from 1924 to 1927; B. H. Pendleton, former city councillor from the old downtown Fifth Ward, Chamber director from 1918 to 1922, and Chamber water committee member and transportation committee chair in 1924; downtown retailers R. A. Leet and H. C. Capwell (the latter vice president of the Athens Athletic Club); and Stuart Hawley, investment broker and Athens Athletic Club director. In 1926, Jones, Leet, and Hawley all served simultaneously on the port board and the Chamber harbor committee. Hawley was replaced on the permanent board by former governor George Pardee. *Observer,* December 31, 1921; "Harbor Program of Oakland Seals City's Destiny," *Oakland Tribune Yearbook* (Oakland: Tribune Publishing Company, 1927), p. 33; DeWitt Jones, ed., *Port of Oakland* (Oakland: State Emergency Relief Administration, 1934), pp. 142–154; "Oakland, Chamber of Commerce 1909–1929" files, Oakland History Room, Oakland Public Library, Oakland; Office of the City Clerk, *Elections 1852 to the Present,* p. 34.

64. Mullins oral history, pp. 10, 24. *Oakland Tribune,* June 27, 1927; Peter Conmy, *Seventy Years of Service, 1902–1972* (Los Angeles: California Knights of Columbus, 1972), p. 233; city council candidates' statements, 1931, in "Oakland—Elections" file, Oakland History Room, Oakland Public Library, Oakland.

65. Mullins was close to Judge Tyrrell, and both were active in the Knights of Columbus. Mullins oral history, pp. 1–11; Jahnsen oral history, pp. 46–48; Warren, *The Memoirs,* pp. 67–69; Leo Katcher, *Earl Warren: A Political Biography* (New York: McGraw-Hill, 1967), pp. 44–46.

66. *Observer,* January 17 and April 25, 1925.

67. *Observer,* September 18 and December 4, 1926.

68. Jahnsen oral history, pp. 34, 38.

69. Warren, *The Memoirs,* pp. 83–85; Mary Shaw, "Perspectives of a Newspaperwoman," an oral history conducted 1970, in *Perspectives on the Alameda County District Attorney's Office,* Regional Oral History Office, Bancroft Library, University of California, Berkeley, 1972, pp. 12–15; *Oakland Times,* August 6, 1925; *Observer,* March 6, 1926; *Oakland Tribune,* November 3 and 4, 1926, and February 20, 1927; *San Francisco Examiner,* November 3 and 4, 1926; Merritt, *History of Alameda County,* pp. 102, 517–518. Oakland and Alameda County Political Scrapbooks, 1910–1930, vol. 2, Oakland History Room, Oakland Public Library, Oakland.

70. *Oakland Tribune*, April 3, 1927; *Observer*, April 9, 1927; B. Hill to B. A. Forester, May 10, 1927, J. R. Knowland Papers, Carton 28, Bancroft Library, University of California, Berkeley.

71. *Oakland Tribune*, April 18, 1927. See also *Oakland Times*, April 8, 11, 12, and 15, 1927.

72. *Oakland Times*, April 8, 11, and 15, 1927.

73. *Oakland Tribune*, April 18 and May 4 and 7, 1927; *Oakland Post-Enquirer*, April 15, 1927; *Oakland Times*, May 9, 1927; *Observer*, May 24, 1930.

74. *Oakland Post-Enquirer*, February 11, 1930; *Oakland Tribune*, October 31, 1927.

75. *California v. Garbutt*, case file no. 11369; and *California v. Parker*, case file no. 11399, both from the Criminal Division, California Superior Court, Alameda County, 1930.

76. Warren, *The Memoirs*, pp. 86ff.; *California v. Becker*, case file no. 11359; *California v. Ormsby*, case file no. 11359; and *California v. Shurtleff*, case file no. 11360, Criminal Division, California Superior Court, Alameda County, 1930.

77. Chief Sanitary Inspector Ernest Engler and Chief Food Inspector Harry Smith were linked to alcohol and gambling interests through their membership on the board of a promotional club, while City Treasurer Jake Croter was sued for nonsupport by a woman who claimed that he had fathered her illegitimate son. All three were discharged from their posts. *Oakland Tribune*, October 25 and 31, and November 1, 3, 4, 8, and 9, 1927.

78. Blutza, "Oakland's Commission and Council-Manager Plans," pp. 227–232; Harding had been vice president of the Oakland Bank and in 1928 became vice president of the American Trust Company. Harding was succeeded as president of the Lions in 1929 by C. J. Struble, vice president of the Oakland Title Insurance and Guaranty Corporation, who then went on the become president of the Chamber of Commerce in 1931.

79. Blutza, "Oakland's Commission and Council-Manager Plans," pp. 234–235, 247–257.

80. Ibid., p. 262.

81. Ibid.; Warren, *The Memoirs*, pp. 99–100.

82. Warren himself endorsed the manager amendments in the November election, declaring, "the commission form of government is a failure"; Blutza, "Oakland's Commission and Council-Manager Plans," pp. 288, 356–357.

83. Ibid., pp. 265, 278, 355; *San Francisco Chronicle*, March 20, 1930. In March, the Lions Club passed a resolution thanking the *Tribune* for its "articles and forceful editorials" in favor of the manager reform; *Oakland Tribune*, March 28 and October 16 and 23, 1930.

84. The Citizens' Freeholder Committee included representatives from the Italian American Federation, the Western Waterfront Industries Association, and the Central Labor Council, whose secretary, William Spooner, chaired the committee. The Council-Manager League chose not to run candidates against the freeholders' slate, but instead concentrated on the amendments; Blutza, "Oakland's Commission and Council-Manager Plans," pp. 282–285.

85. Ibid., pp. 290–308; J. Paul St. Sure, *Some Comments on Employer Organizations and Collective Bargaining in Northern California since 1934,* an oral history conducted 1957, Institute for Industrial Relations, University of California, Berkeley, 1957, pp. 359–363; Gothberg, "The Local Influence of J. R. Knowland's *Oakland Tribune.*"

CHAPTER 4. ECONOMIC CRISIS AND CLASS HEGEMONY

1. On department stores and consumer culture in the first half of the twentieth century, see Susan P. Benson, *Counter Cultures: Saleswomen, Managers, and Customers in American Department Stores, 1890–1940* (Urbana: University of Illinois Press, 1986).

2. Interview with Jean Stewart, November 3, 1994, Oakland; telephone interview with Shirley Massengill, November 10, 1994; telephone interview with Sally Wehe, November 2, 1994.

3. *San Francisco Call-Bulletin,* December 4, 1946.

4. Glen Elder Jr., *Children of the Great Depression: Social Change and Life Experience* (Chicago: University of Chicago Press, 1974), pp. 19, 51; *East Bay Labor Journal,* October 9 and 23, 1931; Beth Bagwell, *Oakland: Story of a City* (Oakland: Oakland Heritage Alliance, 1994 [orig. 1982]), p. 217; John Modell, "Levels of Change over Time," *Historical Methods* 8, no. 4 (September 1975): 116–127, n. 9; "Rotating Unemployed Abused in Oakland, Few Receive Work," *East Bay Labor Journal,* February 12, 1932.

5. U.S. Bureau of the Census, *Census of Population: 1950,* vol. 2: *Characteristics of the Population,* part 5: *California* (Washington, D.C.: GPO, 1952), p. 10.

6. Commonwealth Club of California, *The Population of California* (San Francisco: Parker, 1946), pp. 97–98. Figures in this section do not include the comparatively small number of foreign immigrants to the state during the period (about 54,000).

7. Ibid., pp. 97–98, 101–106; U.S. Bureau of the Census, *Sixteenth Census of the United States, 1940: Population—Internal Migration 1935 to 1940: Color and Sex of Migrants* (Washington, D.C.: GPO, 1943), pp. 96–114; see also James Gregory, *American Exodus: The Dust Bowl Migration and Okie Culture in California* (Oxford: Oxford University Press, 1989).

8. Commonwealth Club, *The Population of California,* pp. 105–109; U.S. Bureau of the Census, *Internal Migration 1935 to 1940: Color and Sex of Migrants,* p. 24; idem, *Sixteenth Census of the United States, 1940: Population—Internal Migration 1935 to 1940: Economic Characteristics of Migrants* (Washington, D.C.: GPO, 1946), p. 204.

9. Idem, *Current Population Reports,* series P-51, no. 24: *Labor Force Characteristics of the San Francisco–Oakland Metropolitan District* (Washington, D.C.: GPO, 1947).

10. All figures for the U.S. are nonfarm. Idem, *Sixteenth Census of the United States,* vol. 3: *The Labor Force* (Washington, D.C.: GPO, 1943), parts 1 and 2.

11. Laton McCartney, *Friends in High Places: The Bechtel Story* (New York: Simon and Schuster, 1988), pp. 50–51; David Weber, *Oakland: Hub of the West* (Tulsa: Continental Heritage Press, 1981), p. 138; A. M. Rosenson, "Origin and Nature of the CIO Movement in Alameda County, California" (master's thesis, University of California, Berkeley, 1937), pp. 124–126; Ruth Hendricks Willard, *Alameda County, California Crossroads: An Illustrated History* (Northridge, Calif.: Windsor Publications, 1988), pp. 77–78.

12. Port of Oakland, *Sixty Years: A Chronicle of Progress* (Oakland: Board of Port Commissioners, 1987); "Bridge—S.F. Bay (proposed)," and "Bridge—S.F. Oakland," files, Joseph R. Knowland Papers, Carton 38, Bancroft Library, University of California, Berkeley; Joseph Moore and James Moore, oral history interview conducted for the documentary film *Crossroads: A Story of West Oakland*, Cypress Freeway Replacement Project, CALTRANS District 4, Oakland, 1995.

13. Edgar Hinkel and William McCann, *Oakland, 1852–1938: Some Phases of the Social, Political, and Economic History of Oakland, California* (Oakland: Works Progress Administration, 1939), pp. 119, 198; Port of Oakland, *Sixty Years: A Chronicle of Progress*, pp. 9–11; California Department of Transportation, *Historic Property Survey Report: For the Proposed I-880 Reconstruction Project* (San Francisco: CALTRANS District 4, 1990), vol. 4: *Historic Architecture Survey Report*, part 7, D: "Oakland Army Base," and part 7, E: "Naval Supply Center, Oakland."

14. On the institutional division of functions in local government, see Roger Friedland, Frances Fox Piven, and Robert Alford, "Political Conflict, Urban Structure, and the Fiscal Crisis," in *Comparing Public Policies: New Concepts and Methods*, ed. Douglas Ashford (Beverly Hills, Calif.: Sage, 1977), pp. 197–225.

15. Judith V. May, "Progressives and the Poor: An Analytic History of Oakland" (MS, Institute of Governmental Studies Library, University of California, Berkeley, 1970); Marilynn Johnson, *The Second Gold Rush: Oakland and the East Bay in World War II* (Berkeley: University of California Press, 1993), p. 187; J. Paul St. Sure, *Some Comments on Employer Organizations and Collective Bargaining in Northern California since 1934*, an oral history conducted 1957, Institute for Industrial Relations, University of California, Berkeley, 1957, pp. 361–362.

16. In addition to its original members (see chapter 3), early appointees to the port commission included department store owner Sherwood Swan and former Good Government League city commissioners Frank Colbourn and Leroy Goodrich. In addition to Knowland, the San Francisco–Oakland Bay Bridge Advisory Committee included executive members C. J. Struble of the Oakland Chamber of Commerce, Charles Truman of the Property Owners Division of the Oakland Real Estate Board, and Frank Hanna of the Oakland Lions Club; Port of Oakland, *Sixty Years: A Chronicle of Progress*, pp. 2–3; "Bridge—S.F. Bay (proposed)," and "Bridge—S.F. Oakland," files, Joseph R. Knowland Papers, Carton 38, Bancroft Library, University of California, Berkeley. City council members in the '30s included gift shop owner Fred Morcom; movie theater owner-

operator Herbert Beach; Mrs. Wilhelmine Yoakum, housewife and vice president of a real-estate investment firm; physician John Slavich; dentist William McCracken; and James DePaoli and Walter Jacobsen, president and secretary-manager, respectively, of the Retail Grocers Association. City council candidates' statements, 1931, in "Oakland—Elections" file, Oakland History Room, Oakland Public Library, Oakland; *East Bay Labor Journal,* May 5 and 12, 1933.

17. Oakland City Clerk, *Elections 1852 to the Present* (Office of the City Clerk, Oakland, n.d.).

18. John Dykstra, "A History of the Physical Development of the City of Oakland: The Formative Years, 1850–1930" (master's thesis, University of California, Berkeley, 1967), pp. 228–236.

19. Elder, *Children of the Great Depression;* Modell, "Levels of Change over Time."

20. Elder, *Children of the Great Depression,* pp. 5, 17, 44–45, 318–321.

21. Ibid., pp. 45–48.

22. Ibid., pp. 47, 53–57, 60–61.

23. *Glenview News* (Oakland), July 1933 and August 1935.

24. Delores Nason McBroome, *Parallel Communities: African Americans in California's East Bay, 1850–1963* (New York: Garland, 1993), pp. 33–38; Lawrence Crouchette, Lonnie Bunch III, and Martha K. Winnacker, *Visions toward Tomorrow: A History of the East Bay Afro-American Community 1852–1977* (Oakland: Northern California Center for Afro-American History and Life, 1989), p. 23; Eric Brown, "Black Ghetto Formation in Oakland, 1852–1965," *Research in Community Sociology* 8 (1998): 255–274; William Brown Jr., "Class Aspects of Residential Development and Choice in the Oakland Black Community" (Ph.D. diss., University of California, Berkeley, 1970), p. 98 n.

25. Donald Hausler, "Blacks in Oakland: 1852–1987" (MS, Oakland History Room, Oakland Public Library, Oakland, 1987), p. 84.

26. Albert Broussard, "Organizing the Black Community in the San Francisco Bay Area, 1915–1930," *Arizona and the West* 23, no. 4 (1981): 335–354; Gloria Harrison, "The National Association for the Advancement of Colored People in California" (master's thesis, Stanford University, 1949), p. 46; *Western American,* March 9, 1928; Crouchette et al., *Visions toward Tomorrow,* p. 26.

27. Crouchette et al., *Visions toward Tomorrow,* p. 33.

28. Joseph Rodriguez, "From Personal Politics to Party Politics: The Development of Black Leadership in Oakland, California, 1900–1950" (master's thesis, University of California, Santa Cruz, 1983), p. 21.

29. In 1923, the San Francisco wing split off from the Northern California branch, which was renamed the Alameda County branch in 1933; Broussard, "Organizing the Black Community," p. 346; Harrison, "The National Association for the Advancement of Colored People," p. 50.

30. Hausler, "Blacks in Oakland," p. 84.

31. Figures for 1930 include males and females ten years and older, for 1940 males and females fourteen years and older. U.S. Bureau of the Census, *Fifteenth*

Census of the United States: Population, vol. 4: *Occupations* (Washington, D.C.: GPO, 1933), p. 202; idem, *Sixteenth Census of the United States,* vol. 3: *The Labor Force* (Washington, D.C.: GPO, 1943), part 2, p. 205. See also Crouchette et al., *Visions toward Tomorrow,* pp. 35, 42; Rodriguez, "From Personal Politics to Party Politics," pp. 27, 31.

32. The Dining Car Cooks and Waiters Union, Local 456, led by black journalist and activist William McFarland, organized black food service workers on the railroads. *East Bay Labor Journal,* November 5, 1926, and February 11, 1927.

33. Crouchette et al., *Visions toward Tomorrow,* p. 37; C. L. Dellums, *International President of the Brotherhood of Sleeping Car Porters and Civil Rights Leader,* an oral history conducted 1970–1971, Regional Oral History Office, University of California, Berkeley, 1971, pp. 15–49, 87–89; "Porters Postpone Strike," *Alameda County Union Labor Record,* June 6, 1928. Albrier lived in neighboring Berkeley but was active in civil rights politics throughout the East Bay; Mary Frances Albrier, *Determined Advocate for Racial Equality,* an oral history conducted 1977–1978, Regional Oral History Office, University of California, Berkeley, 1979, pp. 98–102.

34. Elder, *Children of the Great Depression,* p. 48.

35. Paul Zingg and Mark Medeiros, *Runs, Hits, and an Era: The Pacific Coast League, 1903–58* (Urbana: University of Illinois Press, 1994), pp. 30–31; Richard Boyden, "The San Francisco Machinists from Depression to Cold War, 1930–1950" (Ph.D. diss., University of California, Berkeley, 1988).

36. David Selvin, *A Terrible Anger: The 1934 Waterfront and General Strikes in San Francisco* (Detroit: Wayne State University Press, 1996), pp. 35–42, 54; Harvey Schwartz, *The March Inland: Origins of the ILWU Warehouse Division, 1934–1938* (Los Angeles: Institute of Industrial Relations, University of California, Los Angeles, 1978), pp. 2–8, 66.

37. Selvin, *A Terrible Anger,* p. 185; Dellums oral history, pp. 136–138; McBroome, *Parallel Communities,* pp. 74–75.

38. Selvin, *A Terrible Anger,* pp. 214–215, 238–239; Bagwell, *Oakland: Story of a City,* p. 219.

39. After their strike, the warehouse local donated a thousand dollars a week to the maritime strikers, who settled on favorable terms a month later; Schwartz, *The March Inland,* pp. 26, 76–98.

40. Selvin, *A Terrible Anger,* pp. 238–239; Rosenson, "Origin and Nature of the CIO Movement"; Schwartz, *The March Inland;* Rodriguez, "From Personal Politics to Party Politics," pp. 51–57.

41. *Oakland Post-Enquirer,* March 30, 1937.

42. *Oakland Post-Enquirer,* April 1, 1937.

43. *East Bay Labor Journal,* March 26 and April 9 and 30, 1937.

44. Dellums oral history, p. 67; see also Edward France, "Some Aspects of the Migration of the Negro to the San Francisco Bay Area since 1940" (Ph.D. diss., University of California, Berkeley, 1962), pp. 43–44; *Oakland Tribune,* September 15, 1939.

45. Johnson reports that the Housing Authority board appointed by the city

council included several past presidents of the Alameda County Apartment House Owners Association and the California Rental Association; *The Second Gold Rush*, pp. 97–98. See also Mary Praetzellis, ed., *West Oakland: A Place to Start From*, Research Design and Treatment Plan, Cypress I-880 Replacement Project, vol. 1: *Historical Archaeology* (Oakland: CALTRANS District 4, 1994), pp. 169–170; "Low Cost House Models Drawn," *Oakland Tribune*, April 9, 1939; California Department of Transportation, *Historic Property Survey Report: For the Proposed I-880 Reconstruction Project* (San Francisco: CALTRANS District 4, 1990), vol. 3: *Historic Resources Inventory*, pp. 53–54; Dellums oral history, pp. 68–72.

46. Rosenson, "Origin and Nature of the CIO Movement," p. 183.

47. Selvin, *A Terrible Anger*, p. 215; Albert Vetere Lannon, *Fight or Be Slaves: The History of the Oakland–East Bay Labor Movement* (Lanham, Md.: University Press of America, 2000), p. 66; Harvey Lyon, *Oakland Moving and Storage Entrepreneur, Rotarian, and Philanthropist*, an oral history conducted 1973, Regional Oral History Office, Bancroft Library, University of California, Berkeley, 1973, pp. 54–56.

48. Rosenson, "Origin and Nature of the CIO Movement," p. 180; Paul Heide, "A Warehouseman's Reminiscences," an oral history conducted 1970, in *Labor Looks at Earl Warren*, Regional Oral History Office, Bancroft Library, University of California, Berkeley, 1970, p. 13; *East Bay Labor Journal*, January 29 and March 12, 1937.

49. St. Sure oral history, pp. 421–432, 528–543; Clark Kerr, "Collective Bargaining on the Pacific Coast," *Monthly Labor Review* 64, no. 4 (April 1947): 650–674.

50. Richard E. Jay, "A Case Study in Retail Unionism: The Retail Clerks in the San Francisco East Bay Area (Alameda County)" (Ph.D. diss., University of California, Berkeley, 1953), pp. 273–275; Robert Ash, "Alameda County Central Labor Council during the Warren Years," an oral history conducted 1976, in *Labor Leaders View the Warren Era*, Regional Oral History Office, Bancroft Library, University of California, Berkeley, 1976, p. 19.

51. *East Bay Labor Journal*, April 22, 1932, and May 12, 1933; St. Sure oral history, p. 364.

52. Rosenson, "Origin and Nature of the CIO Movement," pp. 125–126; *Oakland Post-Enquirer*, September 24, 1938.

53. Rosenson, "Origin and Nature of the CIO Movement," pp. 7–8; *East Bay Labor Journal*, March 10, 1933, and February 26, March 12, and April 16, 1937.

54. Local 70 grew from twelve hundred members in 1931 to twenty-two hundred in 1937; *East Bay Labor Journal*, April 3, 1931; Robert M. Robinson, "A History of the Teamsters in the San Francisco Bay Area, 1850–1950" (Ph.D. diss., University of California, Berkeley, 1951), p. 320.

55. This section is much indebted to Richard Boyden, "The Oakland General Strike of 1946" (MS in possession of the author, May 1981).

56. Donald Garnel, *The Rise of Teamster Power in the West* (Berkeley: Uni-

versity of California Press, 1972), pp. 104–115; Jay, "A Case Study," pp. 352–353; *East Bay Labor Journal*, January 26, 1950; Ash oral history, pp. 15–16; St. Sure oral history, pp. 365–366.

57. *East Bay Labor Journal*, August 6, 1926, and April 8, 1949; Boyden, "The Oakland General Strike of 1946," pp. 15, 47–48; Schwartz, *The March Inland*, pp. 118–124.

58. Robinson, "A History of the Teamsters," p. 314.

59. Rosenson, "Origin and Nature of the CIO Movement," pp. 73–77, 95–104; Robinson, "A History of the Teamsters," pp. 309–331; Schwartz, *The March Inland*, 135–140; Charter Restoration Committee, "The Facts about the Revocation of the Charter of Your Central Labor Council," Alameda County Central Labor Council File, Labor Collection, Social Science Library, University of California, Berkeley, 1937.

60. *Bay City Blues* (audio recording produced by Craig Gordon, Ed Schoenfeld, and Ken Russell, New American Movement Radio Project, and Vic Rubin and Tim Reagan, Oakland Study Group, n.d.); St. Sure oral history, pp. 421–432; Ash oral history, pp. 16–20; Robinson, "A History of the Teamsters," pp. 432–435.

61. Jay, "A Case Study," pp. 309–311.

62. *East Bay Labor Journal*, August 6 and 27, 1937; Johnson, *The Second Gold Rush*, p. 23.

CHAPTER 5. WORKING-CLASS COLLECTIVE AGENCY

1. Marilynn Johnson, *The Second Gold Rush: Oakland and the East Bay in World War II* (Berkeley: University of California Press, 1993), p. 28.

2. U.S. Bureau of Labor Statistics, *Indexes of Production Worker Employment in Manufacturing by Metropolitan Area* (Washington, D.C.: GPO, 1942–1946); Katharine Archibald, *Wartime Shipyard: A Study in Social Disunity* (Berkeley: University of California Press, 1947), p. 4.

3. Johnson, *The Second Gold Rush*, pp. 31–34; Beth Bagwell, *Oakland: Story of a City* (Oakland: Oakland Heritage Alliance, 1994 [orig. 1982]), pp. 236–237; California Department of Transportation, *Historic Property Survey Report: For the Proposed I-880 Reconstruction Project* (San Francisco: CALTRANS District 4, 1990), vol. 4: *Historic Architecture Survey Report*, part 7, D: "Oakland Army Base," and part 7, E: "Naval Supply Center, Oakland"; U.S. Bureau of the Census, *Special Reports*, Series CA-3, no. 3: *Characteristics of the Population, Labor Force, Families and Housing, San Francisco Bay Congested Area: April, 1944* (Washington, D.C.: GPO, 1944), p. 10.

4. Less than 5 percent of all recent migrants into Oakland in 1940 were from Oklahoma, Arkansas, Texas, or Louisiana. Commonwealth Club of California, *The Population of California* (San Francisco: Parker, 1946), pp. 105–120; U.S. Bureau of the Census, *Special Reports*, pp. 7, 14; idem, *Sixteenth Census of the United States, 1940: Population—Internal Migration 1935 to 1940: Color and Sex of Migrants* (Washington, D.C.: GPO, 1943), pp. 96–114.

5. Commonwealth Club, *The Population of California*, p. 169; U.S. Bureau of the Census, *Special Census of Oakland, California: October 9, 1945* (Washington, D.C.: GPO, 1946).

6. U.S. Bureau of the Census, *Special Reports*, p. 10; Archibald, *Wartime Shipyard*, p. 30. Manufacturing increased from 15 percent of Bay Area women's employment in 1940 to 27 percent in 1945, while service industries excluding domestic service fell from 34 percent to 19 percent; U.S. Department of Labor, Women's Bureau, "Women Workers in Ten War Production Areas and Their Postwar Employment Plans," Bulletin no. 209 (Washington, D.C.: GPO, 1946), p. 35.

7. Adult war migrants in the Bay Area had even higher marital rates than nonmigrants: 72 percent were married in 1944, compared to 66 percent of nonmigrants; U.S. Bureau of the Census, *Special Reports*, pp. 14–15.

8. One survey of East Bay shipyard workers found that 45 percent of the migrant workers definitely planned to stay in the Bay Area, and another 24 percent planned to stay if they could get work; Oakland Postwar Planning Committee, *Oakland's Formula for the Future* (Oakland: Postwar Planning Committee, 1945). Among migrant female workers in the Bay Area, 56 percent planned to continue living in the area and 46 percent planned to continue working there. Overall, 61 percent of Bay Area working women in 1945 planned to continue living and working in the Bay Area. This represented a 22 percent increase over the total number of Bay Area working women in 1940. Finally, 95 percent of employed Bay Area nonwhite women hoped to continue working after the war. U.S. Department of Labor, Women's Bureau, "Women Workers," pp. 31–47. Davis McEntire and Julia Tarnopol also report that while black women in the Bay Area had extremely high postwar unemployment rates (40 percent in 1948), they did not want to return to the traditional types of work available to them; McEntire and Tarnopol, "Postwar Status of Negro Workers in San Francisco Area," *Monthly Labor Review* 70, no. 6 (June 1950): 617.

9. Johnson, *The Second Gold Rush*, pp. 84–85; Gretchen Lemke-Santangelo, *Abiding Courage: African American Migrant Women and the East Bay Community* (Chapel Hill: University of North Carolina Press, 1996), p. 80.

10. Lawrence Crouchette, Lonnie Bunch III, and Martha E. Winnacker, *Visions toward Tomorrow: A History of the East Bay Afro-American Community 1852–1977* (Oakland: Northern California Center for Afro-American History and Life, 1989), p. 45.

11. Edward France, "Some Aspects of the Migration of the Negro to the San Francisco Bay Area since 1940" (Ph.D. diss., University of California, Berkeley, 1962), p. 45; Lemke-Santangelo, *Abiding Courage*, pp. 86–87; Johnson, *The Second Gold Rush*, pp. 97–109.

12. Johnson, *The Second Gold Rush*, pp. 144–150.

13. Ibid., p. 169; Crouchette et al., *Visions toward Tomorrow*, p. 51.

14. The figure is speculative, but perhaps half of the AFL members on strike in December 1946 had not belonged to unions before the war; see Archibald, *Wartime Shipyard*, p. 130.

15. Estimates report thirty thousand AFL and fifteen thousand CIO members in Alameda County in 1937, and one hundred thousand AFL and thirty thousand CIO members in 1946; A. M. Rosenson, "Origin and Nature of the CIO Movement in Alameda County, California" (master's thesis, University of California, Berkeley, 1937), p. 183; Philip Wolman, "The Oakland General Strike of 1946," *Southern California Quarterly* 57, no. 2 (1975): 147, 168.

16. Archibald, *Wartime Shipyard*, pp. 142–149; Lester Rubin, William Swift, and Herbert Northrup, *Negro Employment in the Maritime Industries* (Philadelphia: University of Pennsylvania Press, 1974), vol. 1, p. 38.

17. Crouchette et al., *Visions toward Tomorrow*, p. 47; Delores Nason McBroome, *Parallel Communities: African Americans in California's East Bay, 1850–1963* (New York: Garland, 1993), pp. 100–107; C. L. Dellums, *International President of the Brotherhood of Sleeping Car Porters and Civil Rights Leader*, an oral history conducted 1970–1971, Regional Oral History Office, Bancroft Library, University of California, Berkeley, 1971, pp. 97–98.

18. Crouchette et al., *Visions toward Tomorrow*, pp. 47–48; McBroome, *Parallel Communities*, pp. 107–108; Johnson, *The Second Gold Rush*, pp. 69–73.

19. Archibald, *Wartime Shipyard*, pp. 81, 142–149; Charles Wollenberg, *Marinship at War* (Berkeley: Western Heritage Press, 1990), p. 80; Johnson, *The Second Gold Rush*, pp. 74–75; Fred Stripp, "The Relationships of the San Francisco Bay Area Negro-American Worker with the Labor Unions Affiliated with the American Federation of Labor and the Congress of Industrial Organizations" (Th.D. thesis, Pacific School of Religion, Berkeley, 1948), pp. 118, 125, 133–135. In 1936, the Oakland Machinists' Lodge 284 withdrew from the International Association of Machinists over the latter's attempt to break a local strike over job classifications, and affiliated with the CIO Steel Workers' Organizing Committee to become the "Steel" Machinists Local 1304; Richard Boyden, "The San Francisco Machinists and the National War Labor Board," in *American Labor and the Era of World War II*, ed. Sally Miller and Daniel Cornford (Westport, Conn.: Praeger, 1995), pp. 105–119.

20. Albert Vetere Lannon, *Fight or Be Slaves: A History of the Oakland–East Bay Labor Movement* (Lanham, Md.: University Press of America, 2000), p. 102; Jim Rose, "Collaboration with a Dual Union: Oakland AFL Political Practice, 1943–1947" (MS in possession of the author, 1990), pp. 9–14; Johnson, *The Second Gold Rush*, p. 190.

21. Rose, "Collaboration with a Dual Union," pp. 16–22; Johnson, *The Second Gold Rush*, pp. 195–196.

22. Archibald, *Wartime Shipyard*, pp. 129, 142.

23. Joel Seidman, *American Labor from Defense to Reconversion* (Chicago: University of Chicago Press, 1953); Nelson Lichtenstein, *Labor's War at Home: The CIO in World War Two* (Cambridge: Cambridge University Press, 1982).

24. Rose, "Collaboration with a Dual Union," p. 16; U.S. Bureau of Labor Statistics, *Indexes of Production Worker Employment*; U.S. Department of Labor, "Indexes of Consumer Prices in Large Cities, November 1946," *Monthly Labor Review* 64, no. 1 (1947).

25. U.S. Bureau of the Census, *Current Population Reports,* series P-51, no. 24: *Labor Force Characteristics of the San Francisco–Oakland Metropolitan District* (Washington, D.C.: GPO, 1947).

26. Unemployment among returning war veterans was also low, compared to other major port cities on the East and Gulf Coasts. In the spring of 1947, unemployment for returning male veterans in the Bay Area was 6 percent, compared to 9 percent in New Orleans, 11 percent in Philadelphia, 12 percent in New York, and 13 percent in Boston; U.S. Bureau of the Census, *Current Population Reports,* series P-51, no. 35: *Labor Force Characteristics of Metropolitan Districts: Summary Report* (Washington, D.C.: GPO, 1947).

27. U.S. Department of Commerce, *Business Establishments, Employment, and Taxable Payrolls under OASI* [County Business Patterns] *First Quarter, 1947,* part 2: *California* (Washington, D.C.: GPO, 1948); see also Richard E. Jay, "A Case Study in Retail Unionism: The Retail Clerks in the San Francisco East Bay Area (Alameda County)" (Ph.D. diss., University of California, Berkeley, 1953), p. 158.

28. Department store managers, of course, were usually men; U.S. Bureau of the Census, *Sixteenth Census of the United States, 1940: Population,* vol. 3: *The Labor Force* (Washington, D.C.: GPO, 1943), part 2, pp. 333–334.

29. U.S. Department of Labor, Women's Bureau, "Women Workers," p. 41; Susan P. Benson, *Counter Cultures: Saleswomen, Managers, and Customers in American Department Stores, 1890–1940* (Urbana: University of Illinois Press, 1986); Jay, "A Case Study," p. 238. From the 1970s on, efforts by numerous historians, the author included, have failed to locate or interview the female workers active in the clerks' strike. One reason for this may be the age of the women involved: Department store clerks were described by observers as typically older or middle-aged women, who may not have survived by the time the research took place. According to census data, in 1940 fully half of the "saleswomen" in Oakland were over the age of thirty-five, nearly twice the proportion (26 percent) as in the United States as a whole. See Fred Glass, "We Called It a Work Holiday: The Oakland General Strike of 1946," *Labor's Heritage* 8, no. 2 (Fall 1996): 25; U.S. Bureau of the Census, *Sixteenth Census of the United States,* vol. 3: *The Labor Force,* parts 1 and 2.

30. This summary is drawn from detailed accounts of the strike in Frank Douma, "The Oakland General Strike" (master's thesis, University of California, Berkeley, 1951); Wolman, "The Oakland General Strike of 1946"; Jay, "A Case Study"; Robert Ash, "Alameda County Central Labor Council during the Warren Years," an oral history conducted 1976, in *Labor Leaders View the Warren Era,* Regional Oral History Office, Bancroft Library, University of California, Berkeley, pp. 19–37; J. Paul St. Sure, *Some Comments on Employer Organizations and Collective Bargaining in Northern California since 1934,* an oral history conducted 1957, Institute for Industrial Relations, University of California, Berkeley, pp. 449–469; and the local daily newspapers of the time. The validity of the latter must be evaluated with care. Jay reports ("A Case Study," p. 321 n.):

In a confidential conversation with the writer, one of the leading persons in employer affairs in Oakland stated that the [Retail Merchants Association] had an "informal understanding" with the local daily press dating from the days of the San Francisco General Strike in 1934 that editorial and news coverage of labor disputes in which the Association was involved would present the merchants in the best possible light. As a result . . . the writer was advised by this informant not to seek accurate accounts of labor disputes in the daily local press.

31. *East Bay Labor Journal,* November 1, 15, 22, and 29, 1946; "1946 Retail Clerks' Strike," pamphlet files, Oakland History Room, Oakland Public Library, Oakland.

32. *Oakland Tribune,* November 12, 17, 21, and 26, 1946. During the shoe store strike, the RMA had run newspaper ads depicting union leaders as children playing with machine guns; Jay, "A Case Study," p. 310.

33. Ash oral history, p. 21; Douma, "The Oakland General Strike," p. 20; St. Sure oral history, p. 457.

34. In some accounts, Brown himself was the driver of the streetcar; see Wolman, "The Oakland General Strike," pp. 154–155; Douma, "The Oakland General Strike," p. 28. Teamsters leader Real happened to be out of town throughout the events of the General Strike, though it is doubtful whether he could have prevented it.

35. *San Francisco Call-Bulletin,* December 3 and 4, 1946; *San Francisco Chronicle,* December 4, 1946.

36. Wolman, "The Oakland General Strike," pp. 172–173; Ash oral history, p. 30; *San Francisco Chronicle,* December 4, 1946, 7–8; *San Francisco News,* December 3, 1946, 4–5.

37. Teamster quote from Richard Boyden, "The Oakland General Strike of 1946" (MS in possession of the author, May 1981), p. 28. Stan Weir, "American Labor on the Defensive: A 1940's Odyssey," *Radical America* 9, nos. 4–5 (1975): 178.

38. *East Bay Labor Journal,* December 6, 1946.

39. Ash oral history, p. 30.

40. Jay, "A Case Study," p. 325; Ash oral history, p. 29.

41. *San Francisco News,* December 5, 1946. On Wednesday morning, Mayor Beach called the city council into special session and was granted emergency powers to take personal command of the police, to impose a curfew, or to ask for the state militia or National Guard, none of which actions was ever actually ordered. Asked what he intended to do with his authority, the mayor replied, "A general does not reveal his plans"; Wolman, "The Oakland General Strike," pp. 169–170.

42. *San Francisco Chronicle,* December 6, 1946.

43. Local 70 president Jim Marshall allegedly kept a telegram from IBT president Tobin containing a back-to-work order in his back pocket for more than

a day, refusing to issue the order to his members; Boyden, "The Oakland General Strike of 1946," pp. 36–37.

44. Ash oral history, p. 32; Wolman, "The Oakland General Strike," p. 165.

45. Ash oral history, pp. 27, 31. Whether the local CIO was really prepared to join the strike is also subject to debate; see Boyden, "The Oakland General Strike of 1946," p. 49ff.; Weir, "American Labor on the Defensive," pp. 179–183.

46. Douma, "The Oakland General Strike," pp. 163–168. Banner headlines in the council's newspaper read, "Labor Takes Holiday in Protest to Smashing of Their Individual Rights" and "AFL Unions Win Fight to Restore Civil Liberties in Oakland." *East Bay Labor Journal*, December 6, 1946.

47. Ash oral history, p. 34; Jay, "A Case Study," pp. 362–372; Douglas Simpson, "The Retail Clerks in the East Bay Area" (master's thesis, University of California, Berkeley, 1963).

48. Hassler had just returned from wartime service and was awaiting reappointment as manager when the General Strike broke out. Among the victories the unions said they had won was "the immediate appointment of [a new] City Manager [Hassler] who holds the respect and confidence of organized labor that we will get fair and just treatment for our movement and that is all the AFL has ever asked, fair and just treatment"; *East Bay Labor Journal*, December 6, 1946.

49. One newspaper reported, "The situation was so confused last night that one leading participant in the negotiations which led to abandonment of the general tie-up said: 'Just now, everybody is standing around with a knife at everybody else's back. The situation is ripe to break out all over again'"; *San Francisco Chronicle*, December 6, 1946. See also Douma, "The Oakland General Strike," p. 68.

50. Rose, "Collaboration with a Dual Union," p. 27; Ash oral history, p. 36. Al Kidder, a rank-and-file picket captain for the clerks, recalled, "[The General Strike] gave the working people, the people in unions, an indication of their strength that they had if they stood together . . . it gave them a greater sense of power"; "Oakland General Strike of 1946," *Bay City Blues* (audio recording produced by Craig Gordon, Ed Schoenfeld, and Ken Russell, New American Movement Radio Project, and Vic Rubin and Tim Reagan, Oakland Study Group, n.d.).

51. Rose, "Collaboration with a Dual Union," pp. 28–29.

52. Wolman, "The Oakland General Strike," pp. 173–175; Frank Roesch, "The 1947 Oakland Municipal Elections" (MS, Institute of Governmental Studies Library, University of California, Berkeley, 1970); Johnson, *The Second Gold Rush*, pp. 204–221.

53. Roesch, "The 1947 Oakland Municipal Elections," p. 4. The OVL campaign newspaper *Voters' Herald* claimed that both the *Tribune* and Kahn's paid lower property taxes in 1945–1946 than in 1929–1930; "Homes and Small Business Carry Oakland Tax Load," *Oakland Voters' Herald*, May 9, 1947, 2.

54. *Oakland Voters' Herald*, May 9, 1947, 4; See also Marilynn Johnson, "Mobilizing the Homefront: Labor and Politics in Oakland, 1941–1951," in

Working People of California, ed. Daniel Cornford (Berkeley: University of California Press, 1995), pp. 357–358.

55. Robert Self, "Shifting Ground in Metropolitan America: Class, Race, and Power in Oakland and the East Bay, 1945–1977" (Ph.D. diss., University of Washington, 1998), p. 117; *East Oakland Times*, December 26, 1947.

56. Roesch, "The 1947 Oakland Municipal Elections," p. 3; *Oakland Tribune*, May 6 and 7, 1947; *Oakland Observer*, April 5, 1947.

57. Roesch, "The 1947 Oakland Municipal Elections," p. 6; telephone interview with Valmar and Evelyn Schaff, May 31, 1995; Rose, "Collaboration with a Dual Union," p. 32; Johnson, "Mobilizing the Homefront," p. 345; *Labor Herald*, April 9 and May 6 and 20, 1947; *Daily People's World*, May 14, 1947.

58. Rose, "Collaboration with a Dual Union," pp. 30–33.

59. Roesch, "1947 Oakland Municipal Elections"; *Observer*, May 17, 1947.

60. Self, "Shifting Ground," pp. 118–119; *East Oakland Times*, December 3, 17, and 24, 1948, and January 14 and 21, February 11 and 18, March 18, and April 25, 1949; "Braga and Linotto Backed for Council; Horstmann as Auditor," *East Bay Labor Journal*, March 25, 1949.

61. Johnson, "Mobilizing the Homefront," p. 359; France, "Some Aspects of the Migration of the Negro," pp. 45–46.

62. *East Bay Labor Journal*, April 8, 1949; Hausler, "Blacks in Oakland," p. 171; *Oakland Tribune*, July 21 and 30, 1949.

63. Voting for the housing proposal were Councillors Smith, Pease, Weakley, Frank Youell, and Douglas Sweeney; opposed were Mayor Cliff Rishell and Councillors Fred Morcom, Florence Fletcher, and Frank Shattuck; *East Bay Labor Journal*, September 2 and 23, 1949; *Oakland Tribune*, July 30, 1949; Johnson, *The Second Gold Rush*, pp. 218–219.

64. Councillors Youell and Sweeney were exempt from recall because they had not yet been in office more than six months when the recall petition was circulated; *Observer*, January 21, 1950; *San Francisco Chronicle*, February 27, 1950.

65. The ramifications of the Oakland campaign spread rapidly across the state. A month after the recall, Oakland contractor John Hennessey, secretary of the Home Builders' Council of California and treasurer of the Oakland Committee for Home Protection, organized a petition drive for what became Proposition 10, a state constitutional amendment that would require a local election to authorize construction of any public housing. Among the first to sign the petition was Clausen. Despite opposition from the unions, the American Legion, the Veterans of Foreign Wars, and religious and community groups, the committee vastly outspent its opponents, and Proposition 10 passed by thirty-seven thousand votes. *San Francisco Chronicle*, March 2, 5, and 15, 1950; *Oakland Tribune*, February 10 and April 21, 1950; Johnson, *The Second Gold Rush*, pp. 220–221.

66. Stripp, "The Relationships."

67. Robert M. Robinson, "A History of the Teamsters in the San Francisco

Bay Area, 1850–1950" (Ph.D. diss., University of California, Berkeley, 1951), pp. 440–444; *San Francisco Chronicle,* February 16, 1950; Johnson, *The Second Gold Rush,* p. 221.

68. Contract files, Hotel Employees and Restaurant Employees Local 2850, Oakland. On small business as an avenue of blue-collar occupational mobility, see Seymour Martin Lipset and Reinhard Bendix, *Social Mobility in Industrial Society* (Berkeley: University of California Press, 1959), pp. 171–173.

69. Interview with Gus Billy, July 23, 1999, Oakland.

CHAPTER 6. RECONSTITUTING THE URBAN REGIME

1. Luigi Laurenti, *Property Values and Race: Studies in Seven Cities* (Berkeley: University of California Press, 1960), p. 124; William Brown Jr., "Class Aspects of Residential Development and Choice in the Oakland Black Community" (Ph.D. diss., University of California, Berkeley, 1970), pp. 129, 142; Edward Hayes, *Power Structure and Urban Policy* (New York: McGraw-Hill, 1972), p. 125 n. 10.

2. U.S. Bureau of the Census, *Special Census of Oakland, California: October 9, 1945* (Washington, D.C.: GPO, 1946); idem, *1970 Census of the Population, Supplementary Report: Negro Population in Selected Places and Selected Counties* (Washington, D.C.: GPO, 1971), p. 5.

3. J. M. Regal, *Oakland's Partnership for Change* (Oakland: City Department of Human Resources, 1967), p. 15; Joseph Rodriguez, "From Personal Politics to Party Politics: The Development of Black Leadership in Oakland, California, 1900–1950" (master's thesis, University of California, Santa Cruz, 1983), pp. 36–37.

4. *San Francisco Chronicle,* December 29 and 31, 1949, and January 5 and 6, 1950; *San Francisco Examiner,* January 5 and 7, 1950; *Oakland Tribune,* January 7, 1950. Robert Powers, *Law Enforcement, Race Relations: 1930–1960,* an oral history conducted 1971, Regional Oral History Office, Bancroft Library, University of California, Berkeley, 1971, pp. 55–63; Delores Nason McBroome, *Parallel Communities: African Americans in California's East Bay, 1850–1963* (New York: Garland, 1993), p. 135.

5. Mary Praetzellis, ed., *West Oakland: A Place to Start From,* Research Design and Treatment Plan: Cypress I-880 Replacement Project, vol. 1: *Historical Archaeology* (Oakland: CALTRANS District 4, 1994), pp. 170–172.

6. Brown, "Class Aspects of Residential Development," p. 139.

7. Gretchen Lemke-Santangelo, "Deindustrialization, Poverty and Community Response" (MS in possession of the author, n.d.), pp. 6–8. A survey of black workers throughout the Bay Area in 1948 found unemployment rates of 15 percent for men and up to 40 percent for women; Davis McEntire and Julia Tarnopol, "Postwar Status of Negro Workers in San Francisco Area," *Monthly Labor Review* 70, no. 6 (June 1950): 612–617. In 1950, joblessness among nonwhites in Oakland was 20 percent for men and 22 percent for women, more than double the rate for whites; U.S. Bureau of the Census, *Census of Population:*

1950, vol. 2: *Characteristics of the Population,* part 5: *California* (Washington, D.C.: GPO, 1952), pp. 62, 262.

8. Gretchen Lemke-Santangelo, *Abiding Courage: African American Migrant Women and the East Bay Community* (Chapel Hill: University of North Carolina Press, 1996), pp. 160–161.

9. "Men of Tomorrow" files, African American Museum and Library at Oakland.

10. *Oakland Tribune,* February 24 and 27, 1974; William Lunch, "Oakland Revisited: Stability and Change in an American City" (MS, Environmental Design Library, University of California, Berkeley, 1970), p. 65.

11. Seymour Adler, *Redundancy in Public Transit,* part 3: *The Political Economy of Transit in the San Francisco Bay Area, 1945–1963* (Washington, D.C.: U.S. Department of Transportation, Urban Mass Transit Administration, 1980).

12. Oakland City Planning Department, *Oakland's Housing Supply: Cost, Condition, Composition, 1960–1966* (Oakland: City Planning Department, 701 Division, 1968).

13. Port of Oakland, *Sixty Years: A Chronicle of Progress* (Oakland: Board of Port Commissioners, 1987).

14. Harriet Sternsher, "The Oakland–Alameda County Coliseum Complex" (MS, Institute of Governmental Studies Library, University of California, Berkeley, 1967).

15. Gayle Montgomery and James Johnson, *One Step from the White House: The Rise and Fall of Senator William F. Knowland* (Berkeley: University of California Press, 1998), pp. 228–254; Lunch, "Oakland Revisited," pp. 65–66.

16. Jeffrey Pressman, *Federal Programs and City Politics: The Dynamics of the Aid Process in Oakland* (Berkeley: University of California Press, 1975), pp. 37–38.

17. Arnold Meltsner, *The Politics of City Revenue* (Berkeley: University of California Press, 1971), pp. 60–71, 86–131.

18. Mari Malvey and Aaron Wildavsky, "The Citizens of Oakland Look at their City" (MS, Institute of Governmental Studies Library, University of California, Berkeley, 1971), p. 8; Citizens for Responsive Government, "Summary of Proposition M Voting Analysis," December 1968, in "Oakland Elections, 1968–1969" file, Oakland History Room, Oakland Public Library, Oakland; David Kirp, *Just Schools: The Idea of Racial Equality in American Education* (Berkeley: University of California Press, 1982), p. 220.

19. Oakland Redevelopment Agency, *West Oakland General Neighborhood Renewal Plan* (Oakland: Redevelopment Agency, 1958); *Oakland Tribune,* January 8, 1959; Michael Marans, "Relocation in Acorn: A Focal Point for the Study of the Transition in Urban Renewal Policy and Politics in Oakland" (MS, Institute of Governmental Studies, University of California, Berkeley, 1969).

20. *Oakland Tribune,* October 1, 2, 14, and 22, and November 5, 1959.

21. *Oakland Tribune,* November 5, 10, and 11, 1959.

22. Other members appointed by Rilea included Sol Gilberg of the Oakland

Real Estate Board, Housing Authority members Jack Kronenberg and Don Henderson, Margo Margossian of the Housing Advisory and Appeals Board, Baptist minister Rev. O. P. Smith, small businessman George Miller, and Lamar Childers of the AFL-CIO County Building Trades Council; *Oakland Tribune*, November 25, 1959.

23. *Oakland Tribune*, January 14 and 17, 1960.

24. *Oakland Tribune*, January 7 and 20, 1960.

25. The 1966 total was less than 1 percent of the city's housing stock and only 8 percent of its low-rent supply, and it represented a reduction from the 2,298 combined temporary and permanent units Oakland had in 1960; Oakland City Planning Department, *Oakland's Housing Supply*, pp. 61–62.

26. *Oakland Tribune*, October 12, 1961.

27. Among those speaking in favor of the project were OCCUR chairman Robert Turner, Sherwood Swan for the Central Business District Association, Lamar Childers of the AFL-CIO Building Trades Council, Hiawatha Roberts of the MOT, and black real-estate agent Albert McKee; *Oakland Tribune*, November 1 and 22, 1961.

28. *Oakland Tribune*, May 3 and 4, and June 16, 1962.

29. Marans, "Relocation in Acorn," section 3, p. 4.

30. *Oakland Tribune*, August 17, October 4, and December 21, 1961.

31. *Oakland Tribune*, February 18, April 6, and May 17, 1962.

32. *Oakland Tribune*, August 16, 1962.

33. *The Montclarion* [Oakland], July 7, 1982; *Oakland Tribune*, January 23, 1966.

34. *Oakland Tribune*, March 19 and April 7, 16, and 21, 1964.

35. *Oakland Tribune*, May 2 and December 2, 1964, and February 4, 1965. Vaughns and Foster were founders, and Goady a member, of the Men of Tomorrow. "Men of Tomorrow" files, African American Museum and Library at Oakland.

36. Wayne Thompson, "Quit Treating Symptoms," *National Civic Review* 53, no. 8 (1964): 423–428.

37. This section and the remainder of the chapter are greatly indebted to Judith V. May, "Struggle for Authority: A Comparison of Four Social Change Programs in Oakland, California" (Ph.D. diss., University of California, Berkeley, 1973), pp. 120–158, 192–492. The Associated Agencies later added the Alameda County Welfare Department and the Alameda County Health Department in 1959, the City Building and Housing Department in 1962, and the Alameda County District Attorney's Office in 1963.

38. May, "Struggle for Authority," p. 117; Wayne Thompson, "Organizing Cities to Solve 'People Problems,'" (Berkeley: Institute for Local Self-Government, 1966), p. 12.

39. White members of the committee included Philip Ennis of the Retail Merchants Association, *Tribune* publisher William Knowland, three Kaiser executives, real-estate agent Sol Gilberg, the manager of the Chamber of Commerce, City Councillors Osborne and Rilea, Mayor Houlihan, and Municipal

Judge Robert Kroninger, president of the Council of Social Planning. Black members included NAACP—Oakland branch president McCullum, Municipal Judge Wilson, and Dr. Norvel Smith, director of research for the Alameda County School Department; May, "Struggle for Authority," pp. 192–197, 248 n.

40. The Castlemont area consisted of that part of the Castlemont High School attendance area lying below MacArthur Boulevard, between Seminary Avenue and the city line of San Leandro, down to the Oakland Airport and San Leandro Bay. The portion below East Fourteenth Street corresponded to what later became the East Oakland Target Area under the Office of Economic Opportunity poverty program; Regal, *Oakland's Partnership for Change*, pp. 22, 71–74.

41. May, "Struggle for Authority," pp. 200–203; Regal, *Oakland's Partnership for Change*, p. 6.

42. May, "Struggle for Authority," p. 192.

43. Ibid., pp. 214, 225; Regal, *Oakland's Partnership for Change*, p. 23.

44. The Ford Foundation had asked for $589,000 in local contributions but accepted a compromise whereby local matching costs could be met with "redirected funds," i.e., money taken from already existing city programs or from state or federal grants. This allowed city government to avoid raising taxes for the program; May, "Struggle for Authority," pp. 210–215; Regal, *Oakland's Partnership for Change*, p. 4.

45. Ennis and Wilson had served on the Committee to Support the Ford Proposal. Black attorneys Clinton White and Carl Metoyer were appointed to the advisory committee in June 1963; May, "Struggle for Authority," pp. 218–220, 237.

46. Thompson, "Organizing Cities to Solve 'People Problems,'" pp. 24–25.

47. May, "Struggle for Authority," pp. 149, 243; Regal, *Oakland's Partnership for Change*, pp. 37, 81.

48. May, "Struggle for Authority," pp. 239–243.

49. Ibid., p. 194.

50. Ibid., pp. 228–234, 267, 278–279; Regal, *Oakland's Partnership for Change*, p. 55.

51. To be designated a depressed area under the statute, a city must have had at least 6 percent unemployment the previous calendar year, and its unemployment rate must have been significantly higher than the national average over several preceding years. Jeffrey Pressman and Aaron Wildavsky, *Implementation*, 3d ed. (Berkeley: University of California Press, 1984 [orig. 1973]), p. 10.

52. Regal, *Oakland's Partnership for Change*, pp. 96–97; Ralph Kramer, *Participation of the Poor: Comparative Community Case Studies in the War on Poverty* (Englewood Cliffs, N.J.: Prentice-Hall, 1969), pp. 110–111.

53. May, "Struggle for Authority," pp. 283–284; Kramer, *Participation of the Poor*, pp. 108–109.

54. May, "Struggle for Authority," p. 295. Black members included attorneys McCullum and White of the NAACP—Oakland branch, Oakland School Board member Barney Hilburn, and Judge Wilson, among others.

55. May, "Struggle for Authority," p. 296; Kramer, *Participation of the Poor*, p. 110.

56. *Oakland Tribune*, February 15, 1965; May, "Struggle for Authority," p. 295.

57. Kaiser Industries executive Norman Nicholson was elected vice chair, with Dr. Smith as secretary and City Auditor-Controller Alan Brizee as treasurer; May, "Struggle for Authority," pp. 297–298; Kramer, *Participation of the Poor*, p. 112.

58. May, "Struggle for Authority," pp. 311–312, 317; Kramer, *Participation of the Poor*, pp. 125–126.

59. May, "Struggle for Authority," pp. 315–317, 321; Kramer, *Participation of the Poor*, pp. 111–112.

60. May, "Struggle for Authority," pp. 315–317, 332, 338–339.

61. Ibid., pp. 314–320; Kramer, *Participation of the Poor*, pp. 115–118.

62. Kramer, *Participation of the Poor*, pp. 111–114; May, "Struggle for Authority," p. 332.

63. Dr. Smith and other OEDC leaders opposed TAAC operation of programs as contrary to their role as conduits of information and feedback between the community and the poverty program as a whole. The TAACs ultimately accommodated this concern by setting up independent nonprofit corporations, with boards of directors drawn from their members; May, "Struggle for Authority," pp. 315, 329–330; Regal, *Oakland's Partnership for Change*, p. 104; Kramer, *Participation of the Poor*, p. 119.

64. May, "Struggle for Authority," pp. 327–328.

65. Kramer, *Participation of the Poor*, pp. 130–133.

66. The McCullum committee recommended that twenty members of the OEDC be elected from the TAACs and nineteen appointed at-large by the mayor, as follows: three elected officials, two business and industry, two labor, two private agencies, three religious organizations, two NAACP, one CORE, one black business and professional, one Mexican American, one Native American, and one Asian American; May, "Struggle for Authority," pp. 356–359.

67. After the 1966 target area elections, all TAAC chairs and fourteen of twenty target area representatives to the OEDC were black. TAAC membership became almost exclusively black (except for the Spanish Speaking Advisory Committee); Kramer, *Participation of the Poor*, p. 144.

68. May, "Struggle for Authority," pp. 365–366; Kramer, *Participation of the Poor*, pp. 135–136.

69. Meltsner, *The Politics of City Revenue*, p. 50.

CHAPTER 7. BUREAUCRATIC INSULATION
AND RACIAL CONFLICT

1. Jeffrey Pressman and Aaron Wildavsky, *Implementation*, 3d ed. (Berkeley: University of California Press, 1984 [orig. 1973]), p. 150; J. M. Regal, *Oakland's Partnership for Change* (Oakland: City Department of Human Re-

sources, 1967), p. 97; Marc Johnson, "Report to the Oakland Adult Minority Project Advisory Committee" (California Department of Employment, October 1968), p. 10, in Edgar F. Kaiser Papers, Carton 55, file 8, Bancroft Library, University of California, Berkeley.

2. Jeffrey Pressman, *Federal Programs and City Politics* (Berkeley: University of California Press, 1975), p. 20.

3. Regal, *Oakland's Partnership for Change*, pp. 56–57; William Woodson, "Final Report of the Oakland Adult Project Follow-up Study" (Department of Human Resources, Oakland, September 1967), pp. 1–2, in Edgar F. Kaiser Papers, Carton 55, file 9, Bancroft Library, University of California, Berkeley.

4. Judith V. May, "Struggle for Authority: A Comparison of Four Social Change Programs in Oakland, California" (Ph.D. diss., University of California, Berkeley, 1973), pp. 394–399; Oakland Economic Development Council, "Oakland's War on Poverty, 1965–1966," Oakland History Room, Oakland Public Library, Oakland; Johnson, "Report," p. 8; *Oakland Tribune*, December 11, 1965.

5. Regal, *Oakland's Partnership for Change*, p. 60; *Oakland Tribune*, December 18, 1965. Amory Bradford says the State Employment Service and Skills Center planning was dominated by the unions, but the initial proposal was approved at a MDTA advisory committee meeting from which the principal union member was absent, and the CSES skills survey was conducted without union participation. Much of the Central Labor Council's anger was directed at the CSES, over the council's exclusion from its decisions; Bradford, *Oakland's Not for Burning* (New York: David McKay, 1968), pp. 98–104; also letter from Robert Ash to Albert Tieburg regarding Skills Center, July 20, 1966; letter from Norman Amundsen to Willard Wirtz et al., June 13, 1966; and Central Labor Council press release, May 10, 1966, in Central Labor Council of Alameda County Collection, Box 102, Labor Archives and Research Center, San Francisco State University.

6. Less than 10 percent of job orders came to the project through its own solicitation (rather than normal CSES channels), even after two job development specialists were hired in October 1965; Woodson, "Final Report," section 3, p. 20.

7. Regal, *Oakland's Partnership for Change*, pp. 58–59; Woodson, "Final Report," section 5, pp. 33–34, section 7, pp. 5–7, and section 8, pp. 6–8.

8. Joseph Rodriguez, "Rapid Transit and Community Power: West Oakland Residents Confront BART," *Antipode* 31, no. 2 (1999): 212–228; Bradford, *Oakland's Not for Burning*, pp. 46–52, 150–158; Ralph Kramer, *Participation of the Poor: Comparative Community Case Studies in the War on Poverty* (Englewood Cliffs, N.J.: Prentice-Hall, 1969), pp. 146–147; *Flatlands*, March 26, April 9, May 7–21, June 5–18, and June 18–July 1, 1966; *California Voice*, July 21 and 28, 1967.

9. Bradford, *Oakland's Not for Burning*, pp. 158–165; Pressman and Wildavsky, *Implementation*, pp. 28–30, 40–58.

10. *Los Angeles Times*, March 16, 1969.

11. Members of the mayor's Manpower Commission included representa-

tives from Kaiser Industries, World Airways, Capwell's department stores, and other Oakland business and educational institutions; Charles Goady of Pacific Gas and Electric and the Urban League; Robert Ash of the Central Labor Council, Lamar Childers of the Building Trades and William York of the Teamsters; and OEDC members Don McCullum and Judge Lionel Wilson, with Carl Metoyer as chair; May, "Struggle for Authority," pp. 456–458.

12. Ibid., pp. 461–474.

13. *San Francisco Examiner,* March 31, 1967.

14. Federal Executive Board, Oakland Task Force, *An Analysis of Federal Decision-Making and Impact: The Federal Government in Oakland,* vol. 2 (Washington, D.C.: U.S. Department of Commerce, Economic Development Administration, 1969), pp. 122–124.

15. U.S. Bureau of the Census, *Census of the Population: 1970,* series PHC 3–45: *Employment Profiles of Selected Low Income Areas: Oakland, California* (Washington, D.C.: GPO, 1971), p. 5.

16. Bradford, *Oakland's Not for Burning,* pp. 131–137; California State Advisory Committee to the U.S. Commission on Civil Rights, "Civil Rights in Oakland, California" (MS, Doe Library, University of California, Berkeley, 1967).

17. Although the regional OEO office advised the OEDC that the police review proposal would likely be rejected, since it served the entire community and not just the poor, the Ford Foundation had previously said it would consider proposals ineligible for federal funds; May, "Struggle for Authority," pp. 436–439; Regal, *Oakland's Partnership for Change,* p. 105; Kramer, *Participation of the Poor,* p. 128.

18. *Oakland Tribune,* March 4 and 9, 1966; May, "Struggle for Authority," pp. 298–299.

19. Pressman and Wildavsky, *Implementation,* p. 27; Arnold Meltsner, *Politics of City Revenue* (Berkeley: University of California Press, 1971), pp. 53, 60; Bradford, *Oakland's Not for Burning,* pp. 85, 95, 138; *Oakland Tribune,* April 6, 1966.

20. May, "Struggle for Authority," p. 439; *Oakland Tribune,* March 4 and 9, 1966.

21. Members of the committee included Judge Wilson; white Protestant minister Rev. Darby Betts; black Protestant minister Rev. A. S. Jackson; Ralph Williams, chair of the West Oakland Advisory Committee; Richard Groulx, executive secretary of the Central Labor Council; and William Lowe of the North Oakland Advisory Committee (Lowe was subsequently removed); May, "Struggle for Authority," pp. 444–445.

22. Ibid., pp. 446–447; Kramer, *Participation of the Poor,* p. 139.

23. May, "Struggle for Authority," pp. 483–491; Kramer, *Participation of the Poor,* pp. 139, 142.

24. Pressman, *Federal Programs and City Politics,* p. 41.

25. Mari Malvey and Aaron Wildavsky, "The Citizens of Oakland Look at Their City" (MS, Institute of Governmental Studies Library, University of California, Berkeley, 1971), p. 36; *Black Panther Inter-Communal News Service,* De-

cember 23, 1972; U.S. Bureau of the Census, *Census of Population: 1960,* vol. 1: *Characteristics of the Population,* part 6: *California* (Washington, D.C.: GPO, 1963), p. 138; idem, *1970 Census of the Population,* vol. 1: *Characteristics of the Population,* part 6: *California* (Washington, D.C.: GPO, 1973), p. 104; Warren Hinckle, "Metropoly: The Story of Oakland, California," *Ramparts* 4, no. 6 (February 1966): 25–50.

26. Hilburn was a member of the Republican state central committee and ran for the Republican nomination for Congress from the Seventh District in 1968. Goady was appointed to the Oakland Civil Service Commission in 1964, and to the School Board in 1968. Goady and Patterson ran the Small Business Development Center, funded by the OEDC, as well as their own business services company. All were members of the Alameda County Republican Group in 1967, of which Patterson was president; *California Voice,* February 12, 1965, and March 29, 1968; *Oakland Post,* April 5, 1967, and April 10, 1969; *Oakland Tribune,* December 18, 1968; E. A. Daly, "Alameda County Political Leader and Journalist," an oral history conducted 1971, in *Perspectives on the Alameda County District Attorney's Office,* Regional Oral History Office, Bancroft Library, University of California, Berkeley, 1972, p. 27.

27. David Kirp, *Just Schools: The Idea of Racial Equality in American Education* (Berkeley: University of California Press, 1982), p. 220; program, 1967 Freedom Fund Banquet, NAACP—Oakland branch, in Joshua Rose papers, African American Museum and Library at Oakland; Port of Oakland, *Sixty Years: A Chronicle of Progress* (Oakland: Board of Port Commissioners, 1987), p. 4. Berkley was also the second black member appointed to the School Board (after Hilburn), but stepped down and nominated Republican Charles Goady as his replacement. One year after his appointment to the Port Commission, in 1970, Berkley's *Post* endorsed Ronald Reagan for governor; *Oakland Post,* October 29, 1970; interview with Thomas Berkley, July 27, 1999, Oakland.

28. Program, 1967 Men of Tomorrow conference retreat, "Men of Tomorrow" files, African American Museum and Library at Oakland.

29. Kramer, *Participation of the Poor,* p. 252; Bradford, *Oakland's Not for Burning,* p. 9; Pressman and Wildavsky, *Implementation,* p. 14; *California Voice,* August 4, 1967.

30. By 1970, more than two thousand black male Vietnam War veterans were living in the low-income target areas in the Oakland flats; U.S. Bureau of the Census, *Census of the Population: 1970,* series PHC 3–45, p. 2.

31. Bobby Seale, *Seize the Time* (New York: Vintage, 1968); Gilbert Moore, *Rage* (New York: Carroll and Graf, 1993 [orig. 1971]); "What We Want, What We Believe," in *The Black Panthers Speak,* ed. Philip S. Foner (New York: Da Capo Press, 1995), pp. 2–4.

32. Clayborne Carson, "Foreword," in *The Black Panthers Speak,* ed. Foner, pp. ix–xviii.

33. Jimmy Mori, "The Ideological Development of the Black Panther Party," *Cornell Journal of Social Relations* 12, no. 2 (Fall 1977): 137–155; Seale, *Seize the Time,* pp. 211–222; Moore, *Rage,* p. 73.

34. Designed by the architectural firm of Roche and Dinkeloo, the museum was completed in September 1969. The new Laney College opened its doors in 1970; Mel Scott, *Partnership in the Arts: Public and Private Support of Cultural Activities in the San Francisco Bay Area* (Berkeley: Institute of Governmental Studies, University of California, Berkeley, 1963), pp. 35–36; Michael Dobrin, "The Oakland Museum: Garden and Gallery," *Journal of the West* 18, no. 3 (1979): 91–94; *Redevelopment in Oakland: Weekly Summary* (Oakland: Redevelopment Agency, May 26, 1967); Annual Report for year 1967, ORA files, in Division of Records, Office of the City Clerk, Oakland, California.

35. *Oakland Tribune* publisher William Knowland chaired the plan's advisory committee, as well as a committee of the Central Business District Association, which contributed $20,000 to help finance the Planning Commission's study; *Oakland Tribune*, November 30, 1965, and February 17 and March 10, 1966; *Redevelopment in Oakland: Weekly Summary* (Oakland: Redevelopment Agency, June 16 and 30, 1967); *Draft Environmental Impact Report: Oakland City Center* (Oakland: Redevelopment Agency, 1973).

36. *Oakland Tribune*, May 19, 1966.

37. *Oakland Tribune*, February 24, March 4, 11, and 23, and April 29, 1965.

38. Michael Marans, "Relocation in Acorn: A Focal Point for the Study of the Transition in Urban Renewal Policy and Politics in Oakland" (MS, Institute of Governmental Studies, University of California, Berkeley, 1969), section 7, p. 1; *Oakland Tribune*, April 6 and August 16, 1966; *California Voice*, December 29, 1967.

39. Oakland City Planning Department, *West Oakland: A 701 Subarea Report* (Oakland: City Planning Department, 701 Division, May 1969).

40. May, "Struggle for Authority," p. 481.

41. Federal Executive Board, Oakland Task Force, *Federal Decision-Making and Impact*, vol. 2, pp. 38–39.

42. Ibid., vol. 2, pp. 37, 43–45, 51.

43. *Redevelopment in Oakland: Weekly Summary* (Oakland: Redevelopment Agency, April 21, 1967); May, "Struggle for Authority," p. 504; Federal Executive Board, Oakland Task Force, *Federal Decision-Making and Impact*, vol. 2, pp. 187–196.

44. *California Voice*, July 31, 1964; May, "Struggle for Authority," pp. 508–509; Federal Executive Board, Oakland Task Force, *Federal Decision-Making and Impact*, vol. 2, pp. 198–201.

45. Federal Executive Board, Oakland Task Force, *Federal Decision-Making and Impact*, vol. 2, pp. 206–209.

46. Ibid., p. 211.

47. May, "Struggle for Authority," pp. 513–516; Edward Hayes, *Power Structure and Urban Policy* (New York: McGraw-Hill, 1972), p. 123.

48. May, "Struggle for Authority," pp. 517, 520–521, 549; Federal Executive Board, Oakland Task Force, *Federal Decision-Making and Impact*, vol. 2, pp. 210–215.

49. *California Voice*, December 8, 1967; May, "Struggle for Authority," p.

525; Federal Executive Board, Oakland Task Force, *Federal Decision-Making and Impact,* vol. 2, p. 218.

50. May, "Struggle for Authority," pp. 525–526; Federal Executive Board, Oakland Task Force, *Federal Decision-Making and Impact,* vol. 2, p. 224.

51. Federal Executive Board, Oakland Task Force, *Federal Decision-Making and Impact,* vol. 2, p. 241.

52. Ibid., pp. 62–64, 243–244.

53. The screening committee to select the project director was set at six members, three each from the city and the community, on condition that Redevelopment Agency director John Williams serve as one of the city members. The city manager would select the project director from a list of three names agreed upon by at least five of the six committee members. The project director would be responsible to the city manager on administrative matters, and to the steering committee for "policy," while the city manager would channel approved proposals from the WOPC to the city council, but was enjoined from altering policy contents; May, "Struggle for Authority," pp. 533–535; Federal Executive Board, Oakland Task Force, *Federal Decision-Making and Impact,* vol. 2, pp. 249–250.

54. Federal Executive Board, Oakland Task Force, *Federal Decision-Making and Impact,* vol. 2, p. 252; May, "Struggle for Authority," p. 553.

55. May, "Struggle for Authority," pp. 536–539; Federal Executive Board, Oakland Task Force, *Federal Decision-Making and Impact,* vol. 2, pp. 251–256.

56. Reginald Major, *A Panther Is a Black Cat* (New York: William Morrow, 1971), pp. 12–15; May, "Struggle for Authority," p. 540; idem, field notes on police-community relations, April–June 1968, pp. 28–29, Oakland Project (Institute of Governmental Studies Library, University of California, Berkeley); Federal Executive Board, Oakland Task Force, *Federal Decision-Making and Impact,* vol. 2, pp. 261–263.

57. Federal Executive Board, Oakland Task Force, *Federal Decision-Making and Impact,* vol. 2, pp. 262–267, 272–273.

58. May, "Struggle for Authority," p. 553; Milton Viorst, *The Citizen Poor of the 1960s* (New York: Charles Kettering Foundation, 1977), pp. 21–22.

59. *Oakland Redevelopment News,* spring 1969 and summer–fall 1969; and Redevelopment Agency, 1971–1972 Progress Report, "Oakland Is a Progressive City," in "Oakland—City Center, 1970–1979, other than clippings" file, Oakland History Room, Oakland Public Library, Oakland.

60. Total construction contracts awarded through the agency for 1970–1974 were $35 million; Lawrence Pearl, "The Other City," *HUD Challenge* (April 1975): 6–13.

61. Pressman and Wildavsky, *Implementation,* pp. 82–86; Oakland Redevelopment Agency, minutes of annual meeting, December 16, 1970, in Division of Records, Office of the City Clerk, Oakland, California; *Oakland Redevelopment News,* February 1972, and *Patterns of Growth: A Summary of Redevelopment in Oakland,* 1974, Y-4, in "Oakland—City Center, 1970–1979, other than clippings" file, Oakland History Room, Oakland Public Library, Oakland.

62. The five groups were the WOPC, the West Oakland Health Council, the GSCA, the United Taxpayers and Voters Union, and OCNA. MORHI also employed black architects Kinnard and Silver, attorney Donald McCullum as legal counsel, and Trans-Bay Engineers, Inc., as the builder for what was said to be the first high rise built by a black firm in the western United States. *Oakland Redevelopment News,* spring 1969, summer–fall 1969, and February 1972; "Oakland Is a Progressive City" and *Patterns of Growth,* M-1, in "Oakland— City Center, 1970–1979, other than clippings" file, Oakland History Room, Oakland Public Library, Oakland.

63. "Oakland City Center," Grubb and Ellis Development Company, 1971, in "Oakland—City Center, 1970–1979, other than clippings" file, Oakland History Room, Oakland Public Library, Oakland; *Patterns of Growth,* G-1. The City Center developer, Grubb and Ellis, signed a marketing agreement with black real-estate agents S. B. Odell, C. J. Patterson, and Percy Provost, along with James Jackson; *Oakland Tribune,* January 6, 1974. Black directors on the City Center economic development corporation board included McCullum, Dr. Smith, Reverend J. L. Richard, Leon Miller, Elijah Turner, Charles Goady, C. J. Patterson, Burton Lewis, and Judge Wilson, along with Latino members Joe Coto and James Delgadillo; *Draft Environmental Impact Report: Oakland City Center,* in "Oakland—City Center, 1970–1979, other than clippings" file, Oakland History Room, Oakland Public Library, Oakland.

64. *Oakland Tribune,* November 3, 1967, January 16, July 4, October 28, and December 29, 1969, and January 10, March 23, July 8, and August 8, 1970; *Oakland Post,* July 10, 1969.

65. *Oakland Tribune,* November 7, 1969, and January 10, June 6, 25, and 29, July 8, August 15, and October 13, 1970.

66. *Oakland Tribune,* June 24, July 3, August 28, September 30, and November 19 and 26, 1969, and July 23 and December 29, 1970.

67. Oakland Citizens' Committee for Urban Renewal, *Annual Report, 1983– 1984* (Oakland: Citizens' Committee for Urban Renewal, 1984), p. 9.

68. *Oakland Tribune,* December 19, 1970; Rufus Browning, Dale Rogers Marshall, and David Tabb, *Protest Is Not Enough* (Berkeley: University of California Press, 1984), p. 64; Frank J. Thompson, *Personnel Policy in the City: The Politics of Jobs in Oakland* (Berkeley: University of California Press, 1975), pp. 114–119.

69. *Oakland Tribune,* May 21 and 26,1969; Jesse McCorry, *Marcus Foster and the Oakland Public Schools* (Berkeley: University of California Press, 1978), pp. 2–26; Interview with David Creque, December 21, 1995, Oakland. The trials of the Oakland Five ended with acquittal or dismissal of most charges and the defendants pleading no contest to a single misdemeanor of blocking an aisle in a public place. Roland Warren, Stephen Rose, and Ann Bergunder, *The Structure of Urban Reform* (Lexington, Mass.: D. C. Heath, 1974), pp. 137–138.

70. McCorry, *Marcus Foster and the Oakland Public Schools,* pp. 33–36; *San Francisco Examiner,* April 16, 1969.

71. OEDCI director Moore and officers Charles Jackson and Virtual Mur-

rell were expelled from the Black Caucus, while caucus members Elijah Turner and Gaye Cobb were fired from their jobs with the poverty program; *Oakland Tribune*, November 25 and December 10, 17, and 19, 1970, and January 10 and 22, 1971; *Inter-City Express*, December 17, 1970; Pressman, *Federal Programs and City Politics*, pp. 78–79.

72. *Oakland Tribune*, February 18, 24, and 25, and April 13, 1971.

73. *Oakland Tribune*, March 2 and 3, April 25, and May 19 and 21, 1971.

74. David Hilliard and Lewis Cole, *This Side of Glory: The Autobiography of David Hilliard and the Story of the Black Panther Party* (Boston: Little, Brown, 1993), pp. 236, 248; Carson, "Foreword," in *The Black Panthers Speak*, ed. Foner, pp. xiv–xv; Hugh Pearson, *The Shadow of the Panther: Huey Newton and the Price of Black Power in America* (Reading, Mass.: Addison-Wesley, 1994), pp. 206, 235; Charles Jones, "The Political Repression of the Black Panther Party, 1966–1971: The Case of the Oakland Bay Area," *Journal of Black Studies* 18, no. 4 (June 1988): 415–434; Huey P. Newton, *Revolutionary Suicide* (New York: Harcourt Brace Jovanovich, 1973), pp. 328–330.

75. Philip S. Foner, "Introduction," in *The Black Panthers Speak*, ed. Foner, p. xxiv; Pearson, *The Shadow of the Panther*, pp. 210, 221–222.

76. As early as October 1968, the party under Bobby Seale had begun giving free breakfasts for children; Hilliard and Cole, *This Side of Glory*, pp. 211, 326–327; Rod Bush, *We Are Not What We Seem* (New York: New York University Press, 1999), pp. 201–202; Elaine Brown, *A Taste of Power: A Black Woman's Story* (New York: Pantheon, 1992), pp. 276–281.

77. Huey P. Newton, *To Die for the People* (New York: Random House, 1972), pp. 109–111; Pearson, *The Shadow of the Panther*, pp. 238–246; Brown, *A Taste of Power*, pp. 331–333.

78. *Black Panther Inter-Communal News Service*, May 20 and August 12, 1972; Pearson, *The Shadow of the Panther*, p. 247.

79. Brown, *A Taste of Power*, pp. 321–326; Robert DeLeon, "Showdown in Oakland: Bobby Seale and Otho Green Battle to Become Mayor," *Jet* (April 12, 1973); interview with Shirley Burton, July 27, 1999, Oakland; Alan Ware, *The Breakdown of Democratic Party Organization, 1940–1980* (Oxford: Oxford University Press, 1985), pp. 221–222.

80. Brown, *A Taste of Power*, p. 324; "Organizing a People's Campaign," *Co-evolution Quarterly* 3 (September 23, 1974): 53–60.

81. Interview with John Sutter, July 13, 1999, Oakland; DeLeon, "Showdown in Oakland"; Pearson, *The Shadow of the Panther*, p. 272; *Oakland Tribune*, July 1, 1973. Among black activists, OCNA leader Love endorsed Reading; "Verified Statements of Candidates for Office at the City of Oakland Nominating Election, April 17, 1973," in "Oakland—Elections" file, Oakland History Room, Oakland Public Library, Oakland.

82. *Oakland Tribune*, May 20 and July 1, 1973; Oakland City Clerk, *Elections: 1852 to the Present* (Oakland: Office of the City Clerk, n.d.); "Election Results," Office of the City Clerk, Oakland.

83. Rod Bush, *The New Black Vote: Politics and Power in Four American*

Cities (San Francisco: Synthesis, 1984), pp. 323–324; Brown, *A Taste of Power,* pp. 350–353; Pearson, *The Shadow of the Panther,* pp. 264–268; Ware, *Breakdown of Democratic Party Organization,* p. 223.

84. Browning et al., *Protest Is Not Enough,* pp. 61–65, 113.

85. John Williams had been touted by some as a potential mayoral candidate, but he died suddenly of cancer in October 1976. Lionel Wilson, *Attorney, Judge, and Oakland Mayor,* an oral history conducted 1985 and 1990, Regional Oral History Office, Bancroft Library, University of California, Berkeley, 1992, pp. 52–53; R. Stanley Oden, "A Sociological Study of the Political Incorporation of People of Color in Oakland, California, 1966–1996" (Ph.D. diss., University of California, Santa Cruz, 1999), p. 137.

86. Rufus Browning, Dale Rogers Marshall, and David Tabb, *Racial Politics in American Cities,* 2d ed. (White Plains, N.Y.: Longman, 1997 [orig. 1990]); Norman Fainstein and Susan Fainstein, "Urban Regimes and Black Citizens: The Economic and Social Impacts of Political Incorporation in US Cities," *International Journal of Urban and Regional Research* 20, no. 1 (1996): 22–37.

CHAPTER 8. FROM SOCIAL MOVEMENTS
TO SOCIAL CHANGE

1. Jeffrey Pressman and Aaron Wildavsky, *Implementation,* 3d ed. (Berkeley: University of California Press, 1984 [orig. 1973]), p. 66.

2. Arnold Meltsner, *The Politics of City Revenue* (Berkeley: University of California Press, 1971), p. 49.

3. Paul Peterson, *City Limits* (Chicago: University of Chicago Press, 1981), pp. 115–116; Paul Starr, "How They Fail," *Working Papers for a New Society* 6 (March–April 1978): 70.

4. Doug McAdam, "Micromobilization Contexts and Recruitment to Activism," *International Social Movement Research* 1 (1988): 125–154; Alberto Melucci, *Nomads of the Present* (Philadelphia: Temple University Press, 1989), p. 60; Bert Klandermans, "The Formation and Mobilization of Consensus," *International Social Movement Research* 1 (1988): 173–196.

5. Kathleen Thelen, "Historical Institutionalism in Comparative Politics," *Annual Review of Political Science* 2 (1999): 369–404.

6. Judith V. May, "Two Model Cities: Negotiations in Oakland," *Politics and Society* 2, no. 1 (Fall 1971): 57–88.

7. Amy Bridges, *Morning Glories: Municipal Reform in the Southwest* (Princeton, N.J.: Princeton University Press, 1997), pp. 95, 152–157.

8. William Grimshaw, *Bitter Fruit: Black Politics and the Chicago Machine, 1931–1991* (Chicago: University of Chicago Press, 1992); John Mollenkopf, "New York: The Great Anomaly," in *Racial Politics in American Cities,* ed. Rufus Browning, Dale Rogers Marshall, and David Tabb, 2d ed. (White Plains, N.Y.: Longman, 1997), pp. 97–116.

9. Steven Erie, *Rainbow's End: Irish Americans and the Dilemmas of Ur-*

ban Machine Politics, 1840–1985 (Berkeley: University of California Press, 1988), pp. 161–164.

10. Arnold Hirsch, *Making the Second Ghetto* (Cambridge: Cambridge University Press, 1983).

11. Clarence Stone, *Regime Politics: Governing Atlanta, 1946–1988* (Lawrence: University Press of Kansas, 1989), pp. 30–37.

12. Joshua Freeman, *Working Class New York: Life and Labor since World War Two* (New York: New Press, 2000); Thomas Sugrue, *The Origins of the Urban Crisis: Race and Inequality in Postwar Detroit* (Princeton, N.J.: Princeton University Press, 1996).

13. Adolph Reed, "The Black Urban Regime: Structural Origins and Constraints," in *Power, Community, and the City,* ed. Michael P. Smith, Comparative Urban and Community Research 1 (New Brunswick, N.J.: Transaction, 1988), pp. 138–189.

14. Sharon Watson, "Mayoral Leadership Changes and Public Policy: Exploring the Influence of Black Urban Governance" (Ph.D. diss., Northwestern University, 1982), p. 170.

15. Watson, "Mayoral Leadership," pp. 165–169; Rufus Browning, Dale Rogers Marshall, and David Tabb, *Protest Is Not Enough* (Berkeley: University of California Press, 1984), pp. 156–163; Albert Kevin Williams, "Crime and Community Security as Political Issues: Citizens' Demands and Government Responses in Oakland, Richmond and San Francisco" (Ph.D. diss., University of California, Berkeley, 1986), p. 65; Donald Hausler, "Blacks in Oakland: 1852–1987" (MS, Oakland History Room, Oakland Public Library, Oakland, 1987), pp. 182–184; Rufus Browning, Dale Rogers Marshall, and David Tabb, eds., *Racial Politics in American Cities,* 2d ed. (White Plains, N.Y.: Longman, 1977), pp. 30–31.

16. Browning et al., *Protest Is Not Enough,* p. 66; Mark Foster, *Henry J. Kaiser: Builder of the American West* (Austin: University of Texas Press, 1989), pp. 254, 281; Gayle Montgomery and James Johnson, *One Step from the White House: The Rise and Fall of Senator William F. Knowland* (Berkeley: University of California Press, 1998), pp. 278–279, 291–306.

17. U.S. Bureau of the Census, *1970 Census of Population and Housing: General Demographic Trends for Metropolitan Areas, 1960 to 1970,* series PHC 2–6: *California* (Washington, D.C.: GPO, 1971), pp. 6–30; idem, *1990 Census of Population and Housing: Population and Housing for Census Tracts and Block Numbering Areas: San Francisco–Oakland–San Jose, CA,* section 1: *Oakland PMSA* (Washington, D.C.: GPO, 1993), p. 282.

18. Roger Kemp, *Coping with Proposition 13* (Lexington, Mass.: D. C. Heath, 1980), pp. 116–132.

19. James Phillip Thompson III, "The Impact of the Jesse Jackson Campaigns on Local Black Political Mobilization in New York City, Atlanta, and Oakland" (Ph.D. diss., City University of New York, 1990), pp. 228–234. Other black political leaders made the same conservative turn: As early as 1974, Paul Cobb was

describing himself as a "right wing nationalist"; Milton Viorst, *The Citizen Poor of the 1960s* (New York: Charles Kettering Foundation, 1977), p. 17.

20. David Weber, *Oakland: Hub of the West* (Tulsa: Continental Heritage Press, 1981), p. 191; U.S. Bureau of the Census, *Major Retail Centers in Standard Metropolitan Statistical Areas: California, 1977 Census of Retail Trade* (Washington, D.C., GPO, 1980), pp. 5–259; idem, *Geographic Area Series: California, 1987 Census of Retail Trade* (Washington, D.C.: GPO, 1989), CA-83.

21. "Oakland Pushes City Center," *San Francisco Chronicle*, December 1, 1986.

22. D. Slater, "A Tale of Two Cities," *East Bay Express*, May 20, 1994; "Mammoth Development Proposed," *Oakland Tribune*, February 9, 2000; "Another Grand Plan to Revive Oakland's Run-down Uptown," *San Francisco Chronicle*, February 9, 2000; Ruth Hendricks Willard, *Alameda County, California Crossroads: An Illustrated History* (Northridge, Calif.: Windsor Publications, 1988), p. 125; *San Francisco Chronicle*, June 24, 1998.

23. *The Montclarian* (Oakland), March 29, 1978.

24. "Lionel Wilson, Ex-Mayor of Oakland, Dies," *San Francisco Chronicle*, January 29, 1998; D. Slater, "The Life and Times of Mayor Wilson," *East Bay Express*, October 9, 1989.

25. "Curtain Rises on New Oakland," *San Francisco Chronicle*, August 3, 1995; "Construction Begins on New State Building," *San Francisco Chronicle*, November 21, 1995; *The Oakland Strategic Plan* (Oakland: Oakland—Sharing the Vision, 1992), p. 105.

26. "Shorenstein Co. Hopes to Make It in Tough Market," *San Francisco Chonicle*, March 18, 1997; "Redevelopment Pact Rejected," *Oakland Tribune*, March 5, 1997; "Oakland OKs $4 Million Loan for 'Urban Village,'" *San Francisco Chronicle*, March 5, 1997. In a separate deal, the city loaned $11 million to a promoter in 1995 to build a commercial ice rink at the corner of Seventeenth Street and San Pablo Avenue. The rink was built, but the owners quickly went out of business, and the city was forced to absorb the loss; "Oakland Council Takes Control of Faltering Ice Rink," *San Francisco Chronicle*, April 2, 1997.

27. M. McGrath and M. Thomas, "The Rise and Fall of the Port of Oakland," *East Bay Express*, July 5, 1991; D. Slater, "Oakland's Once and Future Port," *East Bay Express*, October 9, 1998.

28. U.S. Bureau of the Census, *1970 Census of the Population*, vol. 1: *Characteristics of the Population*, part 6: *California* (Washington, D.C.: GPO, 1973), pp. 6–627; idem, *1990 Census of Population and Housing: Population and Housing Characteristics for Census Tracts and Block Numbering Areas*, section 1: *Oakland, CA PMSA* (Washington, D.C.: GPO, 1993), p. 1052.

29. D. Slater, "The Life and Times of Mayor Wilson," *East Bay Express*, October 9, 1989, 16; Willard, *Alameda County, California Crossroads*, p. 107.

30. *The Oakland Strategic Plan*, pp. 102, 107; "City of Change," *Oakland Tribune*, September 13, 1992; U.S. Bureau of the Census, *1980 Census of Population and Housing: Census Tracts, San Francisco–Oakland Calif., SMSA*

(Washington, D.C.: GPO, 1983), table P-15, p. 731; idem, *1990 Census of Population and Housing,* pp. 1025, 1052.

31. "Prisoner to Stand Trial for Murder of Felix Mitchell," *Oakland Tribune,* May 31, 1991.

32. "How Drugs Create Islands of Fear," *Oakland Tribune,* December 9, 1984; "Homicides Hit 12-Year Low in Oakland," *San Francisco Chronicle,* December 24, 1996.

33. Hugh Pearson, *The Shadow of the Panther: Huey Newton and the Price of Black Power in America* (Reading, Mass.: Addison-Wesley, 1994), pp. 304–315.

34. *San Francisco Chronicle,* January 4, 2000.

35. In the 1980s, the black population in Oakland rose by 2.6 percent, but it increased by 49 percent in the rest of Alameda County; Julia Hansen, "Residential Segregation of Blacks by Income Group: Evidence from Oakland," *Population Research and Policy Review* 15 (August 1996): 369–389. See also D. Gaither, "Oakland Ponders the Effect of Black Flight," *East Bay Express,* September 5, 1997.

36. "Alameda County: Profile of Ethnic and Immigrant Populations," Newcomer Information Clearinghouse, International Institute of the East Bay, Oakland, 1993, p. 42; D. Slater, "Getting It down in Black and White," *East Bay Express,* January 15, 1999.

37. *The Oakland Strategic Plan,* p. 115; Oakland Citizens' Committee for Urban Renewal, "Neighborhood Profile: Oakland Hills," Oakland.

38. *San Francisco Chronicle,* June 27, 1995, and November 11, 1998.

39. "Oakland Has Rich History of Black-Owned Media," *Oakland Tribune,* February 1, 1993.

40. *San Francisco Chronicle,* July 27 and October 27, 1995, September 12, 15, and 16, 1996, and July 8 and 27, 1998; *Oakland Tribune,* June 13, 2001.

41. *San Francisco Chronicle,* January 20 and June 3 and 4, 1998; D. Slater, "The Race for Second Place," *East Bay Express,* May 29, 1998.

42. *San Francisco Chronicle,* June 6 and August 16, 1998.

43. *San Francisco Chronicle,* November 4, 1998.

44. *San Francisco Chronicle,* March 3 and 20, July 19, and November 6, 1999, and April 12, 2000.

45. *San Francisco Chronicle,* June 8, October 27, November 5, and December 1, 1999, and March 8, 21, and 30, 2000.

46. Lee Hubbard, "Oakland's Black Power Decline," *SF Bay View,* June 1999.

47. *San Francisco Chronicle,* July 9 and 13, October 30, and November 10, 1999, and August 17, 2000.

48. *San Francisco Chronicle,* February 9, 2000, and January 21, 2001; *Oakland Tribune,* February 9, 2000, and January 7, 2001.

49. *Oakland Tribune,* April 22 and October 8, 1999, and February 2, 2001.

50. *San Francisco Chronicle,* March 14 and August 17, 2000; *Oakland Tribune,* May 9, 2001.

51. *Oakland Tribune,* March 22 and April 6, 2000; *San Francisco Chronicle,* February 2, 2000.

52. *San Francisco Chronicle,* June 7, 1999; *San Francisco Examiner,* July 12, 1999.

53. *San Francisco Chronicle,* May 1, 2000; *Oakland Tribune,* May 9, 2001.

54. *San Francisco Chronicle,* June 29, 2000; *San Francisco Examiner,* June 29, 2000.

55. Interview with David Kramer, July 27, 1999, Oakland; U.S. Bureau of the Census, *2000 Census of Population and Housing: Profiles of General Demographic Characteristics, Geographic Area: Oakland City, California* (http://www.factfinder.census.gov), May 25, 2001.

56. *San Francisco Chronicle,* November 1, 1999.

57. Michel Laguerre, *The Informal City* (London: Macmillan, 1994), pp. 85–87; *San Francisco Chronicle,* July 21, 1997, December 10, 1998, and January 2 and February 21, 2001.

58. Interview with Rev. J. Alfred Smith Sr., July 21, 1999, Oakland; Michael Covino, "The Mission," *Image* (March 22, 1987): 14–21; "Excellence in the Ministry of Jesus" (Allen Temple Baptist Church, Oakland, n.d.).

59. Unity Council, "Fruitvale Community Profile" (http://www.unity council.org/html/community profile.html), June 21, 2001.

60. Interview with Arabella Martinez, July 28, 1997, Oakland; Community Development Corporation Oral History Project, "Spanish Speaking Unity Council (SSUC)," Pratt Institute for Community and Environmental Development, Brooklyn, New York; Unity Council, "Transit Village," "Main Street," and "Parks and Open Space" (http://www.unitycouncil.org/index.html), June 21, 2001.

61. East Bay Asian Local Development Corporation, "About EBALDC" (http://www.ebaldc.org/organization/about.html), June 21, 2001; idem, "Lower San Antonio Initiative—Year End Report, July 1998" (http://www.ebaldc.org/organization/econ/report98/report7–98.html), June 21, 2001.

62. Richard Wood, "Religious Culture and Political Action," *Sociological Theory* 17, no. 3 (November 1999): 307–332; Tony Molatorre, "East Oakland: Pathways to Community Revitalization" (MS, vertical files, "Elmhurst District," Oakland History Room, Oakland Public Library, Oakland, n.d.).

63. "Looking forward and Back," *Minority Trendsletter* 2, no. 1 (Spring 1989); Gary Delgado, "Building Multiracial Alliances: The Case of the People United for a Better Oakland," in *Mobilizing the Community: Local Politics in the Era of the Global City,* ed. R. King and J. Kling (Newbury Park, Calif.: Sage, 1993), pp. 103–127; John Anner, "Linking Community Safety with Police Accountability," in *Beyond Identity Politics,* ed. J. Anner (Boston: South End Press, 1996), pp. 119–134.

64. *Oakland Tribune,* June 11 and 26 and November 7, 2002.

65. Interview with Judy Goff, July 22, 1999, Oakland; interview with David Kramer, July 27, 1999, Oakland; *East Bay Labor Journal* 46, no. 11 (May 19, 1972), and 50, no. 2 (September 1976).

66. *East Bay Labor Journal* 71, no. 1 (March 1997).

67. *San Francisco Chronicle,* March 20 and 21, 1996.

68. *San Francisco Chronicle,* March 26, 1998, and August 19, 1999; Elisabeth Sara Jacobs, "Waging Justice: Navigating Community in the Shifting Economic Landscape of an American City" (MS in possession of the author, 1999).

69. Todd Harvey et al., "Gentrification and West Oakland" (http://www.comm-org.utoledo.edu/papers2000/gentrify/gentrify.html), June 21, 2001.

70. Daniel Patrick Moynihan, *Maximum Feasible Misunderstanding* (New York: Free Press, 1969), pp. 107, 136–137, 164; see also Jeffrey Berry, Kent Portney, and Ken Thompson, *The Rebirth of Urban Democracy* (Washington, D.C.: Brookings Institution, 1993), pp. 22–34.

71. Samuel P. Huntington, "The United States," in *The Crisis of Democracy,* by Michel Crozier, Samuel P. Huntington, and Joji Watanuki (New York: New York University Press, 1975), p. 114.

72. William Kornhauser, *The Politics of Mass Society* (Glencoe, Ill.: Free Press, 1959); Neil Smelser, *Theory of Collective Behavior* (New York: Free Press of Glencoe, 1962); Seymour Martin Lipset, *Political Man* (Garden City, N.Y.: Doubleday, 1960), pp. 216–218.

73. U.S. Department of Labor, Bureau of Labor Statistics, "Union Membership in 1999," News release USDL 00–16, January 19, 2000; Joel Rogers, "Don't Worry, Be Happy: The Postwar Decline of Private Sector Unionism in the United States," in *The Challenge of Restructuring: North American Labor Movements Respond,* ed. Jane Jenson and Rianne Mahon (Philadelphia: Temple University Press, 1993), pp. 59–114.

74. Richard Freeman, "What Does the Future Hold for U.S. Unionism?" in *The Challenge of Restructuring: North American Labor Movements Respond,* ed. Jane Jenson and Rianne Mahon (Philadelphia: Temple University Press, 1993), pp. 361–380; Bruce Western, *Between Class and Market: Postwar Unionization in Capitalist Democracies* (Princeton, N.J.: Princeton University Press, 1997).

75. Walter Galenson reports that in 1955, 6,171 unfair labor practice charges were filed in 4,215 elections covering 515,995 employees. In 1990, 33,833 charges were filed out of 4,210 elections covering about half as many employees (261,385); Galenson, *The American Labor Movement, 1955–1995* (Westport, Conn.: Greenwood Press, 1996), p. 82.

76. Kate Bronfenbrenner, "Employer Behavior in Certification Elections and First-Contract Campaigns: Implications for Labor Law Reform," in *Restoring the Promise of American Labor Law,* ed. S. Friedman, R. Hurd, R. Oswald, and R. Seeber (Ithaca, N.Y.: ILR/Cornell University Press, 1994), pp. 75–89; Kate Bronfenbrenner and Tom Juravich, "It Takes More Than Housecalls: Organizing to Win with a Comprehensive Union-Building Strategy," in *Organizing to Win: New Research on Union Strategies,* ed. K. Bronfenbrenner, S. Friedman, R. Hurd, R. Oswald, and R. Seeber (Ithaca, N.Y.: ILR/Cornell University Press, 1998), pp. 19–36.

77. Dan Clawson and Mary Ann Clawson, "What Has Happened to the U.S. Labor Movement? Union Decline and Renewal," *Annual Review of Sociology* 25 (1999): 95–119.

78. Martina Morris and Bruce Western, "Inequality in Earnings at the Close of the Twentieth Century," *Annual Review of Sociology* 25 (1999): 623–657.

79. Lawrence Mishel, Jared Bernstein, and John Schmitt, *The State of Working America, 1996–97,* Economic Policy Institute Series (Armonk, N.Y.: M. E. Sharpe, 1997), pp. 46, 140–144.

80. Peter Passell, "Benefits Dwindle along with Wages for the Unskilled," *The New York Times,* June 14, 1998, 1; Richard Freeman, *The New Inequality* (Boston: Beacon Press, 1999).

81. Morris and Western, "Inequality in Earnings." Economist Richard Freeman estimated that for male workers, declining unionization explained about 25 percent of the increase in inequality between high school- and college-educated workers, and 50 percent of the increase between blue- and white-collar men; Freeman, "What Does the Future Hold for U.S. Unionism?" Another study estimates that deunionization, together with the decline in the value of the minimum wage, explains 36 percent of the growth of overall wage inequality among men between 1979 and 1992 and 44 percent of the growth of inequality among women; Mishel et al., *The State of Working America,* p. 203.

82. Gary King, John Bruce, and Andrew Gelman, "Racial Fairness in Legislative Redistricting," in *Classifying by Race,* ed. Paul Peterson (Princeton, N.J.: Princeton University Press, 1995), pp. 85–110; William O'Hare, "City Size, Racial Composition and Election of Black Mayors inside and outside the South," *Journal of Urban Affairs* 12 (1990): 307–313. The problem of black underrepresentation led to a controversial policy debate over redistricting reform and the isolation versus the dilution of the black vote; see Alex Willingham, "The Voting Rights Movement in Perspective," in *Without Justice for All,* ed. Adolph Reed Jr. (Boulder, Colo.: Westview Press, 1999), pp. 235–254; and the chapters by Guinier, Benoit and Schepsle, and Lublin in *Classifying by Race,* ed. Paul E. Peterson (Princeton, N.J.: Princeton University Press, 1995).

83. Browning et al., *Racial Politics in American Cities;* Timothy Bates and Darrell Williams, "Racial Politics: Does It Pay?" *Social Science Quarterly* 74 (1993): 507–522; David Jacobs and Robert O'Brien, "The Determinants of Deadly Force: A Structural Analysis of Police Violence," *American Journal of Sociology* 103 (1998): 837–862; Adolph Reed, "Demobilization and the New Black Political Regime," in *The Bubbling Cauldron,* ed. M. P. Smith and J. R. Feagin (Minneapolis: University of Minnesota Press, 1995), pp. 182–208.

84. M. V. Lee Badgett and Heidi Hartmann, "The Effectiveness of Equal Employment Opportunity Policies," in *Economic Perspectives on Affirmative Action,* ed. Margaret Simms (Washington, D.C.: Joint Center for Political and Economic Studies, 1995); Cedric Herring, "African Americans, the Public Agenda, and the Paradoxes of Public Policy: A Focus on the Controversies Surrounding Affirmative Action," in *African Americans and the Public Agenda: The Paradoxes of Public Policy,* ed. Cedric Herring (Thousand Oaks, Calif.: Sage, 1997), pp. 3–24; Sharon Collins, *Black Corporate Executives: The Making and Breaking of a Black Middle Class* (Philadelphia: Temple University Press, 1997).

85. Mishel et al., *The State of Working America,* p. 49.

86. Ibid., pp. 243, 313.

87. Reynolds Farley, *The New American Reality* (New York: Russell Sage Foundation, 1996), p. 348.

88. Lydia Chavez, *The Color Bind: California's Battle to End Affirmative Action* (Berkeley: University of California Press, 1998); Gwendolyn Mink, *Welfare's End* (Ithaca, N.Y.: Cornell University Press, 1998).

89. George Sanchez, "Face the Nation: Race, Immigration and the Rise of Nativism in Late Twentieth Century America," *International Migration Review* 31 (1997): 1009–1030.

90. Gregory Huber and Thomas Espenshade, "Neo-Isolationism, Balanced-Budget Conservatism, and the Fiscal Impacts of Immigrants," *International Migration Review* 31 (1997): 1031–1054; James Johnson Jr., Walter Farrell Jr., and Chandra Guinn, "Immigration Reform and the Browning of America: Tensions, Conflicts and Community Instability in Metropolitan Los Angeles," *International Migration Review* 31 (1997): 1055–1095; Michael Bazely, "State's Voters Speak Strongly against Teaching in Two Languages," *San Jose Mercury-News,* June 3, 1998.

91. Neil Smith, "Scales of Terror: The Manufacturing of Nationalism and the War for U.S. Globalism," and Arturo Ignatio Sanchez, "From Jackson Heights to *Nuestra America: 9/11* and Latino New York," both in *After the World Trade Center: Rethinking New York City,* ed. Michael Sorkin and Sharon Zukin (New York: Routledge, 2002), pp. 97–108 and 143–152, respectively.

92. Stephen Craig, "The Angry Voter: Politics and Popular Discontent in the 1990s," in *Broken Contract? Changing Relationships between Americans and Their Government,* ed. Stephen Craig (Boulder, Colo.: Westview Press, 1996), pp. 46–66; Stephen Nichols, David Kimball, and Paul A. Beck, "Voter Turnout in the 1996 Election: Resuming a Downward Spiral?" in *Reelection 1996: How Americans Voted,* ed. Herbert Weisberg and Janet Box-Steffensmeier (Chappaqua, N.Y.: Chatham House, 1999), pp. 23–44.

93. William Schambra, "By the People: The Old Values of the New Citizenship," *National Civic Review* 84, no. 2 (Spring 1995): 101–113; National Commission on Civic Renewal, *A Nation of Spectators: How Civic Disengagement Weakens America and What We Can Do about It* (College Park, Md.: National Commission on Civic Renewal, 1998); Dan Coats and Rick Santorum, "Civil Society and the Humble Role of Government," in *Community Works: The Revival of Civil Society in America,* ed. E. J. Dionne (Washington, D.C.: Brookings Institution, 1998). See also Lynn Staeheli, Janet Kodras, and Colin Flint, eds., *State Devolution in America: Implications for a Diverse Society* (Thousand Oaks, Calif.: Sage, 1997).

94. Roger Waldinger, "The Other Side of Embeddedness: A Case-Study of the Interplay of Economy and Ethnicity," *Racial and Ethnic Studies* 18, no. 3 (July 1995): 555–580; Alejandro Portes and Patricia Landolt, "The Downside of Social Capital," *The American Prospect* 7, no. 26 (May–June 1996): 18–21.

95. Michael Schudson, "What If Civic Life Didn't Die?" *The American Prospect* 7, no. 25 (May–June 1996): 17–20; Debra Minkoff, *Organizing for Equal-*

ity (New Brunswick, N.J.: Rutgers University Press, 1995); Jeffrey Berry, *The New Liberalism: The Rising Power of Citizen Groups* (Washington, D.C.: Brookings Institution, 1999).

96. Theda Skocpol, with the assistance of Marshall Ganz, Ziad Munson, Bayliss Camp, Michele Swers, and Jennifer Oser, "How Americans Became Civic," in *Civic Engagement in American Democracy*, ed. Theda Skocpol and Morris Fiorina (Washington, D.C.: Brookings Institution, 1999), pp. 27–80. See also Sheri Berman, "Civil Society and Political Institutionalization," *American Behavioral Scientist* 40, no. 5 (March–April 1997): 562–574.

97. Theda Skocpol, "Advocates without Members: The Recent Transformation of American Civic Life," in *Civic Engagement in American Democracy*, ed. Theda Skocpol and Morris Fiorina (Washington, D.C.: Brookings Institution, 1999), pp. 461–509; idem, "Unraveling from Above," *The American Prospect* 7, no. 25 (March–April 1996): 20–26.

98. Sidney Verba, Kay Lehman Schlozman, and Henry Brady, *Voice and Equality: Civic Voluntarism in American Politics* (Cambridge, Mass.: Harvard University Press, 1995); idem, "Civic Participation and the Equality Problem," in *Civic Engagement in American Democracy*, ed. Theda Skocpol and Morris Fiorina (Washington, D.C.: Brookings Institution, 1999), pp. 427–459.

METHODOLOGICAL APPENDIX:
TELLING STORIES ABOUT ACTORS AND EVENTS

1. Thompson himself described his book as "a biography of the English working class from its adolescence to its early manhood [*sic*]"; E. P. Thompson, *The Making of the English Working Class* (New York: Vintage, 1963), pp. 10–11, 194.

2. Drake and Cayton write, "We shall use the term Bronzeville for Black Metropolis because it seems to express the feeling that the people have about their own community. They *live* in the Black Belt and to them it is more than the 'ghetto' revealed by statistical analysis"; St. Clair Drake and Horace Cayton, *Black Metropolis* (New York: Harcourt Brace, 1945), p. 385.

3. Andrew Abbott, "What Do Cases Do? Some Notes on Activity in Sociological Analysis," in *What Is a Case?* ed. Charles Ragin and Howard S. Becker (Cambridge: Cambridge University Press, 1992), p. 62; David Hull, "Central Subjects and Historical Narratives," *History and Theory* 14, no. 3 (1975): 253–274.

4. George Steinmetz, "Reflections on the Role of Social Narratives in Working Class Formation: Narrative Theory in the Social Sciences," *Social Science History* 16, no. 3 (Fall 1992): 489–516.

5. Paul Gilroy, "One Nation under a Groove: The Cultural Politics of 'Race' and Racism in Britain," in *Anatomy of Racism*, ed. David Goldberg (Minneapolis: University of Minnesota Press, 1990), pp. 263–282.

6. Perry Anderson, *Arguments within English Marxism* (London: Verso, 1980), p. 42; see also Terry N. Clark, Seymour M. Lipset, and Mike Rempel, "The Declining Political Significance of Social Class," *International Sociology* 8, no. 3 (September 1993): 293–316.

7. Doug McAdam, Sidney Tarrow, and Charles Tilly, *Dynamics of Contention* (Cambridge: Cambridge University Press, 2001), pp. 56, 141.

8. Margaret Somers, "Citizenship and the Place of the Public Sphere: Law, Community, and Political Culture in the Transition to Democracy," *American Sociological Review* 58 (October 1993): 595. See also idem, "Deconstructing and Reconstructing Class Formation Theory: Narrativity, Relational Analysis, and Social Theory," in *Reworking Class,* ed. John R. Hall (Ithaca, N.Y.: Cornell University Press, 1997), pp. 73–105.

9. Somers, "Citizenship and the Place of the Public Sphere," p. 595; see also Judith Garber, "The City as Heroic Public Sphere," in *Democracy, Citizenship, and the Public Sphere,* ed. Engin Isin (New York: Routledge, 2000), pp. 257–274.

10. William Sewell, "Three Temporalities: Toward an Eventful Sociology," in *The Historic Turn in the Human Sciences,* ed. T. McDonald (Ann Arbor: University of Michigan Press, 1996), pp. 245–280; Fernand Braudel, "History and the Social Sciences: The Longue Durée," in his *On History* (Chicago: University of Chicago Press, 1980), pp. 25–54.

11. Rogers Smith notes the congruence between neo-institutionalist theory and Braudel's scale of "conjunctural" time: "Political Jurisprudence, the 'New Institutionalism,' and the Future of Public Law," *American Political Science Review* 82, no. 1 (March 1988): 89–108. Likewise, Michael Omi and Howard Winant speak of *trajectories* in describing periods of institutional development of the racial state: *Racial Formation in the United States: From the 1960s to the 1990s,* 2d ed. (New York: Routledge, 1994).

12. Larry Isaac, "Transforming Localities: Reflections on Time, Causality, and Narrative in Contemporary Historical Sociology," *Historical Methods* 30, no. 1 (Winter 1997): 4–12; Andrew Abbott, "On the Concept of a Turning Point," *Comparative Social Research* 16 (1997): 85–105.

13. Ronald Aminzade, "Historical Sociology and Time," *Sociological Methods and Research* 20, no. 4 (May 1992): 456–480; Walter W. Powell, "Expanding the Scope of Institutional Analysis," in *The New Institutionalism in Organizational Analysis,* ed. Walter W. Powell and Paul DiMaggio (Chicago: University of Chicago Press, 1991), pp. 183–203; Arthur Stinchcombe, *Constructing Social Theories* (Chicago: University of Chicago Press, 1968), pp. 108–118.

14. Abbott, "On the Concept of a Turning Point," p. 88; Larry Griffin, "Temporality, Events, and Explanation in Historical Sociology," *Sociological Methods and Research* 20, no. 4 (May 1992): 403–427.

15. Sewell, "Three Temporalities," p. 271.

16. Jeffrey Haydu, "Making Use of the Past: Time Periods as Cases to Compare and as Sequences of Problem Solving," *American Journal of Sociology* 102, no. 2 (September 1998): 339–371.

17. Kathleen Thelen, "Historical Institutionalism in Comparative Politics," *Annual Review of Political Science* 2 (1999): 369–404; James Mahoney, "Path Dependency in Historical Sociology," *Theory and Society* 29 (2000): 507–548; Paul Pierson, "Not Just What, but When: Timing and Sequence in Political Processes," *Studies in American Political Development* 14 (Spring 2000): 79–92.

18. Karen Orren and Stephen Skowrenek, "Institutions and Intercurrence: Theory Building in the Fullness of Time," in *Political Order*, ed. Ian Shapiro and Russell Hardin, Nomos 38 (New York: New York University Press, 1996), pp. 111–146.

19. Aminzade, "Historical Sociology and Time," p. 467.

20. Michael Schwartz and Shuva Paul, "Resource Mobilization versus the Mobilization of People: Why Consensus Movements Cannot Be Instruments of Change," in *Frontiers in Social Movement Theory*, ed. Aldon Morris and Carol Mueller (New Haven, Conn.: Yale University Press, 1992), p. 206.

Bibliography

ARCHIVAL COLLECTIONS

African American Newspapers Collection. Oakland Public Library, Oakland.
Alameda County. Politics and Government Files. Bancroft Library, University of California, Berkeley.
Bueno, Floyd. Papers. Walter P. Reuther Library, Archives of Labor and Urban Affairs, Wayne State University, Detroit.
Central Labor Council, Alameda County. Papers. Labor Archives and Research Center, San Francisco State University, San Francisco.
Davie, John. Scrapbooks. Oakland History Room, Oakland Public Library, Oakland.
Dellums, C. L. Papers. African American Museum and Library at Oakland.
Hotel Employees and Restaurant Employees Local 2850. Contract Files. Oakland.
Kaiser, Edgar F. Papers. Bancroft Library, University of California, Berkeley.
Knowland, Joseph R. Papers. Bancroft Library, University of California, Berkeley.
Men of Tomorrow. Papers. African American Museum and Library at Oakland.
Merritt, Frank. Scrapbooks. Oakland History Room, Oakland Public Library, Oakland.
Oakland and Alameda County. Political Scrapbooks, 1910–1930. Oakland History Room, Oakland Public Library, Oakland.
Oakland History Vertical Files. Oakland History Room, Oakland Public Library, Oakland.
Oakland Redevelopment Agency. Records, 1962–1972. Office of the City Clerk, Oakland.
Office of the City Clerk. Election Files. Oakland.
Rose, Joshua. Papers. African American Museum and Library at Oakland.

NEWSPAPERS AND PERIODICALS

Alameda County Union Labor Record.
Black Panther Inter-Communal News Service.

California Voice.
East Bay Express.
East Bay Labor Journal.
East Oakland Times.
Flatlands [Oakland].
Oakland Daily Record.
Oakland Post-Enquirer.
Oakland Tribune.
Oakland Tribune Yearbooks.
Observer [Oakland].
San Francisco Call-Bulletin.
San Francisco Chronicle.
San Francisco Examiner.
Tri-City Labor Review.
World, The [Oakland].

ORAL HISTORIES

Albrier, Mary Frances. 1979. *Determined Advocate for Racial Equality,* an oral history conducted 1977–1978 by Malca Chall, Regional Oral History Office, Bancroft Library, University of California, Berkeley.

Ash, Robert. 1976. "Alameda County Central Labor Council during the Warren Years," an oral history conducted 1976 by Miriam Stein and Amelia Fry, in *Labor Leaders View the Warren Era,* Regional Oral History Office, Bancroft Library, University of California, Berkeley.

Breed, Arthur. 1977. *Alameda County and the California Legislature: 1935–1958,* an oral history conducted 1973 by Gabrielle Morris, Regional Oral History Office, Bancroft Library, University of California, Berkeley.

Daly, E. A. 1972. "Alameda County Political Leader and Journalist," an oral history conducted 1971 by Joyce A. Henderson, in *Perspectives on the Alameda County District Attorney's Office,* Regional Oral History Office, Bancroft Library, University of California, Berkeley.

Dellums, C. L. 1971. *International President of the Brotherhood of Sleeping Car Porters and Civil Rights Leader,* an oral history conducted 1970–1971 by Joyce Henderson, Regional Oral History Office, Bancroft Library, University of California, Berkeley.

Denahy, William. 1982. *The Irish in West Oakland,* an oral history conducted 1982 by Kathryn Hughes, Padraigin McGillicuddy, Pamela Morton, and Sally Thomas, Neighborhood History Project, Oakland History Room, Oakland Public Library, Oakland.

Heide, Paul. 1970. "A Warehouseman's Reminiscences," an oral history conducted 1970 by Frank Jones, in *Labor Looks at Earl Warren,* Regional Oral History Office, Bancroft Library, University of California, Berkeley.

Jahnsen, Oscar. 1976. *Enforcing the Law against Gambling, Bootlegging, Graft,*

Fraud, and Subversion, an oral history conducted 1970 by Alice King and Miriam Stein, Regional Oral History Office, Bancroft Library, University of California, Berkeley.

Lyon, Harvey. 1973. *Oakland Moving and Storage Entrepreneur, Rotarian, and Philanthropist,* an oral history conducted 1973 by Rosemary Levenson, Regional Oral History Office, Bancroft Library, University of California, Berkeley.

Mockel, Donald. 1981. *Tape-Recorded Interview,* an oral history conducted 1981 by Sally Thomas and Padraigin McGillicuddy, Neighborhood History Project, Oakland History Room, Oakland Public Library, Oakland.

Moore, Joseph, and James Moore. 1995. An oral history interview by Bill Jersey of Quest Productions and/or Marjorie Dobkin for the documentary film *Crossroads: A Story of West Oakland,* Cypress Freeway Replacement Project, CALTRANS District 4, Oakland.

Mullins, John F. 1972. "How Earl Warren Became District Attorney," an oral history conducted 1963 by Amelia Fry, in *Perspectives on the Alameda County District Attorney's Office,* Regional Oral History Office, Bancroft Library, University of California, Berkeley.

Powers, Robert. 1971. *Law Enforcement, Race Relations: 1930–1960,* an oral history conducted 1971 by Amelia Fry, Regional Oral History Office, Bancroft Library, University of California, Berkeley.

St. Sure, J. Paul. 1957. *Some Comments on Employer Organizations and Collective Bargaining in Northern California since 1934,* an oral history conducted 1957 by Corinne Gilb, Institute for Industrial Relations, University of California, Berkeley.

Shaw, Mary. 1972. "Perspectives of a Newspaperwoman," an oral history conducted 1970 by Miriam Feingold, in *Perspectives on the Alameda County District Attorney's Office,* Regional Oral History Office, Bancroft Library, University of California, Berkeley.

Wilson, Lionel. 1992. *Attorney, Judge, and Oakland Mayor,* an oral history conducted 1985 and 1990 by Gabrielle Morris, Regional Oral History Office, Bancroft Library, University of California, Berkeley.

INTERVIEWS CONDUCTED BY THE AUTHOR

Berkley, Thomas. July 27, 1999. Oakland.
Billy, Gus. July 23, 1999. Oakland.
Burke, Fedora. September 20, 1997. Oakland.
Burton, Shirley. July 27, 1999. Oakland.
Butler, Steve. November 20, 1994. Berkeley.
Creque, David. December 21, 1995. Oakland.
Dickson, Melvin. August 3, 1999. Oakland.
Egan, Joe. July 1, 1995. By telephone.
Goff, Judy. July 22, 1999. Oakland.

Hoopes, Lorenzo. July 28, 1999. Oakland.

Johnson, Phyllis. July 28, 1999. Oakland.

Kidder, Al. March 27, 1995. By telephone.

Kramer, David. July 27, 1999. Oakland.

Kushman, Jean. November 5, 1994. Oakland.

Lowe, William. July 30, 1993. Oakland.

Martin, Fern. September 20, 1997. Oakland.

Martinez, Arabella. July 28, 1999. Oakland.

Massengill, Shirley. November 10, 1994. By telephone.

Price, Electra. July 14, 1999. Oakland.

Ramirez, Frank. November 23, 1994. Oakland.

Schaff, Valmar, and Evelyn Schaff. May 31, 1995. By telephone.

Small, Dr. Tolbert. August 4, 1999. Oakland.

Smith, Rev. J. Alfred, Sr. July 21, 1999. Oakland.

Stewart, Jean. November 3, 1994. Oakland.

Sutter, John. July 13, 1999. Oakland.

Thompson, Wayne. February 16, 1994. Oakland.

Wehe, Sally. November 2, 1994. By telephone.

White, Clinton. August 4, 1999. Oakland.

UNPUBLISHED SOURCES

"Alameda County: Profile of Ethnic and Immigrant Populations." 1993. New-comer Information Clearinghouse, International Institute of the East Bay, Oakland.

Blutza, Steven. 1978. "Oakland's Commission and Council-Manager Plans—Causes and Consequences." Ph.D. diss. University of California, Berkeley.

Boyden, Richard. 1981. "The Oakland General Strike of 1946." Manuscript in possession of the author.

———. 1988. "The San Francisco Machinists from Depression to Cold War, 1930–1950." Ph.D. diss. University of California, Berkeley.

Brown, William, Jr. 1970. "Class Aspects of Residential Development and Choice in the Oakland Black Community." Ph.D. diss. University of California, Berkeley.

California State Advisory Committee to the U.S. Commission on Civil Rights. 1967. "Civil Rights in Oakland, California." Manuscript, Doe Library, University of California, Berkeley.

California v. Becker. Case file no. 11359. Criminal Division, California Superior Court, Alameda County, 1930.

California v. Garbutt. Case file no. 11369. Criminal Division, California Superior Court, Alameda County, 1930.

California v. Ormsby. Case file no. 11359. Criminal Division, California Superior Court, Alameda County, 1930.

California v. Parker. Case file no. 11369. Criminal Division, California Superior Court, Alameda County, 1930.

California v. Shurtleff. Case file no. 11360. Criminal Division, California Superior Court, Alameda County, 1930.

Charter Restoration Committee. 1937. "The Facts about the Revocation of the Charter of Your Central Labor Council." Alameda County Central Labor Council File, Labor Collection, Social Science Library, University of California, Berkeley.

Community Development Corporation Oral History Project. 1997. "Spanish Speaking Unity Council SSUC." Pratt Institute for Community and Environmental Development, Brooklyn, New York.

Douma, Frank. 1951. "The Oakland General Strike." Master's thesis. University of California, Berkeley.

Dykstra, John. 1967. "A History of the Physical Development of the City of Oakland: The Formative Years, 1850–1930." Master's thesis. University of California, Berkeley.

East Bay Asian Local Development Corporation. "About EBALDC." http://www.ebaldc.org/organization/about.html. June 21, 2001.

———. "Lower San Antonio Initiative—Year End Report, July 1998." http://www.ebaldc.org/organization/econ/report98/report7-98.html. June 21, 2001.

Eli J. Coon et al. v. Fidelity and Deposit Company of Maryland, Inc. Case file no. 101707. Civil Division, California Superior Court, Alameda County, 1928.

Eli J. Coon et al. v. H. Sephton et al. Case file no. 107549. Civil Division, California Superior Court, Alameda County, 1929.

"Excellence in the Ministry of Jesus." n.d. Allen Temple Baptist Church, Oakland.

Fisher, James. 1972. "A History of the Political and Social Development of the Black Community in California, 1850–1950." Ph.D. diss. State University of New York, Stony Brook.

France, Edward. 1962. "Some Aspects of the Migration of the Negro to the San Francisco Bay Area since 1940." Ph.D. diss. University of California, Berkeley.

Hallinan, Tim. 1964. "The Portuguese of California." Master's thesis. University of California, Berkeley.

Harrison, Gloria. 1949. "The National Association for the Advancement of Colored People in California." Master's thesis. Stanford University.

Harvey, Todd, et al. 2001. "Gentrification and West Oakland." http://www.comm-org.utoledo.edu/ papers2000/gentrify/gentrify.html.

Hausler, Donald. 1987. "Blacks in Oakland: 1852–1987." Manuscript. Oakland History Room, Oakland Public Library, Oakland.

Jacobs, Elisabeth Sara. 1999. "Waging Justice: Navigating Community in the Shifting Economic Landscape of an American City." Manuscript in possession of author.

Jay, Richard E. 1953. "A Case Study in Retail Unionism: The Retail Clerks in the San Francisco East Bay Area (Alameda County)." Ph.D. diss. University of California, Berkeley.

Knights of the Ku Klux Klan, Inc., v. East Bay Club of Alameda County et al. Case file no. 82470. Civil Division, California Superior Court, Alameda County, 1925.

Knights of the Ku Klux Klan, Inc., v. Leon C. Francis et al. Case file no. 81118. Civil Division, California Superior Court, Alameda County, 1925.

Knights of the Ku Klux Klan, Inc., v. Leon C. Francis et al. Case file no. 81245. Civil Division, California Superior Court, Alameda County, 1925.

Knights of the Ku Klux Klan, Inc., v. Leon C. Francis et al. Case file no. 82491. Civil Division, California Superior Court, Alameda County, 1925.

Lemke-Santangelo, Gretchen. n.d. "Deindustrialization, Poverty and Community Response." Manuscript in possession of the author.

Lunch, William. 1970. "Oakland Revisited: Stability and Change in an American City." Manuscript. Environmental Design Library, University of California, Berkeley.

Malvey, Mari, and Aaron Wildavsky. 1971. "The Citizens of Oakland Look at their City." Manuscript, Institute of Governmental Studies Library, University of California, Berkeley.

Map of Central Terrace. 1915. Mutual Realty Company, Oakland, California. Earth Sciences and Map Library, University of California, Berkeley.

Marans, Michael. 1969. "Relocation in Acorn: A Focal Point for the Study of the Transition in Urban Renewal Policy and Politics in Oakland." Manuscript, Institute of Governmental Studies, University of California, Berkeley.

May, Judith V. 1968. Field Notes, Oakland Project. Institute of Governmental Studies Library, University of California, Berkeley.

———. 1970. "Progressives and the Poor: An Analytic History of Oakland." Manuscript. Institute of Governmental Studies Library, University of California, Berkeley.

———. 1973. "Struggle for Authority: A Comparison of Four Social Change Programs in Oakland, California." Ph.D. diss. University of California, Berkeley.

Molatorre, Tony. n.d. "East Oakland: Pathways to Community Revitalization." Manuscript. Vertical files, "Elmhurst District," Oakland History Room, Oakland Public Library, Oakland.

Oakland Chamber of Commerce. 1923. "Industrial Oakland." Oakland Public Library, Oakland.

Oakland Citizens' Committee for Urban Renewal. "Neighborhood Profile: Oakland Hills." n.d. Oakland.

Oakland City Clerk. n.d. *Elections 1852 to the Present* [continuously updated file]. Office of the City Clerk, Oakland.

"Oakland General Strike of 1946." n.d. *Bay City Blues.* Audio recording produced by Craig Gordon, Ed Schoenfeld, and Ken Russell, New American Movement Radio Project, and Vic Rubin and Tim Reagan, Oakland Study Group.

Oakland Police Department. 1985? *Oakland Police Department History—1919,* parts 1–3. Oakland History Room, Oakland Public Library, Oakland.

Oakland Redevelopment Agency. 1958. *West Oakland General Neighborhood Renewal Plan.* Oakland: Redevelopment Agency.

Oakland Strategic Plan, The. 1992. Oakland—Sharing the Vision, Inc., Oakland.

Oden, R. Stanley. 1999. "A Sociological Study of the Political Incorporation of People of Color in Oakland, California, 1966–1996." Ph.D. diss. University of California, Santa Cruz.

Plat of Maxwell Park: Owned and Recorded by John P. Maxwell; Conner and Milner, Selling Agents, East Oakland, California, 1910. Earth Sciences and Map Library, University of California, Berkeley.

Robinson, Robert M. 1951. "A History of the Teamsters in the San Francisco Bay Area, 1850–1950." Ph.D. diss. University of California, Berkeley.

Rodriguez, Joseph. 1983. "From Personal Politics to Party Politics: The Development of Black Leadership in Oakland, California, 1900–1950." Master's thesis. University of California, Santa Cruz.

Roesch, Frank. 1970. "The 1947 Oakland Municipal Elections." Manuscript. Institute of Governmental Studies Library, University of California, Berkeley.

Rose, Jim. 1990. "Collaboration with a Dual Union: Oakland AFL Political Practice, 1943–1947." Manuscript in possession of author.

Rosenson, A. M. 1937. "Origin and Nature of the CIO Movement in Alameda County, California." Master's thesis. University of California, Berkeley.

Rotary Club of Oakland. 1969. "Rotarily Yours: A History of the Rotary Club of Oakland." Booklet produced in Oakland.

Self, Robert. 1998. "Shifting Ground in Metropolitan America: Class, Race, and Power in Oakland and the East Bay, 1945–1977." Ph.D. diss. University of Washington.

Shaffer, Ralph. 1962. "Radicalism in California, 1869–1929." Ph.D. diss. University of California, Berkeley.

Simpson, Douglas. 1963. "The Retail Clerks in the East Bay Area." Master's thesis. University of California, Berkeley.

Smythe, Dallas. 1939. "An Economic History of Local and Interurban Transportation in the East Bay Cities with Particular Reference to the Properties Developed by F. M. Smith." Ph.D. diss. University of California, Berkeley.

Sternsher, Harriet. 1967. "The Oakland–Alameda County Coliseum Complex." Manuscript, Institute of Governmental Studies Library, University of California, Berkeley.

Stripp, Fred. 1948. "The Relationships of the San Francisco Bay Area Negro-American Worker with the Labor Unions Affiliated with the American Federation of Labor and the Congress of Industrial Organizations." Th.D. thesis. Pacific School of Religion, Berkeley.

Thompson, James Phillip, III. 1990. "The Impact of the Jesse Jackson Campaigns on Local Black Political Mobilization in New York City, Atlanta, and Oakland." Ph.D. diss. City University of New York.

Thompson, Wayne. 1966. "Organizing Cities to Solve 'People Problems.'" Berkeley: Institute for Local Self-Government.

Unity Council. "Fruitvale Community Profile," "Transit Village," "Main Street," and "Parks and Open Space." http://www.unitycouncil.org/index.html. June 21, 2001.

Waldron, Gladys. 1956. "Antiforeign Movements in California, 1919–1929." Ph.D. diss. University of California, Berkeley.

Watson, Sharon. 1982. "Mayoral Leadership Changes and Public Policy: Exploring the Influence of Black Urban Governance." Ph.D. diss. Northwestern University.

W. F. Courtney et al. v. John L. McVey et al. Case file no. 82948. Civil Division, California Superior Court, Alameda County, 1925.

Williams, Albert Kevin. 1986. "Crime and Community Security as Political Issues: Citizens' Demands and Government Responses in Oakland, Richmond and San Francisco." Ph.D. diss. University of California, Berkeley.

PUBLISHED SOURCES

Abbott, Andrew. 1992. "From Causes to Events: Notes on Narrative Positivism." *Sociological Methods and Research* 20, no. 4 (May): 428–455.

———. 1992. "What Do Cases Do? Some Notes on Activity in Sociological Analysis." In *What Is a Case?* edited by C. Ragin and H. S. Becker, pp. 53–82. Cambridge: Cambridge University Press.

———. 1997. "On the Concept of a Turning Point." *Comparative Social Research* 16: 85–105.

Adler, Seymour. 1980. *Redundancy in Public Transit,* part 3: *The Political Economy of Transit in the San Francisco Bay Area, 1945–1963.* Washington, D.C.: U.S. Department of Transportation, Urban Mass Transit Administration.

Almond, Gabriel, and Sidney Verba. 1963. *The Civic Culture.* Princeton, N.J.: Princeton University Press.

Aminzade, Ronald. 1992. "Historical Sociology and Time." *Sociological Methods and Research* 20, no. 4 (May): 456–480.

Anderson, Perry. 1980. *Arguments within English Marxism.* London: Verso.

Anner, John. 1996. "Linking Community Safety with Police Accountability." In *Beyond Identity Politics,* edited by J. Anner. Boston: South End Press.

Archibald, Katharine. 1947. *Wartime Shipyard: A Study in Social Disunity.* Berkeley: University of California Press.

Arnesen, Eric. 1990. *Waterfront Workers of New Orleans: Race, Class and Politics, 1863–1923.* Oxford: Oxford University Press.

Badgett, M. V. Lee, and Heidi Hartmann. 1995. "The Effectiveness of Equal Employment Opportunity Policies." In *Economic Perspectives on Affirmative Action,* edited by M. Simms. Washington, D.C.: Joint Center for Political and Economic Studies.

Bagwell, Beth. 1994 [orig. 1982]. *Oakland: Story of a City.* Oakland: Oakland Heritage Alliance.

Baker, Joseph E., ed. 1914. *Past and Present of Alameda County, California.* 2 vols. Chicago: S. J. Clarke.

Bates, Timothy, and Darrell Williams. 1993. "Racial Politics: Does It Pay?" *Social Science Quarterly* 74: 507–522.

Beem, Christopher. 1999. *The Necessity of Politics*. Chicago: University of Chicago Press.

Bendix, Reinhard, and Seymour Martin Lipset. 1957. "Political Sociology." *Current Sociology* 6: 79–99.

Benson, Susan P. 1986. *Counter Cultures: Saleswomen, Managers, and Customers in American Department Stores, 1890–1940*. Urbana: University of Illinois Press.

Berman, Sheri. 1997. "Civil Society and Political Institutionalization." *American Behavioral Scientist* 40, no. 5 (March–April): 562–574.

Berry, Jeffrey. 1999. *The New Liberalism: The Rising Power of Citizen Groups*. Washington, D.C.: Brookings Institution.

Berry, Jeffrey, Kent Portney, and Ken Thompson. 1993. *The Rebirth of Urban Democracy*. Washington, D.C.: Brookings Institution.

Blee, Kathleen. 1991. *Women of the Klan: Racism and Gender in the 1920s*. Berkeley: University of California Press.

Boyden, Richard. 1995. "The San Francisco Machinists and the National War Labor Board." In *American Labor in the Era of World War II*, edited by S. Miller and D. Cornford, pp. 105–119. Westport, Conn.: Praeger.

Bradford, Amory. 1968. *Oakland's Not for Burning*. New York: David McKay.

Braudel, Fernand. 1980. *On History*. Chicago: University of Chicago Press.

Bridges, Amy. 1997. *Morning Glories: Municipal Reform in the Southwest*. Princeton, N.J.: Princeton University Press.

Bronfenbrenner, Kate. 1994. "Employer Behavior in Certification Elections and First-Contract Campaigns: Implications for Labor Law Reform." In *Restoring the Promise of American Labor Law*, edited by S. Friedman, R. Hurd, R. Oswald, and R. Seeber, pp. 75–89. Ithaca, N.Y.: ILR/Cornell University Press.

Bronfenbrenner, Kate, and Tom Juravich. 1998. "It Takes More Than Housecalls: Organizing to Win with a Comprehensive Union-Building Strategy." In *Organizing to Win: New Research on Union Strategies*, edited by K. Bronfenbrenner, S. Friedman, R. Hurd, R. Oswald, and R. Seeber, pp. 19–36. Ithaca, N.Y.: ILR/Cornell University Press.

Bronfenbrenner, Kate, S. Friedman, R. Hurd, R. Oswald, and R. Seeber, eds. 1998. *Organizing to Win: New Research on Union Strategies*. Ithaca, N.Y.: ILR/Cornell University Press.

Broussard, Albert. 1981. "Organizing the Black Community in the San Francisco Bay Area, 1915–1930." *Arizona and the West* 23, no. 4: 335–354.

Brown, Elaine. 1992. *A Taste of Power: A Black Woman's Story*. New York: Pantheon.

Brown, Eric. 1998. "Black Ghetto Formation in Oakland, 1852–1965." *Research in Community Sociology* 8: 255–274.

Browning, Rufus, Dale Rogers Marshall, and David Tabb. 1984. *Protest Is Not Enough*. Berkeley: University of California Press.

———, eds. 1997. *Racial Politics in American Cities.* 2d ed. White Plains, N.Y.: Longman.

Bunje, E. T. H. 1939. "Oakland Industries, 1848–1938." Oakland: Works Progress Administration.

Burawoy, Michael. 1989. "Two Methods in Search of Science: Skocpol versus Trotsky." *Theory and Society* 18: 759–805.

Burke, Robert E., ed. 1983. *The Diary Letters of Hiram Johnson, 1917–1945.* New York: Garland.

Burner, David. 1968. *The Politics of Provincialism.* New York: Knopf.

Bush, Rod. 1984. *The New Black Vote: Politics and Power in Four American Cities.* San Francisco: Synthesis.

———. 1999. *We Are Not What We Seem.* New York: New York University Press.

Calhoun, Craig, ed. 1992. *Habermas and the Public Sphere.* Cambridge, Mass.: MIT Press.

California Department of Transportation. 1990. *Historic Property Survey Report: For the Proposed I-880 Reconstruction Project,* vol. 1, appendix A: "Archaeological Survey Report." San Francisco: CALTRANS District 4.

———. 1990. *Historic Property Survey Report: For the Proposed I-880 Reconstruction Project,* vol. 3: *Historic Resources Inventory.* San Francisco: CALTRANS District 4.

———. 1990. *Historic Property Survey Report: For the Proposed I-880 Reconstruction Project,* vol. 4: *Historic Architecture Survey Report,* part 7, C: "Southern Pacific Railroad Property"; part 7, D: "Oakland Army Base"; and part 7, E: "Naval Supply Center, Oakland." San Francisco: CALTRANS District 4.

Castells, Manuel. 1983. *The City and the Grassroots: A Cross-Cultural Theory of Urban Social Movements.* Berkeley: University of California Press.

Chalmers, David. 1965. *Hooded Americanism: The First Century of the Ku Klux Klan, 1865–1965.* New York: Doubleday.

Chavez, Lydia. 1998. *The Color Bind: California's Battle to End Affirmative Action.* Berkeley: University of California Press.

Chudacoff, Howard. 1975. *The Evolution of American Urban Society.* Englewood Cliffs, N.J.: Prentice-Hall.

Clark, Terry N., Seymour M. Lipset, and Mike Rempel. 1993. "The Declining Political Significance of Social Class." *International Sociology* 8, no. 3 (September): 293–316.

Clawson, Dan, and Mary Ann Clawson. 1999. "What Has Happened to the U.S. Labor Movement? Union Decline and Renewal." *Annual Review of Sociology* 25: 95–119.

Clemens, Elisabeth. 1993. "Organizational Repertoires and Institutional Change: Women's Groups and the Transformation of U.S. Politics, 1890–1920." *American Journal of Sociology* 98, no. 4 (January): 755–798.

Coats, Dan, and Rick Santorum. 1998. "Civil Society and the Humble Role of

Government." In *Community Works: The Revival of Civil Society in America,* edited by E. J. Dionne. Washington, D.C.: Brookings Institution.

Coben, Stanley. 1994. "Ordinary White Protestants: The KKK of the 1920s." *Journal of Social History* 28 (Fall): 157–165.

Cocoltchos, Christopher. 1992. "The Invisible Empire and the Search for the Orderly Community." In *The Invisible Empire in the West,* edited by Shawn Lay, pp. 97–120. Urbana: University of Illinois Press.

Cohen, Jean. 1995. "Interpreting the Notion of Civil Society." In *Toward a Global Civil Society,* edited by Michael Walzer, pp. 35–40. Providence, R.I.: Berghahn Books.

————. 1999. "Does Voluntary Association Make Democracy Work?" In *Diversity and Its Discontents,* edited by N. Smelser and J. Alexander, pp. 263–291. Princeton, N.J.: Princeton University Press.

Collins, Sharon. 1997. *Black Corporate Executives: The Making and Breaking of a Black Middle Class.* Philadelphia: Temple University Press.

Commonwealth Club of California. 1946. *The Population of California.* San Francisco: Parker.

Conmy, Peter. 1961. *The Beginnings of Oakland, California, A.U.C.* Oakland: Oakland Public Library.

————. 1972. *Seventy Years of Service, 1902–1972.* Los Angeles: California Knights of Columbus.

Covino, Michael. 1987. "The Mission." *Image* (March 22): 14–21.

Craig, Stephen. 1996. "The Angry Voter: Politics and Popular Discontent in the 1990s." In *Broken Contract? Changing Relationships between Americans and Their Government,* edited by Stephen Craig, pp. 46–66. Boulder. Colo.: Westview Press.

Cross, Ira. 1974 [orig. 1935]. *A History of the Labor Movement in California.* Berkeley: University of California Press.

Crouchette, Lawrence, Lonnie Bunch III, and Martha K. Winnacker. 1989. *Visions toward Tomorrow: A History of the East Bay Afro-American Community 1852–1977.* Oakland: Northern California Center for Afro-American History and Life.

Cummings, G. A., and E. S. Pladwell. 1942. *Oakland: A History.* Oakland: Grant Miller Mortuaries.

Dahl, Robert. 1961. *Who Governs? Democracy and Power in an American City.* New Haven, Conn.: Yale University Press.

————. 1967. *Pluralist Democracy in the United States: Conflict and Consent.* Chicago: Rand McNally.

Danziger, Sheldon, and Peter Danziger. 1995. *America Unequal.* Cambridge, Mass.: Harvard University Press.

DeLeon, Robert. 1973. "Showdown in Oakland: Bobby Seale and Otho Green Battle to Become Mayor." *Jet* (April 12).

Delgado, Gary. 1993. "Building Multiracial Alliances: The Case of the People United for a Better Oakland." In *Mobilizing the Community: Local Politics in the Era of the Global City*, edited by R. King and J. Kling, pp. 103–127. Newbury Park, Calif.: Sage.

Deverell, William. 1994. *Railroad Crossing: Californians and the Railroad, 1850–1910*. Berkeley: University of California Press.

Dobrin, Michael. 1979. "The Oakland Museum: Garden and Gallery." *Journal of the West* 18, no. 3: 91–94.

Domhoff, G. William. 1990. *The Power Elite and the State*. New York: Aldine de Gruyter.

Drake, St. Clair, and Horace Cayton. 1945. *Black Metropolis*. New York: Harcourt Brace.

Elder, Glen, Jr. 1974. *Children of the Great Depression: Social Change and Life Experience*. Chicago: University of Chicago Press.

Eley, Geoff. 1992. "Nations, Publics, and Political Cultures: Placing Habermas in the Nineteenth Century." In *Habermas and the Public Sphere*, edited by C. Calhoun, pp. 289–339. Cambridge, Mass.: MIT Press.

Elkin, Stephen. 1985. "Twentieth Century Urban Regimes." *Journal of Urban Affairs* 7, no. 2: 11–28.

Emirbayer, Mustafa, and Mimi Sheller. 1998. "Studying Publics in History." *Comparative and Historical Sociology* 11 (Fall): 5–6.

Erie, Steven. 1988. *Rainbow's End: Irish Americans and the Dilemmas of Urban Machine Politics, 1840–1985*. Berkeley: University of California Press.

Fainstein, Norman, and Susan Fainstein. 1996. "Urban Regimes and Black Citizens: The Economic and Social Impacts of Political Incorporation in US Cities." *International Journal of Urban and Regional Research* 20, no. 1: 22–37.

Fainstein, Susan, and Norman Fainstein. 1985. "Economic Change, National Policy, and the System of Cities." In *Restructuring the City*, edited by S. Fainstein, pp. 1–26. 2d ed. New York: Longmans.

Farley, Reynolds. 1996. *The New American Reality*. New York: Russell Sage Foundation.

Federal Executive Board, Oakland Task Force. 1969. *An Analysis of Federal Decision-Making and Impact: The Federal Government in Oakland*, vol. 2. Washington, D.C.: U.S. Department of Commerce, Economic Development Administration.

Foner, Philip S., ed. 1995. *The Black Panthers Speak*. New York: Da Capo Press.

Foster, Mark. 1989. *Henry J. Kaiser: Builder of the American West*. Austin: University of Texas Press.

Fraser, Nancy. 1992. "Rethinking the Public Sphere: A Contribution to the Critique of Actually Existing Democracy." In *Habermas and the Public Sphere*, edited by C. Calhoun, pp. 109–142. Cambridge, Mass.: MIT Press.

Frazer, Elizabeth. 1999. *The Problems of Communitarian Politics*. Oxford: Oxford University Press.

Freeman, Joshua. 2000. *Working Class New York: Life and Labor since World War Two*. New York: New Press.

Freeman, Richard. 1993. "What Does the Future Hold for U.S. Unionism?" In *The Challenge of Restructuring: North American Labor Movements Respond*, edited by J. Jenson and R. Mahon, pp. 361–380. Philadelphia: Temple University Press.

———. 1999. *The New Inequality*. Boston: Beacon Press.

Friedland, Roger, and Robert Alford. 1991. "Bringing Society Back In: Symbols, Practices, and Institutional Contradictions." In *The New Institutionalism in Organizational Analysis*, edited by W. W. Powell and P. DiMaggio, pp. 232–263. Chicago: University of Chicago Press.

Friedland, Roger, Frances Fox Piven, and Robert Alford. 1977. "Political Conflict, Urban Structure, and the Fiscal Crisis." In *Comparing Public Policies: New Concepts and Methods*, edited by Douglas Ashford, pp. 197–225. Beverly Hills, Calif.: Sage.

Friedman, S., R. Hurd, R. Oswald, and R. Seeber, eds. 1994. *Restoring the Promise of American Labor Law*. Ithaca, N.Y.: ILR/Cornell University Press.

Galenson, Walter. 1996. *The American Labor Movement, 1955–1995*. Westport, Conn.: Greenwood Press.

Garber, Judith. 2000. "The City as Heroic Public Sphere," in *Democracy, Citizenship, and the Public Sphere*, edited by Engin Isin, pp. 257–274. New York: Routledge.

Garnel, Donald. 1972. *The Rise of Teamster Power in the West*. Berkeley: University of California Press.

Garner, Roberta Ash, and Mayer Zald. 1987. "The Political Economy of Social Movement Sectors." In *Social Movements in an Organizational Society*, edited by M. Zald and J. McCarthy, pp. 293–317. New Brunswick, N.J.: Transaction.

Gilroy, Paul. 1990. "One Nation under a Groove: The Cultural Politics of 'Race' and Racism in Britain." In *Anatomy of Racism*, edited by D. Goldberg, pp. 263–282. Minneapolis: University of Minnesota Press.

Glass, Fred. 1996. "We Called It a Work Holiday: The Oakland General Strike of 1946." *Labor's Heritage* 8, no. 2 (Fall): 4–25.

Glazer, Nathan, and Daniel Moynihan. 1970. *Beyond the Melting Pot: The Negroes, Puerto Ricans, Jews, Italians, and Irish of New York*. 2d ed. Cambridge, Mass.: MIT Press.

Goldberg, Robert. 1981. *Hooded Empire: The Ku Klux Klan in Colorado*. Urbana: University of Illinois Press.

Goldfield, Michael. 1987. *The Decline of Organized Labor in the United States*. Chicago: University of Chicago Press.

Gothberg, John. 1968. "The Local Influence of J. R. Knowland's *Oakland Tribune*." *Journalism Quarterly* 43, no. 3 (Autumn): 487–495.

Greenstone, J. David, and Paul Peterson. 1973. *Race and Authority in Urban Politics: Community Participation and the War on Poverty*. New York: Russell Sage Foundation.

Gregory, James. 1989. *American Exodus: The Dust Bowl Migration and Okie Culture in California*. Oxford: Oxford University Press.

Griffin, Larry. 1992. "Temporality, Events and Explanation in Historical Sociology." *Sociological Methods and Research* 20, no. 4 (May): 403–427.

———. 1993. "Narrative, Event-Structure Analysis, and Causal Interpretation in Historical Sociology." *American Journal of Sociology* 98 (March): 1094–1133.

Grimshaw, William. 1992. *Bitter Fruit: Black Politics and the Chicago Machine, 1931–1991.* Chicago: University of Chicago Press.

Guigni, Marco, Doug McAdam, and Charles Tilly, eds. 1999. *How Social Movements Matter.* Minneapolis: University of Minnesota Press.

Habermas, Jürgen. 1989. *Structural Transformation of the Public Sphere.* Cambridge, Mass.: MIT Press.

Hansen, Julia. 1996. "Residential Segregation of Blacks by Income Group: Evidence from Oakland." *Population Research and Policy Review* 15 (August): 369–389.

Haydu, Jeffrey. 1998. "Making Use of the Past: Time Periods as Cases to Compare and as Sequences of Problem Solving." *American Journal of Sociology* 102, no. 2 (September): 339–371.

Hayes, Edward. 1972. *Power Structure and Urban Policy.* New York: McGraw-Hill.

Hays, Samuel P. 1957. *The Response to Industrialism 1885–1914.* Chicago: University of Chicago Press.

Held, David. 1989. *Political Theory and the Modern State.* Cambridge: Polity Press.

Herring, Cedric. 1997. "African Americans, the Public Agenda, and the Paradoxes of Public Policy: A Focus on the Controversies Surrounding Affirmative Action." In *African Americans and the Public Agenda: The Paradoxes of Public Policy,* edited by Cedric Herring, pp. 3–24. Thousand Oaks, Calif.: Sage.

———, ed. 1997. *African Americans and the Public Agenda: The Paradoxes of Public Policy.* Thousand Oaks, Calif.: Sage.

Herring, Cedric, and Sharon Collins. 1995. "Retreat from Equal Opportunity? The Case for Affirmative Action." In *The Bubbling Cauldron: Race, Ethnicity and the Urban Crisis,* edited by M. P. Smith and J. R. Feagin, pp. 163–181. Minneapolis: University of Minnesota Press.

Higham, John. 1971 [orig. 1955]. *Strangers in the Land.* New York: Atheneum.

Hilliard, David, and Lewis Cole. 1993. *This Side of Glory: The Autobiography of David Hilliard and the Story of the Black Panther Party.* Boston: Little, Brown.

Hinckle, Warren. 1966. "Metropoly: The Story of Oakland, California." *Ramparts* 4, no. 6 (February): 25–50.

Hinkel, Edgar, and William McCann. 1939. *Oakland, 1852–1938: Some Phases of the Social, Political, and Economic History of Oakland, California.* Oakland: Works Progress Administration.

Hirsch, Arnold. 1983. *Making the Second Ghetto.* Cambridge: Cambridge University Press.

Hofstadter, Richard. 1977 [orig. 1955]. *The Age of Reform: From Bryan to FDR.* New York: Knopf.

Huber, Gregory, and Thomas Espenshade. 1997. "Neo-Isolationism, Balanced-Budget Conservatism, and the Fiscal Impacts of Immigrants." *International Migration Review* 31: 1031–1054.

Hull, David. 1975. "Central Subjects and Historical Narratives." *History and Theory* 14, no. 3: 253–274.

Huntington, Samuel P. 1975. "The United States." In *The Crisis of Democracy,* edited by M. Crozier, S. P. Huntington, and J. Watanuki, pp. 59–118. New York: New York University Press.

———. 1981. *American Politics: The Promise of Disharmony.* Cambridge, Mass.: Harvard University Press.

Isaac, Larry. 1997. "Transforming Localities: Reflections on Time, Causality, and Narrative in Contemporary Historical Sociology." *Historical Methods* 30, no. 1 (Winter): 4–12.

Jackson, Kenneth. 1967. *The Ku Klux Klan in the City, 1915–1930.* New York: Oxford University Press.

———. 1985. *Crabgrass Frontier: The Suburbanization of the United States.* New York: Oxford University Press.

Jacobs, David, and Robert O'Brien. 1998. "The Determinants of Deadly Force: A Structural Analysis of Police Violence." *American Journal of Sociology* 103: 837–862.

Jenkins, J. Craig. 1995. "Social Movements, Political Representation, and the State: An Agenda and Comparative Framework." In *The Politics of Social Protest,* edited by J. C. Jenkins and B. Klandermans, pp. 14–38. Minneapolis: University of Minnesota Press.

Jenkins, J. Craig, and Bert Klandermans, eds. 1995. *The Politics of Social Protest.* Minneapolis: University of Minnesota Press.

Jenkins, William. 1990. *Steel Valley Klan: The Ku Klux Klan in Ohio's Mahoning Valley.* Kent, Ohio: Kent State University Press.

Jenson, Jane, and Rianne Mahon, eds. 1993. *The Challenge of Restructuring: North American Labor Movements Respond.* Philadelphia: Temple University Press.

Johnson, James, Jr., Walter Farrell Jr., and Chandra Guinn. 1997. "Immigration Reform and the Browning of America: Tensions, Conflicts and Community Instability in Metropolitan Los Angeles." *International Migration Review* 31: 1055–1095.

Johnson, Marilynn. 1993. *The Second Gold Rush: Oakland and the East Bay in World War II.* Berkeley: University of California Press.

———. 1995. "Mobilizing the Homefront: Labor and Politics in Oakland, 1941–1951." In *Working People of California,* edited by D. Cornford, pp. 344–368. Berkeley: University of California Press.

Jones, Charles. 1988. "The Political Repression of the Black Panther Party, 1966–1971: The Case of the Oakland Bay Area." *Journal of Black Studies* 18, no. 4 (June): 415–434.

Jones, DeWitt, ed. 1934. *Port of Oakland*. Oakland: State Emergency Relief Administration.

Judge, David, Gerry Stoker, and Harold Wolman, eds. 1995. *Theories of Urban Politics*. Thousand Oaks, Calif.: Sage.

Kasdin, Steven, ed. 1992. *The Collected Jack London*. New York: Barnes & Noble.

Katcher, Leo. 1967. *Earl Warren: A Political Biography*. New York: McGraw-Hill.

Katznelson, Ira. 1981. *City Trenches: Urban Politics and the Patterning of Class in the United States*. Chicago: University of Chicago Press.

Katznelson, Ira, and Aristide Zolberg, eds. 1986. *Working Class Formation*. Princeton, N.J.: Princeton University Press.

Kemp, Roger. 1980. *Coping with Proposition 13*. Lexington, Mass.: D. C. Heath.

Kerr, Clark. 1947. "Collective Bargaining on the Pacific Coast." *Monthly Labor Review* 64, no. 4 (April): 650–674.

Kimeldorf, Howard. 1988. *Reds or Rackets? The Making of Radical and Conservative Unions on the Waterfront*. Berkeley: University of California Press.

King, Gary, John Bruce, and Andrew Gelman. 1995. "Racial Fairness in Legislative Redistricting." In *Classifying by Race*, edited by P. Peterson, pp. 85–110. Princeton, N.J.: Princeton University Press.

Kirp, David. 1982. *Just Schools: The Idea of Racial Equality in American Education*. Berkeley: University of California Press.

Klandermans, Bert. 1988. "The Formation and Mobilization of Consensus." *International Social Movement Research* 1: 173–196.

Knight, Robert. 1960. *Industrial Relations in the San Francisco Bay Area, 1900–1918*. Berkeley: University of California Press.

Koopmans, Ruud. 1993. "The Dynamics of Protest Waves: West Germany, 1965 to 1989." *American Sociological Review* 58 (October): 637–658.

Kornhauser, William. 1959. *The Politics of Mass Society*. Glencoe, Ill.: Free Press.

Kramer, Ralph. 1969. *Participation of the Poor: Comparative Community Case Studies in the War on Poverty*. Englewood Cliffs, N.J.: Prentice-Hall.

Kriesi, Hanspeter. 1995. "The Political Opportunity Structure of New Social Movements: Its Impact on Their Mobilization." In *The Politics of Social Protest*, edited by C. Jenkins and B. Klandermans, pp. 167–198. Minneapolis: University of Minnesota Press.

Kriesi, Hanspeter, and Dominique Wisler. 1999. "The Impact of Social Movements on Political Institutions: A Comparison of the Introduction of Direct Legislation in Switzerland and the United States." In *How Social Movements Matter*, edited by M. Guigni, D. McAdam, and C. Tilly, pp. 42–65. Minneapolis: University of Minnesota Press.

Laguerre, Michel. 1994. *The Informal City*. London: Macmillan.

Lannon, Albert Vetere. 2000. *Fight or Be Slaves: A History of the Oakland–East Bay Labor Movement*. Lanham, Md.: University Press of America.

Laurent, Luigi. 1960. *Property Values and Race: Studies in Seven Cities*. Berkeley: University of California Press.

Lay, Shawn. 1992. "Imperial Outpost on the Border: El Paso's Frontier Klan No.

100." In *The Invisible Empire in the West,* edited by S. Lay, pp. 67–95. Urbana: University of Illinois Press.

———, ed. 1992. *The Invisible Empire in the West.* Urbana: University of Illinois Press.

Lemke-Santangelo, Gretchen. 1996. *Abiding Courage: African American Migrant Women and the East Bay Community.* Chapel Hill: University of North Carolina Press.

Lichtenstein, Nelson. 1982. *Labor's War at Home: The CIO in World War Two.* Cambridge: Cambridge University Press.

Lichtenstein, Nelson, and Howell John Harris, eds. 1993. *Industrial Democracy in America: The Ambiguous Promise.* Cambridge: Cambridge University Press.

Lipset, Seymour Martin. 1960. *Political Man.* Garden City, N.Y.: Doubleday.

Lipset, Seymour Martin, and Reinhard Bendix. 1959. *Social Mobility in Industrial Society.* Berkeley: University of California Press.

Lipset, Seymour Martin, and Earl Raab. 1970. *The Politics of Unreason: Right-Wing Extremism in America, 1790–1990.* New York: Harper & Row.

Lipsitz, George. 1981. *Class and Culture in Cold War America: "A Rainbow at Midnight."* New York: Praeger.

Logan, John, and Harvey Molotch. 1987. *Urban Fortunes.* Berkeley: University of California Press.

Lubell, Samuel. 1965. *The Future of American Politics.* 3d ed. New York: Harper & Row.

Luckingham, Bradford. 1982. *The Urban Southwest.* El Paso: Texas Western Press.

Ma, L. Eve Armentrout, with Jeong Huei Ma. 1982. *The Chinese of Oakland.* Oakland: Chinese History Research Committee.

MacLean, Nancy. 1994. *Behind the Mask of Chivalry.* Oxford: Oxford University Press.

Mahoney, James. 2000. "Path Dependency in Historical Sociology." *Theory and Society* 29: 507–548.

Major, Reginald. 1971. *A Panther Is a Black Cat.* New York: William Morrow.

Map of the City of Oakland. 1900. Oakland: J. H. MacDonald.

March, James G., and Johan P. Olsen. 1989. *Rediscovering Institutions: The Organizational Basis of Politics.* New York: Free Press.

Massey, Doreen. 1984. *Spatial Divisions of Labor: Social Structures and the Geography of Production.* London: Macmillan.

Massey, Douglas, and Nancy Denton. 1993. *American Apartheid.* Cambridge, Mass.: Harvard University Press.

Masters, R. S., R. C. Smith, and W. E. Winters. 1927. *An Historical Review of the East Bay Exchange.* San Francisco: Pacific Telephone and Telegraph.

May, Judith V. 1971. "Two Model Cities: Negotiations in Oakland." *Politics and Society* 2, no. 1 (Fall): 57–88.

McAdam, Doug. 1982. *Political Process and the Development of Black Insurgency.* Chicago: University of Chicago Press.

————. 1988. "Micromobilization Contexts and Recruitment to Activism." *International Social Movement Research* 1: 125–154.

McAdam, Doug, and Ronelle Paulsen. 1993. "Specifying the Relationship between Social Ties and Activism." *American Journal of Sociology* 99: 640–667.

McAdam, Doug, Sidney Tarrow, and Charles Tilly. 2001. *Dynamics of Contention.* Cambridge: Cambridge University Press.

McBroome, Delores Nason. 1993. *Parallel Communities: African Americans in California's East Bay, 1850–1963.* New York: Garland.

McCarthy, John. 1996. "Constraints and Opportunities in Adopting, Adapting and Inventing." In *Comparative Perspectives on Social Movements,* edited by D. McAdam, J. McCarthy, and M. Zald, pp. 141–151. Cambridge: Cambridge University Press.

McCartney, Laton. 1988. *Friends in High Places: The Bechtel Story.* New York: Simon and Schuster.

McCorry, Jesse. 1978. *Marcus Foster and the Oakland Public Schools.* Berkeley: University of California Press.

McDonald, Terence, ed. 1996. *The Historic Turn in the Human Sciences.* Ann Arbor: University of Michigan Press.

McEntire, Davis, and Julia Tarnopol. 1950. "Postwar Status of Negro Workers in San Francisco Area." *Monthly Labor Review* 70, no. 6 (June): 612–617.

Meltsner, Arnold. 1971. *The Politics of City Revenue.* Berkeley: University of California Press.

Melucci, Alberto. 1989. *Nomads of the Present.* Philadelphia: Temple University Press.

Merritt, Frank C. 1928. *History of Alameda County.* Chicago: S. J. Clarke.

Merton, Robert. 1968 [orig. 1949]. *Social Theory and Social Structure.* Rev. ed. New York: Free Press.

Mink, Gwendolyn. 1998. *Welfare's End.* Ithaca, N.Y.: Cornell University Press.

Minkoff, Debra. 1995. *Organizing for Equality.* New Brunswick, N.J.: Rutgers University Press.

Mishel, Lawrence, Jared Bernstein, and John Schmitt. 1997. *The State of Working America, 1996–97.* Economic Policy Institute Series. Armonk, N.Y.: M. E. Sharpe.

Model, Suzanne. 1993. "The Ethnic Niche and the Structure of Opportunity: Immigrants and Minorities in New York City." In *The Underclass Debate: Views from History,* edited by M. Katz, pp. 161–193. Princeton, N.J.: Princeton University Press.

Modell, John. 1975. "Levels of Change over Time." *Historical Methods* 8, no. 4 (September): 116–127.

Mollenkopf, John. 1983. *The Contested City.* Princeton, N.J.: Princeton University Press.

————. 1997. "New York: The Great Anomaly." In *Racial Politics in American Cities,* edited by R. Browning, D. Rogers Marshall, and D. Tabb, pp. 97–116. 2d ed. White Plains, N.Y.: Longman.

Montejano, David. 1987. *Anglos and Mexicans in the Making of Texas, 1836–1986.* Austin: University of Texas Press.

Montgomery, Gayle, and James Johnson. 1998. *One Step from the White House: The Rise and Fall of Senator William F. Knowland.* Berkeley: University of California Press.

Moore, Gilbert. 1993 [orig. 1971]. *Rage.* New York: Carroll and Graf.

Moore, Leonard. 1990. "Historical Interpretations of the 1920's Klan: The Traditional View and the Populist Revision." *Journal of Social History* 24 (Winter): 341–357.

———. 1991. *Citizen Klansmen: The Ku Klux Klan in Indiana, 1921–1928.* Chapel Hill: University of North Carolina Press.

Mori, Jimmy. 1977. "The Ideological Development of the Black Panther Party." *Cornell Journal of Social Relations* 12, no. 2 (Fall): 37–155.

Morone, James. 1990. *The Democratic Wish: Popular Participation and the Limits of American Government.* New Haven, Conn.: Yale University Press.

Morris, Aldon. 1984. *The Origins of the Civil Rights Movement.* New York: Free Press.

———. 1992. "Political Consciousness and Collective Action." In *Frontiers in Social Movement Theory,* edited by A. Morris and C. Mueller, pp. 351–373. New Haven, Conn.: Yale University Press.

———. 1999. "A Retrospective on the Civil Rights Movement: Political and Intellectual Landmarks." *Annual Review of Sociology* 25: 517–539.

Morris, Aldon, and Carol Mueller, eds. 1992. *Frontiers in Social Movement Theory.* New Haven, Conn.: Yale University Press.

Morris, Martina, and Bruce Western. 1999. "Inequality in Earnings at the Close of the Twentieth Century." *Annual Review of Sociology* 25: 623–657.

Mowry, George. 1963 [orig. 1951]. *The California Progressives.* Chicago: Quadrangle Books.

Mowry, George, and Blaine Brownell. 1981. *The Urban Nation: 1920–1980.* Rev. ed. New York: Hill and Wang.

Moynihan, Daniel Patrick. 1969. *Maximum Feasible Misunderstanding.* New York: Free Press.

National Commission on Civic Renewal. 1998. *A Nation of Spectators: How Civic Disengagement Weakens America and What We Can Do about It.* College Park, Md.: National Commission on Civic Renewal.

Newton, Huey P. 1972. *To Die for the People.* New York: Random House.

———. 1973. *Revolutionary Suicide.* New York: Harcourt Brace Jovanovich.

Nichols, Stephen, David Kimball, and Paul A. Beck. 1999. "Voter Turnout in the 1996 Election: Resuming a Downward Spiral?" In *Reelection 1996: How Americans Voted,* edited by H. Weisberg and J. Box-Steffensmeier, pp. 23–44. Chappaqua, N.Y.: Chatham House.

Oakland Citizens' Committee for Urban Renewal. 1984. *Annual Report, 1983–1984.* Oakland: Oakland Citizens' Committee for Urban Renewal.

Oakland City Planning Department. 1968. *Oakland's Housing Supply: Cost,*

Condition, Composition, 1960–1966. Oakland: City Planning Department, 701 Division.

———. 1969. *West Oakland: A 701 Subarea Report.* Oakland: City Planning Department, 701 Division, May.

———. 1992. *Oakland Cultural Heritage Survey,* vol. 32: *West Oakland Survey, Oak Center Redevelopment Area.* Oakland: City Planning Department.

Oakland Postwar Planning Committee. 1945. *Oakland's Formula for the Future.* Oakland: Postwar Planning Committee.

O'Hare, William. 1990. "City Size, Racial Composition, and Election of Black Mayors inside and outside the South." *Journal of Urban Affairs* 12: 307–313.

Omi, Michael, and Howard Winant. 1994. *Racial Formation in the United States: From the 1960s to the 1990s.* 2d ed. New York: Routledge.

Orren, Karen, and Stephen Skowrenek. 1996. "Institutions and Intercurrence: Theory Building in the Fullness of Time." In *Political Order,* edited by I. Shapiro and R. Hardin, pp. 111–146. Nomos 38. New York: New York University Press.

Pearl, Lawrence. 1975. "The Other City." *HUD Challenge* (April): 6–13.

Pearson, Hugh. 1994. *The Shadow of the Panther: Huey Newton and the Price of Black Power in America.* Reading, Mass.: Addison-Wesley.

Peterson, Paul. 1981. *City Limits.* Chicago: University of Chicago Press.

———, ed. 1995. *Classifying by Race.* Princeton, N.J.: Princeton University Press.

Pierson, Paul. 2000. "Not Just What, but When: Timing and Sequence in Political Processes." *Studies in American Political Development* 14 (Spring): 79–92.

Polk's Oakland City Directory. 1918, 1924, 1925, 1929, 1930. Oakland: R. L. Polk.

Portes, Alejandro, and Patricia Landolt. 1996. "The Downside of Social Capital." *The American Prospect* 7, no. 26 (May–June): 18–21, 94.

Port of Oakland. 1987. *Sixty Years: A Chronicle of Progress.* Oakland: Board of Port Commissioners.

Powell, Walter W. 1991. "Expanding the Scope of Institutional Analysis." In *The New Institutionalism in Organizational Analysis,* edited by W. W. Powell and P. DiMaggio, pp. 183–203. Chicago: University of Chicago Press.

Powell, Walter W., and Paul DiMaggio, eds. 1991. *The New Institutionalism in Organizational Analysis.* Chicago: University of Chicago Press.

Powers, Madelon. 1998. *Faces along the Bar: Lore and Order in the Workingman's Saloon, 1870–1920.* Chicago: University of Chicago Press.

Praetzellis, Mary, ed. 1994. *West Oakland: A Place to Start From.* Research Design and Treatment Plan: Cypress I-880 Replacement Project, vol. 1: *Historical Archaeology.* Oakland: CALTRANS District 4.

Pressman, Jeffrey. 1975. *Federal Programs and City Politics: The Dynamics of the Aid Process in Oakland.* Berkeley: University of California Press.

Pressman, Jeffrey, and Aaron Wildavsky. 1984 [orig. 1973]. *Implementation.* 3d ed. Berkeley: University of California Press.

Przeworski, Adam. 1985. *Capitalism and Social Democracy.* Cambridge: Cambridge University Press.

Putnam, Robert. 1995. "Bowling Alone: America's Declining Social Capital." *Journal of Democracy* 6, no. 1 (January): 65–78.

———. 1996. "The Strange Disappearance of Civic America." *The American Prospect* 7, no. 24 (Winter): 34–48.

———. 2000. *Bowling Alone: The Collapse and Revival of American Community.* New York: Simon and Schuster.

Quadagno, Jill. 1994. *The Color of Welfare.* Oxford: Oxford University Press.

Quadagno, Jill, and Stan Knapp. 1992. "Have Historical Sociologists Forsaken Theory?" *Sociological Methods and Research* 20, no. 4: 481–507.

Ragin, Charles. 1987. *The Comparative Method.* Berkeley: University of California Press.

Ragin, Charles, and Howard S. Becker, eds. 1992. *What Is a Case?* Cambridge: Cambridge University Press.

Reed, Adolph. 1988. "The Black Urban Regime: Structural Origins and Constraints." In *Power, Community, and the City,* edited by Michael P. Smith, pp. 138–189. Comparative Urban and Community Research 1. New Brunswick, N.J.: Transaction.

———. 1995. "Demobilization and the New Black Political Regime." In *The Bubbling Cauldron,* edited by M. P. Smith and J. R. Feagin, pp. 182–208. Minneapolis: University of Minnesota Press.

———. 1999. *Without Justice for All.* Boulder, Colo.: Westview Press.

Regal, J. M. 1967. *Oakland's Partnership for Change.* Oakland: City Department of Human Resources.

Reis, Elizabeth. 1985. "Cannery Row: The AFL, the IWW, and Bay Area Italian Cannery Workers." *California History* 64, no. 3 (Summer): 175–191.

Rice, Arnold. 1972. *The Ku Klux Klan in American Politics.* New York: Haskell House.

Rodriguez, Joseph. 1999. "Rapid Transit and Community Power: West Oakland Residents Confront BART." *Antipode* 31, no. 2: 212–228.

Rogers, Joel. 1993. "Don't Worry, Be Happy: The Postwar Decline of Private Sector Unionism in the United States." In *The Challenge of Restructuring: North American Labor Movements Respond,* edited by J. Jenson and R. Mahon, pp. 48–71. Philadelphia: Temple University Press.

Rogin, Michael. 1970. "Nonpartisanship and the Group Interest." In *Power and Community,* edited by P. Green and S. Levinson, pp. 112–141. New York: Pantheon.

Rubin, Lester, William Swift, and Herbert Northrup. 1974. *Negro Employment in the Maritime Industries.* Philadelphia: University of Pennsylvania Press.

Rueschemeyer, Dietrich, Evelyn Huber Stephens, and John Stephens. 1992. *Capitalist Development and Democracy.* Oxford: Polity Press.

Sanchez, Arturo Ignatio. 2002. "From Jackson Heights to *Nuestra America:* 9/11 and Latino New York," in *After the World Trade Center: Rethinking New York City,* edited by Michael Sorkin and Sharon Zukin, pp. 143–152. New York: Routledge.

Sanchez, George. 1997. "Face the Nation: Race, Immigration, and the Rise of

Nativism in Late Twentieth Century America." *International Migration Review* 31: 1009–1030.

Saxton, Alexander. 1971. *The Indispensable Enemy: Labor and the Anti-Chinese Movement in California*. Berkeley: University of California Press.

———. 1990. *The Rise and Fall of the White Republic*. London: Verso.

Schambra, William. 1995. "By the People: The Old Values of the New Citizenship." *National Civic Review* 84, no. 2 (Spring): 101–113.

Schlesinger, Arthur, Jr. 1960. *The Age of Roosevelt: The Politics of Upheaval*. Boston: Houghton-Mifflin.

———. 1992. *The Disuniting of America*. New York: W. W. Norton.

Schudson, Michael. 1996. "What If Civic Life Didn't Die?" *The American Prospect* 7, no. 25 (March–April): 17–20.

Schwartz, Harvey. 1978. *The March Inland: Origins of the ILWU Warehouse Division, 1934–1938*. Los Angeles: Institute of Industrial Relations, University of California, Los Angeles.

Schwartz, Michael, and Shuva Paul. 1992. "Resource Mobilization versus the Mobilization of People: Why Consensus Movements Cannot Be Instruments of Change." In *Frontiers in Social Movement Theory*, edited by A. Morris and C. Mueller, pp. 205–223. New Haven, Conn.: Yale University Press.

Scott, Mel. 1959. *The San Francisco Bay Area: A Metropolis in Perspective*. Berkeley: University of California Press.

———. 1963. *Partnership in the Arts: Public and Private Support of Cultural Activities in the San Francisco Bay Area*. Berkeley: Institute of Governmental Studies, University of California, Berkeley.

Seale, Bobby. 1968. *Seize the Time*. New York: Vintage.

Seidman, Joel. 1953. *American Labor from Defense to Reconversion*. Chicago: University of Chicago Press.

Selvin, David. 1975. *Sky Full of Storm*. Rev. ed. San Francisco: California Historical Society.

———. 1996. *A Terrible Anger: The 1934 Waterfront and General Strikes in San Francisco*. Detroit: Wayne State University Press.

Sewell, William. 1996. "Three Temporalities: Toward an Eventful Sociology." In *The Historic Turn in the Human Sciences*, edited by T. McDonald, pp. 245–280. Ann Arbor: University of Michigan Press.

Shefter, Martin. 1986. "Trade Unions and Political Machines: The Organization and Disorganization of the American Working Class in the Late Nineteenth Century." In *Working Class Formation*, edited by I. Katznelson and A. Zolberg, pp. 197–276. Princeton, N.J.: Princeton University Press.

Siegel, Frederick. 1997. *The Future Once Happened Here: New York, D.C., L.A., and the Fate of America's Big Cities*. New York: Free Press.

Simms, Margaret, ed. 1995. *Economic Perspectives on Affirmative Action*. Washington, D.C.: Joint Center for Political and Economic Studies.

Skocpol, Theda. 1985. "Bringing the State back In: Strategies of Analysis on Current Research." In *Bringing the State back In*, edited by P. Evans, D. Rueschemeyer, and T. Skocpol, pp. 3–37. Cambridge: Cambridge University Press.

———. 1987. "A Society without a 'State'? Political Organization, Social Conflict, and Welfare Provision in the United States." *Journal of Public Policy* 7, no. 4: 349–371.

———. 1996. "Unraveling from Above." *The American Prospect* 7, no. 25 (March–April): 20–25.

———. 1999. "Advocates without Members: The Recent Transformation of American Civic Life." In *Civic Engagement in American Democracy*, edited by T. Skocpol and M. Fiorina, pp. 461–509. Washington, D.C.: Brookings Institution.

Skocpol, Theda, and Morris Fiorina. 1999. "Making Sense of the Civic Engagement Debate." In *Civic Engagement in American Democracy*, edited by T. Skocpol and M. Fiorina, pp. 1–23. Washington, D.C.: Brookings Institution.

Skocpol, Theda, and Morris Fiorina, eds. 1999. *Civic Engagement in American Democracy*. Washington, D.C.: Brookings Institution.

Skocpol, Theda, with the assistance of Marshall Ganz, Ziad Munson, Bayliss Camp, Michele Swers, and Jennifer Oser. 1999. "How Americans Became Civic." In *Civic Engagement in American Democracy*, edited by T. Skocpol and M. Fiorina, pp. 27–80. Washington, D.C.: Brookings Institution.

Smelser, Neil. 1962. *Theory of Collective Behavior*. New York: Free Press of Glencoe.

Smith, Michael P., ed. 1988. *Power, Community, and the City*. Comparative Urban and Community Research 1. New Brunswick, N.J.: Transaction.

Smith, Michael Peter, and Joe R. Feagin, eds. 1995. *The Bubbling Cauldron: Race, Ethnicity, and the Urban Crisis*. Minneapolis: University of Minnesota Press.

Smith, Neil. 2002. "Scales of Terror: The Manufacturing of Nationalism and the War for U.S. Globalism," in *After the World Trade Center: Rethinking New York City*, edited by Michael Sorkin and Sharon Zukin, pp. 97–108. New York: Routledge.

Smith, Rogers. 1988. "Political Jurisprudence, the 'New Institutionalism,' and the Future of Public Law." *American Political Science Review* 82, no. 1 (March): 89–108.

Smith, Stephen Samuel, and Jessica Kulynich. 2002. "It May Be Social, but Why Is It Capital? The Social Construction of Social Capital and the Politics of Language." *Politics and Society* 30, no. 1 (March): 149–186.

Snow, David, and Robert Benford. 1992. "Master Frames and Cycles of Protest." In *Frontiers in Social Movement Theory*, edited by A. Morris and C. Mueller, pp. 133–155. New Haven, Conn.: Yale University Press.

Snow, David, et al. 1986. "Frame Alignment Processes, Micromobilization, and Movement Participation." *American Sociological Review* 51: 464–481.

Somers, Margaret. 1993. "Citizenship and the Place of the Public Sphere: Law, Community, and Political Culture in the Transition to Democracy." *American Sociological Review* 58 (October): 587–620.

———. 1997. "Deconstructing and Reconstructing Class Formation Theory: Narrativity, Relational Analysis, and Social Theory." In *Reworking Class*, edited by J. R. Hall, pp. 73–105. Ithaca, N.Y.: Cornell University Press.

Staeheli, Lynn, Janet Kodras, and Colin Flint, eds. 1997. *State Devolution in America: Implications for a Diverse Society*. Thousand Oaks, Calif.: Sage.

Starr, Paul. 1978. "How They Fail." *Working Papers for a New Society* 6 (March–April): 70.

Steinmetz, George. 1992. "Reflections on the Role of Social Narratives in Working Class Formation: Narrative Theory in the Social Sciences." *Social Science History* 16, no. 3 (Fall): 489–516.

Stinchcombe, Arthur. 1968. *Constructing Social Theories*. Chicago: University of Chicago Press.

———. 1978. *Theoretical Methods in Social History*. New York: Academic Press.

Stoker, Gerry. 1995. "Regime Theory and Urban Politics." In *Theories of Urban Politics*, edited by D. Judge, G. Stoker, and H. Wolman, pp. 54–71. Thousand Oaks, Calif.: Sage.

Stone, Clarence. 1989. *Regime Politics: Governing Atlanta, 1946–1988*. Lawrence: University Press of Kansas.

———. 1993. "Urban Regimes and the Capacity to Govern: A Political Economy Approach." *Journal of Urban Affairs* 15, no. 1: 1–28.

Sugrue, Thomas. 1996. *The Origins of the Urban Crisis: Race and Inequality in Detroit*. Princeton, N.J.: Princeton University Press.

Taylor, Verta, and Nancy Whittier. "Collective Identity in Social Movement Communities: Lesbian Feminist Mobilization." In *Frontiers in Social Movement Theory*, edited by A. Morris and C. Mueller, pp. 104–129. New Haven, Conn.: Yale University Press.

Thelen, Kathleen. 1999. "Historical Institutionalism in Comparative Politics." *Annual Review of Political Science* 2: 369–404.

Thernstrom, Stephen, and Abigail Thernstrom. 1997. *America in Black and White*. New York: Simon and Schuster.

Thompson, E. P. 1963. *The Making of the English Working Class*. New York: Vintage.

Thompson, Frank J. 1975. *Personnel Policy in the City: The Politics of Jobs in Oakland*. Berkeley: University of California Press.

Thompson, Wayne. 1964. "Quit Treating Symptoms." *National Civic Review* 53, no. 8: 423–428.

Tilly, Charles. 1979. "Repertoires of Contention in America and Britain, 1750–1830." In *The Dynamics of Social Movements*, edited by M. Zald and J. McCarthy, pp. 126–155. Cambridge, Mass.: Winthrop.

———. 1992. "How to Detect, Describe, and Explain Repertoires of Contention." Working Paper 150. New York: Center for Studies of Social Change, New School for Social Research.

———. 1997. "Means and Ends of Comparison in Macrosociology." *Comparative Social Research* 16: 43–53.

———. 1998. *Durable Inequality*. Berkeley: University of California Press.

Timberlake, James. 1963. *Prohibition and the Progressive Movement, 1900–1920*. Cambridge, Mass.: Harvard University Press.

Tomlins, Christopher. 1985. *The State and the Unions: Labor Relations, Law, and the Organized Labor Movement in America, 1880–1960.* Cambridge: Cambridge University Press.

Truman, David. 1953. *The Governmental Process.* New York: Knopf.

U.S. Bureau of Labor Statistics. 1942–1946. *Indexes of Production Worker Employment in Manufacturing by Metropolitan Area.* Washington, D.C.: GPO.

U.S. Bureau of the Census. 1913. *Abstract of the Thirteenth Census of the United States, 1910.* Washington, D.C.: GPO.

———. 1913. *Thirteenth Census of the United States: Reports by States, Supplement for California.* Washington, D.C.: GPO.

———. 1919. *Census of Religious Bodies, 1916,* part 1: *Summary and General Tables.* Washington, D.C.: GPO.

———. 1921. *Fourteenth Census of the United States, 1920,* vol. 1: *Population.* Washington, D.C.: GPO.

———. 1923. *Abstract of Fourteenth Census of the United States, 1920.* Washington, D.C.: GPO.

———. 1923. *Fourteenth Census of the United States, 1920: Population,* vol. 4: *Occupations.* Washington, D.C.: GPO.

———. 1930. *Census of Religious Bodies, 1926,* vol. 1: *Summary and Detailed Tables.* Washington, D.C.: GPO.

———. 1933. *Abstract of Fifteenth Census of the United States, 1930.* Washington, D.C.: GPO.

———. 1933. *Fifteenth Census of the United States, 1930: Population,* vol. 3, part 1: *Population;* vol. 4: *Occupations;* vol. 6: *Families.* Washington, D.C.: GPO.

———. 1943. *Sixteenth Census of the United States,* vol. 3: *The Labor Force,* parts 1 and 2. Washington, D.C.: GPO.

———. 1943. *Sixteenth Census of the United States, 1940: Population—Internal Migration 1935 to 1940: Color and Sex of Migrants.* Washington, D.C.: GPO.

———. 1944. *Special Reports,* Series CA-3, no. 3: *Characteristics of the Population, Labor Force, Families and Housing, San Francisco Bay Congested Area: April, 1944.* Washington, D.C.: GPO.

———. 1946. *Sixteenth Census of the United States, 1940: Population—Internal Migration 1935 to 1940: Economic Characteristics of Migrants.* Washington, D.C.: GPO.

———. 1946. *Special Census of Oakland, California: October 9, 1945.* Washington, D.C.: GPO.

———. 1947. *Current Population Reports,* Series P-51, no. 24: *Labor Force Characteristics of the San Francisco–Oakland Metropolitan District.* Washington, D.C.: GPO.

———. 1947. *Current Population Reports,* Series P-51, no. 35: *Labor Force Characteristics of Metropolitan Districts: Summary Report.* Washington, D.C.: GPO.

———. 1952. *Census of Population: 1950,* vol. 2: *Characteristics of the Population,* part 5: *California.* Washington, D.C.: GPO.

———. 1952. *Seventeenth Census of the United States, 1950: Population*, vol. 2, part 5: *California*. Washington, D.C.: GPO.

———. 1963. *Census of Population: 1960*, vol. 1: *Characteristics of the Population*, part 6: *California*. Washington, D.C.: GPO.

———. 1971. *Census of the Population: 1970*, Series PHC 3–45: *Employment Profiles of Selected Low Income Areas: Oakland, California*. Washington, D.C.: GPO.

———. 1971. *1970 Census of Population and Housing: General Demographic Trends for Metropolitan Areas, 1960 to 1970*, Series PHC 2–6: *California*. Washington, D.C.: GPO.

———. 1971. *1970 Census of Population, Supplementary Report: Negro Population in Selected Places and Selected Counties*. Washington, D.C.: GPO.

———. 1973. *1970 Census of the Population*, vol. 1: *Characteristics of the Population*, part 6: *California*. Washington, D.C.: GPO.

———. 1980. *Major Retail Centers in Standard Metropolitan Statistical Areas: California, 1977 Census of Retail Trade*. Washington, D.C.: GPO.

———. 1983. *1980 Census of Population and Housing: Census Tracts, San Francisco–Oakland Calif., SMSA*. Washington, D.C.: GPO.

———. 1989. *Geographic Area Series: California, 1987 Census of Retail Trade*, CA-83. Washington, D.C.: GPO.

———. 1993. *1990 Census of Population and Housing: Population and Housing Characteristics for Census Tracts and Block Numbering Areas*, section 1: *Oakland PMSA*. Washington, D.C.: GPO.

———. 1993. *1990 Census of Population and Housing: Population and Housing for Census Tracts and Block Numbering Areas: San Francisco–Oakland–San Jose, CA*, section 1: *Oakland PMSA*. Washington, D.C.: GPO.

———. 2001. *2000 Census of Population and Housing: Profiles of General Demographic Characteristics, Geographic Area: Oakland City, California*. http://www.factfinder.census.gov. May 25, 2001.

U.S. Department of Commerce. 1948. *Business Establishments, Employment, and Taxable Payrolls under OASI* [County Business Patterns], *First Quarter, 1947*, part 2: *California*. Washington, D.C.: GPO.

U.S. Department of Labor. 1947. "Indexes of Consumer Prices in Large Cities, November 1946." *Monthly Labor Review* 64, no. 1: 1.

U.S. Department of Labor, Bureau of Labor Statistics. 2000. "Union Membership in 1999." News release USDL 00-16, January 19, 2000.

U.S. Department of Labor, Women's Bureau. 1946. "Women Workers in Ten War Production Areas and Their Postwar Employment Plans." Bulletin no. 209. Washington, D.C.: GPO.

Verba, Sidney, Kay Lehman Schlozman, and Henry Brady. 1995. *Voice and Equality: Civic Voluntarism in American Politics*. Cambridge, Mass.: Harvard University Press.

———. 1999. "Civic Participation and the Equality Problem." In *Civic Engagement in American Democracy*, edited by T. Skocpol and M. Fiorina, pp. 427–459. Washington, D.C.: Brookings Institution.

Viorst, Milton. 1977. *The Citizen Poor of the 1960s.* New York: Charles Kettering Foundation.

Voss, Kim. 1988. "Labor Organization and Class Alliance: Industries, Communities and the Knights of Labor." *Theory and Society* 17: 329–364.

Wald, Kenneth. 1980. "The Visible Empire: The Ku Klux Klan as an Electoral Movement." *Journal of Interdisciplinary History* 11, no. 2 (Autumn): 217–234.

Waldinger, Roger. 1995. "The Other Side of Embeddedness: A Case-Study of the Interplay of Economy and Ethnicity." *Racial and Ethnic Studies* 18, no. 3 (July): 550–580.

———. 1995. "When the Melting Pot Boils Over: The Irish, Jews, Blacks, and Koreans of New York." In *The Bubbling Cauldron,* edited by M. P. Smith and J. R. Feagin, pp. 265–281. Minneapolis: University of Minnesota Press.

———. 1996. *Still the Promised City: African Americans and New Immigrants in Post-Industrial New York.* Cambridge, Mass.: Harvard University Press.

Walton, John. 1992. *Western Times and Water Wars.* Berkeley: University of California Press.

Walzer, Michael. 1983. *Spheres of Justice.* New York: Basic Books.

Warde, Alan. 1985. "Spatial Change, Politics and the Division of Labor." In *Social Relations and Spatial Structures,* edited by D. Gregory and J. Urry, pp. 190–212. London: Macmillan.

Ware, Alan. 1985. *The Breakdown of Democratic Party Organization, 1940–1980.* Oxford: Oxford University Press.

Warren, Earl. 1977. *The Memoirs of Earl Warren.* New York: Doubleday.

Warren, Roland, Stephen Rose, and Ann Bergunder. 1974. *The Structure of Urban Reform.* Lexington, Mass.: D. C. Heath.

Weber, David. 1981. *Oakland: Hub of the West.* Tulsa: Continental Heritage Press.

Weber, Max. 1949. "'Objectivity' in Social Science and Social Policy." In his *The Methodology of the Social Sciences,* translated and edited by E. A. Shils and H. A. Finch, pp. 49–112. New York: Free Press.

Weir, Stan. 1975. "American Labor on the Defensive: A 1940's Odyssey." *Radical America* 9, nos. 4–5: 165–185.

Western, Bruce. 1997. *Between Class and Market: Postwar Unionization in Capitalist Democracies.* Princeton, N.J.: Princeton University Press.

Willard, Ruth Hendricks. 1988. *Alameda County, California Crossroads: An Illustrated History.* Northridge, Calif.: Windsor Publications.

Willingham, Alex. 1999. "The Voting Rights Movement in Perspective." In *Without Justice for All,* edited by A. Reed Jr., pp. 235–254. Boulder, Colo.: Westview Press.

Wilson, William J. 1980. *The Declining Significance of Race.* 2d ed. Chicago: University of Chicago Press.

Wollenberg, Charles. 1990. *Marinship at War.* Berkeley: Western Heritage Press.

Wolman, Philip. 1975. "The Oakland General Strike of 1946." *Southern California Quarterly* 57, no. 2: 147–179.

Wood, Richard. 1999. "Religious Culture and Political Action." *Sociological Theory* 17, no. 3 (November): 307–332.

Young, Iris Marion. 1999. "State, Civil Society and Social Justice." In *Democracy's Value,* edited by I. Shapiro and C. Hacker-Cordon, pp. 141–162. Cambridge: Cambridge University Press.

Zald, Mayer, and John D. McCarthy. 1987. "Social Movement Industries: Conflict and Cooperation among SMOs." In *Social Movements in an Organizational Society,* edited by M. Zald and J. McCarthy, pp. 161–180. New Brunswick, N.J.: Transaction.

———, eds. 1987. *Social Movements in an Organizational Society.* New Brunswick, N.J.: Transaction.

Zingg, Paul, and Mark Medeiros. 1994. *Runs, Hits, and an Era: The Pacific Coast League, 1903–58.* Urbana: University of Illinois Press.

Index

accommodation, pluralist, 13, 195
ACORN (Association of Community Organizations for Reform Now), 194
Acorn Project, *122 (map)*, 127–31; affirmative action in, 163; Alameda County Building Trades Council in, 164; Beneficial Development Group in, 156; black middle class in, 131, 133; demolition under, 132; displacements from, 128, 129; hearings on, 130; NAACP and, 129; protest against, 130; supporters of, 244n27
Adams, Edson, 26
Ad Hoc Committee to Preserve Black Business, 168, 169
advocacy groups, professional, 199
affirmative action, 196; in city hiring, 183; implementation of, 163; initiatives against, 197
AFL: alliances with business elites, 89; in Bay Area, 40, 41; Boilermakers Local 681, 101; BSCP in, 84; cooperation with CIO, 101; in Kahn's and Hastings strike, 104–5; membership of, 88, 237n15; militancy of, 111; Painters Local 1175, 100; postwar membership drive by, 103–4; race barriers in, 47; rivalry with CIO, 21, 103, 108; Shipwrights Local 1149, 100; socioeconomic base of,

117; split from CIO, 91–93, 94; steering committee of, *fig. 16;* voluntarism of, 41, 109; in wartime, 100
AFL Central Labor Council, 40, 47; Alameda County Central Labor Council, 91, 92; alliances of, 111; challenge to business regime, 176, 177; decline in membership, 193; in General Strike, 106, 108, 109; job training programs of, 147; in Kahn's and Hastings strike, 105; liberalism of, 118; in public housing controversy, 2, 115; in recall campaign (1912), 41; reorganization of, 92; in San Francisco General Strike, 86
African Americans: in antipoverty programs, 138–40, 142, 143, 145, 177; as bureaucratic clients, 136, 179; bureaucratic incorporation of, 160, 163–67, 172; challenge to developmental regime, 176; cultural institutions of, 202; in Democratic Party, 84, 153; economic integration for, 150, 196; elites, 82; employers of, 217n11; in ethnic hierarchy, 37; in ethnic patronage systems, 181; family income of, 197; group formation of, 74; in labor force, 83, 232n31; in labor unions, 47, 83–84, 100–1; lumpen-proletariat of, 154; mobilization of, 22, 123, 144, 145, 176, 179;

Text:	10/13 Aldus
Display:	Aldus
Compositor:	Integrated Composition Systems
Printer and Binder:	Edwards Brothers, Inc.